AMERICAN INDIAN POLICY
IN THE FORMATIVE YEARS

AMERICAN
INDIAN POLICY
IN THE
FORMATIVE YEARS

THE INDIAN TRADE
AND INTERCOURSE ACTS
1790 - 1834

FRANCIS PAUL PRUCHA

UNIVERSITY OF NEBRASKA PRESS · LINCOLN

First Bison Book printing: July, 1970

Most recent printing shown by first digit below:

4   5   6   7   8   9   10

Bison Book edition published by arrangement with Harvard University Press,
the publisher of the clothbound edition

To Frederick Merk

PREFACE

One of the difficulties in writing history is that often no definite patterns emerge which can be used to explain all that happened. This is especially true in such a complex matter as United States Indian policy. There were too many factors involved, too many different viewpoints toward the Indians, too many hindrances in carrying out an established policy to permit easy generalizations. American Indian policy grew bit by bit. Principles were worked out from time to time as experience deepened and as circumstances changed.

It would be easy in dealing with Indian matters to adopt a dramatic theme and write about it — to write about "savagism" or a "century of dishonor" or of "a continent lost — a civilization won." Such an approach, however, could give an oversimplified view of what actually took place. It might easily obscure the fact that Indian policy did not spring full-blown from some statesman's brow, but rather was a slow growth, developing under the press of circumstances and the pressures of diverse groups. A reviewer of a recent work on American economic history said of the author's treatment that it lacked "the sparkle and simplicity that dogmatism could give it." The present study may also suffer from a lack of sparkle and simplicity: I can only hope that the deficiency will be charitably attributed to my attempt to avoid dogmatism, and that a calm investigation of the laws which expressed American Indian policy in the formative years of our nation's existence may enrich our knowledge and our understanding of Indian-white relations in American history.

In quoting documents from manuscript or printed sources I have endeavored to transcribe the originals exactly, except in some cases where I have added or modified punctuation or provided capitals at the beginning of sentences.

My thanks are due to the Social Science Research Council, whose Faculty Research Grant for nine months permitted me to devote full time to research on Indian policy, and to the staffs of the Harvard University Library, the National Archives, and the

Library of Congress, who so kindly and patiently aided me in the pursuit of the data that are the stuff of written history. Nathan Einhorn, W. Stitt Robinson, and Reginald Horsman read large sections of the manuscript and offered most helpful criticisms.

Francis Paul Prucha, s.j.

Marquette University
September 1961

CONTENTS

AMERICAN INDIAN POLICY
IN THE FORMATIVE YEARS

IA FR	Office of Indian Affairs, Field Office Records, in National Archives, Record Group 75
IA LR	Office of Indian Affairs, Letters Received, in National Archives, Record Group 75
IA LS	Office of Indian Affairs, Letters Sent, in National Archives, Record Group 75
IT LS	Office of Indian Trade, Letters Sent, in National Archives, Record Group 75
SW IA LR	Office of the Secretary of War, Letters Received, Indian Affairs, in National Archives, Record Group 75
SW IA LS	Office of the Secretary of War, Letters Sent, Indian Affairs, in National Archives, Record Group 75
SW LR	Office of the Secretary of War, Letters Received, in National Archives, Record Group 107
SW LS	Office of the Secretary of War, Letters Sent, in National Archives, Record Group 107

INTRODUCTION

The Indians themselves are an anomaly upon the face of the earth; and the relations, which have been established between them and the nations of Christendom, are equally anomalous. Their intercourse is regulated by practical principles, arising out of peculiar circumstances.

— Lewis Cass, in *The North American Review*, 1830

The condition of the Indians in relation to the United States is perhaps unlike that of any other two people in existence.

— John Marshall, in *Cherokee Nation* vs. *Georgia*, 1831

The relation of the Indian tribes living within the borders of the United States, both before and since the Revolution, to the people of the United States has always been an anomalous one and of a complex character.

— Samuel F. Miller, in *United States* vs. *Kagama*, 1886

The basic Indian policy of the United States was formulated during the first decades of our national existence, as the federal government sought solutions to the problems caused by the presence of the Indians. These problems the new nation inherited from Great Britain when it acquired its independence; they grew out of the given fact that the Indians were here when the white man arrived and that their presence on the land formed an obstacle to the westward advance of the white settlers.

The immediate difficulty facing the United States after the Revolution was the establishment of peace with the tribes, who had been allies of the British, but there were also other basic problems: determining the precise authority of the states and of the national government in managing Indian affairs, extinguishing in an orderly way the Indian title to the land so that the expanding settlements might find unencumbered room, restraining aggressive frontiersmen from encroaching upon country still claimed by the Indians, regulating the contacts between the two races that grew out of trade, providing adequate means to protect the rights of the red man, and fulfilling the responsibility that the Christian whites had to aid the savage pagans along the path toward civilization.

For the management of these Indian affairs the United States by the 1830's had determined a set of principles which became the standard base lines of American Indian policy. The fundamental elements of the federal program were the following:

(1) Protection of Indian rights to their land by setting definite boundaries for the Indian Country, restricting the whites from entering the area except under certain controls, and removing illegal intruders.

(2) Control of the disposition of Indian lands by denying the right of private individuals or local governments to acquire land from the Indians by purchase or by any other means.

(3) Regulation of the Indian trade by determining the conditions under which individuals might engage in the trade, prohibiting certain classes of traders, and actually entering into the trade itself.

(4) Control of the liquor traffic by regulating the flow of intoxicating liquor into the Indian Country and then prohibiting it altogether.

(5) Provision for the punishment of crimes committed by members of one race against the other and compensation for damages suffered by one group at the hands of the other, in order to remove the occasions for private retaliation which led to frontier hostilities.

(6) Promotion of civilization and education among the Indians, in the hope that they might be absorbed into the general stream of American society.

This Indian policy of the government was expressed in the formal treaties made with the Indian tribes, but it took shape primarily in a series of federal laws "to regulate trade and intercourse with the Indian tribes, and to preserve peace on the frontier." The first of these laws was passed in 1790, the final and enduring one in 1834. In them appeared the legislative statement of the decisions made by the United States as it was feeling its way toward satisfactory solutions to the problems resulting from the presence of uncultured tribesmen in the path of aggressive and land-hungry whites. On occasion, too, special programs such as the system of government trading factories were established in separate, but related, laws.

The goal of American statesmen was the orderly advance of the frontier. To maintain the desired order and tranquility it was necessary to place restrictions on the contacts between the whites and the Indians. The intercourse acts were thus restrictive and prohibitory in nature — aimed largely at restraining the actions of the whites and providing justice to the Indians as the means of preventing hostility. But if the goal was an *orderly* advance, it was nevertheless *advance* of the frontier, and in the process of reconciling the two elements, conflict and injustice were often the result.

The policy that the United States set forth in the Indian intercourse acts was not the total expression of American attitudes toward the Indians. Behind the laws on the statute books there were deep-running and divergent currents of thought about the character of the Indian and his rights. One of these currents was represented by official government policy; it found expression in the laws passed by Congress, which in large part followed the recommendations and reports of the presidents, the secretaries of war, and other executive officials, in the directives and regulations issued by the War Department and in the decisions of the courts. The other was the frontiersmen's position, a popular attitude of hostility toward the red man, which spurred the ruthless drive against the Indians and made it impossible for the government to carry out its policy with anything like complete effect. The full history of Indian relations in the United States is the history of the interaction of these two currents. It is my intention to trace the development of the policy of the federal government, considering the often-vociferous expressions of the frontier attitudes only insofar as the enforcement of the federal laws was hampered by the intransigence of the Indian-hating frontiersmen and their disregard for Indian rights.

There was solid continuity in American Indian policy as it developed step by step, despite the fact that the anomaly of Indian relations never failed to impress American statesmen. While it is true that there were no set legal precedents to govern the relations between the whites and the Indians and that the policy of the United States had to be refined and changed as circumstances proved the inutility of the old and the necessity of something new, there was over a century and a half of colonial experience to look to, with some basic elements in United States policy inherited from pre-Revolutionary days. The United States government itself moved slowly until, in 1834, came a culmination and codification of laws that had been enacted during the preceding years. In the organic act establishing the Indian department and in the new intercourse act of that year was distilled the wisdom that came with experience — the experience of the English colonists in the seventeenth and eighteenth centuries, the British Board of Trade as it tried to solve the Indian problem by imperialization of control, Congress under the Articles of Confederation, Indian agents and superintendents, army officers on the frontier, men like Benjamin Hawkins, long-time agent to the Creeks who was accused of being too sympathetic with his charges, and Andrew Jackson, who relied on force of arms to banish the Indians beyond the cultivated and civilized sections of the country. The acts bore traces of the complaints of the Indians as the white tide bore down upon them. They reflected the *faits accomplis* of the frontiersmen, who moved unbidden into Indian lands. They were colored by the humanitarian cares of New Englanders for the "poor Indian" and by the awareness of legislators of the weakness of human nature, especially as it was exhibited by the ill-famed, unscrupulous, fly-by-night Indian traders. The acts marked the end of the formative period of American Indian policy. For a full century after the passage of the final intercourse act there was no comparably comprehensive law touching on Indian matters.

Because of the complexity of the laws and the many elements that made up American Indian policy, I have chosen to treat the subject topically, except for three initial chapters, which describe briefly the Indian policy of the colonial and Confederation periods and the early years under the Constitution, and a final chapter, which concerns the legislation of 1834.

⸰⸰ I ⸰⸰

COLONIAL AND IMPERIAL INDIAN POLICY

The Indians frequently repeat that Trade was the foundation of their Alliance or Connexions with us & that it is the chief Cement wch binds us together. And this should undoubtedly be the first Principle of our whole System of Indian Politics.
— Peter Wraxall's *Abridgment*

. . . it is just and reasonable, and essential to our Interest, and the Security of our Colonies, that the several Nations or tribes of Indians with whom We are connected, and who live under our Protection, should not be molested or disturbed in the Possession of such Parts of our Dominions and Territories as, not having been ceded to or purchased by Us, are reserved to them, or any of them, as their Hunting Grounds.
— The Proclamation of 1763

The United States in 1776 did not have a *tabula rasa* on which to sketch out its Indian policy. Heavy lines were already etched in, to be further deepened in some cases by American decisions or rubbed out when changes seemed imperative. All the English colonies had an Indian problem and had adopted measures for regulating the relations between the Indians and the whites.[1] Although there was no uniform policy, as decade after decade each colony was left to manage its own Indian affairs, certain basic procedures became fixed in all the colonies. The Indians, after all, were a class apart, distinguished by their primitive culture, their savagery, and their color. The English, like the French and the Spanish, were forced to develop some rationale on which to base their relations with these strange aborigines, but, whatever the theological and philosophical theories that evolved, it was soon apparent that the two races were not going to live in peace easily. The peace, rather, had to be maintained

[1] The general sources for colonial Indian policy are indicated in the Bibliographical Note, No. 8.

and safeguarded by public authority, and gradually a body of restrictions developed, designed to prevent or regulate contact between the whites and the Indians at crucial and dangerous points, which foreshadowed in some degree the later action of the United States.

There was of course some intermixture, as is inevitable when two races come in contact, but by and large it was replacement of the Indians on the land by the whites, not intermingling, that marked the English colonization. This became ultimately the real basis of conflict, as the natives were relentlessly pushed back by the ever-advancing Europeans.

From the very beginning abuses marred the transfer of land titles from the Indians to individuals among the English colonists, and colonial laws struck at the difficulty by declaring null and void all bargains made with the Indians that did not have governmental approval.[2] Not only did such laws seek to remove causes of resentment among the Indians by preventing unjust and fraudulent purchases, but they aimed as well at preserving the rights of the crown or the proprietor to the land, which would be seriously impaired by extinguishment of Indian titles in favor of just anybody. The preamble of the South Carolina act of December 18, 1739, called attention to this double motivation behind the restrictive legislation of the colonial governments, for it noted that "the practice of purchasing lands from the Indians may prove of very dangerous consequence to the peace and safety of this Province, such purchases being generally obtained from Indians by unfair representation, fraud and circumvention, or by making them gifts or presents of little value, by which practices, great resentments and animosities have been created amongst the Indians towards the inhabitants of this Province," and that "such practices tend to the manifest prejudice of his Majesty's just right and title to the soil of this Province, vested in his Majesty by the surrender of the late Lords Proprietors." [3]

Bargaining with the Indians for land was but one aspect of the transactions between the two races. Trade in general was the great point of contact with the Indians, and the exchange of

[2] *The Colonial Laws of Massachusetts* (Boston, 1889), p. 161; *The Colonial Laws of New York from the Year 1664 to the Revolution* (5 vols., Albany, 1894–1896), I, 149; James T. Mitchell and Henry Flanders, eds., *The Statutes at Large of Pennsylvania from 1682 to 1801* (16 vols., Harrisburg, 1896–1911), IV, 154–156; Thomas Cooper, ed., *The Statutes at Large of South Carolina* (10 vols., Columbia, 1836–1841), III, 526.

[3] *Statutes of South Carolina*, III, 525–526.

goods became a complex mixture of economic, political, and military elements. Two items in the trade, because of their explosive potentialities, were of critical importance in the efforts to preserve the peace — firearms and liquor. Just as the colonists were not free to buy land from the Indians, neither were they free to sell them arms or rum. For obvious enough reasons it was necessary to prevent the supplying of hostile Indians with weapons, and laws were enacted for that purpose, especially in the early days of the colonies, when survival against the Indians was of primary concern.[4]

Of far greater moment, however, were the restrictions placed on the sale of liquor to the natives. The propensity of the Indian for strong drink and the disastrous results that inevitably followed were universal phenomena. The traders throughout the long history of the fur trade relied upon rum and whiskey in their dealings with Indians. The unscrupulous trader did not hesitate to debauch the red man with liquor, in order to cheat him of his furs. And the Indians' revenge more often than not was taken out indiscriminately upon the settlers close at hand. Governor George Thomas of Pennsylvania sensed the danger that was common to all the colonies. "I cannot but be apprehensive," he told the assembly in 1744, "that the Indian trade as it is now carried on will involve us in some fatal quarrel with the Indians. Our Traders in defiance of the Law carry Spirituous Liquors amongst them, and take Advantage of their inordinate Appetite for it to cheat them out of their skins and their wampum, which is their Money, and often to debauch their wives into the Bargain. Is it to be wondered at then, if when they Recover from the Drunken fit, they should take severe revenges?"[5]

In an attempt to meet the difficulty the colonies enacted prohibitions against the sale of rum and other liquors to the Indians. Often enough the prohibition was absolute. Stiff fines were provided for violators and forfeiture of stores was common, and in some cases general authorization was given to destroy the liquor. Such absolute prohibitions against supplying liquor to the Indians met with opposition, however, even from the respectable traders, who could not then compete with the irregular traders or the

[4] Francis X. Moloney, *The Fur Trade in New England, 1620–1676* (Cambridge, Mass., 1931), pp. 102–104; *Archives of Maryland* (62 vols., Baltimore, 1883–1945), I, 346.

[5] Quoted in George A. Cribbs, "The Frontier Policy of Pennsylvania," *Western Pennsylvania Historical Magazine*, II (1919), 25.

Dutch and the French. Prohibitions were often relaxed and sometimes removed altogether.[6]

Unfortunately, the whole business of restriction was largely
futile, for the Indians' thirst would be quenched by foul means
if fair means were denied. The moral fiber of the general run of
traders was too frayed to permit a stand against liquor when the
profits were so enticing, and even the colonial authorities at times
found it necessary, or at least expedient, to give the Indians rum.
The experience of the colonies seemed to teach nothing but the
perversity of the traders and the insatiable thirst of the Indians.

The whole Indian trade, of which the sale of liquor to the
Indians was only one part, was of inestimable importance to the
colonies. The fur trade was for many years a lucrative enterprise,
and the colonial governments sought to protect the interests of
the commonwealth against uncontrolled private gain on the part
of individuals. Since fraud and illegal practices on the part of
traders stirred up Indian indignation and anger, they led to frequent retaliations against the white community. In an attempt
to prevent abuses, multifarious legislation regulating the conditions of the trade was enacted. Different systems were tried,
modified, abandoned, and tried again. Sometimes a strict public
monopoly of the trade was set up; more often the trade was in
the hands of private traders, who were hedged about by strict
and detailed regulations. Because the fur trade had such close
bearing on the public welfare, the colonial governments insisted
on strict measures of control.[7]

The universal means of regulation was a licensing system. It
was the only way to keep the trade open to all qualified persons
and at the same time provide protection against traders of bad
character. The need for such protection was manifest, for, as a
South Carolina law of 1707 declared, "the greater number of
those persons that trade among the Indians in amity with this
Government, do generally lead loose, vicious lives, to the scandal
of the Christian religion, and do likewise oppress the people
among whom they live, by their unjust and illegal actions, which
if not prevented may in time tend to the destruction of this Prov-

---

[6] *Colonial Laws of Massachusetts*, p. 161; *Statutes of South Carolina*, II, 190;
Statutes of Pennsylvania, II, 168–170; *Colonial Laws of New York*, I, 657, 888.
See Moloney, *Fur Trade in New England*, pp. 104–108, for discussion of liquor
in the New England fur trade.

[7] See Verner W. Crane, *The Southern Frontier, 1670–1732* (Durham, 1928),
for details on the vacillation between private trade and public monopoly in South
Carolina.

ince." [8] Often bond was required of the traders, and violators of the regulations were punished by revocation of license, forfeiture of bond and stores, or some specified fine. Frequently the trade was restricted to designated localities, the better to enforce the licensing system. Commissioners and agents were appointed to manage the trade, issue the licenses, enforce the provisions of the laws, and to adjudicate disputes arising from the trade.[9]

However important the trade may have been economically, political considerations came overshadow all else. Peace and at times the very existence of the colonies depended on Indian attachment to the English. Presents to the Indians were long a favored method of ensuring the allegiance of the tribes, and the constant efforts to prevent abuses in dealing with the Indians aimed to secure peace on the frontiers. But the fundamental policy in Indian affairs was to make the Indians dependent on the English in their trade. The colonists were instructed to encourage the Indians to trade with them "so THAT they may apply themselves to the English trade and NATION rather than to any other OF EUROPE." [10] This was eminently true in the case of the Iroquois, whom the English determined to attach to themselves at all costs in their conflict with the French. Since trade became the great means of cementing political alliance, the object was to get the trade; it was less important whether the furs were needed or not.[11] Unfortunately, the rivalry to capture the Indian trade was not limited to that between the European nations in the New World. It existed, too, between the English colonies.

Despite all the concern, regulation of the Indian trade by the colonies was a failure. The frontiers were too extensive and the

[8] *Statutes of South Carolina*, II, 309–316.
[9] An example of an orderly and comprehensive law was the South Carolina "Act for the better regulation of the Indian Trade, and for appointing a Commissioner for that purpose" of August 20, 1731. It came after years of controversy between various elements in the colony for control of the trade and bitter experience with Indian wars resulting from ill-managed affairs. *Ibid.*, III, 327–334. Crane, *Southern Frontier*, pp. 202–203, asserts that under this law the regulation of the Indian trade was "probably as well planned and as efficiently enforced as any such system could have been under colonial conditions, and in view of the vast extent of the Carolina Indian country." The law became an Indian trading code for the whole southern frontier since Georgia modeled its regulations upon it.
[10] Leonard W. Labaree, ed., *Royal Instructions to British Colonial Governors, 1670–1776* (2 vols., New York, 1935), II, 464.
[11] See the "Introduction" in Peter Wraxall, *An Abridgment of the Indian Affairs Contained in Four Folio Volumes, Transacted in the Colony of New York, from the Year 1678 to the Year 1751*, Charles H. McIlwain, ed. (Cambridge, Mass., 1915).

inhabitants too widely scattered to permit adequate control of intercourse with the Indians. The Indians could not be induced or forced to bring their furs to central markets where the trade could be supervised and regulations enforced, so that trade was left practically free and unrestricted. Anyone could engage in it by obtaining a license. The fur trade was thus in the hands of a great number of individuals, many of whom were lawless, unprincipled, and vicious. Even if one leaves out of the picture the ill-famed traders and focuses his attention on the respectable merchants and colonial officials, he still finds little to praise, for Indian regulation could become hopelessly entangled in factional politics. There was no uniformity among the colonies, no two sets of regulations alike. Abuses prohibited by one colony were tolerated by the next, and the conditions could hardly be amended while each colony was left to govern its own trade and to be guided in part by rivalry with its neighbors for the trade.

The failure was apparent to all. The corruption, the fraud, the mischievous dealings of the traders — who were described by those who came in contact with them as the scum of the earth — continually aroused the resentment of the Indians. Furthermore, not only did the Indians resent being made the dupes of the traders, but the steady pressure of the white settlers on their hunting grounds could not escape their attention. It is difficult to explain the slowness with which the British government came to realize the danger of these white encroachments upon the Indian lands. Continuing to rely on presents in order to keep the Indians attached to the English cause, the British officials only slowly awakened to the realization that the way to keep the Indians happy was to remove the causes of their resentment and discontent — namely, the abuses practised upon them by the traders and the encroachment upon their lands by the hunters and settlers.

The conferences between the Indians and the Albany Congress in 1754 emphasized the point, for the Indians made known their resentment in unmistakable terms. "We told you a little while ago," said one speaker for the Mohawks, "that we had an uneasiness on our minds, and we shall now tell you what it is; it is concerning our land." Again and again in the course of the conferences, the Indians complained of the steady encroachment of the whites onto their lands through purchases which the Indians refused to acknowledge or without any semblance of title at all.[12] No matter how great the presents made to the tribes,

[12] E. B. O'Callaghan, ed., *Documents Relative to the Colonial History of the*

the gifts could not cover over the fundamental reasons for Indian hostility to the English.

Strictly speaking, of course, it might have been possible for the individual colonies to handle Indian affairs. Had the colonial leaders been prompted by a far-seeing, humanitarian outlook, or able to eliminate the selfishness that marked the rivalry of one colony with another, or able to devise some means to control or remove from the trade the worst sort of trader, then the demand for imperialization of Indian affairs might never have arisen. We must, however, accept the affairs as they were. There was no question that in fact the colonial management had failed. The trade was not adequately controlled; the English colonists steadily encroached upon the lands of the Indians; the Indians were resentful and showed their ill humor by incessant attacks upon the settlements.

The hardest fact of all had to be faced: the Indians by and large adhered to the French in the imperial war that broke out between England and France in 1754.

In 1755 the first step was taken to remove Indian affairs from the incompetent hands of the colonists and center political control in the hands of the British government. On April 15 of that year William Johnson, long-time friend of the Iroquois, was appointed superintendent of Indian affairs for the northern department, and in the following year Edmond Atkin was named to a similar post in the South, to be replaced in 1762 by the more famous John Stuart. The superintendents were to have full charge of the political relations between the British and the Indians. Their responsibilities were widespread — protecting the Indians as well as they could from the traders and speculators, negotiating the boundary lines that were called for after 1763, distributing the presents given to the Indians in the attempt to gain and maintain their good will, and enlisting the Indians in wartime to fight on the side of the British. The superintendents, too, exercised what control they could over the fur trade, although theoretically, and to a great extent practically, the management of the trade remained in colonial hands.[13]

State of New-York (15 vols., Albany, 1853–1887), VI, 853–892 — hereafter cited as *New York Colonial Documents.*

[13] John R. Alden, *John Stuart and the Southern Colonial Frontier: A Study of Indian Relations, War, Trade, and Land Problems in the Southern Wilderness, 1754–1775* (Ann Arbor, 1944), treats fully of Stuart's career. Chapter IX gives a

The purchase of Indian lands also engaged the attention of the Board of Trade. The colonies themselves, in order to prevent fraud and other abuses, had sought to prohibit the purchase of Indian lands by individuals without license or permission, but the attempt was not successful. An individual colony could not grasp the over-all picture of the pressure along the frontier, and the provincial governments themselves were causing alarm among the Indians by their own purchase of lands. Imperial control was imperative if peace and harmony with the Indians were to be maintained.

As early as 1753, in its instructions to Sir Danvers Osborne, governor of New York, the Board of Trade foreshadowed a new policy in regard to the purchase of Indian lands. The governor was instructed to permit no more purchases of land by private individuals, "but when the Indians are disposed to sell any of their lands the purchase ought to be made in his Majesty's name and at the publick charge." The measure was also proposed at the Albany Congress for improving the regulation of Indian affairs. Then on December 2, 1761, a general order was issued to the governors in the colonies under royal control, which forbade them, under threat of royal displeasure and removal from office, to issue grants to any Indian lands. All requests to purchase land from the Indians were to be forwarded to the Board of Trade and were to depend upon directions received from the Board. The governors, furthermore, were to order all persons who "either wilfully or inadvertently" had settled on Indian lands to remove at once, and to prosecute all persons who had secured titles to such lands by fraud.[14]

The problem of Indian trade also began to receive consideration, but the Board of Trade proceeded very slowly because of the pressure of other business and the intricate nature of the trade problem, which, the Board realized, needed more careful study. Nor could the sensitiveness of the colonies be overlooked; their good will was essential during the war with France, and they might not be happy to have withdrawn from them the control of the fur trade which had been their prerogative for so many decades. Although indications of the movement toward

good discussion of the office of superintendent. For other references on the superintendents, see Bibliographical Note, No. 8.

[14] Oliver M. Dickerson, American Colonial Government, 1696–1765: A Study of the British Board of Trade in Its Relation to the American Colonies, Political, Industrial, Administrative (Cleveland, 1912), p. 340; Labaree, Royal Instructions, II, 467–468; New York Colonial Documents, VII, 478–479.

imperialization of trade can be seen in declarations of the Board of Trade, nothing substantial had been done by 1763.

⁓

To meet the new situation George III issued on October 7 the famous Proclamation of 1763.[15] It was, in a way, an emergency measure, whose consequent shortcomings have been repeatedly pointed out. Yet it was not a surprise move that departed from established patterns, nor did it lie outside the general course of policy. Its roots were deep in previous imperial policy and it was nurtured by the proximate discussions of the Board of Trade, which began months before the Proclamation itself came forth.

The document proclaimed three things: it established the boundaries and the government for the new colonies, offered specific encouragement to settlement in the newly acquired areas, and established a new policy in Indian affairs. The last of these was foremost in the minds of the Lords of Trade in the summer months of 1763.

The great departure from the past, the new turn in Indian policy found in the Proclamation of 1763, was the boundary line drawn between the lands of the Indians and those of the whites. In earlier colonial days there had been no distinct "Indian Country." Indian ownership of land was recognized — Massachusetts quoted Scripture in support of that principle — and care was taken to regularize the purchase of lands from the natives. In some colonies, indeed, clearly marked reservations were set aside for the Indians, but in many places the Indian families lived side by side with the whites, as they were induced to embrace the white man's way of life and civilization. When the Indians were close at hand, one could go out to buy game from them or sell them household manufactures, a personal, family-size trade expressly guaranteed in colonial legislation. Off to the indefinite west were the unlimited hunting grounds of the Indians and the source of their furs and deerskins. No one saw any need to declare these lands off limits to the whites. There was little occasion at first for a strictly drawn boundary line to separate the red men in the West from the whites in the East. It was in the Proclamation of 1763 that the first official delineation and definition of the Indian Country was made.

[15] The Proclamation of 1763 is printed in Adam Shortt and Arthur G. Doughty, eds., *Documents Relating to the Constitutional History of Canada, 1759–1791* (Ottawa, 1907), pp. 119–123 — hereafter cited as *Canadian Constitutional Documents.*

First of all, by this proclamation, the governors and commanders in chief of the new colonies were forbidden to issue any
warrants for survey or patents for lands beyond the boundaries
set for their colonies, and the officials of the older colonies were
forbidden "for the present, and until our further Pleasure be
known," to permit surveys or to grant lands beyond the watershed
of the Appalachians. Secondly, the Proclamation formally reserved the Indian Country for the red men — "all the Lands and
Territories lying to the Westward of the Sources of the Rivers
which fall into the Sea from the West and North West." The
king's subjects were prohibited from making purchases or settlements in the restricted territory, and any person who had already
moved into the Indian Country was ordered to remove at once.

Although this was a new departure, there was a background
from which it grew. Wise men who were acquainted with the
evils existing in Indian affairs in the colonies and who realized
more and more that the great cause of Indian troubles was the
steady encroachment of the whites upon the land of the Indians
had been advocating that a clear line of demarcation be drawn
between the areas of the two races. One fanciful proposal was
that of Dean Tucker, who suggested guarding against Indian
incursions by "clearing away the woods and bushes from a tract
of land, a mile in breadth, and extending along the back of the
colonies," in order to form an open and unproductive buffer to
keep the conflicting races apart. It may well be that this sort
of wild-eyed proposal had no influence on the august Lords of
Trade, but other proposals of more weight came from astute
Indian agents like Sir William Johnson and his first lieutenant,
George Croghan, who in 1763 wrote letters to the Board of Trade
urging the establishment of a boundary line. Although their
letters arrived too late to have direct influence on the action of
the Board of Trade in the preparation of the report that led to
the Proclamation, they indicate the direction of official thought.
Johnson expressed his opinion in the following terms: "I humbly
conceive, that a certain line should be run at the back of the
Northern Colonies, beyond which no settlement should be made,
until the whole Six Nations should think proper of selling part
thereof. This would encourage the thick settlement of the Frontiers, oblige the Proprietors of large grants to get them Inhabited,
and secure the Indians from being further deceived by many who
make a practice of imposing on a few Indians with liquor and fair
promises to sign Deeds, which are generally disavowed by the

Nation." Croghan urged a "natural Boundary . . . between them and us across the frontiers of the British middle Colonies" and declared that "the lands west of such a line should be reserved for the Hunting grounds of the Six Nations, and the several Tribes dependent on them." [16]

There was a precedent, too, for the boundary line. Pennsylvania in 1758 had conciliated the Indians by a solemn assurance that the whites would not interfere with their lands in the fertile Ohio valley. On October 24 of that year, in a formal treaty at Easton, the governor of Pennsylvania returned to the Indians all of the trans-Allegheny lands that had been purchased from the Six Nations in 1754 at Albany. Thus an absolute line was drawn between the whites and the Indians, and neither was to violate the territory of the other. The British ministry ratified this colonial agreement, accepting it under the stress of war, it is true, but binding itself by a solemn commitment that could not be ignored at the conclusion of the hostilities.[17]

Conciliation of the Indians was of prime importance; British officials knew that justice in the treatment of the Indians was a prerequisite and that this justice demanded strong measures to restrain, if not prevent, the encroachment on the Indian lands. In January 1763 Lord Egremont, secretary of state for the Southern Department, asserted the king's desire "to conciliate the affection of the Indian nations, by every act of strict justice, and by affording them his royal protection from any incroachment on the lands they have reserved to themselves, for their hunting grounds, & for their own support & habitation." On July 4 a general instruction was sent to the governors of the colonies in America, which forbade encroachment by the whites and warned the colonial officials that they could make grants of such lands only under the pain of highest royal displeasure and dismissal from their posts.[18]

The Proclamation of 1763 was strongly influenced by a document drawn up in May entitled "Hints Relative to the Division

[16] The quotation from Tucker is in Max Farrand, "The Indian Boundary Line," *American Historical Review*, X (1905), 783. The statements of Johnson and Croghan are in *New York Colonial Documents*, VII, 578, 603.

[17] Lawrence H. Gipson, *The British Empire Before the American Revolution*, Volume IX, *The Triumphant Empire: New Responsibilities Within the Enlarged Empire, 1763–1766* (New York, 1956), p. 51. A facsimile reproduction of Benjamin Franklin's printing of "Minutes of Conferences, held at Easton, In October, 1758," is in Carl Van Doren, ed., *Indian Treaties Printed by Benjamin Franklin, 1736–1762* (Philadelphia, 1938), pp. 213–243.

[18] Alden, *John Stuart*, p. 241, n. 2; Gipson, *British Empire*, IX, 51.

and Government of the Conquered and Newly Acquired Countries in America." The document expressed the views of Egremont and can properly be considered his, although the authorship has also been attributed to Henry Ellis. Since the "Hints" antedated the letters of Johnson and Croghan, it was the first explicit proposal for an Indian boundary line along the western edge of the colonies. The text runs as follows: "It might also be necessary to fix upon some Line for a Western Boundary to our ancient provinces, beyond which our People should not at present be permitted to settle, hence as their Numbers increased, they would emigrate to Nova Scotia, or to the provinces on the Southern Frontier, where they would be usefull to their Mother Country, instead of planting themselves in the Heart of America, out of the reach of Government, and where, from the Difficulty of procuring European Commodities, they would be compelled to commence Manufacturs to the infinite prejudice of Britain." [19]

Although the idea of Indian Country set off by a sharp line is clearly stated, the paper says nothing about placating the Indians as a motive for the boundary line. The argument is, instead, mercantilistic. The line of demarcation was to be a barrier to the westward expansion to the colonies, not to prevent injustice to the Indians, but to forestall the formation of western colonies, which would not fit in well with a mercantilist scheme of empire.

The declaration that this line was "for the present" indicated that the author himself thought of the line as a temporary measure, but others wished for a permanent barrier. There were in fact two groups in the ministry — the expansionists, who were eager for the spread of the colonists to the west, and the antiexpansionists, who wished to restrict the settlements to the seaboard. The boundary line was agreed to by both, the latter looking upon it as a permanent western wall along the back of the colonies, the former as a temporary expedient, needed at once to placate the Indians, and to be the basis from which an ordered and regulated movement toward the west could be made.[20]

A second preliminary document was the "Sketch of a Report

[19] Verner W. Crane, ed., "Hints Relative to the Division and Government of the Conquered and Newly Acquired Countries in America," *Mississippi Valley Historical Review*, VIII (1922), 371; R. A. Humphreys, "Lord Shelburne and the Proclamation of 1763," *English Historical Review*, XLIX (1934), 246.

[20] See chapters VI–VIII in Clarence W. Alvord, *The Mississippi Valley in British Politics: A Study of the Trade, Land Speculation, and Experiments in Imperialism Culminating in the American Revolution* (Cleveland, 1917), I, 157–228. This book is valuable on all phases of imperial Indian policy.

Concerning the Cessions in Africa and America at the Peace of 1763," drawn up by John Pownall, secretary to the Lords of Trade. The "Sketch," too, considered it wise to limit the present colonies lest the difficulties of transportation to remote settlements force them to begin their own manufactures and lest there be a "separation of interests and connections" with the mother country. Pownall, however, tied this reasoning to a second consideration: the need to appease the Indians. He proposed that all the country lying between the ridge of the Appalachians and the Mississippi be considered "as lands belonging to the Indians, the dominion of which to be protected for them by forts and military establishments in proper places, and with full liberty to all your Majesty's subjects in general to trade with the said Indians upon some general plan and under proper regulation and restrictions." Pownall admitted three exceptions to the natural boundary line: places where the Iroquois and the southern Indians had possessions to the east that must be safeguarded and where Virginia had already made settlements in the upper Ohio valley. The Board of Trade itself completed its report on June 8, incorporating much of Egremont's "Hints" and Pownall's "Sketch." [21]

Then suddenly the deliberations were interrupted by news from America, which, though not changing the basic direction in which British policy was moving, gave an emergency stamp to the Proclamation. Word arrived in August of Pontiac's Conspiracy, with its threat of disaster to the whole back country. Sir William Johnson wrote to the Lords of Trade on July 1 reporting the blockade of Detroit, the defeat of a detachment on the way there from Niagara, the destruction of the fort at Sandusky with its garrison (and the apprehension that a similar fate had befallen the other outposts), the cutting off of the communications to Fort Pitt, the destruction of several settlements, the murder of many traders, and in general "an universal pannic throughout the Frontiers." [22]

This was no time for debating where the line should be drawn, for running a carefully surveyed boundary, or for solving the disputed point about the wisdom of westward expansion of the colonies. Some action was needed at once to pacify the Indians.

---

[21] "Mr. Pownall's Sketch of a Report Concerning the Cessions in Africa and America at the Peace of 1763," *English Historical Review,* XLIX (1934), 260; Humphreys, "Shelburne and the Proclamation of 1763," *ibid.,* 248–249; Report of June 8, 1763, in *Canadian Constitutional Documents,* pp. 97–107.
[22] *New York Colonial Documents,* VII, 526.

They must be convinced that the encroachment of the whites was at an end and that they could return with confidence to their peaceful ways, assured that they need no longer fear a steady and ruthless expulsion from their hunting grounds. They must be convinced that the British government meant to honor the commitments made to the Indians in both the north and the south. On August 5, 1763, the Lords of Trade proposed to the king that a proclamation be issued immediately indicating the king's "fixed Determination to permit no grant of Lands nor any settlements to be made within certain fixed Bounds, under pretense of Purchase or any other Pretext whatever, leaving all that Territory within it free for the hunting Grounds of those Indian Nations Subjects of Your Majesty, and for the free trade of all your Subjects, [and] to prohibit strictly all Infringements or Settlements to be made on such grounds. . . ." They urged the king, as a means of restraining settlement to the west, to encourage settlement in the new colonies.[23]

A boundary needed to be drawn quickly, and a plan was already at hand. Pownall's proposal of the Appalachian mountains was accepted as the dividing line, but the haste in preparation of the Proclamation eliminated his three exceptions. The watershed was simply made the line. Since it was considered temporary by the president of the Board of Trade, Lord Shelburne, and by a majority of the Board, refinements and modifications could be arranged at a more convenient time in the future. What was needed at once was a dramatic statement to appease the warring tribes in the West. The natural line was the obvious solution. Thus the Indian Country came into being.

The Appalachian boundary line proclaimed in 1763 was provisional, occasioned by the war whoop of the Indians in the West. The Lords of Trade realized that the ordinary process of instructions to the governors was too slow for a time of crisis. They knew, too, that it was impossible during an Indian war (especially one as serious as the uprising of Pontiac) to proceed with the detailed surveying necessary for laying out the line itself. But the point-by-point negotiation with the Indians over the location of the line was not abandoned, only postponed. In 1764, in its outline of a plan for the management of Indian affairs, the Board of Trade emphasized the necessity of the carefully drawn line, to be worked out by the agents with the Indians.[24]

[23] Lords of Trade to the King, Aug. 5, 1763, in *Canadian Constitutional Documents*, pp. 110–112.
[24] *New York Colonial Documents*, VII, 641. The British government aug-

Almost immediately the laborious work began. In 1765 the line was marked out in South Carolina and continued into North Carolina in 1767. During 1768–69 the line was drawn west of Virginia — with some reluctance on the part of Virginia, which did not want to appear to give up its claims to the western regions. By a series of treaties a continuous boundary line was marked, beginning at a point near the southern boundary of Virginia, running south and west at the back of the Carolinas, turning somewhat east in Georgia, and including the tidewater limits of East Florida.²⁵

In the north the responsibility lay with Sir William Johnson, whose experience in Indian affairs had taught him the difficulty of the task. "The ascertaining and defining the precise and exact Boundaries of Indian Lands," he had written to the Board of Trade in 1764, "is a very necessary, but a delicate point. . . . I must beg leave to observe, that the Six Nations, Western Indians, ettc, having never been conquered, either by the English or French, nor subject to the Laws, consider themselves as a free people. I am therefore induced to think it will require a good deal of caution to point out any boundary, that shall appear to circumscribe their limits too far." He proceeded with the necessary caution, however, and in the spring of 1765 at a conference with the Six Nations he brought up the subject and got the approbation of the Indians. Then in 1768, by the Treaty of Fort Stanwix, he settled the northern boundary line. The line started in northern New York near the eastern end of Lake Ontario, ran in a southerly direction to the Delaware River, then west till it touched the Allegheny River, down that river to the Ohio, and west along the Ohio to the mouth of the Tennessee.²⁶

In 1768 the boundary line extended from Canada to Florida, determined by solemn agreements with the Indians. The concept of such a line by then had become ineradicable; but the

---

mented the Proclamation by special instructions to the colonial governors to enforce its restrictions. See instructions to the governors of East Florida, West Florida, and Quebec, 1763, and instructions to the governors of Virginia and Pennsylvania, Oct. 24, 1765, in Labaree, *Royal Instructions*, II, 473–474, 479–480.

²⁵ Farrand, "Indian Boundary Line"; John C. Parish, "John Stuart and the Cartography of the Indian Boundary Line," in *The Persistence of the Westward Movement and Other Essays* (Berkeley, 1943), pp. 131–146. Parish concludes that on extant contemporary maps the southern boundary line of 1768 and the modifications made in the next decade can be completely traced out.

²⁶ Sir William Johnson to Lords of Trade [October 1764], in *New York Colonial Documents*, VII, 665. Johnson's conferences with the Indians and the Treaty of Fort Stanwix are printed *ibid.*, VIII, 111–137.

line itself moved constantly westward as new treaties and new purchases drove the Indians back before the advancing whites.

⸲◉

The Proclamation of 1763 did not represent a fully worked out western policy and was at best a framework upon which such a policy could be built. The boundary line idea was definitely settled upon; there seems to have been no disagreement about it, although there may well have been different reasons for it in the minds of different men. But the line described in the Proclamation was temporary, to stand only until more definite agreements could be made with the Indians, new lands purchased by the government, and distinct boundaries run by the surveyors.

The government to be provided for the Indian Country was another problem. Lord Egremont suggested that the area be placed under the control of the government of the province of Quebec. The Lords of Trade, however, were unwilling to accept the recommendation. They feared that such a provision might give weight to future French claims that the English title to the trans-Appalachian area came only from the cession, whereas the king's title "to the Lakes and circumjacent Territory as well as to the Sovereignty over the Indian Tribes, particularly of the six Nations, rests on a more solid and even a more equitable Foundation." They feared, too, that it would give the northern province an advantage in the fur trade and that the governor of Canada, on account of the number of troops under his command, would become virtually the military governor of America. The Lords proposed instead that a commission for the government of the Indian Country be issued to the commander in chief of the troops in America. Thus the whole West was placed under the military authority.[27]

The powers intended for the general were military, however, not judicial. The Proclamation itself empowered military officers and agents to seize criminals from the established colonies who fled into the Indian Country for refuge and to send them back to the colonies for trial, but no provision was made for crimes actually committed within the reservation itself. General Thomas Gage soon became aware of the gravity of this omission, and the matter was taken care of by a special clause added to the Mutiny

[27] Lords of Trade to the King, Aug. 5, 1763, in *Canadian Constitutional Documents*, pp. 110–111. See Alvord, *Mississippi Valley in British Politics*, I, 181n., on the question of whether or not the commission was actually issued.

Act of 1765. The act authorized all persons to arrest criminals and empowered military officers to send them to the nearest province for trial.[28]

The crucial debate about westward expansion was not resolved by the Proclamation. In the minds of the ministry, the line was not considered a permanent barrier to the older colonies. It was only a means of providing for a regulated acquisition of the Indian lands in a way that would not stir up the resentment of the Indians, as had the haphazard and often fraudulent methods employed by the individual colonies. Nor was the organization of the important Indian trade provided for by the Proclamation. The problem was intricate and required more study than the Board of Trade had had time to give it. The Lords' intentions, however, were clear. The boundary line and the regulation of the Indian trade were two parts of a single plan, for the Board realized the necessity "of speedily falling upon some method of regulating Indian commerce & polity, upon some more general and better established system than has hitherto taken place." To attain this end it had proposed to the king the immediate need for a proclamation of a boundary line. At the same time it undertook to gather information on which to build an adequate set of regulations for the trade, writing to Sir William Johnson and to John Stuart for their opinions and proposals on the very day on which the proclamation was suggested to the king.[29]

The issuing of the Proclamation could not wait for the replies; opinions were divided, moreover, as to the wisdom of imperialization of Indian affairs. The imperialists wanted to create a complete imperial machinery for the regulation of the fur trade; the anti-imperialists preferred to leave to the local authorities the control of the West. All that the Proclamation could do was to assert the principle of freedom of the trade and to demand that all traders obtain licenses from their respective governors and give security that they would follow whatever regulations might be made in the future.[30]

The confusion in colonial Indian trade regulations, therefore, was not removed by the Proclamation of 1763, and when the reports from the Indian superintendents were in, the Board of Trade set about to formulate a comprehensive imperial program

[28] Alvord, *Mississippi Valley in British Politics*, I, 205–206.
[29] Lords of Trade to Sir William Johnson, Aug. 5, 1763, in *New York Colonial Documents*, VII, 535–536.
[30] Alvord, *Mississippi Valley in British Politics*, I, 216–218; Gipson, *British Empire*, IX, 54.

for the fur trade. On July 10, 1764, it proposed a plan that had for its object "the regulation of Indian Affairs both commerical and political throughout all North America, upon one general system, under the direction of Officers appointed by the Crown, so as to sett aside all local interfering of particular Provinces, which has been one great cause of the distracted state of Indian affairs in general." [31] The plan would have set up an imperial department of Indian affairs independent both of the military commander in America (whose control had irked the Indian superintendents) and of the colonial governments. The Board honestly faced the problems that existed in America and provided a competent set of rules for carrying on an orderly and peaceful trade. It was a great misfortune that the rules were never formally adopted. The plan nevertheless foreshadowed later legislation, as its chief provisions indicate.

The fur trade was declared to be free and open to all British subjects, and to better regulate the trade two districts were designated, with appended lists of tribes that were to be considered in each district. For the southern district, all trade was to be carried on at the Indian towns; in the north, fixed posts for the trade were to be designated.

The Indian trade was to be taken completely out of the hands of the colonies, all colonial laws regulating Indian affairs repealed, and control placed in the hands of the agent or superintendent of each district, who was to be assisted by deputies, commissaries, interpreters, smiths, and missionaries. So that the superintendents might have a free hand, interference in the conduct of Indian affairs was expressly forbidden to the commander in chief of His Majesty's forces in America and to the governors and military commanders of the separate colonies, although the cooperation of these officials was enjoined. The agents or their deputies were to visit the tribes yearly and were empowered to act as justices of the peace.

"For the better regulations of the Trade with the said Indians, conformable to their own requests and to prevent those Frauds and Abuses which have been so long and so loudly complained of in the manner of carrying on such Trade," all trade was to be

---

[31] Lords of Trade to Sir William Johnson, July 10, 1764, in *New York Colonial Documents*, VII, 634–636. The "Plan for the Future Management of Indian Affairs" is printed *ibid.*, 637–641. This Plan of 1764 was sent to Johnson and Stuart for their criticisms and "further lights" and to numerous other colonial officials as well.

under the direction and inspection of the superintendents and their deputies. Persons wishing to trade would be required to obtain licenses from the governor or commander of their respective colonies and to give security for the due observance of the regulations. The licenses were to run for one year only and each trader was required to specify in his license the post at which he intended to trade. Fines and imprisonment were provided for those trading without a license. The trade with the Indians was to be governed by tariffs of prices "established from time to time by the commissaries . . . in concert with the Traders and Indians." No trader might sell or supply the Indians with rum or other spirituous liquors, with swan shot or rifled guns, or give the Indians credit for goods beyond the sum of fifty shillings.

The plan placed a prohibition on the purchase of Indian lands, and proper measures were to be taken "with the consent and concurrence of the Indians" to define the exact boundary of the Indian lands, beyond which no settlement was to be allowed.

Affairs drifted for several years. The Plan of 1764 was not adopted, but the superintendents used it, nevertheless, as their guide in the conduct of Indian affairs. Finally in 1768 the plan was officially abandoned. The superintendents were retained in their political capacity, the boundary line was again approved, quick ratification by the British Government of the lines was recommended, and the colonies were urged to pass laws providing proper punishments for settlement beyond the line. But control and regulation of the Indian trade was returned to the colonies. "No one general plan of Commerce & Policy is or can be applicable to all the different Nations of Indians of different interests and different situations," the Lords of Trade argued. They saw difficulties, too, in confining trade to specified points in the north and west, as the Plan of 1764 provided, and they were disturbed by the expense of the Plan, which might "exceed the value of the object to which it applies." [32] It was this final point that was crucial. The sum of twenty thousand pounds a year, which the plan was estimated to cost, was too heavy for the British government to bear, and the Stamp Act troubles had shown the impossibility of raising the money in the colonies. Colonial opposi-

---

[32] "Representation of Lords of Trade on the State of Indian Affairs," March 7, 1768, in *New York Colonial Documents*, VIII, 19–31; Earl of Hillsborough to Sir William Johnson, April 15, 1768, *ibid.*, 57–58; Hillsborough to the Governors in America, April 15, 1768, *ibid.*, 55–56.

tion, too, contributed to the decision to put aside the imperial program and return the affairs to the colonies.

This was a strange reversal, to give back the important matter of regulating the fur trade to the very governments that had botched the job so badly before. The Board was aware that the colonies had previously failed and that the misconduct of the ill-regulated traders had "contributed not a little to involve us in the enormous expences of an Indian war." Undaunted, with eyes consciously or unconsciously blinded to reality, the Board trusted that the ill effects of past neglect and inattention would induce the colonies in the future to more caution and better management.

The results were what might have been expected. The ministry perhaps thought that the Indian boundary line alone would forever remove the causes of friction between the Indians and the English. But the American settlers could not be restrained. Control of the fur trade was no more exact. The failure of the colonies to enact the necessary legislation caused great restlessness among the Indians. Superintendent Stuart described the conditions in his department as chaotic, for the old lawless traders were still at work and settlements were constantly appearing across the boundary line. The problem was too intricate for the colonists to handle without some closer union than existed among them.

The encroachment continued and, although the superintendents did their best, attempts to stop the process were futile. The failure of the colonies to agree upon any sort of general regulations resulted in intolerable conditions in the West. Some interposition of Parliament for the regulation of the fur trade on an imperial basis was necessary, and one last attempt was made. By the Quebec Act of 1774 the western areas were placed under the Quebec government. In this way the Board of Trade hoped to provide the necessary regulation.

The mind of the British ministry was revealed in the instructions sent to Governor Guy Carleton of Quebec at the beginning of January 1775. The freedom of the fur trade for all His Majesty's subjects was again enunciated — a repetition of the Proclamation of 1763 — and the regulations to be drawn up were to have for their object "the giving every possible facility to that Trade, which the nature of it will admit, and as may consist with fair and just dealing towards the Savages." The need for fixed times and places for the trade, for tariffs of prices for goods and furs, and for prohibiting the sale of rum and other liquors was again indicated. Governor Carleton was furnished a copy of the Plan of 1764, which was to serve as his guide when drawing up the necessary rules for the trade.[33] It was a return to the former plan for imperializing the West, but it came too late. The Revolution was about to begin.

[33] Instructions to Governor Guy Carleton, Jan. 3, 1775, in *Canadian Constitutional Documents*, pp. 419–433.

THE CONTINENTAL CONGRESS AND THE ARTICLES OF CONFEDERATION

... the trade with the Indians ought to be regulated, and security be given by the traders, for the punctual observance of such regulations, so that violence, fraud, and injustice towards the Indians, may be guarded against and prevented, and the honor of the federal government and the public tranquility thereby promoted.

— Report of Committee on Indian Affairs, Continental Congress, October 15, 1783

The utmost good faith shall always be observed towards the Indians; their land and property shall never be taken from them without their consent; and in their property, rights and liberty, they shall never be invaded or disturbed, unless in just and lawful wars authorized by Congress; but laws founded on justice and humanity shall from time to time be made, for preventing wrongs done to them, and for preserving peace and Friendship with them.

— The Northwest Ordinance, 1787

The British were given no more time to work out a feasible Indian policy, for the throes of war upset whatever possibilities there might have been for a peaceful solution to the Indian problem. With the coming of the Revolution the Indians became the pawns in the military game between the rebelling colonies and the mother country.

The British had the better position and in large measure retained the allegiance of the Indians. John Stuart and his deputies in the south and the numerous agents in the north made use of their authority and influence with the Indians to prevent them from following the colonists in opposition to the king. In general the British had better agents than the colonists could muster and

had powerful arguments, too, which they did not fail to exploit.[1]
It was plain that the causes of complaint among the Indians —
the abuses of the traders and the encroachment of the white
settlers and hunters — all came from the colonists. It was the
colonists who did the intruding; it was from them that the traders
arose. On the other hand, the British imperial officials had a good
record of trying to deal justly with the Indians, of protecting their
rights to their lands and their furs, and of furnishing the goods
needed for the trade. The Indian agents did not hesitate to call
these facts to the attention of the Indians. One deputy reminded
the Cherokees, "But for the care of the Great King they could not
have had a foot of land left them by the White." John Stuart,
haranguing the Choctaws and Chickasaws at Mobile in May 1777,
urged them to follow the Cherokees in taking up the hatchet
against the Americans. He pointed out the difficulties that the
royal superintendents had had in protecting Indian rights against
the colonists, and he concluded that "as it is the declared intention of the Rebels to possess themselves of your Lands, it also
becomes your duty and interest to unite yourselves with other
nations for your mutual defense and protection and to attach
yourselves firmly to the King's cause, to whose goodness and protection you have been and are so much indebted." [2]

The colonists, of course, could not afford to let Indian
matters drift, and individual colonies sent commissioners to the
Indians. The Indian problem, however, could not be handled
adequately by disparate provincial practices, and on July 12, 1775,
the Continental Congress inaugurated a federal Indian policy
with a report from a committee on Indian affairs. Declaring that
"securing and preserving the friendship of the Indian Nations,
appears to be a subject of the utmost moment to these colonies"
and noting that there was reason to fear that the British would
incite the Indians against the rebelling colonies, the committee
recommended that steps be taken to maintain the friendship of
the Indians. To this end, three departments were established:
northern, including the Six Nations and the Indians to the north
of them; southern, including the Cherokees and all others to the
south of them; and middle, containing the tribes living in between. Commissioners were appointed for each department, five

[1] Walter H. Mohr, *Federal Indian Relations, 1774–1788* (Philadelphia, 1933),
pp. 42–43.
[2] The quotations are in Helen L. Shaw, *British Administration of the Southern Indians, 1756–1783* (Lancaster, Pa., 1931), pp. 96–97, 109–110.

for the southern and three for each of the others (although a fourth was soon added to the northern). The commissioners were to treat with the Indians "in the name, and on behalf of the united colonies"; they were to work to preserve peace and friendship with the Indians and, in the quaint understatement of the report, "to prevent their taking any part in the present commotions." Agents were to be appointed by the commissioners to spy out the conduct of the British superintendents and their agents and to seize any British agents who were stirring up the Indians against the Americans.[3]

Congress the next day appointed the commissioners for the northern and middle departments, but it left the nomination of three for the southern department with the council of safety of South Carolina. That Benjamin Franklin, Patrick Henry, and James Wilson were chosen for the middle department is an indication of the importance attached to the matter.[4]

Indian matters, to be sure, were entwined with the still greater problem of the western lands, since administration of the lands and management of the Indians who were on the lands went hand in hand. As Washington observed in 1783, "the Settlmt. of the Western Country and making a Peace with the Indians are so analogous that there can be no definition of the one without involving considerations of the other." [5] But the questions of managing the Indians and controlling the trade with them did have a separate identity and were considered separately by the Continental Congress. The decisions made by the Congress and the principles incorporated into the Articles of Confederation gave a decisive turn to American Indian policy.

As with all the major questions involved in the formation of the new government, so with the Indian policy the fundamental decision concerned the authority to be given to the federal government. The imperial experiment in the unified management

[3] *Journals of the Continental Congress, 1774–1789* (34 vols., Washington, 1904–1937), II, 174–177.

[4] *Ibid.*, 183, 192, 194.

[5] Washington to James Duane, Sept. 7, 1783, in *The Writings of George Washington from the Original Manuscript Sources, 1745–1799*, John C. Fitzpatrick, ed. (39 vols., Washington, 1931–1934), XXVII, 139–140. See Merrill Jensen, *The Articles of Confederation: An Interpretation of the Social-Constitutional History of the American Revolution* (Madison, 1940), for details of the western land problem and how it was tied in with the Indian question.

of the Indians had made its mark on the minds of the delegates
to Congress, and there was fundamental agreement that Indian
affairs was one area that belonged to the central government.
Benjamin Franklin, the leading personality in the Congress, had
offered a plan of union at Albany in 1754, which provided that
the president-general, with the advice of the grand council, should
control Indian affairs. Now he included the idea in a draft for a
confederation, which he proposed to Congress on July 21, 1775.
He offered two articles. First, no colony could engage in offensive
war against the Indians without the consent of Congress, which
would be the judge of the justice and necessity of the war. Second,
a perpetual alliance, both offensive and defensive, should be
made with the Six Nations. For them, as well as for all other
tribes, boundaries should be drawn, their land protected against
encroachments, and no purchases of land made except by con-
tract drawn between the great council of the Indians and the
Congress. Agents were to reside among the tribes to prevent injustices in the trade and to provide for the "personal Wants and
Distresses" of the Indians by occasional presents. The purchase
of land from the Indians was to be "by Congress for the General
Advantage and Benefit of the United Colonies." [6]

The committee appointed to draft the Articles of Confederation put the task into the hands of the able writer John Dickinson,
a Pennsylvanian like Franklin and an advocate of congressional
control of the western lands. His draft, submitted on July 12,
1776, followed and elaborated the plan submitted by Franklin;
in the general enumeration of powers to be granted the central
government, Dickinson included "Regulating the Trade, and
managing all Affairs with the Indians." [7]

Congressional control of the Indian trade and Indian affairs,
however, was not easily accepted by all. The report of a debate
on July 26 indicated a decided divergence of views. The opposition came chiefly from South Carolina, which wanted to handle
Indian affairs as a colony. Georgia, on the other hand, was quite
willing for Congress to assume the burden, since it itself could
not afford the presents for the Indians which its position as a

---

[6] The 1754 proposal is in *The Writings of Benjamin Franklin*, Albert H.
Smyth, ed. (10 vols., New York, 1905–1907), III, 217–218; the 1775 draft is in
Journals of the Continental Congress, II, 197–198. Jensen, *Articles of Confederation*, p. 152, points out that Franklin's draft reflects his views as a Pennsylvanian
and a land speculator, siding with the landless states in insisting on control of
the western lands by Congress.

[7] Dickinson's draft is in *Journals of the Continental Congress*, V, 546–554.

buffer state against hostile tribes demanded. In the end, the over-all necessities of Indian control prevailed, for, as James Wilson pointed out, the Indians refused to recognize any superior authority and only the United States in Congress assembled could have any hope of dealing with them in an adequate fashion. Above all else, rivalries between colonies in treating with the Indians had to be avoided.[8]

On August 20 an amended draft was agreed to by Congress. The Franklin-Dickinson articles about alliances with the Indians, maintaining their boundaries and purchase of their lands, as well as Dickinson's strong statements about federal control of boundaries of colonies and of the western lands, were omitted. Only the following simple statement appeared: "The United States Assembled shall have the sole and exclusive right and power of . . . regulating the trade, and managing all affairs with the Indians, not members of any of the States." [9]

Even this did not satisfy the advocates of state control, who were jealous of individual state authority within their own territory, and corrective amendments were offered. After two alternative amendments were rejected, the provision was agreed to which appeared in the ratified document. In Article IX, a long enumeration of the powers of Congress, the Articles of Confederation asserted: "The United States in Congress assembled shall also have the sole and exclusive right and power of . . . regulating the trade and managing all affairs with the Indians, not members of any of the States, provided that the legislative right of any State within its own limits be not infringed or violated." [10]

Thus the principle was accepted that the federal government should manage Indian affairs and regulate Indian trade. The principle was enunciated but it was not crystal clear, for the proviso cast a heavy blur over the article and the power that it actually gave to Congress and prohibited to the states. James Madison, in Number XLII of *The Federalist*, poked fun at the article, ridiculing it as "obscure and contradictory," as "absolutely incomprehensible," and as inconsiderately endeavoring to accomplish impossibilities. It must be admitted that Madison was moved to make the Articles of Confederation look black so that the new Constitution might look that much brighter. Practical

---

[8] *Journals of the Continental Congress*, VI, 1077–79; Jensen, *Articles of Confederation*, p. 155; Mohr, *Federal Indian Relations*, pp. 182–184.

[9] *Journals of the Continental Congress*, V, 674–689.

[10] *Ibid.*, IX, 844, 845.

experience, however, gave Madison and other critics of the Articles of Confederation a sound foundation for their criticism. At critical moments some of the colonies refused to abdicate in favor of Congress when it came to dealing with the Indians.

The debates over the Articles of Confederation and the subsequent practice under this frame of government nevertheless did gradually clarify one element of Indian relations. The concept of the Indian Country was strengthened. Not only was the Indian Country that territory lying beyond the boundary lines and forbidden to settlers and to unlicensed traders; but it was also the area over which federal authority extended. Federal laws governing the Indians and the Indian trade took effect in the Indian Country only; outside they did not hold.

♦

The Articles of Confederation were approved in Congress in 1777, but they did not take effect until 1781, for Maryland refused to ratify until the landed states had ceded their western claims to the United States. Meanwhile, the course of the war was in the hands of the Continental Congress and its committees. There was little they could do about the Indians except to treat them as enemies of the colonies in the struggle for freedom. Then, as the war ran its course and peace loomed on the horizon, the problem of the Indians and the western lands again came to the fore.

The ascendency and unique authority of Congress in regard to Indian affairs had to be asserted again and again. The committee appointed to report on the land cessions of the states and on the petitions of various land companies declared on May 1, 1782, that a clearer definition of congressional jurisdiction over Indian affairs was imperative. The recommendations of the committee indicate that the authority given Congress in the Articles of Confederation was not well understood by the states and their citizens. Among a series of resolutions dealing with the creation of new states to the west, the committee felt obliged to include two which reasserted the principle that the sole right of "superintending, protecting, treating with, and making purchases of" the Indian nations living beyond the boundaries of the states belonged to Congress.[11]

The war was now coming to a close. The preliminary peace arrangements were drawn up on November 30, 1782, and on

[11] *Ibid.*, XXII, 230–231.

September 3, 1783, the Peace of Paris was signed with Great Britain. Independence had been won and peace restored, but the hostile Indian allies of the British still had to be pacified. A committee report to Congress on April 21, 1783, recommended suspending all offensive movements against the Indians and informing the Indians of the decision as a preparation for a final peace with them. Four commissioners should be appointed — eastern, northern, western, and southern — and presents should be purchased to be on hand when the Indians assembled for a treaty of peace. Because of the emergency the committee suggested that a special group be appointed until the regular commissioners could be designated, and this group should endeavor to engage the help of respectable inhabitants who knew the Indians to undertake negotiation of an immediate peace. Congress also took action against the steady encroachment taking place on the Indian lands. A proclamation of September 22, 1783, formally forbade settling on lands inhabited or claimed by the Indians outside of state jurisdiction and purchasing or otherwise receiving such lands without the express authority and direction of Congress. It declared moreover that any such purchases or cessions were null and void.[12]

A new report submitted by the committee on Indian affairs on October 15, 1783, proposed a policy for dealing with the Indians of the northern and middle departments only, for the committee disclaimed competency in regard to the southern Indians because of insufficient data.[13] The first problem to be faced was that of drawing the proper boundary lines to designate the lands reserved to the Indians. The lines should be drawn "convenient to the respective tribes, and commensurate to the public wants;" that is, restricting the Indians enough so that lands would be available to fulfill the pledges made to the soldiers during the war for land bounties. This land should be obtained from the Indians without any considerable expenditure to extinguish the Indian claims to the land, an expenditure which the state of public finances would in no case allow. After all, the committee argued, the Indians had been on the losing side in the war. They could with justice be treated as a conquered nation and their

[12] Ibid., XXIV, 264; XXV, 602.
[13] Ibid., XXV, 680–694. The committee which drew up this report relied heavily on the opinions and advice of George Washington, expressed in a letter to the head of the committee, James Duane, September 7, 1783. Much of the wording of the report is identical with that in Washington's letter. Writings of George Washington, XXVII, 133–140.

lands be taken from them by right of conquest. And even if the right of conquest were waived, the destruction wrought by the Indians and the outrages and atrocities they committed required atonement and a reasonable compensation for the expenses which the United States had incurred. The Indians could accomplish this act of justice only by agreeing to the boundaries proposed. The committee, however, was composed of realists, who recommended some compensation for the Indian claims rather than risk another Indian war and the tremendous expense it would bring upon the new nation.

It was further proposed that a general conference should be held with the tribes in order to receive them back into the favor and friendship of the United States. The conference should determine the boundary lines that would divide the white settlements from the villages and hunting grounds of the Indians and thus remove as far as posible the occasion for "future animosities, disquiet and contention." The government commissioners should demand hostages for the return of all prisoners, indicating at the same time to the Indians the nation's preference for clemency instead of rigor in dealing with the defeated Indians. They should tell the Indians that the government was disposed to be kind to them, to supply their wants through trade, and to draw a veil over the past.

The committee drew up in detail the line that should be proposed to the Indians. For the Oneida and Tuscarora tribes, who had adhered to the colonial cause during the war, it recommended special assurances of friendship and recognition of their property rights; and the importance of the Indian trade was not forgotten. To prevent violence, fraud, and injustice towards the Indians the trade must be regulated and the traders required to give security that they would follow the regulations. To this end, the committee recommended that a group be appointed to draw up an ordinance for regulating the Indian trade.

The committee appointed to consider Indian affairs in the south returned an almost identical report on May 28, 1784.[14]

Outlining a policy in the halls of Congress was easy enough; the test came in carrying out the actual negotiations with the Indians. In the north and west this was accomplished shortly by the treaties of Fort Stanwix, October 22, 1784, Fort McIntosh, January 21, 1785, and Fort Finney (at the mouth of the Great

---

[14] *Journals of the Continental Congress*, XXVII, 453–464.

Miami), January 31, 1786. The first, drawn up with the Six Nations, limited them to an area in western New York and distributed goods to them pursuant to "the humane and liberal views of the United States." The second was a treaty with the Delawares, Wyandots, Chippewas, and Ottawas, by which these western Indians were allotted a reservation of land and ceded to the United States other lands formerly claimed by them. The last was a similar agreement made with the Shawnees. In these negotiations the boundary line idea was taken for granted; the basic problems were the exact determination of the line, the conflict of state and federal authority in dealing with the tribes, and the grounds for demanding cessions from the Indians.[15]

The sole and exclusive right of Congress to treat with the Indian tribes was challenged by New York commissioners, who had already come to an agreement with the Six Nations and caused trouble at the Fort Stanwix negotiations, but the federal power was vindicated by the treaty. No provisions were made, however, for trade.[16]

The United States in these first treaties after the Revolution thought it was dealing with conquered tribes or nations. Although Congress spoke of liberality toward the vanquished and realized that some moderation of claims might be necessary to avoid renewal of fighting, its commissioners dictated the boundary lines and offered no compensation for the ceded lands. To this highhanded arrangement the Indians, abetted by the British, continued to object. They had never asked for peace, they insisted, but thought that the Americans desired it, and they had no idea that they were to be treated as conquered peoples.[17]

Furthermore, although the lands west of the boundary lines were guaranteed to the Indians and the United States promised to restrict the encroachment of the whites, white aggressions continued to cause great trouble. Washington, after a tour of the West in 1784, reported the extent of the menace:

Such is the rage for speculating in, and forestalling of Lands on the No. West side of Ohio, that scarce a valuable spot within any tolerable distance

[15] For the treaties see Charles J. Kappler, comp., *Indian Affairs: Laws and Treaties*, Volume II, *Treaties* (Washington, 1904), pp. 5–8, 16–18 — hereafter cited as Kappler, *Treaties*.

[16] For troubles with the New York commissioners see Henry S. Manley, *The Treaty of Fort Stanwix, 1784* (Rome, N. Y., 1932).

[17] Mohr, *Federal Indian Relations*, pp. 93–139; Reginald Horsman, "American Indian Policy in the Old Northwest, 1783–1812," *William and Mary Quarterly*, XVIII (1961), 35–39.

of it, is left without a claimant. Men in these times, talk with as much facility of fifty, a hundred, and even 500,000 Acres as a Gentleman formerly would do of 1000 acres. In defiance of the proclamation of Congress, they roam over the Country on the Indian side of the Ohio, mark out Lands, Survey, and even settle them. This gives great discontent to the Indians, and will unless measures are taken in time to prevent it, inevitably produce a war with the western Tribes.[18]

The government seemed powerless to hold back the onslaughts of the advancing whites, and by 1786 the northwest Indians, out of disgust with the whole policy of the United States, were ready to repudiate all the engagements made with them since the close of the war.

In the south the difficulties were, if anything, even greater because of the tenacity with which the Indians held to their lands, the mounting pressure of the white settlers on the lands, the history of hostility of the tribes against the whites, and the serious interference by state officials in the federal government's handling of Indian affairs. A special committee again reported recommendations for dealing with these southern tribes similar to those proposed a year earlier. Emphasis continued to be placed on the precise determination of the boundary line between Indian country and white and the Indians were authorized to drive off unlawful intruders, who would forfeit the protection of the United States.[19] After troubles with North Carolina and Georgia, which objected to the composition of the board of commissioners, a series of treaties was negotiated with the Cherokees, Choctaws, and Chickasaws at Hopewell at the end of 1785 and the beginning of 1786. These treaties fixed boundaries for the Indian Country, withdrew United States protection from settlers on the Indian lands who would not leave within six months, made arrangements for the punishment of criminals, and declared in solemn tones that "the hatchet shall be forever buried." These treaties stipulated further that "the United States in Congress assembled shall have the sole and exclusive right of regulating the trade with the Indians, and managing all their affairs in such manner as they think proper," and declared that "until the pleasure of Congress

---

[18] Washington to Jacob Read, Nov. 3, 1784, in *Writings of George Washington*, XXVII, 486.
[19] *Journals of the Continental Congress*, XXVIII, 118–120. A detailed account of Georgia's relations with the Creeks is found in Randolph C. Downes, "Creek-American Relations, 1782–1790," *Georgia Historical Quarterly*, XXI (1937), 142–184.

be known," all traders who were citizens of the United States should be entitled to trade with the tribes.[20]

The new nation faced innumerable difficulties and it was imperative that the Indians remain at peace. This happy end could be attained only by a policy of justice toward the Indians and a protection of their rights and property against the unscrupulous traders, avaricious settlers, and speculators. With this in mind, Congress on August 7, 1786, enacted an Ordinance for the Regulation of Indian Affairs. With an eye, no doubt, to North Carolina and Georgia, the sole and exclusive right of Congress under the Articles of Confederation to deal with the Indians was once more reasserted. A southern and a northern Indian department were established, to be divided by the Ohio River. For each district a superintendent of Indian affairs was authorized. These men were to hold office for two years unless sooner removed, reside in or near their districts, and "attend to the execution of such regulations, as Congress shall, from time to time, establish respecting Indian Affairs." The superintendents were placed under the secretary of war and were directed to correspond regularly with him and to obey his instructions. The superintendent of the northern district was authorized to appoint two deputies "to reside in such places as shall best facilitate the regulations of the Indian trade," and the superintendents and the deputies were authorized to grant licenses to trade. They were strictly prohibited, however, from engaging in the trade themselves and were required to take an oath to fulfill their obligations and to post a bond for the faithful discharge of their duties. Only citizens of the United States were permitted to reside among the Indians or to trade with them. A license was required of all traders, good for one year at a fee of fifty dollars, and each trader had to give bond of three thousand dollars for strict observance of the laws and regulations.[21]

Despite the regulations affairs got out of hand. The frontier was too extensive, the enforcing agencies inadequate, the concern with other problems more pressing. Again and again through-

[20] Kappler, *Treaties*, pp. 8–16. Details on the appointment of commissioners are in *Journals of the Continental Congress*, XXVIII, *passim*, and in Merritt B. Pound, *Benjamin Hawkins — Indian Agent* (Athens, Ga., 1951). See also Chapter IV, "The Problems of Peace: Negotiations with the Southern Indians," in Mohr, *Federal Indian Relations*, pp. 139–172.

[21] *Journals of the Continental Congress*, XXXI, 490–493. Objections of the traders to the license fee are reported in Joseph Martin to Henry Knox, July 15, 1788, Papers of the Continental Congress, No. 150, II, 449–451, in General Records of the Department of State, National Archives, Record Group 59.

out the history of Indian affairs, strong statements of the high intentions of justice toward the Indians were issued and re-iterated. The Ordinance of 1786 was backed up in February 1787 by a set of instructions sent to the superintendents of Indian affairs. "The United States are fixed in their determination," the instructions read in part, "that justice and public faith shall be the basis of all their transactions with the Indians. They will reject every temporary advantage obtained at the expence of these important national principles." The superintendents were to seek out the causes of Indian unrest and correct them as much as possible. They were to cultivate the trade with the Indians as an object of special importance but were to allow no traders to engage in the trade without the proper license; they were to investigate the character and the conduct of the traders. To aid in the enforcement of the Ordinance, the commanding officers of the frontier posts were instructed to render such assistance as was necessary and as the state of their commands would allow. These were general instructions; the fine points of treating with the Indians and managing the trade were left to the "prudence, fidelity and judgment" of the agents.[22]

The grand utterances of the general government were largely ignored. Georgia on November 3, 1786, less than three months after the Ordinance had restated the sole and exclusive right of Congress to deal with Indian tribes, signed with the Creeks the Treaty of Shoulderbone, in which a small body of Creeks pretending to speak for the nation signed and gave up the Indian claims to all lands in Georgia east of the Oconee River.[23] The encroachments continued apace, and the trade regulations of the Ordinance were not adhered to, for there is no record of any licenses being issued in the South under its provisions.

Again in the Northwest Ordinance of July 13, 1787, the federal government voiced its position: "The utmost good faith shall always be observed towards the Indians, their lands and property shall never be taken from them without their consent; and in their property, rights and liberty, they shall never be invaded or disturbed, unless in just and lawful wars authorised by Congress; but laws founded in justice and humanity shall from time to time be made, for preventing wrongs being done to them, and for preserving peace and friendship with them." [24]

[22] *Journals of the Continental Congress,* XXXII, 66–69.
[23] Pound, *Benjamin Hawkins,* p. 54.
[24] *Journals of the Continental Congress,* XXXII, 340–341.

The continual reassertion by Congress of its ideas of justice toward the Indians began to have a hollow sound. Part of the problem undoubtedly came from the haziness (at least professed in the minds of some) about the exact authority of Congress, and the intermeddling of the states in Indian affairs aggravated the difficulties of the general government.

Mincing no words, a congressional committee on southern Indian affairs in August 1787 went to the heart of the matter. It insisted on the authority of Congress over independent Indian tribes and condemned the acts of states (specifically Georgia and North Carolina) in dealing with Indian tribes. It demanded that Congress give serious attention to the repeated complaints of the Indians about encroachments upon their lands, "as well because they [the encroachments] may be unjustifiable as on account of their tendency to produce all the evils of a general Indian war on the frontiers." It urged an investigation of the causes of hostilities and a policy of strict justice to both sides. "An avaricious disposition in some of our people to acquire large tracts of land and often by unfair means," the committee noted, "appears to be the principal source of difficulties with the Indians," and it made note of the settlements that were appearing on the lands of the Cherokees and Creeks contrary to treaties made with those tribes.

It was admittedly difficult to determine accurately the titles to land as between the whites and the Indians, but more embarrassing by far was the misunderstanding about the extent of federal power in governing Indian matters. It was on this point that the committee had its strongest say. The constructions placed upon the Articles of Confederation by some of the states were not allowable and were conducive of all manner of evil.

The committee conceive that it has been long the opinion of the country, supported by Justice and humanity, that the Indians have just claims to all lands occupied by and not fairly purchased from them; and that in managing affairs with them, the principal objects have been those of making war and peace, purchasing certain tracts of their lands, fixing the boundaries between them and our people, and preventing the latter settling on lands left in possession of the former. The powers necessary to these objects appear to the committee to be indivisible, and that the parties to the confederation must have intended to give them entire to the Union, or to have given them entire to the State; these powers before the revolution were possessed by the King, and exercised by him nor did they interfere with the legislative right of the colony within its limits. . . . It cannot be supposed, the state has the power mentioned without making the recited clause useless, and without absurdity in theory as well as in practice. . . .[25]

Still the encroachments continued. Henry Knox, secretary of war under the Confederation, reported to Congress in July 1788 the unprovoked and direct outrages against the Cherokee Indians by the inhabitants on the frontiers of North Carolina in open violation of the Treaty of Hopewell. The outrages were of such extent, Knox declared, "as to amount to an actual although informal war of the said white inhabitants against the said Cherokees." The action he blamed on the "avaricious desire of obtaining the fertile lands possessed by said indians of which and particularly of their ancient town of Chota they are exceedingly tenacious," and he urged Congress to take action to uphold the treaty provisions and thus the reputation and dignity of the Union. He recommended that Congress issue a proclamation warning the settlers to depart, and if they did not, to move in troops against them. A suspicion, however, that the whole attempt to maintain order was futile creeps into the remarks of the general. "Your Secretary begs leave to observe," he concluded his report, "that he is utterly at a loss to devise any other mode of correcting effectually the evils specified than the one herein proposed. That he conceives it of the highest importance to the peace of the frontiers that all the indian tribes should rely with security on the treaties they have made or shall make with the United States." [26]

Congress did not disappoint the general. On September 1 it came through with the recommended proclamation — that universal but generally useless prescription for such ills as Knox had described. The proclamation cited the provisions of the Treaty of Hopewell and the boundary lines drawn therein, and it ordered the intrusions and the outrages to cease, enjoining all who had settled on the Cherokee lands to leave at once. It directed the secretary of war to have troops in readiness to disperse the intruders.[27]

That Knox and Congress were not sure of their ground is shown by the deference they both paid to the state of North Carolina. Knox stated in his report his assumption that North

[25] *Ibid.*, XXXIII, 455–462. The precise point at issue was the meaning of the proviso in the Articles of Confederation about not restricting the legislative right of any state within its own borders.

[26] *Journals of the Continental Congress*, XXXIV, 342–344.

[27] *Ibid.*, 476–479.

Carolina would place no obstruction in the way of federal action, but he recommended nevertheless that a special request of concurrence be made of the state. Congress sent special copies of the proclamation to the executives of North Carolina and Virginia, asking their cooperation.

Congress did not retreat from the position that Indian matters were a uniquely federal concern. The hazy proviso in Article IX and the highhanded action of New York and North Carolina caused difficulties, it is true, but the high counsels of state, by constant reiteration of the principle, managed to make it stick. The centrifugal force of state sovereignty and state pride was never strong enough to disintegrate the centralization of Indian control.

The new federal government had to tread with great care and it could not always act according to the theories it propounded. The practical problems of dealing with the Indians at the end of the war had to be met by practicable measures, not high-flown theory. The one basic requirement of the new nation — which never faded from the consciousness of its leaders — was peace on the frontiers. The nation, it was rightly feared, could not survive renewed hostilities with the Indians. The government needed peace in which to get firmly established, and it had to tailor its practice to this great end.

Knox came to realize that agreements with the Indians based upon the right of conquest did not work and that adherence to such a policy would continually endanger the peace of the frontier. The British and colonial practice of purchasing the right of the soil from the Indians was the only method to which the Indians would peaceably agree, and Knox urged a return to that policy. To establish claims by the principle of conquest would mean continuous warfare. He recommended, therefore, that the lands ceded by the northwest Indians be compensated for and that future cessions be acquired by purchase.[28] By the treaties signed at Fort Harmar on January 9, 1789, with the Six Nations and the northwest Indians, the lands granted to the United States at Fort Stanwix and Fort McIntosh were paid for.[29] Small as the payments were, they marked the abandonment of the policy that the lands from the Indians were acquired by right of conquest.

[28] Mohr, *Federal Indian Relations*, p. 132.
[29] Kappler, *Treaties*, pp. 18–25.

THE FIRST YEARS UNDER THE CONSTITUTION

> . . . it is the most ardent desire of the President of the United
> States, and the general government, that a firm peace should be
> established with all the neighbouring tribes of Indians on such
> pure principles of justice and moderation, as will enforce the
> approbation of the dispassionate and enlightened part of man-
> kind. . . . The Indians have constantly had their jealousies
> and hatred excited by the attempts to obtain their lands. I hope
> in God that all such designs are suspended for a long period.
> We may therefore now speak to them with the confidence of
> men conscious of the fairest motives towards their happiness
> and interest in all respects. A little perseverance in such a system
> will teach the Indians to love and reverence the power which
> protects and cherishes them. The reproach which our country
> has sustained will be obliterated and the protection of the help-
> less, ignorant Indians, while they demean themselves peaceably,
> will adorn the character of the United States.
>
> — Secretary of War Henry Knox to Governor
> William Blount, April 22, 1792

After the concern of the Continental Congress with Indian
affairs and the discussion aroused when the Articles of Confederation were drawn up, it is surprising to find so little about
Indian matters in the Constitutional Convention of 1787. It was
almost as if the presence of Indians on the frontiers had slipped
the minds of the Founding Fathers and provisions made for
carrying on relations with the red men only as an afterthought.
The lack of debate on the question indicates, perhaps, how universally it was agreed that Indian affairs were to be left in the
hands of the federal government. It was not the purpose of the
men who wrote the Constitution, of course, to provide explicit
details for congressional or executive action. Grants of powers
and responsibilities were made to the federal government, enabling Congress to work out the detailed laws that were necessary

to achieve the end proposed, but the Constitution is meager indeed on the Indians, and what does appear was not the product of long debate.

The statesmen who gathered in Philadelphia in the summer of 1787 had come together to correct weaknesses in the federal compact. It was natural, then, that disregard of federal authority by the states in Indian matters under the Articles of Confederation should find a place in the discussions. In Madison's mind, at least, the problem was clear, and when the Committee of the Whole discussed the Paterson plan on June 19, Madison asked, "Will it prevent encroachments on the federal authority?" The Articles of Confederation had failed in this regard, and one of the examples adduced by Madison was that "by the federal articles, transactions with the Indians appertain to Congs. Yet in several instances, the States have entered into treaties & wars with them." When the Committee of Detail presented its draft of a constitution to the convention on August 6, however, no provision of any kind was made for dealing with the Indians. To remedy this omission, Madison proposed on August 28 — among other additions to the powers of the federal legislature — that Congress have power "to regulate affairs with the Indians, as well within as without the limits of the United States." His proposal was referred to the Committee of Detail.[1]

This broad grant of power, "to regulate affairs with the Indians," was considerably cut down by the committee, which merely added to the clause granting Congress the power "to regulate commerce with foreign nations, and among the several States" the words, "and with the Indians, within the Limits of any State, not subject to the laws thereof." In the report of the committee of eleven, submitted on September 4, the Indian clause was reduced again, this time to the simple phrase "and with the Indian tribes." The convention agreed to this wording the same day without any opposition.[2]

[1] Max Farrand, ed., *The Records of the Federal Convention of 1787* (4 vols., New Haven, 1911–1937), I, 316, II, 321. Madison had Georgia specifically in mind. In his "Preface to Debates in the Convention of 1787" he wrote: "In certain cases the authy of the Confederacy was disregarded, as in violations not only of the Treaty of peace; but of Treaties with France & Holland, which were complained of to Congs. In other cases the Fedl authy was violated by Treaties & wars with Indians, as by Geo: . . ." *Ibid.*, III, 548.

[2] *Ibid.*, II, 367, 493, 495, 499. There is little evidence that Indian matters entered into the debates over ratification of the Constitution. Georgia, however, seems to have quickly ratified because of a desire to gain stronger protection against hostile Indians. James Jackson, Georgia's representative in Congress, de-

These five words would seem to be scant foundation upon which to build the structure of federal legislation regulating trade and intercourse with the Indian tribes. Yet through them, plus the treaty-making and other powers, Congress has ever since exercised what amounts to plenary power over the Indian tribes. As John Marshall noted in *Worcester* vs. *Georgia,* the Constitution "confers on Congress the powers of war and peace; of making treaties, and of regulating commerce with foreign nations, and among the several states, and with the Indian tribes. These powers comprehend all that is required for the regulation of our intercourse with the Indians. They are not limited by any restrictions on their free actions; the shackles imposed on this power, in the confederation, are discarded." There have been questions about the precise derivation of congressional power over the Indians, of course. Some jurists have emphasized the commerce clause; others find the bulk of congressional power in the treaty clause; some add authority from the general welfare, national defense, and national domain clauses of the Constitution; and in 1886 the Supreme Court spoke of federal power that grew out of the peculiar nature of the relations between the two races, independent of grants of authority in the Constitution. But whatever the ultimate source of congressional power, the federal legislature has never felt hampered for want of authority.[3]

꘎

Congress soon enacted a series of laws specifically designed to express and execute the Indian policy of the United States. The

clared on August 11, 1789, as he was demanding federal aid against the Creeks, that the Georgians "must procure protection here or elsewhere. In full confidence that a good, complete, and efficient Government would succor and relieve them, they were led to an early and unanimous adoption of the Constitution." Quoted in Downes, "Creek-American Relations," pp. 172–173.

[3] An excellent discussion of the constitutional basis for dealing with the Indians is found in W. G. Rice, "The Position of the American Indian in the Law of the United States," *Journal of Comparative Legislation and International Law,* 3d ser., XVI (1934), 78–95. Rice points out the paradox of ending treaty making in 1871: "The federal power over Indians having become firmly settled, Congress thus struck down or admitted to be false the chief constitutional basis of that power." A thorough analysis of the scope of federal power over Indian affairs is in Felix S. Cohen, *Handbook of Federal Indian Law* (Washington, 1942), pp. 89–100. A revision of Cohen's work, *Federal Indian Law* (Washington, 1958), has been issued by the Office of the Solicitor, United States Department of the Interior. My references are all to Cohen's original work, which is more readily available.

See also the arguments in the following decisions of the United States Supreme

architects of this policy were in large part President Washington and Henry Knox, his secretary of war, both men of high integrity, who had had extensive experience in Indian affairs. They understood the frontier situation that confronted the nation in 1789 and proposed to Congress the measures they considered necessary to preserve the well-being and the untarnished honor of the United States.

The first consideration was peace. To achieve and maintain it, two means were possible. The first was renewed military engagement against the hostile tribes, attacks carried on with vigor enough to effect a smashing victory; by absolute conquest the Indians could be destroyed or subdued. Such a policy was rejected by Washington, Knox, and other responsible leaders — though it would appeal to frontiersmen for decades to come — for all-out war was simply impossible. The country, precariously perched among the sovereign nations of the world, could not stand the expense and strain of a long drawn-out Indian war. Nor would such a brutal undertaking accord with the high dictates of humanity and justice demanded by the national character of the United States. The alternative, which had already been frequently propounded in the days following the Revolution, was conciliation of the Indians by negotiation, a show of liberality, express guarantees of protection from encroachment beyond certain set boundaries, and a fostered and developed trade. This program the nation set about to accomplish. Having waived the right of conquest, it determined to compensate the Indians fairly for lands given up and to protect them in the lands they still retained. The Indians' wants would be cared for by a government-fostered trade, and presents would be freely used when necessary to smooth the road toward solid friendship.

The program had in fact begun well before the inauguration of Washington in the treaties signed with the Indians after the Revolution. The policy of good will and guarantees had been laid down for the Cherokees, Choctaws, and Chickasaws in the Treaties of Hopewell in 1785 and 1786. At Fort Harmar in January 1789 the Wyandots and other western Indians had been granted similar terms, and old engagements with the Six Nations had been renewed at the same time and place. Only the Creeks delayed in agreeing to a formal treaty, and they, too, signed in

---

Court: *Cherokee Nation* vs. *Georgia*, 5 Pet. 1 (1831); *Worcester* vs. *Georgia*, 6 Pet. 515 (1832); *United States* vs. *Forty-three Gallons of Whiskey*, 93 U.S. 188 (1876); and *United States* vs. *Kagama*, 118 U.S. 375 (1886).

1790.[4] But the boundary lines established in these treaties and the guarantees of protection to the Indians in their rights were insufficient to restrain the aggressions of the frontier whites.

Washington and Knox were disturbed by the accounts of outrages that came to them from the frontiers, and they systematically carried to Congress reports of the unrest and recommendations for action. For the southern tribes, where the dangers to the tranquillity of the nation for the moment seemed most acute, Washington on August 7, 1789, recommended the appointment of a temporary commission to terminate the differences with the Indians and to lay the foundations for future confidence by an amicable treaty. Two weeks later the President, accompanied by Knox, appeared before the Senate to lay before it the facts about relations with the southern tribes and to call attention to the disorderly conduct of the whites on the frontiers of North Carolina. On August 24 the President returned again to the Senate chamber, where the consideration of the questions was resumed, and the President continued to communicate with the Senate on relations with the hostile Indians.[5] Plainly, something more was needed than the treaties themselves, which had been so largely disregarded.

What Congress supplied in answer to the insistent pleas of the executive was a series of laws "to regulate trade and intercourse with the Indian tribes." These laws, which were originally designed to implement the treaties and enforce them against obstreperous whites, gradually came to embody the basic features of federal Indian policy. The first of these measures became law on July 22, 1790. Continuing the pattern set in the Ordinance of 1786 and earlier colonial legislation, the law first of all provided for the licensing of traders and established penalties for trading without a license. Then it struck directly at the current frontier difficulties. To prevent the steady eating away at the Indian Country by individuals who privately acquired lands from the Indians, it declared the purchase of lands from the Indians invalid unless made by a public treaty with the United States. To put a stop to the outrages committed on the Indians by whites who aggressively invaded the Indian Country, the act made provision

[4] Kappler, *Treaties*, pp. 8–28.
[5] James D. Richardson, comp., *A Compilation of the Messages and Papers of the Presidents, 1789–1897* (10 vols., Washington, 1896–1899), I, 59–60; *Sen. Exec. Jour.*, 1 Cong., 1 sess., pp. 20–24; *American State Papers: Indian Affairs* (2 vols., Washington, 1832–1834), I, 12–16, 54–55.

for the punishment of murder and other crimes committed by whites against the Indians in the Indian Country.[6]

The bill as introduced authorized the appointment of a military officer as superintendent, but strong opposition to this in the House, because it "blended the civil and military characters," caused it to be dropped. In the Senate an article that would have authorized the purchase of trade goods by the government for sale to the Indians through the superintendents and agents was likewise removed.[7] The act in its final form was to be in force "for the term of two years, and from thence to the end of the next session of Congress, and no longer." Congress was feeling its way and was not ready to commit the nation to a permanent measure.

Despite the legislation, frontier disturbances continued in both the north and south, and military force had to be used to restrain the Indians and defend the whites. Washington, however, did not abandon his hope for a rule of law and justice. In his annual message to Congress on October 25, 1791, he laid down basic principles to govern the dealings of the United States with the Indians. The President hoped to avoid all need of coercion in the future, and to this end he sought "to advance the happiness of the Indians, and to attach them firmly to the United States." He offered a six-point program:

1. An "impartial dispensation of justice" toward the Indians.

2. A carefully defined and regulated method of purchasing lands from the Indians, in order to avoid imposition on the Indians and controversy about the reality and extent of the purchases.

3. Promotion of commerce with the Indians, "under regulations tending to secure an equitable deportment toward them."

4. "Rational experiments" for imparting to the Indians the "blessings of civilization."

5. Authority for the President to give presents to the Indians.

6. An "efficacious provision" for punishing those who infringed Indian rights, violated treaties, and thus endangered the peace of the nation.[8]

The President's message was referred to a special committee in the House of Representatives, which in turn reported a bill, but the legislation died without debate or action. Although the act of 1790 still continued in force, its temporary life was about

---

[6] *U.S. Stat.*, I, 137–138.
[7] *Annals of Congress*, 1 Cong., 2 sess., p. 1575 (April 10, 1790).
[8] Richardson, *Messages and Papers*, I, 104–105.

to expire, and Washington in his annual message of 1792 called this fact to the attention of Congress. His report was not optimistic, since troops were being raised and measures taken to put down the continuing hostilities, but he still hoped that legislation could be provided which would eliminate the causes of the conflict, and he again urged the matter upon Congress. It was necessary, first of all, to make sure that the laws were enforced on the frontier and to check the outrages committed by the whites against the Indians, which led only to reprisals on the part of the red men. To this should be added the employment of qualified agents, the promotion of civilization among the friendly tribes, and some plan for carrying on trade with them "upon a scale equal to their wants." [9]

A bill was soon introduced in the House that contained some of the features Washington desired, and as a further means of removing the cause of hostility, stronger provisions were made to prohibit individual acquisitions of Indian lands. The law, which was approved March 1, 1793, was a considerably stronger and more inclusive piece of legislation than its predecessor of 1790. The seven sections of the earlier law were now expanded to fifteen. Part of the increase came from the new sections authorizing the President to give goods and money to the tribes "to promote civilization . . . and to secure the continuance of their friendship," and from a long section that aimed to stop horse stealing, but the bulk of the augmentation came from the detailed provision enacted to stop criminal attacks of whites against the Indians and irregular acquisition of their lands. This act, too, was a temporary one, having the same limitations as to time as the first trade and intercourse act. [10]

A good part of Washington's program was written into these laws; they at least set up the machinery for the protection of Indian rights that the President had asked, and complaints of the Indians about encroachments could be met by prosecutions for violences committed by the whites. Peace, nevertheless, was not yet firmly won, and at the end of 1793 Washington found it necessary to urge further congressional action. In addition to the immediate emergency, which certainly required attention, Washington was looking ahead to measures that would "render tran-

---

[9] *House Jour.*, 2 Cong., 1 sess., pp. 445, 462; Richardson, *Messages and Papers*, I, 125–127. Citations of the *House Journal* for the first thirteen Congresses are in the reprint edition published by Gales and Seaton (9 vols., Washington, 1826).

[10] *U.S. Stat.*, I, 329–332.

quillity with the savages permanent, by creating ties of interest." He came back again to the second part of his two-pronged program. "Next to a rigorous execution of justice on the violators of peace," he said, "the establishment of commerce with the Indian nations, on behalf of the United States, is most likely to conciliate their attachment." Advocating a system of government trading houses which would replace the profit-seeking private traders, he was to hammer at the point again and again until he was heeded by Congress.[11]

The genesis of the first trade and intercourse acts is clear. The laws were necessary to provide a framework for the trade — to establish a licensing system which would permit some control and regulation — but this was merely a restatement of old procedures. The vital sections of the laws dealt with the crisis of the day on the frontier. They sought to provide an answer to the charge that treaties with the Indians, which guaranteed their rights to the territory behind the boundary lines, were not respected by the United States. The laws were not "Indian" laws; they touched the Indian only indirectly, as they limited him in his trade and his sale of land. The legislation was, rather, directed against the lawless whites on the frontier and sought to restrain them from violating the sacred treaties made with the Indians. Even when severe crises were resolved by force — by the crushing of the hostile tribes at Fallen Timbers and Horseshoe Bend, for example — the restrictive elements of the intercourse acts were kept, augmented, refined, and applied to later frontiers.

At first an attempt was made to combine the restrictive or protective features of Washington's program (that is, the regulation of traders, the prohibition of land purchases, the prevention and punishment of outrages against the Indians) with the positive features (the promotion of trade through government trading houses and the civilization of the Indians). But in the course of events the two elements of the President's plan for maintaining peaceful relations with the Indians became embodied in separate series of legislation. The acts "to regulate trade and intercourse with the Indian tribes, and to preserve peace on the frontier," became the main current which carried along the federal Indian policy, which was in large measure a policy of restricting contact between the two races. The essential elements of these acts run in a direct stream up to the present day. There were tributary currents as well, which from time to time marked out other

[11] Richardson, *Messages and Papers*, I, 141.

features of the Indian policy — the government trading houses, the appropriations for civilizing the Indians, and so on. Impressed by Washington's insistence upon trading houses, Congress in 1795 passed a preliminary measure and in the following year established a more sizeable program, which was to continue until 1822,[12] but the program got under way slowly and had little effect on the immediate frontier disturbances at which the trade and intercourse acts were initially aimed.

∞

By the end of 1795 the Indians north of the Ohio had met defeat at the hands of General Wayne, and the focus of Indian trouble was in the Creek and Cherokee nations of Georgia and Tennessee. The largely unrestrained encroachments of the whites upon lands that had been solemnly guaranteed to the tribes caused a constant disruption of the peace, and Washington again asked Congress to act. He reiterated his plea that measures be adopted to protect the Indians from injuries inflicted by inhabitants of the United States and to supply the necessities of the Indians on reasonable terms. The House of Representatives quickly passed resolutions in accord with the President's message and ordered bills to be drawn up pursuant to them. Out of these came the intercourse act of May 19, 1796.[13]

The first section of this new law specified in detail the boundary line between the whites and the Indians — the first designation of the Indian Country in a statute law. The delineation was meant to indicate with added clarity the government's intention to uphold the treaties, and though the boundary line met with opposition in the House, efforts to remove it from the bill failed. More violent was the debate over those sections in the new law which were aimed specifically at intruders on Cherokee lands, but again the supporters of the bill were able to maintain their ground. The bill was the only way, they argued, to satisfy the Indians and prevent encroachment on their lands. As the bill finally emerged, unscathed by the attacks made upon it, it was almost double the length of the one it replaced, with its specification of the boundary line and its additional provisions restricting the whites who looked upon the Indian lands with covetous eyes

---

[12] For a discussion of the factory system, see pages 84–93, below.
[13] Richardson, *Messages and Papers*, I, 185; *House Jour.*, 4 Cong., 1 sess., p. 382.

and upon the Indians themselves with murderous intent. This law, too, was only a temporary measure.[14]

Despite the dissatisfaction with the law on the part of the frontier elements whose encroachments it curtailed, the act was re-enacted with only minor changes in 1799. The law of 1796 did not wreak the havoc on the frontier that its opponents had feared, and it gave assurance to the Indians that the federal government was doing what it could to protect their rights. The 1799 bill was introduced only two days before the old one was due to expire, and it passed both houses without amendment and with little debate.[15]

When Thomas Jefferson sent his first annual message to Congress in December 1801, he could remark that "a spirit of peace and friendship generally prevails" among the Indian tribes. The new President saw no need to depart from the Indian policies of his predecessors, and when the temporary laws for trading houses and for governing trade and intercourse expired, he called Congress's attention to the fact so that appropriate action could be taken to renew them. The only modification he suggested was some restriction upon the liquor traffic among the Indians, which he said the Indians themselves wanted.[16]

Accordingly, on March 30, 1802, a new trade and intercourse act became law.[17] It was for the most part merely a restatement of the laws of 1796 and 1799, but by now the period of trial was over. The act of 1802 was no longer a temporary measure; it was to remain in force, with occasional additions, as the basic law governing Indian relations until it was replaced by a new codification of Indian policy in 1834.

[14] *House Jour.*, 4 Cong., 1 sess., pp. 426, 433, 508, 510; *Sen. Jour.*, 4 Cong., 1 sess., pp. 256–257; *Annals of Congress*, 4 Cong., 1 sess., pp. 286–288, 893–905 (Feb. 2, April 9, 1796); *U.S. Stat.*, I, 469–474. Citations of the *Senate Journal* for the first thirteen Congresses are in the reprint edition published by Gales and Seaton (5 vols., Washington, 1820–1821).

[15] *U.S. Stat.*, I, 743–749; *Sen. Jour.*, 5 Cong., 3 sess., pp. 600, 602; *House Jour.*, 5 Cong., 3 sess., pp. 512–513.

[16] Richardson, *Messages and Papers*, I, 326, 334–335.

[17] *U.S. Stat.*, II, 139–146.

❧ IV ❧

THE INDIAN DEPARTMENT

The motives of the Government for sending Agents to reside with the Indian Nations, are the cultivation of peace and harmony between the U. States, and the Indian Nations generally; the detection of any improper conduct in the Indians, or the Citizens of the U. States, or others relating to the Indians, or their lands, and the introduction of the Arts of husbandry, and domestic manufactures, as means of producing, and diffusing the blessings attached to a well regulated civil Society. . . .
— Instructions to agents, 1802

The committee have sought, in vain, for any lawful authority for the appointment of a majority of the agents and subagents of Indian affairs now in office. For years, usage, rendered colorably lawful only by reference to indirect and equivocal legislation, has been the only sanction for their appointment. Our Indian relations commenced at an early period of the revolutionary war. What was necessary to be done, either for defence or conciliation, was done; and being necessary, no inquiry seems to have been made as to the authority under which it was done.
— Report of House Committee on Indian Affairs, 1834

Enforcement of the intercourse acts depended first of all upon the special personnel within the War Department appointed to deal with the Indians. To the aggregate of these persons the general designation of "Indian department" was applied, a term covering the officials and clerks in the office of the secretary of war who were assigned to Indian matters and the superintendents, agents, subagents, interpreters, and mechanics who carried on the work in the field. It did not necessarily indicate a fixed organization and seems to have been used in the first place as a category for accounting for funds. The term "department," it should be noted, was initially also applied to geographical administrative units, such as the northern and southern districts or departments delineated by the Indian Ordinance of 1786, but the geographical divisions of Indian administration soon came to be known as superintendencies, agencies, and subagencies, corresponding to the designation of the persons in charge. As the laws governing intercourse with the Indians expanded in scope and gained greater clarity of expression, so the official standing and the duties of the men in the Indian department also became more clearly defined, until in 1834 a definitive organization was established by law.[1]

Reference has already been made to the colonial agents sent among the Indians, the British superintendents, the special commissioners sent out by the Continental Congress, and the Indian superintendents authorized by the Indian Ordinance of 1786. All of these were antecedents of the Indian department that eventually took shape. Most directly concerned were the superintendents, for their office was quietly carried over when the new government under the Constitution replaced the Confederation. On September 11, 1789, Congress provided two thousand dollars to be paid to the governor of the Northwest Territory, as his annual salary and "for discharging the duties of superintendent of Indian affairs in the northern department," thus beginning the practice of making territorial governors ex officio superintendents of Indian affairs.[2] In 1790 the act establishing the Territory South of the River Ohio declared that "the powers, duties and emoluments of a superintendent of Indian affairs for the southern department, shall be united with those of the governor." This office of southern superintendent lapsed in 1796 when Tennessee became a state, but in the same year Benjamin Hawkins was appointed "principal temporary agent for Indian affairs south of the Ohio River," and he exercised a wide supervision over the southern Indians, although he was especially responsible for the Creeks. When Mississippi Territory was authorized in 1798, the office of southern superintendent was joined to the office of governor of the new territory. The law of May 7, 1800, which divided the original Northwest Territory and established Indiana Territory, declared that "the duties and emoluments of superintendent of Indian affairs shall be united with those of governor"; the sub-

---

[1] For general accounts of the development of the Indian department, see the works listed in Bibliographical Note, No. 11.
[2] U.S. Stat., I, 50, 54, 68.

sequent laws setting up new territories included a similar clause.[3]

The first intercourse act (July 22, 1790) authorized these superintendents to issue licenses to trade with the Indians, to revoke licenses, and to place the bonds of traders in suit if the laws or conditions of the bonds were violated. There was a reference, furthermore, to "such other person as the President of the United States shall appoint" to issue and recall licenses, but there was no specific provision establishing agencies or appointing agents.[4] To care for particular Indian problems, however, special agents were appointed in 1792. These men — three sent to the southern Indians and one to the Five Nations — were not conceived of as having any connection with the intercourse act. They were charged instead with special diplomatic missions. The agent sent to the Cherokees had as his primary object keeping the southern Indians from joining the warring tribes north of the Ohio and attaching the Indians more firmly to the interests of the United States. The agent sent to the Creeks was to quiet disturbances among them, to see that the Treaty of New York was complied with, and finally to obtain three hundred Creek warriors to join the federal troops against the northern Indians. The duties of the agents sent to the Chickasaws and the New York Indians were of a similar nature.[5]

A new turn in the development of Indian agencies came with the second intercourse act (March 1, 1793). In a section dealing with measures to civilize the Indians, the President was authorized "to appoint such persons, from time to time, as temporary agents, to reside among the Indians, as he shall think proper." [6] The commissions and instructions sent to these agents emphasized their duties in civilizing the Indians by means of agriculture and

[3] *Ibid.*, I, 68, 123, 550, II, 59. For examples of later legislation, see the laws establishing Michigan Territory, Jan. 11, 1805, *ibid.*, II, 309; Louisiana Territory, March 3, 1805, *ibid.*, 331; Illinois Territory, Feb. 3, 1809, *ibid.*, 515. The governor of Orleans Territory, unlike the other territorial governors, was not given the ex officio duties of Indian superintendent by the act for the government of the territory, but he acquired the office by a subsequent act. Acts of March 26, 1804, and March 2, 1805, *ibid.*, 283–289, 322–323. See also William C. C. Claiborne to James Madison, Jan. 27, 1805, in Clarence E. Carter, ed., *The Territorial Papers of the United States* (24 vols. to date, Washington, 1934–), IX 383–384 — hereafter cited as *Territorial Papers*.

[4] *U.S. Stat.*, I, 137.

[5] Instructions to Leonard Shaw, Feb. 17, 1792, in *American State Papers: Indian Affairs*, I, 247–248; Henry Knox to James Seagrove, Feb. 20, 1792, *ibid.*, 249–250; Knox to William Blount, April 22, 1792, *ibid.*, 253; Instructions to Israel Chapin, April 28, 1792, *ibid.*, 231–232.

[6] *U.S. Stat.*, I, 331.

domestic arts and referred to them officially as "temporary agents." The duties assigned them, however, ran the wide range of Indian relations set forth in the intercourse act, and eventually the word "temporary" was dropped from their title, although the instructions remained the same.[7] Under this authorization appeared the permanent Indian agents, assigned to particular tribes or areas, who became indispensable in the management of Indian affairs.

Development of the agents' duties paralleled development of the intercourse acts. At first the duties of the agents were set down in very general terms — to maintain the confidence of the Indians, to keep them attached to the United States, and to impress upon them the government's desire for peace and justice. As the intercourse acts made more specific the means by which peace was to be preserved and justice maintained, the agents' duties were thus also specified, in order to see that the means outlined in the laws were carried out.

The Indian agents were placed under the general superintendence of the territorial governors and were directed to report through them to the War Department, to keep records of the happenings at their agencies, and to note the condition of the Indians, the natural history of the area, and the progress of the Indians in civilization.[8] Subagents were also appointed, but there seems to have been no special authorization for them as distinct from the agents. They were appointed at first as assistants to the agents; then eventually they were assigned to separate locations with duties similar to those of the agents.[9]

By 1818 there were fifteen agents and ten subagents among

---

[7] Benjamin Hawkins in 1796 was appointed "Principal Temporary Agent for Indian Affairs South of the Ohio River," Thomas Lewis in 1799 was appointed "Temporary Indian Agent in the Cherokee Nation," William Lyman in 1801 was appointed "Temporary Agent for Indian Affairs in the Northwestern and Indiana Territories," and Silas Dinsmoor in 1802 was appointed "Temporary Agent for the Choctaw Nation." But the commissions issued to Charles Jouett and Richard Graham in 1815 called them simply "Agent of Indian Affairs." See references in note 12, below.

[8] Dearborn to Governors William C. C. Claiborne, William H. Harrison, and Arthur St. Clair, Feb. 23, 1802, in SW IA LS, vol. A, pp. 166–168; Dearborn to Agents William Lyman, Samuel Mitchell, John McKee, and William Wells, Feb. 27, 1802, ibid., pp. 172–173.

[9] In 1834 eleven of the eighteen Indian agents in office were referred to the act of 1802 for authorization, and twenty-one of the twenty-seven subagents. There was, however, some additional authorization under specific treaty arrangements for agents to the tribes. House Doc. 60, 23 Cong., 1 sess., ser. 255; House Rep. 474, 23 Cong., 1 sess., ser. 263, p. 7.

the Indians, and on April 16 of that year a law was approved which regularized the appointment of these men — they were to be nominated by the President and appointed by and with the advice and consent of the Senate — but the act could hardly be said to establish the agencies which the appointees were to fill. Nor did the act of April 20, 1818, which set the compensation to be allowed the agents and subagents, actually establish the agencies. These laws and the succeeding appropriation bills that provided "for pay of the several Indian agents as allowed by law," merely took the agencies for granted.[10]

In 1822, in an amendment to the intercourse act of 1802, there was repeated mention of agents — their authority in restricting the whiskey traffic, their duties in issuing licenses, and the reports required of them by the War Department. The act, furthermore, authorized the appointment of a superintendent of Indian affairs at St. Louis, having power over the Indians frequenting that place (a necessary arrangement after the admission of Missouri as a state), and a special agent for the tribes in Florida.[11]

However indefinite and insecure their legislative foundation was before 1834, the agents were accepted as a regular part of the Indian service, and the War Department came to rely on them more and more heavily in the enforcement of the Indian policy set forth in the intercourse acts, a reliance explicitly indicated in the instructions and regulations given to the agents. Of these instructions the most important were the detailed ones drawn up for the early agents, which — with some necessary changes in geographical names and territorial officers — continued to be sent to Indian agents until 1815.[12] After a preamble which enjoined upon the agent zealous endeavors to introduce the

[10] U.S. Stat., III, 428, 461.

[11] Ibid., 682–683. In the interval between the end of Missouri Territory with its governor as ex officio superintendent of Indian affairs and the commission to William Clark, who became superintendent under the act of 1822, the Indian agents were charged to correspond directly with the War Department. See John C. Calhoun to Auguste Chouteau, Aug. 4, 1820, in Territorial Papers, XV, 630. This was a general practice, but in some cases agents within states were made subordinate to a nearby territorial governor.

[12] James McHenry to Thomas Lewis, March 30, 1799, in SW IA LS, vol. A, pp. 29–35; Dearborn to Return J. Meigs, May 15, 1801, ibid., pp. 44–49; Dearborn to William Lyman, July 14, 1801, and to Charles Jouett, Sept. 6, 1802, in Territorial Papers, VII, 26–29; Dearborn to Silas Dinsmoor, May 8, 1802, ibid., V, 146–150; A. J. Dallas to Charles Jouett, June 20, 1815, and to Richard Graham, July 14, 1815, ibid., XVII, 190–191, 196–200. The copy of the instructions issued by Secretary of War McHenry in 1799 is the oldest extant copy. It is possible that he merely transcribed instructions that had been issued earlier to other agents.

civilized arts of agriculture and spinning and weaving (an injunction worked into the body of the instructions in the 1815 version), the document directed the agent point by point in his enforcement of the intercourse act and in the records and reports required. The agents and the interpreters they were authorized to appoint were required to take the following oath:

I ——————— do swear, that I will well and truly serve the United States in the office of ——————— and promote, as far as in my power, the execution of the act passed the 3ᵈ of March 1799, entitled "An Act to regulate trade and intercourse with the Indian tribes, and to preserve peace on the frontiers" and all regulations relative thereto proceeding from the President of the United States.

These initial instructions were augmented by specific directions sent to the agents by the War Department, either to promulgate some change in policy or in answer to questions of policy and procedure posed by the agents themselves. From time to time, too, more general directives were issued to the superintendents of Indian affairs for their own guidance and for transmittal to the agents under their charge, and copies of the intercourse act were frequently sent by the War Department to superintendents and agents with the admonition that in the general management of their agencies they were to be guided by the act.[13]

An agent's duties were in large part reportorial. He was to keep an eye out for violations of the intercourse acts and to report them to the superintendents of Indian affairs, to the military commanders of the frontier posts, or to the War Department. Action and further directions to the agent were in most cases to come from these superior officers. But the critical work of dealing with the Indians and the frontier whites devolved upon the agent, and the success of the work depended upon the character of the man, the respect he won from the tribes among whom he lived, and the authority his position had in the eyes of the whites. It was fortunate that the United States had a number of capable and distinguished men of a character and integrity that

[13] For example, see Calhoun to James Miller, Sept. 21, 1819, in *Territorial Papers*, XIX, 102–103; Calhoun to Jean A. Pénières, March 31, 1821, *ibid.*, XXII, 26–27; Calhoun to Abraham Eustis, Aug. 21, 1822, *ibid.*, XXII, 512–513; Calhoun to Lawrence Taliaferro, Dec. 27, 1819, in SW IA LS, vol D, pp. 350–351; Calhoun to William P. DuVal, Lewis Cass, and James Miller, April 20, 1824, in IA LS, vol. 1, p. 46; Thomas L. McKenney to William Clark, April 20, 1824, *ibid.*, p. 47.

gave stature to the office of Indian agent and enabled them by their personal influence alone to ease the conflicts between the whites and Indians without reliance on either civil court procedure or a call upon the military forces.[14]

∿

The work of directing the superintendents and agents rested upon the secretary of war himself and those clerks of his Department whom he chose to assign to the task, for in the first decades of the new nation there was no formally established office charged specifically with Indian affairs. That dealings with the Indians were considered a special category of the Department's activities, however, is indicated by the fact that separate letter books were maintained in the Department for correspondence concerned with Indian matters.

On April 21, 1806, the office of superintendent of Indian trade was established within the War Department.[15] This office pertained to the factory trading system; the superintendent was charged with purchasing goods for the factories, transmitting the stores to the frontier, and in general directing the work of the factors. While he had no responsibilities in the over-all conduct of Indian relations, his office in some ways did become an unofficial focus for Indian affairs, supplying information and advice to the secretary of war and corresponding with citizens who were interested in the Indians. Thomas L. McKenney, who held the office from 1816 to the end of the factory system in 1822, was a zealous promoter of Indian welfare and used his office to further that work.

The abolition of the factory system removed even this semblance of an Indian center in the War Department. But two years later, on March 11, 1824, Secretary of War Calhoun, by his own order and without special authorization from Congress, created in the War Department what he called the Bureau of Indian Affairs. To head the office Calhoun appointed McKenney and assigned him two clerks as assistants. The duties of the new position were set forth in the letter of appointment: to take charge of the appropriations for annuities and current expenses, to examine and approve all vouchers for expenditures, to administer the fund for the civilization of the Indians, to decide on

[14] For general accounts of the work of the agents, see the works of Wesley, Gallaher, Cotterill, and Pound listed in the Bibliographical Note, No. 11.

[15] *U.S. Stat.*, II, 402.

claims arising between Indians and whites under the intercourse acts, and to handle the ordinary Indian correspondence of the War Department.[16]

Despite Calhoun's designation, the new section was not commonly called the Bureau of Indian Affairs. Instead, McKenney headed his correspondence for the first few months with "Indian Office" and then uniformly used the designation "Office of Indian Affairs." Correspondence dealing with Indian matters from the superintendents and agents passed through his hands, as well as correspondence on Indian affairs with persons outside the government. The correspondence was voluminous and McKenney was generally also called upon to prepare the reports on Indian affairs requested by Congress of the secretary of war. He and his clerks formed a sort of Indian secretariat within the War Department, but it did not take McKenney long to become dissatisfied with this setup. The work of handling disbursements, the immense correspondence with the agents, preparation and execution of treaties, care for Indian schools, and regulation of Indian trade all rested with McKenney, but the authority and responsibility still resided in the secretary of war. "It was the weight of these concerns, added to their importance, which led to the creation, *by the Executive*, of this office. But, with its constitution, no power was conveyed," McKenney complained. "The business, though it be arranged, has yet, at every step, to be carried up to the head of the Department, without regard to its importance, otherwise the most unimportant correspondence upon matters of mere detail, is not authorized, *except by the general confidence of the head of the Department in the Officer in charge of the Indian business.*" What McKenney wanted was the creation by Congress of an office of Indian affairs, with a responsible head, to whom would be referred all matters arising out of Indian relations.[17]

McKenney drew up a bill embodying his suggestions, which was introduced in the House of Representatives on March 31,

[16] *House Doc.* 146, 19 Cong., 1 sess., ser. 138, p. 6.

[17] Thomas L. McKenney to James Barbour, Nov. 15, 1825, *ibid.*, pp. 6–9. In an "unofficial" letter of the same date to Barbour, McKenney spoke of his own high qualifications in Indian matters and suggested that a higher salary than the $1600 he was currently receiving was necessary. *Ibid.*, pp. 9–12. McKenney's dissatisfaction with his salary went back to the beginning. He first refused the offer of the job because of the low pay and was persuaded to take it only when Calhoun promised that Congress would be asked to provide for the office with the pay of an auditor. Thomas L. McKenney, *Memoirs, Official and Personal; With Sketches of Travels Among the Northern and Southern Indians* (New York, 1846), pp. 56–57.

1826. It called for the appointment of a "General Superintendent of Indian Affairs," who would have the responsibility for keeping the records on Indian affairs, conducting all correspondence arising out of Indian relations, handling and adjusting financial accounts before transmitting them to the Treasury — and in general for doing all things in relation to Indian affairs which had hitherto rested with the secretary of war directly. The bill was committed to the Committee of the Whole, but it got no further action in that Congress, and subsequent attempts to get the bill passed also failed.[18]

The accounting procedures were always a special problem and seemed to give the officials of the Indian department more trouble than the actual dealings with the Indians. Henry S. Schoolcraft, long-time Indian agent at Sault Ste. Marie, expressed a general view when he wrote graphically in 1828, "The derangements in the fiscal affairs of the Indian department are in the extreme. One would think that appropriations had been handled with a pitchfork. . . . And these derangements are only with regard to the north. How the south and west stand, it is impossible to say. But there is a screw loose in the public machinery somewhere." Such criticisms McKenney was willing to accept; he knew well enough, he said, "how slip-shod almost every thing is," but he insisted that only Congress could remedy the situation.[19]

McKenney's proposal for congressional action was picked up by Governor Cass and General Clark and included in their plan for reorganizing Indian affairs, which they prepared at the behest of the secretary of war in 1829. Then in the Twenty-second Congress the measure was introduced again, this time by the Senate Committee on Indian Affairs, and it passed both houses

[18] *House Jour.*, 19 Cong., 1 sess., ser. 130, p. 394; Original bill (HR 195), 19 Cong., 1 sess., March 31, 1826; *House Jour.*, 20 Cong., 1 sess., ser. 168, pp. 72–73, 105; Original bill (HR 29), 20 Cong., 1 sess., Jan. 2, 1828. McKenney wrote: "At the request of the Chairman of the Committee of Indian Affairs, I prepared a bill, submitted it to the Secretary of War, who wrote on it, in pencil, '*All right — alter not a word.*' I left in it a blank for the committee to fill with the sum they might agree upon for the salary. It was filled with the sum of three thousand dollars. It was reported to the House, and passed to a second reading, and there it stopped, not from objection to it, or its provisions, but because it was taken precedence of, by other matters, deemed by Congress to be of more importance. This was its fate for several successive sessions; I being left, meantime, to get along as well as I might on the *half pay*, which was at the disposal of the department." *Memoirs*, p. 58.

[19] Henry R. Schoolcraft, *Personal Memoirs of a Residence of Thirty Years with the Indian Tribes on the American Frontier* (Philadelphia, 1851), p. 319; McKenney to P. S. Duponceau, Oct. 1, 1828, in IA LS, vol. 5, pp. 140–142.

without difficulty.[20] The bill, which became law on July 9, 1832, authorized the President to appoint a Commissioner of Indian Affairs, under the secretary of war, who was to have "the direction and management of all Indian affairs, and of all matters arising out of Indian relations." The secretary of war was to assign clerks to the new office, without, however, increasing the total number of clerks in the War Department, and an annual salary of three thousand dollars was specified for the Commissioner.[21] It was sadly ironic that the new position was established only after McKenney had been removed from office.

§⦿

The superintendents of Indian affairs and the Indian agents were charged with enforcement of the intercourse acts, but they themselves had no coercive power. They had to rely upon the district attorneys, the marshals, and the courts to bring offenders to justice — and often with only limited success. Within the Indian Country itself, for the apprehension of violators of the law, the examination and seizure of stores suspected of containing liquor, and driving off intruders from the Indian lands, the agent was forced to call upon the commandant of some nearby frontier post.

Traditionally there had been an intimate relationship between the army and Indian matters. Indian affairs were frequently war affairs, and military officers had always played a conspicuous role in dealing with Indians even in peacetime. This is seen in the close connections between the British Indian superintendents and the military commander in America.[22] It is seen, too, in the management of Indian affairs by General Knox under the Confederation, in the placing of Indian affairs under the War Department, and in the explicit authority given for the use of military force in the Indian intercourse acts.

Indian affairs on the American frontier, indeed, can hardly be thought of without taking into consideration the regular army of the United States, for ultimately it was upon the army that responsibility for frontier peace rested. It was the army that quelled outbreaks of Indian hostility; it was the army garrisons along the frontier — a cordon of posts from north to south — that

[20] *Sen. Jour.*, 22 Cong., 1 sess., ser. 211, pp. 155, 309–310, 313; *House Jour.*, 22 Cong., 1 sess., ser. 215, pp. 819, 820, 823, 1029, 1092.

[21] *U.S. Stat.*, IV, 564. The final section of the act authorized the President to discontinue the services of agents, subagents, interpreters, and mechanics if they became unnecessary because of the emigration of the Indians or for other reasons.

[22] See the discussion in Alden, *John Stuart*, pp. 139–155.

overawed the Indians and prevented violence against the whites. More important, the frontier army was the power behind the decisions and polices of the Indian agents and the last resort of the territorial governors in dealing with hostile Indians or recalcitrant whites.

From the very beginning of the government under the Constitution Henry Knox insisted upon a line of garrisons in the Indian Country, in order to enforce the treaties and maintain the peace of the frontier. "The angry passions of the frontier Indians and whites, are too easily inflamed by reciprocal injuries, and are too violent to be controlled by the feeble authority of the civil power," he wrote to Washington on July 7, 1789. "There can be neither justice or observance of treaties, where every man claims to be the sole judge of his own cause, and the avenger of his own supposed wrongs. In such a case, the sword of the republic only, is adequate to guard a due administration of justice, and the preservation of the peace." Knox recommended that at least five hundred troops be assigned to the frontier and that offenders against the treaties be tried by court-martial. The following year Knox, viewing the unsubdued Creeks, the demands of the Cherokees for enforcement of the Treaty of Hopewell, and the need for cultivating the friendship of the Chickasaws and Choctaws, again called for the establishment of a line of military posts on the southern frontier and the augmentation of the number of troops. In 1794 he repeated his call for the line of regular army posts in the Indian Country and for the use of courts-martial to try offenders, both Indians and whites. "If to these vigorous measures," he concluded, "should be combined the arrangement of trade, recommended to Congress, and the establishment of agents to reside in the principal Indian towns, with adequate compensations, it would seem that the Government would then have made the fairest experiments of a system of justice and humanity, which, it is presumed, could not possibly fail of being blessed with its proper effects — an honorable tranquillity of the frontiers." [23]

The line of military posts manned by regular troops that Knox called for became an established part of United States frontier policy. At first there was a string of small garrisons along the Ohio and from the Ohio north to Lake Erie, and a line of posts among the southern tribes stretching from the St. Mary's River

[23] Knox to Washington, July 7, 1789, Jan. 4, 1790, and Dec. 29, 1794, in *American State Papers: Indian Affairs*, I, 53, 60, 544.

to the Ohio. Then as white pressure pushed the frontier west, the line of posts shifted, too; new ones were established deep in the Indian Country or on the line of contact between the Indians and the whites, and older posts faded into oblivion as the troops moved west. The posts were small, and the number of troops that could be squeezed from the civilian-minded and economy-conscious Congress was always inadequate, but the Indian agents and special commissioners who carried on the relations between the government and the Indians always did it under the shadow of the authority and protection of a nearby military garrison.[24]

The instructions sent to the Indian agents uniformly directed them to apply to the military commanders for aid in carrying out their duties, and reciprocally, the army officers received explicit directives time after time from the War Department to assist the agents in the enforcement of the laws and treaties. The legal justification for this assistance was written into the intercourse acts, beginning with the act of May 19, 1796, which provided that the President of the United States could employ such military force as he judged necessary to remove illegal settlers on lands belonging to the Indians or secured to them by treaty, and to apprehend any person found in the Indian Country in violation of the intercourse acts. Furthermore, the act directed the military force of the United States, when called upon by civil magistrates, to assist in arresting offenders against the act and committing them to safe custody for trial according to law.[25]

The recommendation made by Knox and others for trial and punishment by court-martial, however, was never acceded to by Congress. The intercourse acts carefully provided that the military troops, in apprehending persons who were in the Indian Country illegally, were to convey them immediately by the nearest convenient and safe route to the civil authority of the United States in an adjoining state or territory to be tried. The act of 1796 directed that persons thus apprehended by military force could be detained by the military no more than ten days between arrest and removal to the civil authorities. In 1799 the period of detention was reduced to five days, and as a further precaution against tyrannical action, which American frontiersmen always feared and suspected on the part of the military, the law provided that the officers and soldiers having custody of a prisoner should treat

[24] For data on the military posts, see the references listed in the Bibliographical Note, No. 11.
[25] U.S. Stat., I, 470, 473–474.

him "with all the humanity which the circumstances will possibly permit; and every officer and soldier who shall be guilty of maltreating any such person, while in custody, shall suffer such punishment as a court-martial shall direct." Military officers, if requested by the persons in custody, were required to conduct them to the nearest judge of the supreme court of any state, who, if the offense were bailable, might take proper bail if offered. By a special supplement to the intercourse act in 1800, this final provision was extended to justices of inferior or county courts, unless the defendant was charged with murder or some other capital offense.[26]

When the intercourse act of 1802 was augmented by a prohibition against foreigners in the Indian trade, the President was authorized to direct the use of military force in seizing trading goods introduced by foreigners and furs they had collected from the Indians, and the act of 1822 against the introduction of whiskey into the Indian Country specified that military officers as well as Indian superintendents and agents could be directed to search the stores suspected of harboring the contraband liquor.[27]

Intimate cooperation was required of the agents and the military commanders, not only by the intercourse acts themselves, but also by the repeated directives coming from the secretary of war, the general in chief, or the head of the Office of Indian Affairs. Typical of the directives was one sent from Secretary of War Barbour to General Jacob Brown in 1825: "Sir, You will cause an order to be given to the commanding officer of Cantonment Towson, to afford from his command such military aid to Captain Gray, Indian Agent at Sulphur Fork on Red River, as he may from time to time require to enable him to carry into effect the provisions of the intercourse law and the orders of this Department."[28] Official directives, unfortunately, were unable to iron out all the rough edges in human relationships between the military post commanders and the civilian Indian agents. Both groups were subject to the War Department and the direction and surveillance of the secretary of war, but frequent conflicts of authority arose, to the detriment of efficient enforcement of the intercourse acts. Legally, and according to accepted practice, routine peacetime Indian relations were to be in the hands of the civilian superintendents and agents. Troops were to be called

[26] *Ibid.*, I, 748, II, 40.
[27] *Ibid.*, III, 333, 682.
[28] Barbour to Brown, July 11, 1825, in *Territorial Papers*, XX, 93–94.

upon by them only when physical force or the threat of its use was necessary. Alexander Hamilton expressed the policy in a letter to a frontier commander in 1799:

> You are aware that the Governors of the North Western Territory and of the Missisippi Territory are severally *ex officio* Superintendants of Indian Affairs. The management of those affairs under the direction of the Secretary of War appertains to them. The military in this respect are only to be auxiliary to their plans and measures. In saying this, it must not be understood that they are to direct military dispositions and operations; But they are to be the organs of all negociations and communications between the Indians and the Government; they are to determine when and where supplies are to be furnished to those people and what other accommodations they are to have. The military in regard to all such matters are only to aid as far as their Cooperation may be required by the superintendants; avoiding interferences without previous concert with them, or otherwise than in conformity with their views. This will exempt the military from a responsibility which had better rest elsewhere: And it will promote a regular and uniform system of Conduct towards the Indians, which Cannot exist if every Commandant of a Post is to intermeddle separately and independently in the management of the concerns which relate to them.[29]

The army officers were sensitive about taking orders from civilian officers of the government, even from the superintendents and agents who were, like them, under the War Department. Specific orders coming directly from the secretary of war or down through the chain of command to the post commandant were considered necessary before the military officers would heed the requests of the agents for help. Such orders, however, were a normal procedure and the agents were supported by the War Department in their call for military assistance, although the post commanders could be slow to respond and ready in finding excuses for taking no action at all.

Difficulties sometimes arose because of interference in Indian affairs on the part of the army officers, who did not always wait to get a cue from the agents and whose garrisons were at times a point of infection in the Indian Country, to which the Indians flocked for free food and even liquor. One Indian agent recommended to Governor Lewis Cass in 1815 that the relative powers of the agents and the commanding officers be more clearly pointed out. "For want of this definition of powers," he asserted, "the officers of the two departments are very apt to fall out, and the

---

[29] Hamilton to J. F. Hamtramck, May 23, 1799, *ibid.*, III, 24–25.

publick interest receive much injury." [30] Lawrence Taliaferro, the able Indian agent at St. Peter's, for example, had been directed when he assumed his post to consult with the post commander at Fort Snelling and keep him informed of all his proceedings as agent. "It is of the first importance," Calhoun had written him, "that, at such remote posts, there should be a perfect understanding between the officers, civil and military, stationed there, to give energy and effect to their operations." Nevertheless, in his long tenure in the office of agent, Taliaferro was often at odds with the commander of the fort.[31]

The disputes and controversies between agents and officers, however, were more than balanced by the energy and zeal with which most of the frontier commanders undertook to carry out the Indian policy of the federal government. In removing intruders, confiscating liquor, restraining Indian hostilities, and conducting treaties and conferences, the army officers were able and devoted supporters of the government and of the intercourse acts.

[30] Benjamin F. Stickney to Cass, Sept. 27, 1815, *ibid.*, X, 597. For an indication of trouble at Prairie du Chien, see Alfred Brunson, "Memoir of Thomas Pendleton Burnett," *Wis. Hist. Colls.*, II (Madison, 1856), 247–248.

[31] Calhoun to Taliaferro, Dec. 27, 1819, in SW IA LS, vol. D, p. 350. See also the Taliaferro Journals in the library of the Minnesota Historical Society.

◄ V ►

REGULATING THE TRADE IN FURS

For the benefit and comfort of the Indians, and for the prevention of injuries or oppressions on the part of the citizens or Indians, the United States in Congress assembled shall have the sole and exclusive right of regulating the trade with the Indians, and managing all their affairs in such manner as they think proper.

— Treaty of Hopewell with the
Cherokees, 1785

Under the existing regulations, the United States have sustained great injury, by foreigners, and improper characters having been licensed to trade on their own account, with little or no responsibility to any government, and a kind of peddling traders, without license, vending their wares and ardent spirits, not only to the great injury of the savages, but to the peace and safety of our frontier inhabitants.

— Report of Special House Committee, 1819

The fur trade was the most important source of legitimate contact between the Indians and the whites, and from earliest colonial days it had been of great economic and political significance. After the Revolution and especially after the removal of British and Spanish influence over the natives in the early years of the nineteenth century, the political importance of the trade disappeared; it was no longer necessary to win over the Indians from rival allegiances by drawing them into the American circuit of trade. Economically, too, the trade declined in importance, and by 1834 John Jacob Astor, the great fur mogul, withdrew from the business after complaining for years about its economic liabilities. Governmental interest in the trade then tended to become colored more and more by a humanitarian interest in the Indians, by the desire to protect them from the injustices of wily traders and thus assure Indian contentment and peace on the frontiers. But under all the changing conditions trade regulation was an essential element in federal Indian policy.

Congress did not have to look far for a method of regulation. It simply adopted the principles of the licensing system used for decades past, although it softened somewhat the requirements that had been set forth in the Ordinance of 1786. The intercourse act of July 22, 1790, required a license for those who wished to trade with the Indians, to be issued for a period of two years by the superintendent of the department or by some other person appointed by the President. A bond of one thousand dollars was required from the trader for faithful observance of the rules and regulations set up to govern the trade, and the issuing agent was authorized to recall the licenses and put the bonds in suit for violations of the rules. Any person who attempted to trade without a license or who was "found in the Indian country with such merchandise in his possession as are usually vended to the Indians" was subject to forfeiture of his goods, one half to go to the person prosecuting, one half to the United States. Succeeding acts repeated these provisions, with an occasional strengthening of the legislation by additional restrictions or increased fines. The act of 1793 added to the forfeiture of goods of unlicensed traders a fine not to exceed one hundred dollars and imprisonment not to exceed thirty days, at the discretion of the court. It further prohibited the superintendents and agents who issued licenses from engaging in the trade themselves, under the penalty of a thousand-dollar fine and imprisonment up to twelve months. The act of 1796 and subsequent acts provided that military force might be employed to apprehend offenders. In 1822 the limit of the bond was raised to five thousand dollars, proportioned to the amount of capital employed, and fur traders among the remote tribes west of the Mississippi were granted their licenses for terms up to seven years.[1]

These laws supplemented and strengthened the treaties signed with the Indians, which often dealt with trade and the federal government's right to regulate it. Even during the period of the Confederation some trade provisions appeared in the treaties. That of Hopewell with the Cherokees, for example, asserted the exclusive right of Congress to regulate trade with the Indians and to manage Indian affairs. Later treaties were more specific in their trade stipulations. The treaty with the western Indians at Fort

---

[1] *U.S. Stat.*, I, 137–138, 329–330, 473, III, 682.

Harmar on January 9, 1789, provided that no person was to reside in the Indians towns as a trader without a license from the governor of the Northwest Territory or his deputies. The Indians promised in the treaty to protect the licensed traders and to deliver to the governor persons who intruded themselves on the Indian lands without a license. The Treaty of Greenville had substantially the same provision, and in 1804, when a treaty was drawn up in St. Louis with the Sacs and Foxes, a formal statement was included that the laws of the United States governing trade and intercourse with the Indian tribes extended to the country inhabited by these tribes. The tribes agreed to help enforce the law by not allowing unlicensed traders to reside among them and to send to the agents or superintendent from time to time a list of all the traders operating among them.[2]

For the next few years such provisions were omitted from the treaties, but the spate of treaties made in the summer of 1825 with the Indians of the Plains all included two articles about trade. One article reiterated the provision of the law of 1824 which directed that trade be carried on only at certain designated spots and added the requirement that only citizens be allowed as traders. In a subsequent article, the various tribes agreed to protect the licensed traders who were sent among them and to apprehend and turn over to United States authorities all persons who came in to trade illegally.[3]

The laws and the treaty provisions seem unexceptionable as one reads through them. The licensing system was meant to furnish a check on the traders and make them abide by the rules and regulations of the trade. The bond of one thousand dollars was high enough to eliminate the unstable, and the threat of confiscation of goods — with one half to the informer — should have dampened any hopes for profitable trading outside the law.

The facts, however, belied the surface impression. Year after year reports poured in about illegal trading and the inability of anyone to prevent it. In March 1792 the commander of Fort Knox reported to the secretary of war that British traders with goods from Michilimackinac were operating along the Illinois and Wabash rivers, underselling United States traders with goods

[2] Kappler, *Treaties*, pp. 10, 20, 42–43, 76. Similar provisions to those in the Cherokee treaty were written into the treaties with the other southern tribes, but nothing was said about trade in the treaty with the Six Nations at Fort Stanwix in 1784.

[3] Kappler, *Treaties*, pp. 225 ff.

brought in without payment of duty and plying the Indians with strong drink. "There is so much difficulty and ceremony to find them out that not one of them has yet been punished since the civil government has taken place," the officer wrote, and he advocated some sort of military control. "Civil Law," he added "is an admirable institution any where except on a frontier situated in the center of an Indian Country and in a time of War." [4]

Both north and south of the Ohio the territorial governors found it impossible to cope with the illicit trade. Governor William Blount wrote from Knoxville at the end of 1794 to the secretary of war, recommending the establishment of military posts in the Cherokee country and urging that no trade be permitted anywhere except under the shadow of the posts, where the agents could more easily regulate the intercourse. At almost the same time George Turner, who had been appointed one of the judges of the Northwest Territory in 1789, reported from Kaskaskia to Governor Arthur St. Clair at Marietta his complaints about the intercourse act, which was "open to evasions and has, in some instances, been evaded before my Eyes."

Under the present Law [he wrote], the Indian Merchandize is not seizable, unless found in the indian Country — a very indefinite term. Besides us it cannot be supposed that our civil Officers are resident in the Indian Country, but on the contrary in towns and settlements, the first knowledge we usually have of the illicit Trader's arrival with Goods is from himself, on landing at some Town or Settlement to sell them to such Indians as may come in to trade. Others go directly into what I would term the Indian Country, that is not more than 10 or 15 Miles, perhaps, from the Settlements — there they send off runners to invite the Indians, who instantly crowd in to make their purchases. I fancy but few Sherifs could be found hardy enough to face such Traders thus surrounded by savages, who would without hesitation make the traders cause their own. I mean however to make the Experiment soon; but shall take care to have the Sherif supported by the Posse of his County. There have lately gone out from Kakokia to a point at no great distance, 14 or 15 Horses packed with indian merchandize, the property of british traders.

St. Clair forwarded the letter to the secretary of state with the acid remark that he had been obliged to remind the good judge that "the executive and judicial authority and duties are quite

[4] J. F. Hamtramck to Henry Knox, March 31, 1792, in *Territorial Papers*, II, 381.

distinct . . . and that his office is neither inquisitorial nor executive." [5]

With the addition of the Louisiana Purchase the problems of regulating the trade spread over a vaster area and one where the legal lines were even less clearly drawn. Governor William C. C. Claiborne of Orleans Territory reported at the beginning of 1805 that the intercourse between the white citizens and the Indians west of the Mississippi was "at present not subject to much restraint." He noted that several persons had been carrying on trade with the Indians without licenses, but since he had not received instructions on the subject he felt "a delicacy in interfering." Claiborne, however, continued to send instructions governing Indian trade to the army commanders on the frontier and directed them to stop all traders without licenses from the governor, unless they were persons of good character and gave bond of four thousand dollars that they would traffic in peltry only.[6]

At St. Louis William Clark called the intercourse act "a little defective, and not as well Calculated for this Territory as for other parts of the U. States in which it was intended to have its effect." He noted several violations and contempts of the law and related in some detail the case of an unlicensed trader whose goods were seized and who was bound in eight thousand dollars to appear before the September term of the court. The grand jury could not be induced to indict the man, even on the oath of two very respectable persons, and it was feared that the agent who had apprehended the trader would be made to pay for his "solisitude to do a service to his Country." Clark feared that the principle would be established that no punishment could be expected for infringement of the intercourse laws and that an agent might be imprisoned for attempting to enforce the law. The fact that the law applied strictly only to the Indian Country — territory where the Indian title had not yet been extinguished — caused confusion and disruption, for the lines were not well marked and were only imaginary barriers that were freely crossed back and forth. Even the agents of the Indian department were

[5] Blount to Knox, Nov. 10, 1794, *ibid.*, IV, 368; St. Clair to the Secretary of State, May 4, 1795, *ibid.*, II, 515–518.

[6] Claiborne to James Madison, Jan. 27, 1805, *ibid.*, IX, 384; Claiborne to Joseph Bowmar, Jan. 29, 1805, *ibid.*, 387. Unlike the governors of previously organized territories, the governor of Orleans Territory was not given the office of superintendent of Indian affairs by the organic act. The authority was not given until the act of March 2, 1805, became effective.

not clear in their own minds about the distinctions of the law, and missteps in the enforcing of the law weakened their authority.[7]

The problem of enforcing the intercourse acts can be understood and appreciated only in the light of the character of the men with whom the enforcing agents had to contend. The organized and responsible trading companies, of which the American Fur Company stood pre-eminent, were troublesome enough. Some of their business tactics and the character of many of their lesser employees were far from righteous, and they could interfere seriously with the process of the law by their political pressure and their astute discovery of legal technicalities. But coexisting with them on the frontiers was another breed of men — irresponsible, lawless, in many cases depraved — who lived off clandestine intercourse with the Indians, supplying them with whiskey and some trade goods and reaping a harvest of furs in return. They were everywhere condemned, and the documents of the period are filled with epithets that make disheartening reading.

The Missouri Baptist Association memorialized Congress in October 1818, begging for some means of supplying the Indians by fair and honorable means so as to prevent the "base and corrupting intercourse" with the Indian traders. "They are," the Baptists averred, "generally speaking, men who have no principle but *gain*; and being at a distance from the restraints of civilized manners, they give full scope to their corrupt propensities. For gratifying these, they defraud the Indians of their property, corrupt their morals, debauch their manners, and consequently, increase the wretchedness of those already miserable people, and prejudice their minds against our Government, our citizens, and our manners, and lead them to have the most contemptible ideas of our civilization, and religion."[8]

A special committee of Congress reported on January 15, 1819, that a more aggressive and extensive system was needed to civilize the Indians and regulate their trade, for as things stood, foreign traders, licensed traders of bad character, and unlicensed interlopers were debauching and defrauding the savages and threatening the peace and security of the frontier citizens.[9] The

---

[7] Clark to Henry Dearborn, July 17, 1807, in *Territorial Papers*, XIV, 136–137; Richard Graham to William H. Crawford, July 8, 1816, *ibid.*, XVII, 359.

[8] Memorial to Congress, Missouri Baptist Association, Oct. 24, 1818, *ibid.*, XV, 448–440.

[9] *House Doc.* 91, 15 Cong., 2 sess., ser. 22.

very nature of the fur trade called forth a type of man to whom the restraints of more civilized living meant little. These traders went off into the wilderness with their packs of goods and sought out the peltries of the Indians. Often they took Indian wives and adopted Indian ways, yet their loyalties were hardly transferred to the tribe, for they mercilessly exploited the Indians, debauched them with whiskey, and then robbed them of their furs. The fines and forfeitures of the laws meant little to them, for they had no property to lose. If they were temporarily driven off in one area they quickly appeared again in another.

A few historians have come forward to salvage the reputation of these forest men. But romanticizing their life, making them "solitary frontier heroes" and picturing them devouring their daily rations of corn and fat "under the open sky, with the greensward for a tablecloth and the nearby stream for a finger bowl" is hardly convincing in the face of so much contemporary condemnation of their character and their actions. Henry H. Sibley, for many years a respectable trader near Fort Snelling, defended the traders in his reminiscences. "Perhaps no body of men have been so misunderstood and misrepresented . . .," he wrote. "To them have been ascribed not only all the evils and outrages that are the accompaniments of extreme frontier life, where law is unfelt and unknown, but they have been charged with fraud and villainy of every conceivable description. . . . With too much self respect to contradict charges so absurd and improbable, and with an undue contempt for public opinion, it is not surprising that scarcely a voice has been raised, or a pen wielded on his behalf." [10]

The true picture does not come from splitting the difference between the two evaluations and coming up with a genial "average trader," half frontier hero, half unscrupulous wretch. Rather we should divide the traders into two rough classes, found on all the frontiers in all the periods of fur trade history. There were the licensed traders, often attached to some company like the Ameri-

[10] Ida A. Johnson, *The Michigan Fur Trade* (Lansing, 1919), p. 163; Henry Sibley, "Reminiscences: Historical and Personal," *Minn. Hist. Colls.*, I (St. Paul, 1872), 463, quoted with approval in R. Carlyle Buley, *The Old Northwest: Pioneer Period, 1815–1840* (2 vols., Bloomington, 1951), I, 407. Buley speaks of the traders' "energy and a capacity to meet and handle varied problems incidental to their business." He concludes: "The peculiar fascination of this hazardous life, so rarely financially remunerative to the average trader, lay in part, no doubt, in the charm of the surroundings, the romance of wild regions inhabited by savage beasts and men, and the adventures and dangers which gave zest to existence."

can Fur Company, who frequently were substantial men in the frontier community (although often enough their business methods would hardly pass a strict scrutiny) — men like Sibley and Hercules Dousman. But there were also the hordes of independent little traders, large numbers of whom were unlicensed and who made no attempt to adhere to the rules and regulations of the government and its agents. It was these men who appear so numerously in the reports that reached the Indian Office and the War Department. The distinction, of course, did not entirely escape the men of the time. Colonel George Croghan, whose long term of duty as Inspector General brought him into close contact with the frontier, clearly delineated the two classes: "Confound not together the licensed trader and the whiskey dealer of the frontier. The latter is but the unprincipled scoundrel who makes the Indian drunk that he may rob him of his blanket, rifle, traps, and whatever else he can lay his hands on. The former, on the contrary, refuses the Indian whiskey, urges him to leave the settlement of the whites, at the same time providing him with needful articles and in every way encouraging him to exert himself in the hunt, well knowing that they are mutually and gainfully interested in its result." [11]

There was trouble enough from both groups when it came to enforcing the intercourse acts — from the one a total disregard for legalities and from the other lobbying to get favorable laws and interpretations and an intransigence in the local courts against government officials who were too solicitous in the enforcement of the letter of the law.

≫≪

It seemed well-nigh impossible to stop the illegal trading by judicial process through the courts. The intercourse acts provided judicial machinery, designating the action to be taken and the courts to be used, but the machinery was shaky and not very effective. Distances were too great, the time lag too long, and the difficulties of arranging for witnesses too serious to provide an effective deterrent or remedy for the illicit traffic. If some diligent and conscientious officer or agent did make the effort to bring a violator to trial, the chances were that the judges would dismiss

[11] Francis Paul Prucha, ed., *Army Life on the Western Frontier: Selections from the Official Reports Made Between 1826 and 1845 by Colonel George Croghan* (Norman, 1958), pp. 165–166. This George Croghan should not be confused with the Indian trader and agent of the same name, who died in 1782.

the case on a technicality or the jury side with the defendant. Too often the only reward for the officer who attempted to enforce the law was to be called into court himself to answer to charges of illegal trespass or arrest.

Brigadier General Thomas A. Smith laid the matter before the secretary of war in the spring of 1818. Smith had earlier issued instructions to the commanding officers under him to seize all persons found violating the intercourse act. Under these orders, Captain James H. Ballard, the commandant at Fort Edwards, had arrested a number of men for trading illegally with the Indians and sent them under guard to St. Louis, along with witnesses to prove the accusations. All the effort went for naught. Judge Silas Bent declined to act in the case, on the ground that there was no legal evidence before him and that it did not appear that the offense was within the jurisdiction of his court, since it might have been committed within the jurisdiction of the courts of Illinois Territory. Such a rebuff from the courts forced Smith to countermand his orders to the post commanders and to leave the matter entirely in the hands of the Indian agents, who had authority to act but no force to back them. Smith was dissatisfied because the governor had not supported his action against illegal traders, but Clark was well aware of the problem and sought to strengthen the agents in dealing with it. He begged the secretary of war to appoint an agent for the tribes on the Missouri River with extensive powers to seek out illicit traders (especially those distributing liquor), to seize and send down for trial traders operating without license, and to call upon the military to assist the agents. Similar powers should be given to agents on the Mississippi and Arkansas rivers, and Clark further suggested that the agents be furnished with a few regular troops to act as boatmen under their control. "Such a Measure," he argued, "would be reduceing the necessary expenditers, and produce a favourable affect among the Indians; as Soldiers are more respected by the Indians on those rivers than Common Trader or Citizen." The plan had its good points, but Clark showed a strange naiveté in assuming that the army officers and their soldiers would be ready to subordinate themselves in such a degree to the Indian agents.[12]

The secretary of war directed the agent appointed for the Missouri to exercise an uncommon degree of industry and discretion and not to come into collision with the foreign or illicit traders

---

[12] Smith to Calhoun, April 18, 1818, and enclosures, in *Territorial Papers*, XV, 380–383; Clark to Calhoun, May 11, 1818, *ibid.*, 392–393.

who were seeking a monopoly of the trade until the military posts were finally established. At that time, the agent was instructed, "You will give notice, that all trade except that which. is duly licensed by government will be prohibited under the penalty provided by law. To the regular traders you will afford every protection in your power." [13]

Indian agents found little support on the frontier when they tried to prosecute violators of the law. A striking case occurred among the Creeks in 1824. A man had located himself in the Creek Nation as a trader and sold goods without license. He was apprehended by the Indian agent, John Crowell, and was tried in the district court at Savannah. The fact that the man had traded without a license was solidly established before the court. The defendant claimed, however, that he had an Indian wife and was an adopted member of the Nation, and therefore not subject to the trade and intercourse laws, since the Creeks were a sovereign and independent nation. The district attorney destroyed the argument by producing the Treaty of Fort Jackson, which expressly declared that the Creeks would not admit any persons among them as traders except those who were licensed by agents of the United States. Crowell was taken aback by the jury's verdict. "Notwithstanding the offence for which the Deft. was indicted had been established by unimpeachable testimony, and the charge of the Judge to the Jury clear and conclusive," he wrote, "the Jury returned a verdict of not Guilty. If so strong a case as this cannot be prosecuted to effect, it will be worse than useless to attempt the execution of the laws of the U. States in the nation." It was easy, he asserted, for "men of the worst character" to become Indian citizens. [14]

On all parts of the frontier the story was much the same. Florida, too, was not immune from the confusion and uncertainty that marked the operation of the intercourse acts in other areas. Lieutenant Colonel Abraham Eustis, the acting Indian agent, informed the secretary of war in 1822 that there was not a single licensed trader in East Florida, and as a result many Indians brought their skins and other articles of trade into St. Augustine, where they were abundantly supplied with liquor. There were no municipal regulations to prevent it and no power to enforce regulations, anyway. To get things started on an orderly basis Governor William P. DuVal in June 1823 revoked all previous

---

[13] Calhoun to Benjamin O'Fallon, March 8, 1819, *ibid.*, 520–521.
[14] Crowell to Calhoun, Nov. 23, 1824, in IA LR, Creek Agency.

licenses and forbade all persons to trade with the Indians without procuring a new license from him or from the agent for the Indians of the territory. The governor's proclamation, however, apparently had little effect, for the secretary of war was obliged to call him to task when reports reached Washington of wholesale violations of the intercourse act in Florida. "You will therefore immediately instruct the Indian Agents within your superintendency," DuVal was ordered, "rigidly to enforce the intercourse law against all violations of its provisions, as well against those who are not, as those who are licensed to trade with the Indians — the latter of whom not only put at defiance the act of Congress but also the express provisions of their bonds, under which they hold their license." [15]

The mischievous, unscrupulous, unlicensed trader caused untold troubles along the whole frontier, yet he was unorganized, and his total volume of trade was perhaps of little moment. It was his ubiquity and his furtive ways that made him such a nuisance, and it was his reliance on the illegal introduction of liquor to gain his ends that made him cause such consternation. He was not the only plague of the trade, however. More serious in many respects than his infractions were the inroads on the trade made by foreign traders, chiefly the British along the Great Lakes and the upper reaches of the Mississippi and the Missouri.

British traders had infiltrated the Northwest deeply after the French were driven out in 1763. Operating under the direction of powerful companies, they exerted great influence over the Indian tribes, who accepted their presents and depended upon them for goods. The British traders were unmolested after the Revolution, chiefly because the Americans were not prepared to replace them, and Jay's Treaty of 1794 specifically guaranteed their right to be there. Their posts at Michilimackinac and Prairie du Chien were great gathering points for the Indians.

There had always been irritation on account of these foreigners in the heart of the West, and little by little the British traders were pushed out of the trade south of the Lakes, but it was the War of 1812 that fully opened the eyes of the Americans to the danger, for it was through the influence of the traders that the Indians

[15] Abraham Eustis to Calhoun, July 23, 1822, in *Territorial Papers*, XXII, 495–497; Proclamation of Governor DuVal, June 7, 1823, *ibid.*, 694; Calhoun to DuVal, April 20, 1824, *ibid.*, 926–927.

fought with the British against the Americans in the war. Whatever may be the scholars' final decision on the influence that Indian incitation had as a cause of the War of 1812, at the conclusion of the conflict it was clear that many Indians had indeed been loyal to the foreigners and not to the United States. There had been too many evidences of atrocities committed by the Indians to make it possible for the British to continue in the same position as before the war. By the Treaty of Ghent the British were forced, finally, to give up their posts in American territory, but the treaty did not prevent the old traders from continuing to operate within the United States from centers outside or to draw the Indians across the boundary to trade.

It is understandable that agitation should arise to eliminate the British traders altogether. In a general report on Indian affairs, sent to the War Department in July 1815, Governor Lewis Cass of Michigan Territory wrote: "The privilege which British traders have heretofore enjoyed of carrying on a lucrative commerce with the Indians is a subject which will doubtless engage the attention of the Government. To this source may be traced most of the difficulties we have experienced in our intercourse with them." Cass noted that the British seemed to be renewing and intensifying their activity. He recognized, however, that there was a diplomatic question involved which could not be settled in terms of frontier policy alone — that the United States might be forced to grant privileges to British Indian traders in return for "commercial rights more important to the nation at large" — but he urged strong regulations for the British traders if they had to be permitted.[16]

At the end of February 1816 the House Committee on Foreign Relations introduced a bill to supplement the intercourse act of 1802. By the provisions of this measure, which became law on April 29, licenses to trade with the Indians within the territorial limits of the United States were refused to noncitizens, although the President was given discretionary authority to permit such licenses if he thought the public interest demanded it. All goods taken into the Indian Country by foreigners were subject to seizure and forfeiture if not yet traded to the Indians, and all peltries purchased from the Indians by foreigners were liable to seizure while still in the Indian Country. The President was authorized to use military force to seize the goods or furs and

[16] Cass to A. J. Dallas, July 20, 1815, *ibid.*, X, 573–575.

to arrest violators of the act. Even foreigners who wished merely to pass through the Indian lands were required first to obtain a passport from the governor of the state or territory adjoining the Indian Country or from the nearest military commander. Failure to do so made the offender liable to a fine of fifty dollars to one thousand dollars or imprisonment from one to twelve months. Copies of the act were sent to the governors and Indian agents of Michigan, Indiana, Illinois, Missouri, and Mississippi territories and the state of Louisiana two weeks after the passage of the act, accompanied by a circular letter that gave instructions for its administration.[17]

The Indian agent at Michilimackinac, William H. Puthuff, who had developed a lasting hatred of the British traders, caused considerable consternation by the extraordinary zeal with which he put the law into effect. At the same time, the army began to move up the Mississippi to establish the posts of Fort Armstrong at Rock Island and Fort Crawford at Prairie du Chien as a firm step in enforcing its policy against the British influence. When the troops arrived at Prairie du Chien on June 20, 1816, they required the traders to show their licenses and seized the goods of those who could not produce one, much to the dismay of the residents of the Prairie, who complained of this action of the military authority, which disrupted their easygoing ways.[18]

A certain reasonableness prevailed in higher official circles, however, and the discretionary power of the President was invoked to allow some foreigners to continue in the trade. A sudden and absolute cutting off of noncitizens from the trade in the Northwest was impolitic, if not impossible, for there were not Americans enough to fill the vacuum that would have been created. The Indian tribes had to be supplied with the goods on which they had become dependent, and for the time being it was necessary to rely on foreign traders, under strict regulations, however. The President granted authority to the governor of Michigan Territory and to the Indian agents at Michilimackinac, Green Bay, and Chicago to issue licenses to foreigners — but only to reputable characters who were above suspicion and who had not been

[17] *U.S. Stat.*, III, 332–333; William H. Crawford to Cass and agents, May 10, 1816, in *Wis. Hist. Colls.*, XIX (Madison, 1910), 405–407. There was little debate on the measure in Congress and apparently no opposition. *House Jour.*, 14 Cong., 1 sess., pp. 402, 647, 654; *Sen. Jour.*, 14 Cong., 1 sess., p. 603.

[18] Puthuff to Cass, June 27, 1816, in *Territorial Papers*, X, 654–655; John W. Johnson to Francis Bouthilier, June 23, 1816, in *Wis. Hist. Colls.*, XIX, 424–425. For other documents relative to Puthuff's activities, see *ibid.*, *passim.*

charged with smuggling. Bonds equal to one fourth the value of the capital used in the trade were required; and descriptive lists of the persons to whom licenses were granted were to be sent to Indian agents, collectors of customs, and commanding officers of the frontier posts. The licenses were to be granted for a limited period only, in no case to exceed twelve months, although they could be renewed by application to the governor of any territory or to any agent within whose agency the trader happened to be when the original license expired.[19]

It has been suggested, with probability, that John Jacob Astor, who had organized his American Fur Company in 1808, was a moving force behind the restriction on foreigners. He no doubt was glad to be rid of rivals in the trade, but he found that he could not get along without hiring foreigners. Astor went so far as to write to Secretary of State Monroe, asking him to get from the President blank licenses, which the Company could fill in at will, but he was unsuccessful. The secretary of war, however, kept Astor well informed on the steps taken by the department in regard to foreigners and sent him a copy of the special instructions to Cass and the agents.[20]

The presidential discretion in issuing licenses to foreigners was not universally hailed. Early in 1817 the House Committee on Indian Affairs submitted a report condemning the authority granted to the President by the act of 1816. While admitting that the provision might do well enough in theory, in practice it resulted in the admission to the trade of men "of the most inflam-

---

[19] Crawford to Cass, May 10, 1816, ibid., 406–407; George Graham to Cass, Oct. 29, 1816, in Territorial Papers, X, 667–668; Graham to Cass, May 4, 1817, in SW IA LS, vol. D, p. 35.

[20] Kenneth W. Porter, John Jacob Astor: Business Man (2 vols., Cambridge, Mass., 1931), II, 695–696; 702–704; Ramsay Crooks to John Jacob Astor, [March or April] 1817, in American Fur Company Letter Books, vol. 1, p. 12, photostatic copy in State Historical Society of Wisconsin; Crawford to Astor, May 27, 1816, in SW IA LS, vol. C, pp. 367–368. Crooks told Astor, "You must try hard to get clerks & interpreters acting under an improved trader admitted to a reasonable extent, giving assurances that proper care will be taken to keep from among the Indians, all whom there is reason to believe unfriendly to the Government, but should this modification be rejected, it will still be good policy to admit freely & without the least restraint the Canadian Boatmen; these people are indispensable to the successful prosecution of the trade, their places cannot be supplied by Americans, who are for the most part too independent to submit quietly to a proper controul, and who can gain any where a subsistence much superior to a man of the interior and although the body of the Yankee can resist as much hardship as any man, tis only in the Canadian we find that temper of mind, to render him patient, docile and persevering, in short they are a people harmless in themselves, whose habits of submission fit them peculiarly for our business. . . ."

mable and vicious habits." "Either admit or exclude all," the committee insisted, for it feared that partiality would be shown by those who were granted the discretionary authority and that worthy applicants would be refused while "fraudulent speculators" would be admitted. The total exclusion of the foreigners, the committee conceded, would cause a "momentary irritation, and a temporary expense to the nation," but it thought that the trade could be provided for by an expansion of the government trading houses. It reported a bill authorizing the further outlay of two hundred thousand dollars for Indian goods and the erection of eight new factories. This bill would have ended the discretionary power of the President to grant licenses to noncitizens.[21]

Although the bill was not acted on, a stop was soon put to the authority to issue licenses to foreigners, for on November 26, 1817, the President withdrew the power he had granted earlier to Cass and the three agents. The act of April 29, 1816, was now to be carried fully into effect, and no licenses in the future were to be granted to foreigners. Cass, in transmitting the order to the agents, warned them, "The prohibition to be effectual must be universal, and their entrance into the Country either as principals or as engagees must be wholly checked."[22]

The exigencies of the trade, however, would not allow this drastic move. The traders themselves must be American citizens, but where could enough citizens be found to serve as boatmen and interpreters? It was necessary to rely on foreigners for these essential jobs — chiefly men of French extraction but of British citizenship, who congregated at such centers as Mackinac, Green Bay, and Prairie du Chien. The President's decision based on "farther information and reflection," was transmitted to Governor Cass on March 25, 1818. Careful directions were included to ensure tight supervision and to prevent foreigners from creeping into the trade itself under the guise of boatmen or interpreters. A descriptive list was to be furnished of all such foreigners em-

[21] *House Jour.*, 14 Cong., 2 sess., p. 339; House report and bill (HR 103), 14 Cong., 2 sess., Feb. 4, 1817. The report was submitted again on January 22, 1818, *House Rep.* 59, 15 Cong., 1 sess., ser. 7.

[22] George Graham to Cass, Nov. 26, 1817, in SW IA LS, vol. D, p. 101; Cass to Charles Jouett, Jan. 22, 1818, in *Territorial Papers*, XVII, 561–562; Cass to John Bowyer, Jan. 22, 1818, in *Wis. Hist. Colls.*, XX (Madison, 1911), 16–17. "This step had undoubtedly been taken at the instance of the superintendent of the Indian trade, T. L. McKenney, who had been kept informed by his factors of the detrimental activities of British traders among the Indians, and especially of the way in which the trade of American citizens was being ruined." Porter, *John Jacob Astor*, II, 708.

ployed. Bonds in penal sum of five hundred dollars per man were to be given as surety that they were truly boatmen and interpreters and were not intended to be employed in any other capacity. Bonds were required also, in half the amount of the value of the goods, that the goods were the property of American citizens. Finally, foreigners who were "odious to our citizens, on account of their activity or cruelty in the late war" were not to be admitted in any capacity.[23]

There was temporarily some indecision as to just who was and who was not a citizen in the frontier settlements that had existed before the United States took over the area after the Revolution. It was assumed by some that citizens of Green Bay, for example, had automatically become citizens of the United States by Jay's Treaty, and when the agent at Green Bay refused a license to one of the traders there, an appeal was made to the acting governor of Michigan Territory, who granted the license. When the case came before the secretary of war, however, a decision of the attorney general was sought. He decided that the citizenship was not automatic and that it required special court action of naturalization in each case. The acting governor's decision was overruled and the license he had granted was revoked.[24]

By the effects of the restrictive legislation and the steady growth of the power and influence of the American Fur Company, the British were generally forced out of the trade within the territory of the United States, but the elimination was not absolute. In 1821 the agent at St. Peter's was commended by the War Department for the measures he had taken to drive out British traders who were carrying on trade with the Indians near Big Stone Lake, and military explorations of the Minnesota River valley were projected as a means of more effectual control of the Indian trade in that region. For many years the agents of the Hudson's Bay Company caused serious competition to the Americans along the northern border by the introduction of British goods on which no duties were paid and by the use of whiskey to draw the Indians away from the American traders.[25] While the

[23] Calhoun to Cass, March 25, 1818, in SW IA LS, vol. D, pp. 130–131; Cass to agents at Mackinac, Green Bay, and Chicago, April 23, 1818, in *Wis. Hist. Colls.*, XX, 42–46.
[24] Calhoun to Cass, Sept. 6, 1819, in SW IA LS, vol. D, pp. 320–321; Cass to agents, Oct. 11, 1819, in *Wis. Hist. Colls.* XX, 127–128.
[25] Calhoun to Lawrence Taliaferro, Aug. 14, 1821, in SW IA LS, vol. E, p. 144. The Indian Office in 1827 directed Cass to refuse licenses "to all persons, indiscriminately, who may have, *on proof*, been found to have purchased goods of

British required close watching along the northern frontier, Spaniards were also threatening to encroach upon the American trade in the south, although the problem there never reached serious proportions.[26]

The regulatory policy of the government was sometimes obstructed by court action initiated against the military officers and agents who attempted to enforce the laws. One such case arose in 1817 over a question of licensing, and it seriously undermined effective enforcement of the intercourse acts. In the fall of that year two traders of the American Fur Company, Russell Farnham and Daniel Darling, were licensed by William Puthuff, the agent at Michilimackinac, to trade along the Mississippi River. When the traders with their boatmen and interpreters appeared at Prairie du Chien, they were stopped by Lieutenant Colonel Talbot Chambers, in command of Fort Crawford. Chambers insisted that the license from Michilimackinac was insufficient for their trading in Missouri Territory west of the Mississippi. He sent them down to St. Louis to procure a license from Governor Clark and forbade them to trade on the way except for absolute necessities, forewarning Major Willoughby Morgan at Fort Armstrong that the men were coming by. Morgan, ascertaining that the traders intended to begin operations despite Chambers' prohibition, apprehended the men and sent them under guard to St. Louis. Morgan acted under orders from Chambers, his superior officer, but he justified his action to the secretary of war on the basis of enforcing the intercourse act of 1802. He argued that Puthuff had no right to grant the licenses to these men for trading on the Mississippi, that the men had attempted to trade with the Indians without proper licenses, and that he had used the authority granted to the military by section 16 of the act to apprehend the traders in the Indian Country. Morgan admitted, however, that he was somewhat hazy about just how the law was to be interpreted.[27]

The disinterestedness of the army officers' action cannot be easily determined. It has been suggested that they were influenced by the rivalry between the St. Louis traders and those from the

British Traders, on the Frontiers." Thomas L. McKenney to Cass, Feb. 20, 1827, in IA LS, vol. 3, p. 389.

[26] William Bradford to Calhoun, March 28, 1818 [1819], in *Territorial Papers*, XIX, 59–60; Henry Atkinson to Bradford, Dec. 15, 1819, *ibid.*, 128–129.

[27] Morgan to Calhoun, Oct. 12, 1817 [1818], *ibid.*, XV, 312–316. See also the documents following the letter, *ibid.*, 317–319. Other documents on the case are printed in *Wis. Hist. Colls.*, XIX, 477–484.

Lakes, and the officials of the American Fur Company considered the arrest of the traders as an indication of western traders' jealousy.[28] It is not hard to see, however, how antagonism of the American officers to certain notorious members of the traders' party — who were remembered for their pro-British activities during the war — influenced the decision to interrupt the traders' plans. Chambers, in one of his notes to Morgan, spoke of the crew members as "hardened Raschels" and indicated that he did not want the military to be made "the subject of derision by such named Raschels." He asserted that one of the clerks had appeared at Prairie du Chien during the war with three American scalps flying from his boat.[29]

Whatever the cause of the commotion, the outcome was all on the side of the American Fur Company. Representation was made to the secretary of war about the restrictions placed on the licenses obtained on the Lakes, and Calhoun wrote to Chambers and to Clark in St. Louis that they were to pay "proper respect" to the licenses issued by the agents at Green Bay, Chicago, and Michilimackinac and were to protect men trading under such licenses "in every section of the Indian Country whilst in the lawful prosecution of their business." [30]

The reversal of Chambers' decision — which had been seconded by the Indian agent, Benjamin O'Fallon — was not the only rebuff that the army officers had to bear. The American Fur Company brought suit against them for illegal arrest and in 1822 obtained an award of five thousand dollars damages against Chambers. It is questionable whether the Company actually collected the award, however, since in later litigation a charge of only two hundred dollars was made against the officer, but the American Fur Company gained its chief point in winning unrestricted use of the licenses granted on the Lakes and in success-

---

[28] Hiram M. Chittenden, *The American Fur Trade of the Far West* (3 vols., New York, 1902), I, 312–314. Ramsay Crooks wrote to Cass, "Col Chambers has been too undisguised in his hostility toward us to admit of our passing over the affair in silence; for at the very time he ordered the seizure of our Boats, he permitted others exactly in the same situation to proceed unmolested into the Country interdicted to our Agents." Crooks to Cass, April 16, 1818, in American Fur Company Letter Books, vol. 1, pp. 92–93. See also Crooks to Calhoun, March 2, 1819, *ibid.*, p. 166.

[29] Chambers to Morgan, Sept. 19, 1817, in *Wis. Hist. Colls.*, XIX, 478–479.

[30] Calhoun to Clark, March 3, 1819, in *Territorial Papers*, XV, 520. Chambers rather weakly backed down by insisting that he only acted in response to requisitions for aid from the Indian agents. Chambers to Calhoun, April 8, 1819, *ibid.*, 532–533.

fully challenging the action of the military officers.[31] The army officers suffered not only the harassment of the civil suits but also the very real danger of substantial financial loss. For reimbursement they were forced to turn to the War Department to pay the costs of damages assessed against them and the costs of hiring legal counsel.[32]

☙

Against the evils which arose from the uncontrolled traders, whom the restrictive laws seem seldom to have reached, the government attempted a more radical remedy — the government trading houses or factories. Such trading establishments had been one of the basic planks in Washington's Indian policy. Intended by him first of all as a means of supplying the Indians liberally with the white man's goods and thus gaining their friendship, the factories were to accomplish their purpose also by forcing out of the trade the independent traders, who, by preying on the the Indians, continually stirred up their resentment.

The scheme was not completely new, but neither now nor earlier was it pushed to the ultimate position of a government monopoly of the trade. As a result American Indian trade policy was seriously weakened by a dichotomy of principle. On the one hand it was strongly and, it appeared, irrevocably committed to private enterprise. The fur trade, it was asserted, belonged to everyone. It was part of the resources of the nation and as such should be open to any person who had the means to engage in it. Colonial law and colonial practice, while instituting a licensing system for the Indian trade and hedging it about with certain restrictions and regulations, by and large left the trade open to all individuals, or at least to all citizens of the colony. Even the king's Proclamation of 1763, which irritated the colonists with its boundary line and inviolate Indian Country, declared that the trade with the Indians was to be open to all. Yet on the other hand, running parallel to this determination to exclude no one from the benefits of the trade, was a secondary principle, which

[31] See Chittenden, *American Fur Trade*, I, 313–314, and Porter, *John Jacob Astor*, II, 702, 725, 727–728, for discussions of the case. Many details on the litigation are included in a statement by Chambers' lawyers, H. S. Geyer, George F. Struther, and A. L. Magenis, November, 1825, in IA LR, Miscellaneous.

[32] Calhoun to Morgan, Dec. 22, 1818, in SW LS, Military Book No. 10; Calhoun to Chambers, Dec. 16, 1823, in SW IA LS, vol. F, p. 19; Thomas L. McKenney to H. S. Geyer, George F. Struther, and A. L. Magenis, March 2, 1826, in IA LS, vol. 2, p. 460.

now and then forced its way to the front of public policy. This was the idea that the importance of the fur trade made it a direct concern of the state. The call for government participation in the fur trade usually came as a result of the near or utter breakdown of control under a system of private traders. The excesses and abuses which were the regular concomitant of open competition in the trade demanded some amelioration for the protection of the Indian and the consequent preservation of peace with the aborigines.

It was a commonplace that Indian allegiance and friendship depended ultimately on the tenuous ties of trade. With this in mind, the Continental Congress had initiated a program of government-sponsored trade to compensate for the lack of a well-knit private trading enterprise working for the American cause. A special report on Indian affairs urged that Congress exert strenuous efforts to procure the goods that the Indians wanted, and a committee was appointed to devise a scheme for carrying on trade with the Indians and procuring goods for the trade. On January 27, 1776, a plan was instituted "in order to preserve the friendship and confidence of the Indians, and to prevent their suffering for want of the necessaries of life." Indian goods to the value of forty thousand pounds were to be imported by Congress and divided between the three departments that had been set up for Indian affairs in the previous July. The goods, when delivered to the commissioners of Indian affairs for the respective departments, were to be sold to licensed Indian traders, who would sell them in turn to the Indians at prices fixed by the commissioners and at such places only as the commissioners determined. The proviso was carefully added, however, that this congressional enterprise was not intended to prevent private persons from importing goods on their own for the Indian trade. Congress had its finger in the business, but not as a monopoly and only to prevent a stoppage of the flow of goods to the Indians. The resolutions, ineffective as they often were, still showed the realization of the importance of the Indian trade and of the necessity and advisability of government participation in the trade itself.[33]

Under the Continental Congress no further action material-

[33] *Journals of the Continental Congress*, III, 365, 366, IV, 96–98, 318. The measures antecedent to the factory system are discussed briefly in Edgar B. Wesley, *Guarding the Frontier: A Study of Frontier Defense from 1815 to 1825* (Minneapolis, 1935), pp. 32–33, and Ora Brooks Peake, *A History of the United States Indian Factory System, 1795–1822* (Denver, 1954), p. 186.

ized, but as the new government under the Constitution got under way and as the difficulties in the private trade became again more manifest, renewed agitation for government trading houses began. With the frontiers both north and south of the Ohio afire with Indian unrest, Washington in his annual message to Congress of December 3, 1793, urged some method of securing permanent tranquillity by creating ties of interest between the Indians and the whites. "Next to a vigorous execution of justice on the violators of peace," the President declared, "the establishment of commerce with the Indian nations in behalf of the United States is most likely to conciliate their attachment." The trade, he insisted, must be carried on without fraud or extortion, with constant and steady supplies, and at fixed and stated prices. Such an exemplary state of trade could not depend on private traders, who were moved only by hope of profit; it would have to rest upon the United States government itself. In his message of 1794 Washington renewed his recommendation "for the improvement of harmony with all the Indians within our limits by the fixing and conducting of trading houses." [34]

In March of the following year Congress heeded the President's insistent recommendations and passed a trial measure. It appropriated fifty thousand dollars for the purchase of goods to be sold to the Indians within the United States during the year 1795, under the direction of the President. With the limited appropriation only a small beginning could be made; the Creeks and Cherokees were selected for the experiment. The difficulty of getting the proper goods from American merchants, who had exhausted their supplies in providing goods for General Wayne's treaty with the Indians and various Indian annuities, made it necessary to wait for the fall ships from Europe, but in December, 1795, the secretary of war reported that suitable factors had been engaged, the goods sent off, and the experiment gotten under way. After this successful inauguration of the program, Congress established a definite system of government trading houses. By an "act for establishing Trading Houses with the Indian Tribes," of April 18, 1796, the President was authorized to establish factories on the western and southern frontiers or in the Indian Country at places convenient for carrying on a "liberal trade" with the Indians. He was to appoint factors and clerks for the houses, and money and rations were provided for their pay. One

---

[34] Richardson, *Messages and Papers*, I, 141, 167.

hundred and fifty thousand dollars was appropriated, exclusive of the allowances for personnel, and the law provided that prices should be so set that the capital stock furnished by the United States not be diminished.[35]

This law was to run for two years and to the end of the next session of Congress thereafter and was the first in a series of temporary measures that kept the factory system alive until 1822. From time to time the capital was increased, a superintendent of Indian trade was authorized in 1806, and new factories were established as needs dictated. Altogether, in the twenty-seven years of the existence of the factory system, twenty-eight houses were in operation at one time or another.[36]

The reasons for the factory system, both for its inception and for the repeated renewals, are obvious enough. In order to maintain friendship with the Indians and wean them away from adherence to foreign powers it was necessary to establish effective trade relations with them. On two scores private traders were not satisfactory. Sometimes they were inadequate for the job; private American traders in the early years of the nation could not effectively counteract the British traders in the Northwest nor step into the breach left when these foreigners and their supplies were eliminated after the War of 1812. Also the profit motive which induced the private individuals or companies to enter the trade brought in its wake a series of abuses in debauching and defrauding the Indian that defeated the promotion of friendship, which was supposed to flow from trade attachments.

The purposes of the factory system were thus diplomatic, in the attempt to destroy foreign influence over the Indians; economic, in seeking to eliminate British traders from the lucrative business; military, in the hope of controlling the Indians and preventing frontier warfare; and finally and throughout, humanitarian, in seeking to supply the white man's goods, upon which the Indians had come to depend for their very existence, at a fair price and by honest dealing.

Now one, now another of these motives was stressed, according to the temperament of the proponent or the peculiar combination of circumstances at any given time. Jefferson, in recommending the renewal of the factory system in 1803, saw the trading houses

[35] *U.S. Stat.*, I, 443, 452–453; Report of Timothy Pickering, Dec. 12, 1795, in *American State Papers: Indian Affairs*, I, 583–584.

[36] There is an excellent brief account of the succession of laws and of the factories established in Wesley, *Guarding the Frontier*, pp. 35–41.

not only as a means of eliminating private traders — "getting rid of this pest without giving offence or umbrage to the Indians" — but also as a means of civilizing the Indians. By multiplying trading houses among them he hoped to convince them that they could be happier with such elements of domestic comfort as the white man supplied than with the "possession of extensive but uncultivated wilds." Thus drawn to the white man's way of life, they would more readily part with their lands and convert to an agricultural way of life. Jefferson was sly enough, as well, to suggest that when the Indians ran up debts at the trading houses beyond their power to pay, "they become willing to lop them off by a cession of lands." Even severe critics of the factory system like the agents of the American Fur Company realized the essential purpose of the system — to supply goods when private American traders were unable to and to eliminate British traders, and with them foreign influence over the Indians.[37]

The first reports of the trade operations were encouraging, for in the early years of the factory system considerable success met its efforts. There were no strong protests from any private traders, and economically the factories were holding their own. The Indians seemed pleased with the fair treatment they received, and the activities of the British were held somewhat in check, so the system in these years was gradually expanded. The War of 1812, however, caused severe economic loss to the factories, and after the war, with the removal of the British from the Northwest, American activity began to come to life. The factory system no longer had an easy time, because it was more and more strongly attacked by the private individual traders and then by the ever more powerful American Fur Company, which brought strong economic and political pressure to bear against the government trade. It began to fail economically under the pressure, and this failure was used as a further argument for scrapping the whole system.[38]

[37] Jefferson to Congress, Jan. 18, 1803, in Richardson, *Messages and Papers*, I, 352; Jefferson to William Henry Harrison, Feb. 27, 1803, in Logan Esarey, ed., *Messages and Letters of William Henry Harrison*, I (Indianapolis, 1922), 70–71; Jefferson to Henry Dearborn, Aug. 12, 1802, in *Territorial Papers*, VII, 67–70; Ramsay Crooks and Robert Stuart to John Jacob Astor, Jan. 24, 1818, in *Wis. Hist. Colls.*, XX, 26–27.

[38] Katherine Coman, "Government Factories: An Attempt to Control Competition in the Fur Trade," *Bulletin of the American Economic Association*, 4th series, no. 2 (April 1911), p. 370. There is a long series of reports on the operation of the factory system, communicated to the Senate on March 8, 1822, in *American State Papers: Indian Affairs*, II, 326–364.

One difficulty that the system faced was its continuing temporary nature. Each act authorizing its existence or extending its operations had a time limit attached, usually three years. This was eloquent evidence of the uncertain hold the concept of government trading had on the mind of Congress. At each renewal there was a more bitter contest between the proponents and the opposition, and after 1820 there was an all-out attempt on the part of the American Fur Company to have Congress abolish the whole system. Ramsay Crooks, as agent of the Company, expressed his determination in a frank letter to John Jacob Astor, then in Europe.

I shall follow your advice in again visiting Washington, and will use every fair means to obtain a decision on the Public Trading House system. Last session a respectable majority voted against their continuance, but Congress had to rise on the 3d March without having time to act finally on the subject, in consequence of the Government Officers having resorted to every means in their power to delay its consideration. It will be brought forward early this session, and I have reason to think will be warmly supported, for enough is now known of the subject to excite enquiry, and if a thorough investigation is had, the abolition of these useless establishments is in my opinion sure. Great efforts will be made by Mr McKenney, & his friends to save the Factories. His official reports to the Indian Committee will villify the Traders, and whine over the unfortunate & helpless conditions of the poor Indians, who will be left to the mercy of these unprincipled private traders; but all this will avail him little, for his canting is too well known, and his only resource will be falsehood, to which he has more than once resorted. Exposition will become necessary, and may involve us in a paper war, but the consequences must be encountered; for I cannot, and will not tamely submit to his scurilous abuse.[39]

Although the opposition to the factories came chiefly from the traders, there were also disinterested persons who really believed that the system was disadvantageous, if not a failure. Lewis Cass argued that the government suffered in dignity in the eyes of the Indians by engaging in trade. "Our trading factories, and our economy in presents have rendered us contemptible to them," he wrote to the secretary of war in 1814. "The Government should never Come in contact with them, but in cases where its Dignity, its strength or its liberality will inspire them with respect or fear." In 1818, in answer to an inquiry from Calhoun, Cass repeated his opinion. The factory system he believed to be "radically incor-

[39] Crooks to Astor, Nov. 30, 1821, in American Fur Company Letter Books, vol. 2, pp. 177–178.

rect," and he was decidedly in favor of its abolition, since private American capital was able to handle the business. Cass had no sooner written his letter, however, than he had some misgivings about the absolute statements he had made against the government system of trade. In a second letter he backed down from his strong stand and admitted that his opinion was "more speculative than practical." "It may also be found, should the experiment be made," he noted, "that consequences which are not now foreseen, may follow from this abolition equally injurious to the United States and to the Indians. . . . Practical results do not always accord with previous speculations, and it may sometimes be more expedient to continue a doubtful system, rather than hazard effects which can neither be foreseen nor controlled." The Reverend Jedidiah Morse, in his famous survey of the Indian Country in 1820 found, however, that the general consensus was against the system, and he himself advocated its abolition.[40]

On the other hand, advocates of the system were not wanting in high places, and they were strong enough to keep the affair alive long after the opposition had risen in strength against it. Secretaries of War William H. Crawford and John C. Calhoun upheld the factories and they were repeatedly supported by committees of Congress. Crawford sent a long report to the Senate in 1816 on the financial state of the program, which indicated unmistakably the humanitarian motivation of its supporters. An annual loss of capital in the trade did not disturb him, for profits could not be the inducement for continuing the system. "That inducement, if it exists at all," he asserted, "must be found in the influence which it gives the Government over the Indian tribes within our limits, by administering to their wants, increasing their comforts, and promoting their happiness. The most obvious effect of that influence is the preservation of peace with them, and among themselves." Crawford hoped by such trade ties to develop in the Indians a concern for private property, and he urged an expansion of the capital of the factory system. He wanted further regulation of private traders as well, suggesting

[40] Cass to John Armstrong, Sept. 3, 1814, in *Territorial Papers*, X, 476; Cass to Calhoun, Sept. 14, 1818, in *Wis. Hist. Colls.*, XX, 82–86; Cass to Calhoun, Oct. 1, 1818, in IA FR, Michigan Superintendency, Letters Sent by the Superintendent; Jedidiah Morse, *A Report to the Secretary of War of the United States, on Indian Affairs* (New Haven, 1822), pp. 60–61. Chapter XI, "Contemporary Criticism of the United States Indian Trade Factory System," in Peake, *Indian Factory System*, pp. 184–203, gives an extensive survey of the criticism.

that discretion be exercised in licensing applicants and that the traders be required to take an oath to observe the intercourse acts.

These views [he concluded] are substantially founded upon the conviction that it is the true policy and earnest desire of the Government to draw its savage neighbors within the pale of civilization. If I am mistaken in this point — if the primary object of the Government is to extinguish the Indian title, and settle their lands as rapidly as possible, then commerce with them ought to be entirely abandoned to individual interprise, and without regulation. The result would be continued warfare, attended by the extermination or expulsion of the aboriginal inhabitants of the country to more distant and less hospitable regions. The correctness of this policy cannot for a moment be admitted. The utter extinction of the Indian race must be abhorrent to the feelings of an enlightened and benevolent nation. The idea is directly opposed to every act of the Government, from the declaration of independence to the present day. . . . It will redound more to the national honor to incorporate, by a humane and benevolent policy, the natives of our forests in the great American family of freemen, than to receive with open arms the fugitives of the old world, whether their flight has been the effect of their crimes or their virtues.[41]

Strong in support, of course, were the superintendents of Indian trade. John Mason argued ably in 1816 that, although ultimately the factories might be dispensed with, at that date they were an absolute necessity if the Indians were to be adequately supplied, and Thomas L. McKenney, whose humanitarian interest in the Indians deeply colored his outlook, considered the factory system a necessary means of protecting the Indians from the wicked and unscrupulous traders and thus advancing them on the road to civilization.[42]

More and more the argument for the government houses came to rest upon the disrepute of the private trader — of which mounting evidence accumulated. "In the course of my superintendence of the trade established with the several Indian tribes," McKenney wrote in 1818, "it has become part of my duty to take cognizance of such checks as are known to operate against it. Among these,

[41] Report of Crawford to the Senate, March 13, 1816, in *American State Papers: Indian Affairs*, II, 26–28.
[42] Mason to Crawford, March 6, 1816, in IT LS, vol. C, pp. 485–488. McKenney's best statement in defense of the factory system is a report he sent to Henry Johnson, Chairman of the Senate Committee on Indian Affairs, Dec. 27, 1821, in *American State Papers: Indian Affairs*, II, 260–265. Other vigorous defense can be found in McKenney to Calhoun, Aug. 19, 1818, in *Wis. Hist. Colls.*, XX, 66–79; McKenney to Henry Southard, March 19, 1818, *ibid.*, 37–41; McKenney to Southard, Nov. 30, 1820, Dec. 30, 1820, March 17, 1821, in IT LS, vol. F, pp. 99–104, 104–107, 151–153.

and foremost in the train, is the conduct of private traders, than which it is impossible to conceive any thing more obnoxious, if viewed in relation to the morals of the Indians; or more destructive of that pacific result which the U.S. factories are or may be calculated to produce." The power of the factory to control the Indians by granting or withholding supplies was negated by the traders, who not only made the Indians independent of government supplies — even though "at the cost of exactions and the most unexampled debauchery" — but stimulated their hostility to the factory system with the hope of gaining a complete monopoly of the trade.[43]

Such attacks upon the character of the traders were not enough. As the returns from the factories diminished and the original capital could no longer be maintained, the voices of the attackers grew stronger. The American Fur Company and the St. Louis fur trading interests enlisted in their support Senator Thomas Hart Benton, who with vigorous rhetoric and biting sarcasm stormed against the factory system in Congress in 1822. In May of that year an act was passed which brought an end to the system, and special agents were appointed to liquidate the factories. The trade now became the unimpeded domain of the private traders and the powerful fur company. They had sufficient reason for their rejoicing.[44]

Much has been written about the reasons for the economic failure of the factory system. That it had weaknesses is clear, but these weaknesses were not fatal and might have been sufficiently corrected if the factories had been given half a chance. The ineffectiveness of the trading houses, which the opposition charged, was belied by the opposition itself, for the strength and violence of its attacks is indication that the factories were offering serious competition. Had the government system been pushed

---

[43] Reports of Thomas Biddle and Henry Atkinson, 1819, in *American State Papers: Indian Affairs*, II, 201–204; McKenney to Southard, Jan. 6, 1818, in *Wis. Hist. Colls.*, XX, 12–16; McKenney to Calhoun, July 16, 1819, in *Territorial Papers*, XIX, 86.

[44] *U.S. Stat.*, III, 679 680. A summary of Benton's activity is given in Royal B. Way, "The United States Factory System for Trading with the Indians, 1796–1822," *Mississippi Valley Historical Review*, VI (1919), 231–234. Ramsay Crooks wrote to Senator Benton, congratulating him on the overthrow of the factories: "The result is the best possible proof of the value to the country of talents, intelligence, & perseverance; and you deserve the unqualified thanks of the community for destroying the pious monster, since to your unwearied exertions, and sound practical knowledge of the whole subject, the country is indebted for its deliverance from so gross and holy [unholy] an imposition." Crooks to Benton, April 1, 1822, in American Fur Company Letter Books, vol. 2, p. 241.

as a permanent measure, designed to centralize the trade in government hands and thus control that vital relationship with the Indians, instead of leading an insecure existence from Congress to Congress as a temporary expedient, much of the distress of Indian intercourse might have been avoided.[45]

⁂

Since the factory system, in the minds of its supporters, had as a primary end the elimination of the abuses that crept into the Indian trade with private traders, it might have been expected that when the factories were done away with some tightening of trade regulations would replace them. These expectations were not completely fulfilled, but on the same day the law abolishing the factory system was approved an amendment to the intercourse act of 1802 also became law. The new act provided that the bonds of licensed traders might be raised to five thousand dollars, proportionate to the capital employed, and extended the life of the licenses issued for west of the Mississippi to seven years. It required, also, an annual report of all licenses granted, bonds taken, and capital employed to be laid before Congress, and it took a firm step toward elimination of whiskey in the fur trade. To protect the property rights of the Indians in suits with white citizens, Congress declared that in such trials the burden of proof was to rest with the whites in every case where the Indian had a presumption of title based on previous possession and ownership. The law was important, too, because it authorized the appointment of the superintendent of Indian affairs at St. Louis.[46]

The provision of the new law which most interested the secretary of war, however, was a section dealing with accounting for Indian department funds. At least this was the chief point called to the attention of the superintendents and agents when the War Department sent them notice of the law. All persons charged with the disbursement of money or goods for the benefit of the Indians were required to submit a complete account each year as of

---

[45] The two final chapters in Peake, *Indian Factory System*, summarize the various reasons proposed for the failure of the system and give references to the authors. Peake's own conclusions, however, are not convincing. Chittenden saw in the factories or some other sort of monopoly the only solution for the evils that were met with in the trade. *American Fur Trade*, I, 12–16. Porter concluded that the trading houses were "a system which possessed great possibilities for national benefit, and which probably would have enjoyed a reasonable measure of success and undoubtedly a much longer term of existence had it not been for the opposition of Astor's powerful American Fur Company." *John Jacob Astor*, II, 714.

[46] *U.S. Stat.*, III, 682–683.

September 1, and Calhoun asserted that these reports would be rigidly exacted.[47]

Attempts to ameliorate conditions in the fur trade, of course, did not end with the collapse of the factory system. One move was the continuing attempt of Thomas L. McKenney to regularize the organization of the Indian department so that there might be some accurate and ordered information on hand in Washington on which to base decisions in regard to policy and practice. It is difficult to believe the ignorance of basic facts about the trade that existed in the Indian office. When the Senate asked for a report on the "present condition of the Fur Trade within the limits of the United States" in 1829, McKenney was forced to answer that except for the bonds of the traders and reports of agents designating the posts they occupied, "there was not a single document in this office . . . that throws any light on the subject." In 1825 he had urged that some system be adopted to keep the Department informed on the extent and character of the trade, but nothing had been done about it.[48] Congressional requests for information had to be met by writing to the agents for *ad hoc* reports — a far from satisfactory system.

Other recommendations were centered on a tightening of the existing licensing provisions. John Mason declared in 1816 that "the penalties for trading with Indians without license are too light, and the forfeitures too easily evaded to deter persons disposed to violate the law." Calhoun in 1818 feared that the factory system had "relaxed the attention of Government to the system of trade under license." He urged stronger government regulation in order to eliminate the small irresponsible traders — an annual fee of one hundred to five hundred dollars for a license, and regular books to be kept and inspected by the government agents. If the number of traders could be reduced, they could be more closely watched. He argued, too, that regular traders who had paid for their licenses would themselves be more active in preventing the distribution of spirituous liquors on the frontiers.[49]

[47] Calhoun to Clark, May 28, 1822, in SW IA LS, vol. E, pp. 258–261; Calhoun to William P. DuVal, June 11, 1822, in *Territorial Papers*, XXII, 452–455; Calhoun to the territorial governors, March 18, 1823, *ibid.*, XIX, 502. For other similar letters see SW IA LS, vol. E.

[48] McKenney to Peter B. Porter, Jan. 3, 1829, in IA LS, vol. 5, p. 252; McKenney to James Barbour, Nov. 15, 1825, *ibid.*, vol. 2, pp. 235–238.

[49] Mason to Crawford, March 6, 1816, in IT LS, vol. C, pp. 487–488; Report of Calhoun, Dec. 5, 1818, in *House Doc.* 25, 15 Cong., 2 sess., ser. 17. Calhoun based his recommendations largely on a report submitted to him by McKenney on August 19, 1818, in *Wis. Hist. Colls.*, XX, 66–79. A bill containing Calhoun's

A repeated proposal that had considerable force was to authorize discretion on the part of the agents in issuing licenses so that the worst sort of trader could be eliminated. Mason complained in his 1816 report that under the existing interpretations of the laws the superintendents were bound "to give a license to any person whomsoever, foreigner or citizen, that can furnish security for a thousand dollars." The result, he asserted, was that the Indian Country was filled with foreigners hostile to the interests of the United States or with men "off desperate character, who are debasing the habits and destroying the health of the Indians — and at the same time cheating them of their little earnings, by constantly dealing out to them spiritous liquors." He wanted complete discretionary power to be lodged with the President and agents under him for granting or withholding licenses. Mason's wish in regard to foreigners came true, but it was harder to get the authority to withhold licenses from American citizens. In 1817 McKenney, Mason's successor in the Office of Indian Trade, repeated the complaint about the "undue extent" to which licenses were granted. "I am aware of the broadness of the law; and how easy it is to obtain this privilege under its provisions," he wrote to the secretary of war. "Still, however, I apprehend, with all its extent of privilege, the use made of it, in many cases, is at war with its spirit, — and certainly with the design of the Government." [50]

In May, 1820, the Senate passed a bill "for the better regulation of the trade with the Indian tribes," the purpose of which was to place the issuing of licenses directly in the hands of the President, who was to issue them under prescriptions that would ensure the granting of licenses only to men of good moral character. This move seriously frightened the American Fur Company, which renewed its efforts to quash any attempts to give discretionary power in the granting of licenses.

The new-fangled obnoxious Indian system [Ramsay Crooks wrote to Astor], died a natural death; as the House of Representatives pleading a press of much more important business refused to act on the bill from the Senate and from the interest our friends took in the explanations given them . . . I have not the smallest doubt, had the bill been brought forward, but the monster would have been strangled — Now, that nothing can

proposals was introduced in the House of Representatives on January 15, 1819, but was not acted upon. *House Jour.,* 15 Cong., 2 sess., ser. 10, p. 188.

[50] Mason to Crawford, March 6, 1816, in IT LS, vol. C, p. 488; McKenney to George Graham, March 19, 1817, in *Territorial Papers,* XVII, 492–493.

be expected till Congress meets again, I presume the trade will be for this summer continued under the former regulations; but had Mr. Secretary Calhoun carried his point in getting the proposed new law passed, it is no longer concealed that his first step was to license so few traders that the factories were sure of reviving. Another appeal to Congress for an increase of the public trade fund would no doubt have followed; and private trade confined to a limited number of favorites, among whom I hazard but little in saying, the American Fur Company would not have been found; because we will not suffer ourselves to be trampled on with impunity, either by the military or any other power; and because others profiting by our example, have of late shown them their teeth. The suit with Col Chambers is still pending, but it has already done much good, and our traders pursue their business now without interruption; indeed I am told, the officers generally take some pains to appear uncommonly civil.[51]

Ten years later conditions were no better, and Governor Cass recommended again that discretionary authority be given to the agents in issuing licenses so that undesirable traders could be eliminated, and in 1829 Cass and Clark repeated the recommendation in their detailed code for Indian affairs. The criticism of the traders in this recommendation called forth a vigorous defense from Robert Stuart of the American Fur Company and a condemnation of the proposal to place discretionary authority in the hands of the agents. Fearing that Congress might act on the Cass-Clark report, Stuart sent a long series of "Remarks" to the chairmen of the House and Senate committees on Indian affairs. The code of the two Indian superintendents, far from repairing the evils in the trading laws, he charged, would instead increase them. "Do these Gent. really believe that an agent can never do wrong? That he has no passions or prejudices to gratify?" He listed a long series of cases in which the operations of the American Fur Company had been interrupted by agents whom he charges with "tyrannical conduct." To replace the sections of the report which aimed to eliminate traders of bad character — but which to Stuart seemed to imply that the traders were "engaged in a concern which is wholly managed by fraud and chicanery" — Stuart submitted revised articles of his own for consideration by the congressional committees. These remarks were so violent in nature and so obviously far from disinterested

[51] Crooks to Astor, May 30, 1820, in American Fur Company Letter Books, vol. 1, pp. 305–306; *Sen. Jour.*, 16 Cong., 1 sess., ser. 25, pp. 159, 180, 193, 197; Engrossed bill (S 36), 16 Cong., 1 sess., March 1, 1820, in Records of the United States Senate, National Archives, Record Group 46; *House Jour.*, 16 Cong., 1 sess., ser. 30, pp. 273, 324.

that we may presume they swayed the committees little. McKenney kept harping on the need for a change and expressed his approval of the Cass-Clark proposals. They would, he said, remove the "embarrassing situation" in which "unfit persons, altho' *known* to the agent to be so, can . . . *command* a license, and the agent is bound to grant it, or be subject to a suit of law for damages." [52]

The situation plainly needed remedying, as the Indian agent at Green Bay summed it up in 1831: "Granting licenses to traders is, at present, a mere farce; any person, no matter how depraved, can procure a license, and every provision of the law is violated under it. Conscientious & respectable men cannot go into the Indian trade with any chance of success. If they refuse to furnish the Indians with whiskey & to commit other infractions of the law, they cannot compete with the petty, unprincipled trader, who sits down beside them with his supply or ardent spirits, regardless of the law and its consequences. Thus the Intercourse Law, as *custom has rendered* it, only serves to retain bad men among the Indians; & is productive of much injury to the tribe & to the government." [53]

When the trade laws were revised in 1834, discretionary power for the agent in granting licenses had a prominent place.

Another panacea was the proposal to permit trading only at designated sites in the Indian Country. Presumably, with fewer places to keep an eye on, the agents could be more efficient in enforcing the law. The policy had been adopted from time to time in granting licenses to individuals of specifying the spots at which the trading could be done, but gradually there developed a movement to make it a universal law. The governor of Louisiana Territory wrote to the War Department in 1812 that to secure permanent peace with the Indians it was necessary "that Traders should be compelled to Trade, at particular points, where they would be brought under a Police — for many of our difficulties are to be ascribed to the malconduct of some of those people, who under our present regulations, cannot be restrained, completely." The proposal was also part of Calhoun's able suggestions

[52] Cass to Barbour, Feb. 2, 1826, in *American State Papers: Indian Affairs*, II, 658–659; Report of Cass and Clark, Feb. 10, 1829, in *Sen. Doc.* 72, 20 Cong., 2 sess., ser. 181, p. 32; Stuart to H. L. White and to John Bell, Feb. 16, 1831 [1830], in IA LR, Miscellaneous; McKenney to John H. Eaton, Jan. 21, 1830, in IA LS, vol. 6, pp. 237–238.

[53] S. C. Stambaugh to Cass, Nov. 19, 1831, in IA FR, Michigan Superintendency, 1832, no. 1.

for improving the system of Indian trade of 1818 and appeared in the bill introduced in the House on January 15, 1819. No action was taken at the time, and it is impossible to judge the congressional mind on this particular issue, since the proposed measure was only part of a bill to abolish the factory system — a much more controversial matter.[54]

Not until 1824 did the proposal become law, and again it was tucked away in a bill that dealt with other aspects of Indian affairs. The law provided "that it shall be the duty of Indian agents to designate, from time to time, certain convenient and suitable places for carrying on trade with the different Indian tribes, and to require all traders to trade at the places thus designated, and at no other place or places." Calhoun drew up a circular which he sent to the Indian superintendents and agents on June 5, 1824, directing them to carry the law into effect and providing norms for their action. He directed that no more than one site should be selected for each tribe unless special reasons dictated otherwise. The agents were to report the designated locations to the War Department, and when approved the locations were not to be changed without department sanction. The licenses issued were to indicate the places approved, and departure from the terms of the license was to be considered as a forfeiture of the bond.[55]

The new law was variously received. The Creek agent postponed a selection of sites until the Indians gathered for their annuity payments, in order to consult with the chiefs on the most suitable points. He found the Indians highly incensed at this move of the government to further restrict their trading, and the chiefs asked the agent to express their great dissatisfaction with the legislation. The agent selected two spots for the trade — one at Fort Mitchell and the other at the Creek agency — but, he wrote, "I deem it unimportant whether one or a dozen places is selected. The nation being surrounded by a white population,

[54] James McHenry to Arthur St. Clair, April 26, 1800, in *Territorial Papers*, III, 83; Benjamin Howard to William Eustis, March 19, 1812, *ibid.*, XIV, 534; Report of Calhoun, Dec. 5, 1818, in *House Doc.* 25, 15 Cong., 2 sess., ser. 17, p. 7; *House Jour.*, 15 Cong., 2 sess., ser. 16, p. 188.

[55] "An Act to enable the President to hold treaties with certain Indian tribes, and for other purposes," May 25, 1824, *U.S. Stat.*, IV, 35–36; Calhoun to superintendents and agents, June 5, 1824, in IA LS, vol. 1, pp. 96–97. The treaties made with the various tribes of Plains Indians in 1825 declared, "All trade and intercourse . . . shall be transacted at such place or places as may be designated and pointed out by the President of the United States, through his agents." Kappler, *Treaties*, pp. 225 ff.

much the greater part of the Indians will go over the line to trade." [56]

In the Northwest there was an immediate outcry from the traders of the American Fur Company. It was the common opinion of the time that the law had been passed through the influence of John Jacob Astor, who expected it to help his company eliminate smaller rivals, but soon the Company began to agitate for the law's repeal. The circular letter designating locations which Lawrence Taliaferro, the agent at St. Peter's, sent to the traders on April 10, 1825, was unsatisfactory, and the traders forwarded a remonstrance to the secretary of war against the action of the agent. The traders on the Missouri likewise complained about the restrictive nature of the measure, which cut down the number of locations, asserting that the Indians would be the ones to suffer from the new arrangements. The complaints were sent on to the secretary of war by William B. Astor, acting president of the Company, on June 28, 1825. He charged that the action of the agents hardly met the specifications of the law to provide *"convenient* and *suitable* places" for carrying on the trade. The present situation, he asserted, proved "inconvenient to the Indians, detrimental to those engaged in the trade, and vexatious to both." [57]

McKenney met the requests of the traders with remarkable sympathy. He wrote to William Clark to look into the matter and, if he thought the complaints were well-founded, to designate more sites and then report his actions to the Department. In his reply to Astor he reported that the secretary of war desired to "accommodate our enterprizing Citizens who are engaged in the Fur Trade and to accord to them in these locations for Indian Trade whatever facilities may be considered by them to be necessary for the promotion of their interests" — provided they did not conflict with the act of Congress. Clark at St. Louis adopted a liberal view and directed the agents under his supervision to designate additional places within their agencies in order to promote the convenience of the traders and the Indians.

[56] John Crowell to Calhoun, July 31, 1824, in IA LR, Creek Agency.
[57] Robert Stuart to Cass, Aug. 26, 1824, in American Fur Company Letter Books, vol. 3, p. 89; Stuart to John Jacob Astor, Sept. 6, 1824, *ibid.*, pp. 99–100; Stuart to William B. Astor, Oct. 20, 1824, *ibid.*, pp. 130–131; William B. Astor to Barbour, June 28, 1825, enclosing circular of Lawrence Taliaferro to traders, April 10, 1825, remonstrance of the traders to the secretary of war, May 6, 1825, and extract of a letter from Bernard Pratte and Company, June 1, 1825, in IA LR, Miscellaneous. See Porter, *John Jacob Astor*, II, 737–738, for a discussion of the reaction of the American Fur Company to the law of 1824.

He later reported that the agents had designated several new locations but that they found it difficult to please the traders and the Indians.[58]

These adjustments within the law, however, did not satisfy the traders. In 1826 Bernard Pratte and Robert Stuart wrote to the War Department urging complete repeal of the law. It gave an advantage to the British along the northern border, they argued, and to lawless American traders, who sought out the Indians and obtained their furs before they could bring them in to the designated locations, and it worked hardships on the traders in their efforts to plan economically for the trade. Under the law they could not move about easily to adjust to changing conditions in the hunt. "We are firmly of opinion," they concluded, "that no evil can possibly result by permitting free intercourse between the traders and the Indians, and that it would tend greatly to their mutual benefit and accommodation." Their appeal was backed up by Lewis Cass, who declared himself in general agreement with their conclusions and declared that the law could be abolished with safety.[59]

Within a week of Cass's report the House of Representatives directed the Committee on Indian Affairs to inquire into the expediency of modifying or repealing the provision, and instructed the secretary of war to report to the House on the operation of the act and whether it did not "operate to the injury of both the trader and the Indians." The writing of the report was entrusted to McKenney, who penned a vigorous defense of the restriction, particularly as a means of checking the evils of the whiskey traffic. He cited the dramatic account recently received from Colonel Josiah Snelling on the scenes of drunkenness he had witnessed, and argued that such evils could be controlled better if the traders were kept under the eye of the government officials by requiring them to trade at set places only. "If former laws, and printed regulations under them, have proved inoperative, and have fallen short of their object, shall we, for that reason, permit the avenues to remain wide open as heretofore, and take away all our guards; or [should we not rather] seek to narrow the one,

---

[58] McKenney to Clark, July 22, 1825, in IA LS, vol. 2, p. 98; McKenney to William B. Astor, July 22, 1825, *ibid.*, pp. 98–99; Clark to Barbour, Sept. 26, 1825, in IA LR, St. Louis Superintendency. Clark sent a report of the places designated to McKenney on September 30, 1825. A new listing of posts was also made by Taliaferro. Taliaferro to Robert Stuart, April 2, 1826, in IA LR, St. Peter's Agency.

[59] Pratte and Stuart to Barbour, Jan. 28, 1826, and Cass to Barbour, Feb. 2, 1826, in *American State Papers: Indian Affairs,* II, 658–659.

and multiply the other? Does not policy unite with justice and humanity in demanding the adoption of the latter course?" But did the act really help? McKenney hedged a bit on this crucial question. It had not yet been in effect long enough to disclose "any very striking effects in correcting the evils which it was intended to remedy," but McKenney declared that in his opinion the act had helped and if everything hoped for had not been attained, it was due more to the short period in which the law had been in operation than to any defect in the provision itself.[60]

When McKenney's report became public, Stuart immediately came to the defense of the American Fur Company. He denied the charges made against the Company and complained of "the very partial, and uncalled for manner, in which the Officer in charge of the Indian Bureau, has thought proper to *drag* their character under the odium of the Committee on Indian affairs, through his report." McKenney was, however, able to hold his position on the designation of locations. The bill introduced in the House on March 29, 1826, to modify the law of 1824 by providing for the granting of additional locations on application of the traders, was not acted on, and a resolution on December 11 to bring the matter up again got nowhere. The proposed reorganization of the Indian department submitted by Cass and Clark in February 1829 included the measure among its recommendations, and the act of 1834 continued to specify that no trade was to be carried on in the Indian Country "except at certain suitable and convenient places, to be designated from time to time by the superintendents, agents, and sub-agents, and to be inserted in the license." [61]

[60] *House Jour.*, 19 Cong., 1 sess., ser. 130, pp. 236, 240; McKenney to Barbour, Feb. 14, 1826, in *American State Papers: Indian Affairs*, II, 659–661.

[61] Stuart to Barbour, Feb. 24, 1826, in IA LR, Miscellaneous; *House Jour.*, 19 Cong., 1 sess., ser. 130, p. 388; Original bill (HR 189), 19 Cong., 1 sess., March 29, 1826; *House Jour.*, 19 Cong., 2 sess., ser. 147, pp. 38–39; Report of Cass and Clark, *Sen. Doc.* 72, 20 Cong., 2 sess., ser. 181, p. 28; *U.S. Stat.*, IV, 729.

VI

THE CRUSADE AGAINST WHISKEY

It may be that the policy of the government on the subject of
Indian affairs has, in some particulars, justly provoked criticism:
but it cannot be said, that there has not been proper effort, by
legislation and treaty, to secure Indian communities against the
debasing influence of spirituous liquors. The evils from this
source were felt at an early day; and, in order to promote the
welfare of the Indians, as well as our political interests, laws
were passed and treaties framed, restricting the introduction of
liquor among them. That these laws and treaties have not
always secured the desired result, is owing more to the force
of circumstances which the government could not control, than
to any unwillingness to execute them.
— Justice David Davis in *United States* vs.
Forty-three Gallons of Whiskey, 1876

The greatest source of difficulty in the Indian trade was whiskey.
The "ardent spirits" smuggled into the Indian Country made
madmen of the Indians, yet the flow could not easily be stanched.
It was an elemental problem, rooted in uncontrollable human
drives — the Indians' fondness for strong drink and the heartless
avarice of the whites. To protect the Indian from his own weakness it was necessary eventually for the government to clamp
down on the whiskey dealer.

The problem of controlling the liquor traffic was as old as
white settlement in America. In colonial days there had been
restrictions or prohibitions on the distribution of rum to the red
man, although these laws for the most part proved to be quite
ineffective, and the difficulties continued. Despite the universality
of the problem, the first federal laws governing intercourse with
the Indians made no mention of intoxicating liquors, just as there
had been no discussion of the matter in the Continental Congress
and no specific enactments in regard to it. This may seem like
a strange omission in view of the past troubles that had grown

out of laxness in the matter, but it is likely that the legislators hoped the licensing provisions of the laws would provide the necessary restraints. They looked to the superintendents of Indian affairs and to the Indian agents to place the necessary brake upon the liquor trade. It was not clear at the beginning that state or territorial ordinances could not take care of the problem. Officials in the West were in fact well aware of the whiskey menace, and territorial governors and legislators took action in all sectors of the frontier. That their steps were halting was due more to the dim twilight of authority between federal and local governments and to hesitation to act against the economic interests of the infant communities than to any malice toward the Indian or indifference to his plight.

The Territory North West of the River Ohio was still in its first stage of territorial government when the governor and judges enacted a comprehensive law governing Indian trade, not only forbidding under penalty of fine the distribution of intoxicating liquor to the Indians, but excluding foreigners from the trade and setting the high penalty of five hundred dollars for trading without a license. The law set a pattern for ineffectiveness. The acting governor was soon urging the courts and commandants of militia to inquire into delinquencies and to take proper legal action against the "notorious violation" of the law and the "very mischievous Consequences" which ensued. When frequent disturbances from drunken Indians arose at Cincinnati and other places where the Indians gathered, he issued a proclamation directing all judges, commissioners for licensing taverns, justices of the peace, sheriffs, coroners, attorneys for the United States and for the Territory, and all other civil and military officers and good citizens to bring the offenders to justice. There seemed to be an uneasiness about the restrictions, however, and five years after enactment the law was quietly repealed with the notation that the law was "partly supplied by an act of the United States." [1]

The problem quickly arose of distinction between the Indian Country and the land ceded by the Indians to the whites. The governor of the Territory, who was also superintendent of Indian affairs according to law, found that his authority as superintendent in large measure evaporated, because it did not apply to the

---

[1] Theodore C. Pease, ed., *The Laws of the Northwest Territory, 1788–1800* (Springfield, Ill., 1925), pp. 26–28, 256; Letter of Winthrop Sargent, July 22, 1793, in *Territorial Papers*, III, 412; Proclamation of Sargent, Sept. 10, 1794, *ibid.*, 423.

white settlements to which the Indians freely resorted for liquor. The obvious remedy, of course, was for territorial legislation to supply the deficiency, but territorial legislatures were slow to provide for the areas under their jurisdiction the sort of regulations that federal law provided for the Indian Country. Only once more did the legislature of the Northwest Territory notice the problem, when in 1799, to aid the missionary activities of the Society of United Brethren, it prohibited the selling of liquor in the Indian towns in which these missionaries labored.[2]

The inability or unwillingness of the Territory to cope with the whiskey problem brought numerous complaints to the federal officials as the nefarious traffic flourished. Even the Indians themselves, becoming aware of the evil effects of the liquor on their morals, health, and very existence, pleaded with President Jefferson for protection. When Jefferson in turn recommended to Congress that it pass some law to restrict the trade, Congress inserted a special provision in the intercourse act of 1802, which authorized the President "to take such measures, from time to time, as to him may appear expedient to prevent or restrain the vending or distributing of spirituous liquors among all or any of the said Indian tribes." To implement this law, the secretary of war sent a circular of instructions to Indian officials, forbidding traders to vend ardent spirits. He addressed special letters as well to territorial governors, informing them that no traders should be allowed to supply the Indians with spirituous liquors on any pretext whatever and that traders who disturbed the peace and harmony existing between the Indians and the whites were to be deprived of their licenses.[3]

In line with these federal directions, William Henry Harrison, governor of Indiana Territory, issued a proclamation strictly forbidding traders and other persons to sell intoxicating liquors to the Indians, but after a year of operation the restriction had done no good. Harrison wrote to Jefferson at the end of October 1803: "I wish I could inform you that the benevolent intentions of the Government in their indeavours to prevent the use of Ardent Spirits amongst the Indians had been successful — It is my Opin-

---

[2] *Laws of the Northwest Territory*, pp. 415–416.

[3] Jefferson to Congress, Jan. 27, 1802, in Richardson, *Messages and Papers,* I, 334–335; *U.S. Stat.*, II, 146; Henry Dearborn to Indian superintendents and agents, Sept. 14, 1802, in SW IA LS, vol. A, p. 276; Dearborn to Harrison, Sept. 3, 1802, in *Territorial Papers*, VII, 74; Dearborn to William C. C. Claiborne, Sept. 11, 1802, in Dunbar Rowland, ed., *The Mississippi Territorial Archives, 1798–1803*, I (Nashville, 1905), 552.

ion that more Whisky has been Consumed by the Indians &
more fatal Consequences ensued from the Use of it since the
traders have been prohibetted from taking it into the Indian
Country than there ever was before." He urged that the restrictions be tightened to include all persons, not just the Indian
traders.[4]

The distinction between the Indian Country and ceded territory continued to be a major obstacle in the enforcement of the
restrictions on whiskey, for it became accepted opinion that the
regulations of the federal government and of its superintendents
and agents for Indian affairs applied only to the lands still owned
and occupied by the Indians. If the Indian title had been extinguished, the federal laws did not apply; and how easy it was
for the distributors to render themselves immune to legal action
by operating just across the line.

The territories and states needed to take further action themselves to extend the Indian Country prohibitions over the ceded
lands. Governor Harrison had been informed in January 1804 of
the President's opinion that the territorial governments had authority to establish such restrictions under their power to regulate
retailers, and he was urged to see that the territory prevented
unauthorized persons from selling spirituous liquors. Harrison,
whose fair-minded attitude toward the Indians was well known,
accordingly suggested the needed legislation to the first meeting
of the General Assembly on July 29, 1805. After some rhetorical
remarks about the excellent regard which the United States had
always shown the Indians — "a striking contrast to the conduct
of other civilized nations" — he recommended restrictions on liquor traffic to supplement the "entirely ineffectual" measures of
Congress. The governor's good intentions and high idealism were
no doubt sincere, but he little reckoned with the profit motive,
so strong among the inhabitants of the frontier. The General
Assembly dutifully passed a law prohibiting the sale or giving
of intoxicating liquors to Indians; then it added a final section
that negated the whole act by providing for the law to go into
force only after the states of Kentucky and Ohio and the territories of Louisiana and Michigan had passed similar legislation.
The law was to remain in force only so long as these neighboring states kept their laws on the books. Harrison explained that
the legislature thought a law in Indiana Territory alone would

[4] Proclamation of Oct. 24, 1802, in *Messages and Letters of Harrison*, I, 59–60;
Harrison to Jefferson, Oct. 29, 1803, in *Territorial Papers*, VII, 146.

be of little effect if the Indians could go into neighboring areas and bring back liquor for their use. "The citizens," it was argued, "would suffer all the inconveniences of their drunkenness without the advantage of their trade." [5]

The Indiana territorial legislature did, nevertheless, take some steps to restrict the flow of liquor to the Indians. On August 6, 1805, the Assembly authorized the governor to prohibit by proclamation the sale or disposition of ardent spirits to any Indian within thirty miles of a place where a council or conference was being held with the Indians. This was an emergency measure, rushed through because of an impending council to be held at Vincennes, and the governor immediately issued a proclamation putting the law into effect. Harrison made use of the law when later treaties were held, and the law was continued in the revised statutes of the Territory issued in 1807. A general law of 1806, however, which forbade the distribution of liquor to Indians within forty miles of Vincennes, was allowed to lapse.[6]

Since the limited measures enacted by the territorial governments did not effectively prevent the Indians from coming into the white settlements to obtain strong drink, fuller cooperation was needed between the states and territories and the federal government. President Jefferson therefore pleaded with the governors in 1808 to propose to their lawmakers the wisdom and humanity of restraining the citizens from vending spirituous liquors to the Indians. Ohio complied immediately with a law that placed a fine of five to one hundred dollars for selling intoxicating liquor to Indians within the state or helping to convey the liquor out of the state for sale to the Indians. According to the law all articles received from Indians in exchange for liquor were to be returned to them.[7]

In Indiana Governor Harrison placed Jefferson's letter before the General Assembly and in his annual message to the legisla-

[5] Dearborn to Harrison, Jan. 6, 1804, *ibid.*, 164; Harrison to the General Assembly, July 29, 1805, in *Messages and Letters of Harrison*, I, 153–154; Harrison to Dearborn, Sept. 16, 1805, *ibid.*, 166; Act of August 15, 1805, in Francis S. Philbrick, ed., *The Laws of Indiana Territory, 1801–1809* (Springfield, Ill., 1930), pp. 97–98. The law of 1805 was included in the revised statutes of September 17, 1807, but it of course never went into effect.

[6] *Laws of Indiana Territory, 1801–1809*, pp. 91, 216, 497; Gayle Thornbrough and Dorothy Riker, ed., *Journals of the General Assembly of Indiana Territory, 1805–1815* (Indianapolis, 1950), p. 65, n. 32; p. 112, n. 6.

[7] Jefferson to executives, Dec. 31, 1808, in *The Writings of Thomas Jefferson* (memorial edition, 20 vols., Washington, 1903–1904), XII, 223–224; *Laws of Ohio, 1808–1809* (Chillicothe, 1809), pp. 180–181.

ture in 1809 urged the body to follow Ohio's example of obedience to the national government. "The experience of nine years has left a perfect conviction upon my mind," he said, "that the humane and benevolent intentions of the government in relation to the aborigines can never be accomplished as long as the means of indulgence in this fatal liquor is so easily obtained." The gentlemen of the Assembly, however, were not to be hurried. A year later Harrison again addressed them on the subject of Indian trade, calling attention to the fact that the federal regulations had no force within the white settlements and noting the "mischievous effect" that this lack of control had on both the Indians and the whites. The result was a law that not only prohibited the sale or distribution of ardent spirits to Indians "within the part of the territory to which the Indian title is extinguished," but also required a license from the governor to trade with the Indians at all in these areas and confined the trade to places designated by him. The preamble to the act was a noble statement of compliance with the wishes of the general government and indicated a humane interest in saving the Indians from intoxication as well as a desire to facilitate the extinguishment of Indian titles and to prevent depredations.[8]

Following these good examples, the Territory of Illinois in December 1813 prohibited the selling or giving of liquor to Indians and provided for a fine of five to twenty dollars upon conviction. This law was not strong enough to be effective, and a year later the territorial legislature, noting the insufficiency of the law, passed a new one with more specific prohibitions and with judicial proceedings placed in the hands of the justices of the peace. Other territories, too, found it expedient to enact or strengthen existing laws against giving whiskey to the Indians. The governor and judges of the Territory of Louisiana, in May 1806, forbade the giving or selling of liquor to Indians without permission of the superintendent of Indian affairs, with a fine of thirty to one hundred and fifty dollars or imprisonment of ten to thirty days. The Territory of Orleans in the same month included Indians with slaves in its law prohibiting the selling of liquors, under penalty of twenty dollars and forfeiture of tavern license; and in December 1812 the State of Louisiana replaced

[8] Harrison to the General Assembly, Oct. 17, 1809, and Nov. 12, 1810, in *Messages and Letters of Harrison*, I, 382–383, 490–491; Louis B. Ewbank and Dorothy L. Riker, ed., *The Laws of Indiana Territory, 1809–1816* (Indianapolis, 1934), pp. 148–151.

this early act with a more specific prohibition against providing Indians with strong drink. A fine of two hundred dollars was to be imposed on offenders and they were furthermore to be liable for all the injuries and damages done by Indians while in the state of intoxication. Michigan in 1812 and again in 1815 passed laws which restricted the sale of liquor to Indians, and the governor issued a strongly worded proclamation in April 1815 that won the special commendation of the secretary of war. And Mississippi Territory in 1816 in a special act to prevent the sale of spirituous liquors to Indians strengthened an earlier law of 1799 by requiring the grand juries of the counties to present persons violating the law and requiring applicants for licenses to sell spirituous liquors to swear that they would not sell any spirits to Indians or knowingly let it be done on their premises.[9]

∾∾

The laws — federal, state, and territorial — were on the books, and Indian agents were directed to prevent "as far as practicable" the use of ardent spirits among the Indians, allowing no trader to sell or dispose of liquor or keep it at any of the trading stations. Effective enforcement was another matter. William Clark wrote to the President in 1811 from St. Louis that he had used every exertion authorized by law to prevent the sale of whiskey to the Indians, but without effect. "My power under the laws," he lamented, "is not sufficient to affect this object in a country like this, where nine out of ten of the Indian Traders have no respect for our Laws." Clark, nevertheless, did not give up. He sent out to the Indian agents copies of the intercourse acts, the laws of Missouri Territory against spirituous liquors, and a special proclamation; and he set on foot plans to move troops into the area most seriously affected.[10]

Conditions got worse instead of better, and Clark in 1819 received a strong letter from Secretary of War Calhoun, pointing

[9] Francis S. Philbrick, ed., *The Laws of Illinois Territory, 1809–1818* (Springfield, Ill., 1950), pp. 89–90, 154–155; *Laws of the Territory of Louisiana* (St. Louis, 1808), pp. 32–33; Francois-Xavier Martin, ed., *A General Digest of the Acts of the Legislatures of the Late Territory of Orleans and of the State of Louisiana* (3 vols., New Orleans, 1816), II, 434, 438; *Laws of the Territory of Michigan* (4 vols., Lansing, 1871–1884), I, 180–181, 201–202; Proclamation of William Woodbridge, April 14, 1815, in *Territorial Papers*, X, 717; Acts of Feb. 28, 1799, and Dec. 6, 1816, in session laws of Mississippi Territory.

[10] William Eustis to Nicholas Boilvin, March 14, 1811, in *Territorial Papers*, XIV, 444; Clark to Madison, April 10, 1811, *ibid.*, XIV, 445–446; Clark to William L. Lovely, May 2, 1816, *ibid.*, XV, 134–135.

out once again the mischief caused by the introduction of liquor among the Indians. Clark was reminded of his duty and was formally requested to take prompt and efficient steps to prevent the introduction of liquor among the Indians of Missouri Territory, whether by licensed or by other traders, and to enforce the law strictly against all offenders. The stringent law passed by Michigan Territory was called to Clark's attention, and he was reminded that equally rigid laws should obtain over all sections of the Indian Country in order that traders in one part would not have an unfair advantage over traders in another.[11]

At Fort Mitchell in Alabama the Indian agent complained of the introduction of liquor, not by the traders, but by the factor and the sutler at the military post. Private adventurers could not easily be restrained when the factors and sutlers introduced whiskey without restraint. The agent reported seeing in the yard and houses occupied by the factor more than fifty Indians lying about, so drunk as to be perfectly helpless, and many more rioting and fighting. He then issued an order prohibiting the introduction of spirits into the Creek Nation and directed the warriors of each town who were appointed by the nation to execute the laws to enforce his order. For a time the order had some effect.[12]

Through the first two decades of the century hope for ending the whiskey traffic was placed in control of the traders. The condemnations that filled the air against the traders — both licensed and unlicensed — were founded on the traders' reliance upon whiskey to exploit and degrade the Indians. The fight of Thomas L. McKenney and others to tighten the regulations in regard to traders was aimed principally at one thing: to do away with the evils brought in the train of the whiskey keg. The purpose of urging discretionary authority in the granting of licenses was to prevent known whiskey dealers from entering the Indian Country to trade under the legal cover of their license. The designation of a limited number of locations at which the trade must be conducted was intended to strengthen the agents' position when it came to enforcing the provisions of the licenses, which prohibited the use of whiskey. In the minds of McKenney and his humanitarian supporters, the great argument in favor of the factory system was the hope that the government trading houses would squeeze

---

[11] Calhoun to Clark, March 15, 1819, *ibid.*, XV, 527–528.
[12] David B. Mitchell to Calhoun, June 17, 1818, *ibid.*, XVIII, 352–353. A copy of the order is included.

the petty traders completely from the field. To McKenney, in fact, there appeared to be no alternative to the government factories, unless one wished to abandon the Indians altogether to their fate. No other system of regulating the trade so as to protect the Indians from the whiskey venders was deemed possible by him.[13]

The collapse of the factory system before the onslaughts of the traders would leave the Indians largely unprotected from the increasing virulence of the liquor trade. The unceasing reports from the frontier forced Congress to do something to strengthen the federal legislation. As it struck down the factories with one hand, it made an attempt with the other to prevent the introduction of ardent spirits into the Indian Country. In the amendment to the intercourse act of 1802, dated May 6, 1822, which accompanied the act abolishing the trading houses, the President was authorized to direct Indian agents, governors of territories acting as superintendents of Indian affairs, and military officers to cause the stores and packages of goods of all traders to be searched, in case of suspicion or information that ardent spirits were being carried into the Indian Country. If ardent spirits were found among the goods, all the goods were to be forfeited — one half to the use of the informer and one half to the government — and the trader's license was to be cancelled and his bond put in suit. Copies of the act were sent to the commandants of the military posts on the frontier with explicit instructions to follow the letter of the law in searching the stores and packages of all Indian traders if there was reason to believe that whiskey was being introduced. The officers were directed to seize the goods and start libel proceedings against the goods.[14]

The new amendment with its provisions for search and the severe penalty of forfeiture of goods availed little. There were still ambiguities and loopholes in the law, and the powerful trading interests on the frontier were able successfully to thwart the government agents and army officers in the execution of the law.

Of tremendous importance in the question of liquor restriction was the policy of John Jacob Astor and his American Fur Company. At first the Company was opposed to the use of whiskey among the Indians, since it was interested in a steady, year-

---

[13] McKenney to Calhoun, Aug. 19, 1818, in *Wis. Hist. Colls.*, XX, 66–79; McKenney to Henry Southard, March 19, 1818, *ibid.*, 37–41.

[14] *U.S. Stat.*, III, 682–683; Edmund P. Gaines to post commanders, June 12, 1822, in *American State Papers: Military Affairs* (7 vols., Washington, 1832–1861), V, 508.

by-year trade and did not depend upon a year or two of spectac-
ular profits, as did the fly-by-night traders. The Indians, if sober,
would continue to be good hunters for furs, and they would
recognize the excellence of the goods offered by Astor. If need
be, the American Fur Company could squeeze out its rivals by
underselling them, and then make up the difference by raising
prices after it had acquired a monopoly, but all of this policy was
presaged on the assumption that no one had whiskey to offer in
the Indian trade. Such was the overwhelming desire of the Indians
for liquor that even the powerful American Fur Company could
not compete with smaller rivals if the latter used whiskey to
entice the Indians in with their furs. As Thomas L. McKenney
remarked, "The source of all the difficulty is to be found in the
necessity which the traders esteem themselves to be under to carry
spirituous liquors into the Indian country; and it is from this
source that so much wretchedness and so many evils proceed.
There are many persons engaged in this trade whose feelings, no
doubt, revolt at the calamities which a traffic of this sort occasions;
but the forbidden and destructive article is considered so essential
to a lucrative commerce, as not only to still those feelings, but
to lead the traders to brave the most imminent hazards, and evade,
by various methods, the threatened penalties of law. . . . The
trader with the whiskey, it must be admitted, is certain of getting
most furs." [15]

Although the American Fur Company did not immediately
relinquish its initial policy of opposition to whiskey and sought to
have the restrictions enforced against traders who were smuggling
liquor into the Indian Country, keeping the ardent spirits out
seemed to be a total impossibility. [16]

༄

Competition from the British companies along the northern
border was real enough to offer some justification for the Company's request for special permission to take liquor into that
region. On the basis of the discretionary power lodged with the
President by the basic law of 1802 the Company got the privilege

[15] McKenney to James Barbour, Feb. 14, 1826, in *American State Papers:
Indian Affairs*, II, 659–660.

[16] Ramsay Crooks to John Jacob Astor, June 23, 1817, in American Fur Company
Letter Books, vol. 1, p. 30; Crooks and Robert Stuart to Astor, Jan. 24, 1818, in
Wis. Hist. Colls., XX, 21; George Boyd to William Morrison, July 17, 1819, *ibid.*,
116.

of taking in whiskey for posts along the border in order to enable the American traders to compete successfully with the British and thus keep the trade in American hands. In July 1818, after having received word from Robert Stuart that the British North West Company was freely distributing liquor to the Indians with the purpose of "engrossing the whole of the fur trade in that quarter," Governor Lewis Cass authorized the agent at Michilimackinac to permit a small quantity of liquor to be introduced. Cass was cautious in granting permission — he was, he said, "in general utterly opposed to the introduction of spirituous liquors into the Indian Country" — and he insisted that no whiskey was to be admitted unless the British actually resorted to its use. But the beginning was made, and the use of whiskey along the northern border became the accepted practice. As the British continued to use whiskey in the trade, Cass saw only two alternatives: either admit limited quantities of liquor for use by American traders or abandon the fur trade completely to the British. Cass could find no absolute prohibition of the use of liquor in the laws of 1802 and 1822, since they allowed discretion on the part of the executive. He assumed this discretionary authority for himself, authorized Henry R. Schoolcraft, the agent at Sault Ste. Marie, to permit the traders to take whiskey into the area west of Lake Superior, and then wrote to the War Department for confirmation of his action. Secretary of War Calhoun gave his approval.[17]

[17] Cass to William H. Puthuff, July 4, 1818, in *Territorial Papers*, X, 778–779; Cass to Schoolcraft, June 10, 1823, in *Wis. Hist. Colls.*, XX, 306–307; Calhoun to Cass, July 14, 1823, in SW IA LS, vol. E, p. 463. The modus vivendi adopted by the American Fur Company can be seen in the following report of Robert Stuart to William B. Astor, April 25, 1825: ". . . there are several parts of the country we had much better abandon than send without it [liquor]; and in short we must either send some (under all possible precaution) wherever there is opposition, particularly along the frontier, or take my word for it, we must *give* [up] that trade entirely; which altho' it is the least profitable, you will at once see the impropriety of doing — If you think proper to leave this matter to my discretion I feel confident we shall not often get into difficulty; and should you forbid it altogether, rest asured the consequences will be extremely injurious; of this Mr Crooks who you can consult, must be fully sensible, for he cannot have forgotten how much we suffered by not sending liquor in 1817 & 1818, while all our opponents had it in abundance every where and notwithstanding all our efforts we were never able to get the law enforced upon one of them; we then found it to be absolutely necessary, *to do, as we were done by*; and were it not for the bungling of such a sheep as Wallace, but little is ever to be feared — I have an understanding with Gov. Cass & Mr Schoolcraft about the quantity of Liquor deemed sufficient for the Lake Superior Country, which is liberal & quite sufficient — about this place, Lake Michigan, & the Green Bay country, if we do not give the *necessary* supplies, those who will can get three fourths of the skins, and on their own terms — In a business like ours, where much is be-

Limiting the use to cases of absolute necessity, however, proved most difficult. Colonel Josiah Snelling on the upper Mississippi complained violently about the whiskey permitted by the agents on the Lakes to enter the Indian Country. "If the sale of whiskey could be restricted to the vicinity of the British line," Snelling asserted, "the mischief would be comparatively trivial; but if permitted at all, no limits can be set to it." He complained that the permission granted in the north was unfair to the traders along the Mississippi who had no such privilege and declared that in 1825 3300 gallons of whiskey and 2500 gallons of high wines had been delivered to the agent of the American Fur Company at Mackinac. "I will venture to add," he concluded, "that an inquiry into the manner in which the Indian trade is conducted, and especially by the North American Fur Company, is a matter of no small importance to the tranquillity of the borders." The secretary of war, in reply to Snelling's complaints, sent him a copy of the act of 1822 with the instructions that he was to carry out the procedure therein outlined for preventing the introduction of whiskey.[18]

The officers of the American Fur Company, to be sure, did not meekly accept the charges made against them by Colonel Snelling and supplied the secretary of war with a batch of testimonials from Governor Cass, George Boyd, the Indian agent at Mackinac, and Adam D. Steuart, collector of the customs, which stated that the Company was really composed of law-abiding and cooperative people. Yet, however innocent the Company might proclaim itself, it feared investigation of its traders in regions outside the border area itself. When Colonel Snelling began to send out troops to search their consignments of Indian goods for liquor, Astor and his men took the matter up with the secretary of war. Astor in 1826 recalled for the secretary that under his predecessor, the post commanders had been ordered "not to interfere with the

---

yond our immediate control, we must expect some blunders, & even losses, but you may always depend on my conducting every thing with all possible caution & prudence. . . ." American Fur Company Letter Books, vol. 3, p. 165.

[18] Snelling to Calhoun, Jan. 10, 1825, in SW LR, S-163 (19), 1825; Snelling to Barbour, Aug. 23, 1825, in *American State Papers: Indian Affairs*, II, 661; Barbour to Snelling, Sept. 17, 1825, in IA LS, vol. 2, p. 156. William Clark supported Snelling's views and reported that the agents under his jurisdiction had received "pointed instructions, in relation to the introduction of Ardent Spirits among the Indians." He, however, sent them another circular "to remind them of the necessity of exercising the utmost vigilance in detecting & prosecuting, such traders and others, as may attempt a violation or evasion of the laws." Clark to Barbour, Oct. 19, 1825, in IA LR, St. Louis Superintendency.

Indian traders," and hinted at suits against officials of the government like Snelling if they became too insistent on making the Company toe the mark. The War Department acceded to Astor's request that if liquor should by chance be found the seized goods would be released on bond so that the furs would not spoil.[19]

In February 1827 there was a new tightening of the prohibition against liquor. "Upon this point," McKenney wrote to Cass, "any discretion which may have been heretofore given not provided for by law, you will consider as withdrawn. The laws will govern." Cass objected to the order, since he had permitted whiskey only along the boundary to prevent the utter ruin of American trade. Furthermore, Cass pointed out, his use of the discretionary power was not contrary to the laws, but was expressly allowed by the acts of 1802 and 1822, for he considered Calhoun's permission as passing down the presidential discretionary power to himself. Since he assumed that the President's intention, now, however, was to allow no more exceptions, he instructed Schoolcraft to discontinue such licenses. Cass's assumption was correct, as he soon learned from McKenney, whose previous letter had been intended to take away exactly the discretionary power Cass was talking about. It was now deemed useless, Cass was told, to adopt any measures short of an absolute exclusion. "One single licence to exercise *a discretion*, as to *quantity*, you must be aware is equivalent to a universal grant. There is no controlling the evils of the practice short of *an unqualified prohibition*." The word had been passed on to General Clark, too, that he was to prohibit its use *in toto*.[20]

The American Fur Company did not rest content with this rebuff. It soon made renewed application for the privilege that it had previously enjoyed, and on June 15, 1831, Secretary of War John H. Eaton restored to Cass the discretionary power that had been withdrawn in 1827. The Company had made its request in order to compete with the Hudson's Bay Company and Eaton accepted its arguments. "It is impossible to judge fully the effect of granting the application which is made," the secretary wrote,

[19] Robert Stuart to Barbour, Feb. 24, 1826, and enclosures, in IA LR, Miscellaneous; John Jacob Astor to Barbour, May 26, 1826, *ibid.*; McKenney to Clark, May 29, 1826, in IA LS, vol. 3, p. 107; McKenney to Astor, May 29, 1826, *ibid.*, p. 108.

[20] McKenney to Cass, Feb. 20, 1827, *ibid.*, p. 390; Cass to McKenney, March 25, 1827, in IA LR, Michigan Superintendency; McKenney to Cass, April 19, 1827, in IA LS, vol. 4, p. 24; McKenney to Clark, April 13, 1827, *ibid.*, p. 15; McKenney to Barbour, Feb. 15, 1828, *ibid.*, p. 294.

"or to determine what effect may be occasioned to the frontier by it. It is obvious, however, that the interest of this Company cannot be advanced by too freely granting the use of spirits to the Indians. The tendency would be to enervate, and draw them from the chase, whence only the articles they exchange can be procured. I feel a confidence therefore, that the object is as it is represented, to be enabled merely to compete upon fair and equal terms with British traders." [21] It proved to be a temporary respite, for a new law in 1832 destroyed altogether the possibility of a discretionary grant.

There was another way to take liquor into the Indian Country under the protection of authority. Permission was granted to carry in whiskey for the use of the boatmen employed in the trade, since the prohibition under the acts of 1802 and 1822 was only against introducing the article for use in trade with the Indians. The amount of whiskey, of course, was to be limited according to the number of boatmen and the length of their absence, and bond was to be given that the liquor was not sold or given to the Indians. Under this principle William Clark at St. Louis freely granted permits to the traders, but his faith was not well placed. The commandant at Fort Leavenworth estimated that twice as much liquor was taken in as was permitted by the special licenses, that "somewhere about 8000 gallons" a season went up the Missouri — as much "as could be desired for any purpose." One Indian agent claimed in 1831 that for only one out of every hundred gallons taken into the Indian Country was a permit asked of the superintendent. So brazen were the traders that they openly sold the whiskey in the face of the agents, who had no power at their command to prevent it. The agent on the upper Missouri was heard to exclaim that "he wished to the Lord that the traders would not sell or give whiskey to the Indians in his presence." It was reported by the sutler at Fort Leavenworth that thousands of gallons had passed that post in 1831.[22]

Any ruse seemed to succeed. In 1832 William Sublette was permitted to take in four hundred and fifty gallons of whiskey for the use of his boatmen — but in that year the trader took his expedition overland and did not engage a single boatman. And

[21] Eaton to Cass, June 15, 1831, in *Territorial Papers*, XII, 294 and n.
[22] William Davenport to Cass, Sept. 25, 1831, in IA LR, Upper Missouri Agency; Report of Andrew S. Hughes, Oct. 31, 1831, in *Sen. Doc.* 90, 22 Cong., 1 sess., ser. 213, pp. 23–24. A copy of a license to take in whiskey for boatmen issued by Clark, August 22, 1831, is enclosed in Davenport's letter to Cass.

the traders would pad the lists of boatmen in order to increase the available liquor.[23]

The reports which reached the War Department caused an inquiry to be sent to Clark about the state of affairs in his superintendency. His reply displayed an unbecoming naiveté, for he reported that "relying on their good faith," he had not checked up on the traders, neither examining their outfits before they left St. Louis nor having their boats inspected by the officers of the military posts along their route. "This delicate task," he told the secretary of war, "was dispensed with." But finally Clark's eyes opened and he saw the operations of the traders in their true light. He began to notice the increased amounts for which permits were requested and he discovered that instead of whiskey, the traders were taking in alcohol which was diluted many times before being distributed to the Indians. "As those traders have evinced so little good faith, such disrespect to the Government as to violate its most imperative laws, and so little humanity toward the Indians themselves as to disregard the most sacred provision for their protection," he wrote in a new spirit of righteousness, "I shall conceive it my bounden duty to recommend the total and entire prohibition of this article in the Indian country, under any pretence, or for any purpose whatever."[24]

Clark was pictured in a bad light by his own admission. If he knew of these flagarant violations, why did he not bring the offenders into court and put an end to the difficulty? He had his reply ready:

I would answer, that the institution of a suit on a trader's bond, with such an object in view, would be considered as a mere *farce*; as past experience fully shows that, in order to [have] a successful prosecution, there are many things to be proven before a court having cognizance of the offence, which would not occur at the time to the witness testifying. It would prove nothing that he should have witnessed the process of reducing the *alcohol* in the trader's house, and the putting it into casks; that he should have seen the liquor drawn from these same casks, put into kegs, and delivered to Indians, who conveyed the same to their camps, which, after a few hours, exhibited a scene of the most frightful drunkenness: — he must be able to testify that he has *tasted* this liquor, and found it to be spirituous, in order to produce a conviction. And when it is considered that an individual seeking to qualify himself by these means to produce the conviction of the

---

[23] These two examples are cited in Chittenden, *American Fur Trade*, I, 25–26.
[24] Elbert Herring to Clark, Nov. 5, 1831, in IA LS, vol. 7, p. 455; Clark to Cass, Nov. 20, 1831, in *Sen. Doc.* 90, 22 Cong., 1 sess., ser. 213, p. 7.

traders, would at once arouse suspicions which might result in the most serious consequences to himself, the difficulty attending it may be easily imagined.[25]

These pious protestations of Clark to the secretary of war in November 1831, however, lose some of their force when we consider that he was still granting permission to take large quantities of "boatmen's" whiskey up the Missouri in the summer of the following year.

※

A further source of difficulty was the recurring Indian Country problem. When the Indian agent at Green Bay reported that he had prohibited the landing of spirituous liquors at his agency, Lewis Cass approved the action, but then, though agreeing that the "total exclusion of Spirituous liquors from the Indian Country is altogether proper," decided that the settlement at Green Bay was not strictly Indian Country. Since liquors could not be prohibited to the settlers there, Cass recommended restoring any liquors of theirs that were still in the public stores.[26] Cass directed that the agent limit and guard the liquor allowed the settlers in such a manner as to prevent its subsequent transfer to the Indians, but he in fact opened a door for the passage of ardent spirits into the Indian Country.

The peculiar situation of Prairie du Chien offered a similar opportunity for evading the government's prohibition. To figure out the exact legal status of the village taxed the best official minds, for it was an island within the Indian Country, and practical doubts filled the mind of Lieutenant Colonel Willoughby Morgan, the commandant at Fort Crawford, which stood guard at Prairie du Chien. With hostile traders and settlers ready to jump on him if he made the slightest misstep, Morgan wanted an interpretation from higher headquarters before he took action in doubtful cases. There were more problems involved in preventing the introduction of liquor to the Indians than occurred to the minds of Congressmen, and the frontier commander put his finger on some sore points. Did he have authority to prevent citizens at Prairie du Chien from having liquor or from trading liquor to the Indians? Did these citizens have the right to go

[25] Clark to Cass, Nov. 20, 1831, *ibid.*
[26] John Bowyer to Cass, July 22, 1817, in *Wis. Hist. Colls.*, XIX, 466–467; Bowyer to Cass, Dec. 15, 1817, *ibid.*, 487–488; Cass to Bowyer, Jan. 22, 1818, *ibid.*, XX, 16–17.

back and forth into the Indian Country? Was their settlement
considered Indian Country or was it part of the cession made by
the Indians for the military post? Did the intercourse act he was
charged with enforcing pertain to other persons besides licensed
traders? Its wording — about forfeiture of bonds and goods —
seemed to apply only to traders and would thus allow nontraders
to bring in liquor unmolested. Could traders be prosecuted even
though liquor was not actually found among their goods if there
were clear evidence that they had in fact introduced ardent
spirits? And what about the pockets of lead miners settling on the
Galena River? Was he, as army commander, authorized to restrict liquor among them under the intercourse act? The officer
realized well enough that raising such difficulties did not prevent
the flow of liquor, and he approved the policy of the government,
but he did not dare to act until he was sure of the subtleties of
the law. He knew that the traders would not hesitate to attack
him in the courts for the least overextension of his authority.[27]

The response Morgan received was not encouraging. He was
told, in short, that the laws plainly took care of cases in which
liquor was brought into the Indian Country by licensed traders,
that the unlicensed traders were to forfeit all their goods including whiskey, and that the passports granted to other persons to
enter the Indian Country should specify that they could not take
in liquor with them. As for the traders at Prairie du Chien and
elsewhere outside the limits of the Indian Country, there was no
law to prevent them from selling liquors to the Indians. Astor's
men and no doubt other traders, too, made full use of the
irregularity.[28]

[27] Morgan to Edmund P. Gaines, Nov. 15, 1822, *ibid.*, 291–297. Gaines forwarded Morgan's letter to Secretary of War Calhoun and expressed his agreement with Morgan. He was not optimistic about chances of enforcing the laws
since the unlicensed traders would largely evade it, thus forcing the lawful
traders too to resort to the use of liquor. As for "collisions" between the army
officers and the illicit whiskey dealers, Gaines noted past instances and could
understand why the officers tended to enter upon the enforcement of the laws
"with due circumspection, if not with fastidious caution." Gaines to Calhoun,
March 22, 1823, in SW IA LR.
[28] Calhoun to Gaines, May 14, 1823, in SW IA LS, vol. E, pp. 441–442;
Porter, *John Jacob Astor*, II, 800; Clark to Barbour, Oct. 19, 1825, in *Wis.
Hist. Colls.*, XX, 385–387. Clark pointed out the difficulty that "neither the Agent
at that place, or the Officer in command, has the power to prevent the sale of
spirits to the Indians; that being a Town and settlement without the Indian limits,
over which the Government and Laws of Michigan Territory are extended, and
where the Laws in relation to that subject are but little regarded by the civil
authority at that place."

Whatever may have been the original intentions of John Jacob Astor, he and his company succumbed to the pressure of the trade. They could not escape the vicious circle. Because of its financial strength, the Company had no need for whiskey if no other traders were using it. The opposition traders, however, needed to resort to whiskey, without which they could not compete with Astor. Eventually the Company decided that price-cutting was not sufficient and that the use of liquor must be added if rivals were to be eliminated. Astor's agents engaged freely in the liquor trade, in violation of the law, the Indian trading regulations, and their licenses. They made use of all the technicalities possible and all the influence they had in high places to make some claim of legality when they ran into the opposition of the Indian agents and the army officers.[29]

The American Fur Company refused to be treated like ordinary run-of-the-mill traders. When action was taken against one of its traders for violation of the intercourse acts, the wheels began to turn, and the commotion around the heads of Washington officials generally resulted in a victory for the Company against the enforcing agents on the frontier. One such case was the seizure at Fort Wayne in 1824 of American Fur Company goods in the hands of its agent, William H. Wallace. John Tipton, Indian agent at that post on the Maumee, seized the goods of the trader under the laws of 1802 and 1822 because he found intoxicating liquor among them, and he libeled the goods in the federal court. When word of the seizure reached the Company, Astor wrote to the secretary of war, protesting the seizure and charging that Tipton was "more actuated by a desire to injure our Company, than to discharge his duty to the public faithfully." He appealed to Calhoun "to interfere for the protection of our trade before it is ruined by the extraordinary course of Mr. Tipton." Astor requested that at least the War Department should order the release under bond of the goods seized. Although he refused to back down in his charges, Tipton was willing enough to release the goods pending the outcome of the case. He denied any hostility toward the Company or any desire to injure it, but he had proof of illegal action and intended to do his duty, "notwithstanding the fearful odds of talent and influence that the Co. will array against me."[30]

[29] Porter, *John Jacob Astor*, II, 795.
[30] Astor to Calhoun, Oct. 29, 1824, and Nov. 13, 1824, in IA LR, Miscellaneous; Robert Stuart to James Abbott, Nov. 10, 1824, in American Fur Company Letter

The case, brought before the District Court of the United States for the District of Ohio early in 1825, was decided in favor of the agent, and the goods were condemned. The American Fur Company then appealed to the Supreme Court on a writ of error, arguing that the liquor had not been intended for the Indians at all. Meanwhile the Company continued its efforts to have the condemned goods released on bond. Astor himself again appealed to the War Department, and Albert Gallatin wrote to the secretary of war on the Company's behalf. Finally, in July, 1826, Secretary of War James Barbour directed Tipton to release the goods to the agent of the Company on his giving bond to the United States for their value, to be paid in the event of the case being finally decided against Astor. At length, however, in 1829, the Supreme Court reversed the decision of the lower court on the grounds of an improper charge to the jury in regard to the meaning of the term "Indian Country." [31]

❧

The geographical areas covered by the northern and western departments of the American Fur Company were not the only

---

Books, vol. 3, pp. 139–140; Tipton to Calhoun, Nov. 20, 1824, and Dec. 24, 1824, in IA, LR, Fort Wayne Agency. The case is discussed in Porter, *John Jacob Astor*, II, 758–759, 803.

[31] Gallatin to Barbour, June 20, 1826, in IA LR, Miscellaneous; Barbour to Tipton, July 5, 1826, in IA LS, vol. 3, p. 139; Solicitor of the Treasury, Attorneys' Returns, vol. 2, 1821–1830, Indiana, National Archives, Record Group 206; *Sundry Goods, Wares, and Merchandises* vs. *United States*, 2 Pet. 357. See also McKenney to Clark, May 29, 1826, in IA LS, vol. 3, p. 107, in which directions are given to permit the release on bond of goods seized under the laws prohibiting the introduction of whiskey.

McKenney's hostility toward the American Fur Company abated at this time, and he offered to use his influence to settle the Tipton case. Robert Stuart reported McKenney's change to John Jacob Astor and proposed to take full advantage of it. ". . . it is, in my opinion best, that the application go thro' him, or that his aid be solicited, same time touching his vanity a little, about his sense of equity, and particularly *the full knowledge he now possesses*, of the manner in which our business is conducted; this he is very fond of proclaiming everywhere — and takes every oppy: of lauding our humane and correct dealing with the Indians — his excuse for his former conduct is, he 'sees all things' with his own eyes, he is a perfect man of the world, and how far his expressions of friendship &c can be relied upon is a question I dare not undertake to solve — at all events, we are pretty sure of him at present, for he is anxiously trying to establish an independant Dpt for Indian affairs, the full control of which he aspires to, and I *know* that he is very much afraid of your opposition to the measure — this I told him I was confident he need not apprehend. Indeed I believe we could get along with him as well as with any one else; for he has changed his sentiments a good deal about Indians &c, and he is a good hearted, *feather headed* kind of man, we could always keep as our friend, and we have nothing to ask that it

regions disturbed by traders who refused to obey the intercourse acts. Similar problems existed in the Territory of Arkansas, toward which the usual type of traders was drawn as the Cherokees and other southern Indians migrated to the Southwest. In this territory, to which the enterprise of the American Fur Company did not reach, the problem of liquor in the Indian Country was, if anything, greater than on the older frontier of the Northwest. The techniques of the traders were the same and the frustrations that the enforcing officers met were similar. There was as little regard for the law in the south as in the north and west.

The first attempt to bring action against violators of the laws prohibiting the introduction of liquor into the Indian Country showed the seriousness of the situation. In early May 1829, Colonel Matthew Arbuckle of the Seventh Infantry, the commanding officer at Fort Gibson, seized the goods of the trading firm of William DuVal and Peter A. Carnes in accordance with the provisions of the acts of 1802 and 1822. It was clear to the colonel that the traders had been flagrantly violating the provision of the acts prohibiting the distribution of ardent spirits to the Indians. When the stores were searched some liquor was found, and the traders were unable to show a license to trade, although they subsequently produced one. The seizure of the goods began a long controversy between Arbuckle, the traders, and the government, which assumed almost comic-opera complications. The whole affair demonstrated how ineffective the laws were in the face of determined and unscrupulous traders, even when the charges were pushed by as zealous and exact an officer as Colonel Arbuckle.[32]

Arbuckle first began the proceedings by turning over the information to Samuel C. Roane, the United States district attorney for the Territory of Arkansas, so that he might initiate court action as the law provided. Arbuckle posed a number of questions about the disposition of the seized goods, to which the district attorney replied in June, although even he was unsure on some points since this was the first such case in the Territory. Roane

---

would any longer be his interest to refuse." Stuart to Astor, Sept. 26, 1827, in American Fur Company Letter Books, vol. 3, pp. 469–470. See also Stuart to Astor, Aug. 28, 1826, and July 12, 1827, *ibid.*, pp. 358, 445; Stuart to Ramsay Crooks, Nov. 29, 1826, *ibid.*, p. 403.

[32] The pertinent papers dealing with the DuVal and Carnes case are printed in *Territorial Papers*, XXI, 32–36, 36–39, 53–55, 58–60, 70–72, 102–104, 120–127, 181, 285, 286, 292–295, 300, 333–336, 346–348, 349–350, 371–375, 381, 382, 385–386, 390–395.

counseled turning the goods over to the marshal of Arkansas Territory and saw no way to bring the matter to trial before the regular October term of the court. The marshal at first agreed to accept the goods — valued at between eight and ten thousand dollars by the traders — and directed Arbuckle to send them by steamboat down to Little Rock, but on second thought he hesitated, and in a later letter to Arbuckle indicated that he could not receive the goods without being authorized by a court order or directed to do so by the War Department. Roane, meanwhile, had temporarily left the Territory without having instituted any suit against the goods. Arbuckle in July pleaded with the secretary of war that "such instructions in Relation to the Case may be given to the Civil Authorities of the Territory as may best ensure the execution of the laws of the U.S. in the Case." The Attorney General of the United States, to whom the initial questions of Arbuckle about disposition of the goods had been sent for an opinion, wrote a long letter in response, which added up to the fact only that he had nothing to say on the matter.

Before anything further could be done along this line of attack, the matter took a new turn: DuVal and Carnes protested to the secretary of war against the army officer's action. It is evident that they told the secretary of war their own side of the story — and apparently with success. "It appears," Secretary of War Eaton wrote to Arbuckle in September, "that one barrel of Brandy & one of Rum are the only spirituous liquors which he [Carnes] had on hand and for which the seizure was made. Whatever reliance may be placed on the letter of the Law, it does not occur to me, that this was a case intended to be provided for by the Act of Congress. They are not the description of ardent spirits suited to Indian consumption, or which they can purchase in quantities to produce those inconveniences which it was the object and policy of the Law to provide against." He thereupon directed Arbuckle to return the goods to the traders, first making a careful examination to determine what damage had occurred to the goods since the seizure. Eaton enclosed a statement from DuVal and Carnes in which the firm agreed to release Arbuckle or any other officers acting under his authority from any damages resulting from the seizure of the goods — provided that if any loss or damage had occurred, the traders could call upon the government for remuneration.

Arbuckle dutifully acquiesced in the secretary of war's decision and notified the traders that the goods would be restored to them at their convenience, although he protested that Eaton had acted without full knowledge of the situation. The quantity of liquor found at the store at the time of the search was of small account. What mattered was the established policy of DuVal and Carnes of supplying the Indians with large quantities of liquor. If the case had come to trial, Arbuckle asserted, he would have produced proof that the firm had brought in large quantities of liquor and had distributed it to Indians and Indian countrymen, and that since the store had arrived "scarcely a day passed . . . without a number of Indians being drunk at it."

Colonel Arbuckle inspected the goods and returned them to the firm. An army board of inspectors checked the goods against the original invoice and discovered that all was in good order, except for three and a half pounds of chocolate damaged by rats or mice and three blankets somewhat damaged by moths. The total damage they judged to be only five dollars.

The trading firm was by no means satisfied with this award. They took the matter in person to the secretary of war, pointing out the loss they had sustained and saying that their understanding of the release they had signed entitled them to recompense from the War Department if damages had been suffered. "Ten thousand dollars-worth of goods," they cried, "for which there was a ready market at an average profit of 50 per cent Seized upon by force of arms whilst under the protection of our laws, carried into a military garrison and locked up for nine months, and then restored in a defaced condition with damages assessed at five dollars!! The common sense of every man must proclaim it a mere mockery of Justice —"

While Eaton was absent from Washington the merchants reached an agreement with the acting secretary of war. The firm claimed $6662.38 in damages, which was cut down by arbitration to $3838.49. A warrant was issued for this sum to the petitioners and would have been paid except for the lack of funds in the department. When Eaton returned to Washington, however, he quashed the whole proceeding, and DuVal and Carnes had to lay their case before Congress. The legislators in March 1830 awarded the traders the sum agreed to in the arbitration as compensation "for losses and damages sustained by them in consequence of an unlawful seizure of their goods, in the Territory of Arkansas, by Colonel Arbuckle." [33] When Arbuckle got word of

[33] *House Rep.* 74, 21 Cong., 2 sess., ser. 210; *U.S. Stat.,* VI, 466. DuVal and Carnes argued that the seizure was unlawful because their store was

the congressional action he was furious, considering it a public censure of his action, and he criticized the government for acting on incomplete and erroneous information.

Meanwhile the agents of the government on the Arkansas frontier were not freed of DuVal and Carnes. Because the traders continued to supply liquor to the Indians from their store near the line of the Indian Country, the Indian agent for the Cherokees refused to renew their license to trade, although he gave them a temporary permit while he laid their case before the secretary of war. Carnes, in July 1833, took the matter directly to the President, accusing the Indian agent of "over Zele and missionary like conduct." Later in the same month Carnes and DuVal wrote again to the President, this time bringing accusations against Colonel Arbuckle for letting the sutler of his post dispose of whiskey to the Indians, and accusing the sutler himself of being a drunkard.

Arbuckle, his sensitive honor touched, began to gather information in earnest about the whiskey dealings of DuVal and Carnes with the Indians. Addressing letters to numerous Indian agents, army officers, and other residents of the frontier, he sent them copies of the DuVal and Carnes letter to the President and asked them to supply specific details of the disposition of liquor to the Indians. Some of the responses Arbuckle used in laying the whole matter before the commanding general, but the affair seems to have died without further action.

Although the seizure of goods and the proceeding against them in accordance with the intercourse acts might work against weak and individual traders — and even here there was no end of difficulties — it failed dismally against a firm like DuVal and Carnes, who by no means wielded the influence of the American Fur Company, but were knowledgeable enough in Washington to deal personally with the secretary of war and with the President and on the frontier did not hesitate to weaken the position of Colonel Arbuckle by preferring counter charges against him. Arbuckle apparently had enough of the roundabout procedure of the intercourse acts. He wanted to throw over the business of instituting action in the courts, usually at a great distance from the scene of the offense, and wanted authority for the military,

---

actually in Arkansas Territory at the time of the seizure and not in Indian Country. There was considerable confusion on this point arising out of the reduction of Arkansas Territory by the Cherokee treaty of 1828.

after seizing liquor in the Indian Country, to empty the liquor immediately on the ground.[34]

Fort Gibson, where Arbuckle was stationed, was unable to cope with the liquor problem. When a new reservation of land was provided for the Cherokees in 1828, the Indian boundary line was thrown some forty miles to the east of Fort Gibson, which then became isolated in the Indian Country and was no longer on the border of contact between the Indians and the frontier whites. A dozen years earlier the line had been protected by Fort Smith, but as the frontier advanced its troops had been sent up the river to build and garrison Fort Gibson. Now Arbuckle called for the re-establishment of Fort Smith. The intercourse acts could not be enforced in the area, he believed, without a fort at that site again. "In that vicinity," he wrote to Western Department Headquarters, "I am informed, whiskey is kept and sold to Indians and Indian Countrymen by the barrel; and, I have reason to believe that the Indians are furnished with whiskey by almost every Steam-Boat or Boat of any description which passes up the Arkansas, above Fort Smith." Although the colonel was informed that the reoccupation of Fort Smith would be considered, it was not until March 1833 that the post was regarrisoned by Captain John Stuart and a company of the Seventh Infantry.[35]

Meanwhile a grand jury, instituted for the July term, 1832, by the Superior Court of Arkansas Territory in its capacity as a United States court, was inquiring into the enforcement of the intercourse acts. The findings of the grand jury substantiated the worst accounts of the army officers, since witnesses who lived on or near the Indian boundary line described demoralizing practices and extensive intemperance. They told of the ease with which the Indians obtained whiskey, half a dozen barrels or more at a time, and how on one occasion sixty barrels were taken into the Creek Nation. The whiskey was the cause of deaths among the Indians and occasioned great alarm on the frontier. Fort Smith itself was in danger of destruction from drunken Indians who repeatedly set it on fire. Even though the witnesses reported that mercantile establishments at Fort Smith, just across the line from the Indian Country, kept large stocks of whiskey on hand, the grand

[34] Arbuckle to Roger Jones, Jan. 26, 1834, in *Territorial Papers*, XXI, 890–891.
[35] Arbuckle to Edward G. W. Butler, May 4, 1830, *ibid.*, 222; Arbuckle to Eaton, June 26, 1830, *ibid.*, 243; P. G. Randolph to Arbuckle, Aug. 6, 1830, *ibid.*, 247–248.

jury was unable to establish the fact of any selling or delivery of whiskey to the Indians, so clever were the merchants in carrying on their nefarious business. The jurors viewed the situation with alarm, especially as the numbers of Indians coming from the East aggravated the evil. Two "insuperable obstacles," however, prevented their doing anything about it; both were legal technicalities. The jury examined the federal laws of 1802 and 1822 and the territorial law of 1808 (passed by the Louisiana Territory and considered still in force in the region) and found that they could not operate under any of them. The federal laws, argued the jury, give authority to the President to prevent distributing spirituous liquors in the Indian Country, and hence the laws were to be enforced otherwise than by a presentment from the grand jury. Under the territorial law, which should have reached to the action of the traders on the territorial side of the line, the jurors declined to act, because they had been drawn up and sworn as a federal jury, and the territorial law gave authority not to the federal courts but to the circuit courts of the territory. It was absurd impasse.[36]

The United States district attorney sent a copy of the presentment to the secretary of war, commenting on the insufficiency of the laws to prevent the evil that they were intended to correct, and he asked that the matter be laid before the President for proper action. The secretary of war hoped to get evidence from the grand jury so that he could proceed against the flagrant violators of the law, but to his dismay he learned that all the witnesses had given only oral testimony and that none of the evidence had been written down by anyone.[37]

∂◐

However diligent the agents and the army officers were, the whiskey merchants seemed always to be one step ahead. The licensed traders used whatever schemes they could concoct to gain permission to take in the liquor and slipped easily into illegal practices. The unlicensed traders operated altogether beyond the law. No section of the frontier was free of disturbance. From Florida, Alabama, Mississippi, Michigan, Arkansas, and Missouri reports flowed into the War Department from the offi-

---

[36] Grand jury presentment, *ibid.*, 517–519.
[37] Samuel C. Roane to Cass, July 25, 1832, *ibid.*, 523; John Robb to John Pope, Aug. 16, 1832, *ibid.*, 530; Roane to Cass, Sept. 19, 1832, *ibid.*, 543; William S. Fulton to Robb, Oct. 3, 1832, *ibid.*, 554.

cers and agents, lamenting the state of affairs, which all the current laws were quite inadequate to remedy. The legislation to date had concentrated on regulating the trade: licensed traders were not allowed to dispense liquor to the Indians and no one was allowed to trade without a license. Discretionary power had been used to make exceptions to the prohibition on liquor. If such measures were ineffective, the next step was absolute prohibition on spirituous liquor in the Indian Country.

This step was taken in 1832. In a separate article included in the law which established a commissioner of Indian affairs, Congress bluntly declared: "No ardent spirits shall be hereafter introduced, under any pretence, into the Indian country." It was an all-inclusive prohibition which allowed for no exceptions and which applied to traders and nontraders alike.[38]

For a short period the strong prohibition seemed to have a good effect. The War Department sent strongly worded instructions to the Indian agents to carry out the provisions of the new law, and army officers were given a new energy in searching out the forbidden article. At Fort Leavenworth on the Missouri the officers and troops were especially alert, at least against the American Fur Company. When Kenneth McKenzie, the Company's agent on the upper Missouri, tried to take liquor up the river in the spring of 1833, it was all seized by the inspectors at Fort Leavenworth. McKenzie wrote: "We have been robbed of all our liquors, say seven barrels shrub, one of rum, one of wine and all the fine men and sailors' whiskey which was in two barrels. They kicked and knocked about everything they could find and even cut through our bales of blankets which had never been undone since they were put up in England." The distinguished foreign naturalist, Maximilian, Prince of Wied, who was a passenger on the steamboat, noted of Fort Leavenworth: "We were stopped at this place, and our vessel searched for brandy, the importation of which, into the Indian territory, is prohibited; they would scarcely permit us to take a small portion to preserve our specimens of natural history." McKenzie was sure, however, that the competitors of the American Fur Company, Sublette and Campbell, had sneaked by the fort with a hundred flat kegs of alcohol on their steamboat, which they took into the Indian Country for trade.[39]

[38] *U.S. Stat.*, IV, 564.
[39] Chittenden, *American Fur Trade*, I, 357–358; Reuben Gold Thwaites, ed., *Early Western Travels, 1748–1846* (32 vols., Cleveland, 1905), XXII, 253–254.

Optimism, if any genuinely existed in the minds of men who knew the devious ways of the lawless whites, was short-lived. The new prohibition was not as clear as the simple statement in the statute appeared, nor was it generally effective. Along the Arkansas River Captain John Stuart, on regarrisoning Fort Smith, found conditions every bit as bad as Colonel Arbuckle had feared. Stuart was a zealous officer — and not a little loquacious — and he flooded the War Department with long, detailed accounts of the situation on his frontier, furnishing a vivid picture of the whiskey traffic on the raw edge of the frontier and indicating clearly enough why the intercourse acts were so ineffective.

I have now been here a Little more than one Month [he wrote to the secretary of war in May 1833], And have made it my particular Duty, to prevent so far as practicable the Introduction of Ardent Spirits, into the Indian Country, And so far as relates to the passage of this river I Confidently believe that I have Succeeded, but that will by no means put a final Stop to its Introduction. For the Situation of the Country is Such that although it be prevented from passing up the river, It can and will, be Introduced by means of Waggons Pack horses &ct., along the numerous by roads and Paths which cross the Line into the Indian Country, And I am well Convinced from the Knowledge that I have of the Country, And its Inhabitants, on both Sides of the Line, that it is not within the Scope of human possibility to Entirely Prevent its Introduction among the Indians. In the first place, the Inhabitants of the Territory of Arkansas, Particularly Such of them as border on the Indian Country, are either adventurers from different Parts of the world, whose Purpose it is to make money in any way they can, without regard to Laws or they are such as have been all their Lives moving along in Advance of Civilization and good order, And who have for their Governing Principles Self Interest alone, Without regard to Law or honesty — And they will Sell Whiskey to Indians whenever and wherever they can find Purchasers, And I know of no Law by which they can be punished for Selling to them within the Territory. If a Law to that effect did Exist, and could be full and Impartially administered, It would no doubt be Benificial in its Effects. But So Little regard is their paid to Law in this Country — And So much are the Justices of the Peace and Jurors, under the controle of the Lawless traders, And Neighbourhood opinions that it is impossible to get a Legal Decision made against an offender, where Neighbourhood Interest are involved. . . .

The Merchants of this place have their Store houses five or Six in number Erected within the Arkansas Territory. And close to the Choctaw Line, where they Sell Whiskey to the Indians, in full view, And within one hundred Yards of My Quarters — And if I were to attempt to disperse the

For the effect in the northern department of the American Fur Company, see Porter, *John Jacob Astor*, II, 812.

Indians in the Territory or to take from them their whiskey, The Merchants would claim them to be hirelings of theirs, And would Sue me for damages in interfering with the rights and Privileges of the *free* Democratic and *Immaculate* citizens, of the *Sovereign* Territory of Arkansas, for which reason I have not attempted to interfere with the Indians, whilst they are within the Territorial Limits, And when they get their Kegs filled and well Strapped on their back (their usual Manner of carrying the Whiskey which they purchased at this place) they break into the thick brush and underwood, and cross the Line wherever it may suit their convenience and an attempt to catch them with the means which I have, would be as vain as an attempt would be to catch a red Fox with Tistze. — [40]

The obvious impossibilities of the situation did not deter Stuart from attempting what he could. He seized every drop of whiskey that he found in the Indian Country — "except out of the bars of Steam Boats" — taking from different persons at different times amounts varying from a pint to several gallons. By this constant alertness he was able to end the whiskey traffic with the Indians in the immediate area of Fort Smith, although he was unable to control his own soldiers, who sneaked in liquor and kept the post in a constant state of disorder. Having seized the liquor from the traders or the Indians, he was obliged by law to proceed to libel the goods in court action. This became sheer farce. Seizing a pint here, a gallon there, often from men whose names he could not understand, he found it impossible to proceed against each offender individually, so he dumped all the contraband together in a barrel without any accurate account of the seizures. Stuart turned the whiskey over to the marshal of the territory, but the district attorney was at a loss, and wrote to Virgil Maxcy, the solicitor of the Treasury, for instructions as to how to proceed against such a mixture. He doubted the propriety of libeling such small amounts, since the expense of the suits would far exceed the value of the goods. Maxcy replied that he should not attempt to libel each parcel seized but should wait until he had collected enough to make the suit worthwhile. Meanwhile he could store the whiskey in barrels and stow it away for safe keeping. "Happily," Maxcy observed, "it is an article which will be benefitted, rather than injured by age." [41]

The officers at Fort Smith and Fort Gibson continued to seize the liquor and turn it over to the civil authorities for judicial

[40] Stuart to Cass, May 1, 1833, in *Territorial Papers*, XXI, 710–711.
[41] Roane to Maxcy, Jan. 22, 1834, *ibid.*, 887–888; Maxcy to Roane, Feb. 25, 1834, *ibid.*, 913.

action. The district attorney reported in July 1834 that there were no cases of an ordinary character pending at the present term of the Superior Court but that he had seven cases instituted for forfeiture of liquor seized by the officers. The total amount in the cases, however, came to only twenty barrels. This must have been no more than a trickle compared with the whiskey that escaped the military officers.[42]

Despite his efforts, Stuart reported at the beginning of 1834 that the introduction of ardent spirits among the Indians had increased. "The experience of a year," he said, "has appeared to give additional facility to the Whiskey Smugglers in forwarding their lawless & clandestine purposes." He found the masters of steamboats and others transporting merchandise more obstinate and unyielding and making claims that they had an unimpeded right to navigate the rivers in the Indian Country and that the military had authority only to examine the goods of licensed traders. If the military stepped beyond their authority (as this authority was viewed by the frontiersmen), they were liable to suits for damages. The threat was so real that the officers hesitated to act because of the peril. Stuart himself asserted, "I have come to the determination to make over to a Relative all of the little property which I possess, and to Stand Stripped but Strongly nerved between my duty and the Populace." Still doubts about his authority to act gnawed at his conscience, and he wrote for more specific confirmation of his action by the War Department.[43]

On the upper Mississippi the enforcing officers were again running afoul of the fur traders. In July 1832, shortly after the new prohibition of Congress and armed with instructions and orders from the War Department to carry out the law most strictly, Captain William R. Jouett, commandant at Fort Snelling, set out to seize liquor coming up the river. It was a time of crisis in the Northwest. The Black Hawk War was in progress down the Mississippi from Fort Snelling, and the Sioux and Chippewas, hostile to each other, were threatening the peace of the northern area. Jouett knew well the explosive potential of whiskey in such circumstances, and he warned the agents of the American Fur Company and other traders of the danger of taking liquor in

[42] Roane to Maxcy, July 28, 1834, ibid., 960.
[43] Stuart to Cass, Feb. 7 and 17, 1834, ibid., 896–898, 907–908.

among the Indians. But, as Jouett himself reported the story, "when he found that neither warnings nor persuasion could influence, nor danger deter the traders from violating the laws of the country at so critical a period, there was but one course left for him to pursue relative to the subject, and that was, faithfully to execute the orders and instructions he had received." [44]

Accordingly, he searched two Mackinac boats ascending the Mississippi at Lake Pepin. One was the property of the American Fur Company and the other of Joseph Renville; both were loaded with merchandise for the Indian trade. Among the goods the officer found sixteen kegs of alcohol or high wines. These kegs of liquor he seized and stowed away at Fort Snelling, awaiting order for their disposition from the War Department. The American Fur Company and Renville each immediately instituted suit against Jouett for illegal trespass. James D. Doty, erstwhile Supreme Court judge for the additional court of Michigan Territory, who had been ousted from that important post by the influence of frontier army officers who disliked him and his ways, was engaged as attorney by the Company and by Renville. The cases, entered first in the County Court of Crawford County at Prairie du Chien, were removed to the Circuit Court of the United States for the Counties of Iowa and Crawford at Mineral Point, presided over by David Irwin, who held the position recently vacated by Doty. The American Fur Company case was heard in the October term of the court, 1833, at which Jouett was charged with illegal trespass, with assault on the company's employees, and with imprisoning them illegally for fifteen days at Fort Snelling. The Company claimed damages for one thousand dollars for goods converted and disposed of by Jouett, and another two thousand dollars, the value of the services of the employees during the period of their detention at Fort Snelling. Although the Company made use of the old argument that Jouett had not been specifically authorized to make the seizure by the President of the United States as the law demanded, it centered its case on the argument that the Mississippi was not Indian Country and that they had a right to travel on it. They had not intended to take the liquor into the Indian Country, and in fact had not entered the Indian Country with it. When Jouett was upheld by the circuit court, Doty carried the case to the Michigan Supreme Court, but he dropped the proceedings before the case came to

[44] Jouett petition to Congress, Oct. 30, 1833, in *American State Papers: Military Affairs*, V, 507.

trial there. The Renville case was carried over to the October term of the circuit court for the following year, 1834, and again the judgment was in Jouett's favor.[45]

Even though Jouett had won favorable judgments, the situation was not conducive to careful enforcement of the intercourse acts. The inconvenience that Jouett underwent was enough to discourage any further attempts to enforce the law. He had been forced to leave his command to attend the court at Mineral Point, close to three hundred miles from Fort Snelling — for fourteen days in October 1833 and for another eight days in 1834 — and he had had the additional anxiety of expecting the first case to reopen before the Supreme Court of Michigan Territory in Detroit. He had engaged an attorney from Galena to defend him in the two cases, at the cost of three hundred dollars for each case, and he had to pay the court costs adjudged against him in the first trial. His total bill was $642.37, for which he was obliged to ask Congress for reimbursement. When he got no response to his first petition, he requested permission from the War Department to travel to Washington for the purpose of settling his accounts with the government. At length, in March 1835, in a clause tacked on to the act making appropriations for Indian annuities for the year, Jouett got his money.[46]

The officer's discouragement was evident. He complained: "I cannot expect the least indulgence from my adversaries, as there is no doubt that the agent for the company at this place, who manages the cases, will push them to the utmost extremity." When Jouett's immediate superior, Colonel Zachary Taylor, wrote to the adjutant general in behalf of the officer, he painted a dark picture of the trials of the army officers. He chided the War Department for not standing firmly behind the officers in their attempts to enforce the laws, instead of permitting them to be harassed by sheriffs and dragged from place to place to defend themselves as best they could.[47]

The trepidation of the army officers was mirrored in the Indian agent at Prairie du Chien, Joseph M. Street, who had him-

[45] The details of the Jouett case are found in *American State Papers: Military Affairs*, V, 506–511, and William W. Blume, ed., *Transactions of the Supreme Court of the Territory of Michigan* (6 vols. Ann Arbor, 1935–1940), V, 145, 563–569, VI, 357, 387. Note that the case was not quashed until the beginning of January 1836, four and one-half years after Jouett seized the liquor.

[46] *U.S. Stat.*, IV, 791.

[47] Taylor to Jones, July 15, 1834, in *American State Papers: Military Affairs*, V, 510.

self earlier been assessed damages in a suit brought against him when he removed intruders from the Indian lands. When the suits were commenced against Captain Jouett, Street wrote to the secretary of war, announcing that "there is little prostpect of Justice from a Jury, on the part of an officer of the U.S.," and inquiring whether or not he should begin suit against the traders for forfeiture of their bonds, which they had violated in bringing in the ardent spirits. Street's irritation was not lessened as the action against Jouett continued, and he spoke his mind again to Cass: "If something more effectual is not done to protect the officers of Government against the *cupidity of the Traders*, they will be reduced to the *alternative* of deciding between pecuniary ruin, on the one hand, and disobedience of orders on the other." [48]

The arguments of the traders shifted ground somewhat after the passage of the law of 1832 with its absolute prohibition of introduction of liquor into the Indian Country. Earlier the traders had had success in the courts by arguing that the seizures of whiskey under the acts of 1802 and 1822 had not had specific authorization from the President. Even as late as January 1832 Lieutenant Colonel Willoughby Morgan at Prairie du Chien insisted that he had no orders that had sufficient weight to support him in a civil court in the enforcement of the intercourse acts, unless he should first be called upon by the civil authority as provided by section 17 of the act of 1802. The absolute prohibition of the act of 1832, while it did not strengthen the enforcement procedures of the earlier acts, seems nevertheless to have been so clear in its intent that the casuistry of the traders and their attorneys now turned toward a different emphasis. The main argument in the Jouett cases was centered on the definition of Indian Country and on the intention of the traders. It was denied that Lake Pepin and the Mississippi were Indian Country. Jouett's seizure was illegal because it was not done in Indian Country, and there had been no intention of taking the liquor into the forbidden areas. As agent Street phrased it, "Their defense is that they were in no Ind. Country — That the Mississippi is a great open *high way* and open to all — That the having whiskey on it was not a violation of law, or a forfeiture of their bond." The weakness of the plea was apparently evident to the court.[49]

[48] Street to Cass, Oct. 4, 1832, transcript in Joseph M. Street Papers, State Historical Society of Wisconsin; Street to Cass, Dec. 5, 1832, in *Territorial Papers*, XII, 551.
[49] Morgan to Henry Atkinson, Jan. 4, 1832, cited in Edmund P. Gaines to

Whatever the outcome may have been in a single case, the threats of civil action against army officers and Indian agents were a deterrent to effective enforcement. The Company was powerful, it stood behind its traders, and it had the support of the local courts and judges, who generally did not take kindly to the army officers and what the frontiersmen considered their arbitrary, if not tyrannical, action. It was usually an uneven match. The government officials were often isolated and ill-supported by far-off Washington and had little hope of a sympathetic court. It is no wonder that it seemed a rash maneuver to enforce the laws against so powerful an enemy. Whenever the interests of the American Fur Company were at stake the enforcing officers suffered harassment, embarrassment, inconvenience, and often financial loss. It came to be the accepted thing that the officers would get into trouble by enforcing the acts, the offenders brought to trial for violation of the intercourse acts would escape conviction in the frontier courts, and the officers apprehending them would be subjected to a civil prosecution for faithful discharge of their official duties. The secretary of war himself called attention to the difficulty in his annual report in 1829 and suggested that the local courts be bypassed and the cases taken directly to the Supreme Court as a means of preventing "those frequent suits with which our officers are annoyed," a solution that was not judicially feasible.[50]

The situation was so common as to impress itself upon the casual visitor to the frontier. Charles Joseph Latrobe, who visited at several frontier posts in his travels of 1832 and 1833, described conditions as follows:

The officer on the frontiers is now called to defend the Indian against the citizen, and then to protect the citizen against the Indian; and in enforcing the orders of the executive against the encroachment and nefarious dealings of the loose inhabitant of the boundary, he is sure to win the hatred of the latter, who, as a citizen, will always meet with a sympathy, which, however just the cause, will rarely be accorded to the officer. The consequence is, that he is frequently involved personally in the most vexatious suits with the State Jurisdiction, by the execution of orders from his superior; and strange to say, though a refusal on the part of an officer to act, would of

Jones, Feb. 12, 1832, in Western Department Letter Book, vol. VI, National Archives, Record Group 98; Street to Cass, Oct. 4, 1832, transcript in Joseph M. Street Papers.
[50] Report of the Secretary of War, 1829, in American State Papers: Military Affairs, IV, 153.

course subject him to military pains and penalties — the general Government does not appear either ready or able to protect him from civil pains and penalties inflicted by the State, because, in obeying orders received, her laws may have been infringed.[51]

ॐ

On the Missouri, however, the American Fur Company for once was in serious trouble. It was there that it was experiencing the strongest competition from rival American firms as well as from the British. Pierre Chouteau, Jr., wrote to Astor, "The late law prohibiting absolutely the carrying of liquor to our trading establishments will do us an incalculable injury at all posts above the mouth of the Yellowstone," and the Company sought to gain some relaxation in its favor. But Secretary of War Cass declared that he no longer had any discretionary power.[52] In desperation the agents of the Company overstepped the bounds of propriety and good judgment in their attempts to obtain the whiskey they needed to stay abreast of their competitors, and they came close to losing their trading licenses altogether. In the summer of 1832, Clark had authorized Narcisse Leclerc, a new trader who appeared as a rival of the American Fur Company, to take two hundred and fifty gallons of alcohol with him into the Indian Country. The act of July 9, 1832, was already law, and Chouteau, the agent of the American Fur Company, protested against the authorization, for he had been informed at Fort Leavenworth as he came down the river of the new congressional prohibition. Clark, however, would not revoke Leclerc's license, since he had not yet been officially notified of the passage of the law. Indeed, he also gave Chouteau permission to send fourteen hundred gallons with the Company's outfit. Chouteau's liquor was seized at Fort Leavenworth, while Leclerc's managed — by favoritism or by subterfuge — to get by. Finding no other way to stop the advance of their rival, one of the Company's zealous traders, J. P. Cabanné, took matters into his own hands and, usurping the authority of the government, sent an armed force against Leclerc and confiscated his liquor. Leclerc withdrew to St. Louis, where he instituted criminal proceedings against Cabanné and sued the Company. By a compromise settlement, Leclerc was paid $9200, which was charged to the Upper Missouri Outfit.

[51] Charles J. Latrobe, *The Rambler in North America* (2 vols., New York, 1835), II, 231-232. Note that Latrobe generally reflected the opinions and attitudes of the army officers, who were his hosts on the frontier.
[52] Chittenden, *American Fur Trade*, I, 26-29.

Cabanné's action was more than a private wrong against Leclerc. He argued in his own defense, to be sure, that he was only aiding the government in the enforcement of its laws, but the argument was ignored. The Commissioner of Indian Affairs, Elbert Herring, considered it an outrage against the government and directed, "as an atonement for the public wrong," that the trader's license be revoked for at least a year. Cabanné, however, operated under the license of the American Fur Company, and since it was not Herring's intention to deprive the Company of its right to trade, he directed merely that Cabanné was to be ordered out of the Indian Country. In the next year, after Leclerc and the Company had reached their private agreement, Cabanné was permitted to get a license to trade, and he and his subordinate were readmitted to the Indian Country.[53]

McKenzie's inability to get past the fort with his modest supply of liquor was a failure of only part of his program, for he had conceived the daring scheme of setting up a distillery within the Indian Country. The threat of competition was too great to be ignored, and the Company was too conspicuous to sneak into the Indian Country with liquor. Apparently oblivious of a law that had been on the statute books since 1815 forbidding the erection of a distillery in the Indian Country,[54] McKenzie in his anxiety about competition thought he would get around the law which forbade *importation* into the Indian Country. It was an imaginative scheme, but in the end proved a feeble subterfuge. Its discovery drove McKenzie from the trade and nearly caused disaster for the Company. When the *Yellowstone* went up from St. Louis in the spring of 1833, McKenzie shipped on board distilling equipment, which he set up near the mouth of the Yellowstone. With his usual foresight, he put off a force of laborers above Fort Leavenworth to plant corn for the project and probably took a cargo of corn with him from Council Bluffs. The distillery was a great success and McKenzie was rejoicing over his ingenuity, when rival traders sent word of the enterprise to the Indian agent at Fort Leavenworth, who notified General Clark in St. Louis. McKenzie and the Company put forward the lame excuse that the still was meant only to make a little wine

[53] *Ibid.*, 347–350; Clark to Herring, April 2, June 28, 1833, and Aug. 11, 1834, in IA LR, St. Louis Superintendency; Herring to Clark, June 5, July 13, 1833, and Sept. 8, 1834, in IA LS vol. 10, pp. 408–409, vol. 11, p. 47, and vol. 13, p. 366.

[54] *U.S. Stat.*, III, 243–244.

from the wild pears and berries of the region. When the news reached Washington, both through official channels and from the numerous enemies of the Company, the Company came dangerously close to losing its license. In the East, meanwhile, the officials of the American Fur Company never lost their respectability. While McKenzie was planning to distill his corn, Ramsay Crooks was protesting that he would prefer to abandon the business altogether than resort to breaking the laws.[55]

Attempts were made to get permission once more to introduce limited amounts of whiskey as exceptions to the law, but the War Department officials were now adamant. Lewis Cass, who as governor of Michigan Territory had looked with favor upon such requests under the earlier laws, now firmly refused permission, even to his friends of the American Fur Company. It was still the wish of the Department, the commissioner of Indian affairs wrote, "to extend to those, in any measure engaged with it in business transactions, a spirit of accommodation and liberality," but the new act of Congress no longer allowed any discretionary power and to grant requests now would be in open violation of the law.[56]

Cass had no doubts about the intention of Congress to exclude entirely ardent spirits from the Indian Country, but he continued to be bothered about details in the execution of the new law. The brief statement in the statutes needed official interpretation, he thought, so he addressed a series of particular questions to Attorney General Roger B. Taney in April 1833. On the basis of Taney's reply the War Department drew up a detailed circular for the superintendents and agents of Indian affairs, prescribing the procedure they were to follow in seizing and libeling whiskey. The whiskey was not to be destroyed, but stored in some safe place and libeled in the proper court under the direction of the United States district attorney. Care was to be taken not to seize liquor in territory that was not Indian Country and there was to be no military force to prevent the introduction of ardent spirits nor to effect seizure without special authority from the War Department. It was Taney's opinion that the law applied to Indians as well as to whites. The circular represented an attempt

[55] Chittenden, *American Fur Trade*, I, 355–362.
[56] William B. Astor to Cass, July 26, 1832, in IA LR, Miscellaneous; John Robb to Robert Stuart, July 26, Aug. 15, 1832, in IA LS, vol. 9, pp. 93, 162; Cass to Astor, Aug. 17, 1832, *ibid.*, p. 152; Robb to George B. Porter and William Clark, Sept. 11, 1832, *ibid.*, pp. 230–231; Herring to Clark, March 16, 1833, *ibid.*, vol. 10, p. 118.

to so define the legal procedure that questions, hesitations, and missteps could be avoided and some of the earlier hindrances to the effective prohibition on liquor thus be removed. The correspondence between the secretary of war and the attorney general, however, is evidence enough that the statutory provisions were still far from perfect. Taney, in suggesting that the seized liquor be libeled and the offenders indicted, was not sure that the courts would sustain the measures, but he felt that the reasons in their favor were sufficiently strong to justify taking the cases into court. "It is manifest," he concluded, "that further legislation is necessary in order to carry into effect the intention of Congress. The legislation upon the subject has been heretofore too general and vague to accomplish the very desirable object which Congress had in view." [57]

The final sections of the circular requested from the agents a report on the problem of the whiskey traffic, "as the subject will probably be submitted to Congress at its next session for further and more specific legislation." They were to state the extent of the traffic, the number of persons involved, obstacles to efficient enforcement of entire exclusion, the views of the Indians themselves on the subject, and suggestions as to further measures to be taken. Response to the inquiry disappointed Herring, but he got enough replies to indicate general agreement that stronger measures were needed. On the basis of the reports from the field he urged some sort of summary court process to be held in the Indian Country itself, with judgments executed by military force. [58] Whatever might be the final solution, some new and stronger measure was bound to come soon.

[57] Cass to Taney, April 15, 1833, *ibid.*, pp. 246–248; Taney to Cass, Nov. 2, 1832, and May 1, 1833, in Attorney General's Opinions, vol. D, pp. 44, 65–66, National Archives, Record Group 60; Circular issued by Herring, May 6, 1833, in IA LS, vol. 10, pp 332–334. The requirement to obtain special instructions before resorting to the use of military force was considered by Captain Stuart at Fort Smith to lessen the effect of the law. John Stuart to the Secretary of War, Feb. 17, 1834, in *Territorial Papers*, XXI, 907–908.

[58] Report of Herring, Nov. 28, 1833, in *Sen. Doc.* 1, 23 Cong., 1 sess., ser. 238, pp. 201–203.

VII

REMOVAL OF INTRUDERS ON INDIAN LANDS

I hope too that your admonitions against encroachments on the Indian lands will have a beneficial effect — the U.S. find an Indian war too serious a thing, to risk incurring one merely to gratify a few intruders with settlements which are to cost the other inhabitants of the U.S. a thousand times their value in taxes for carrying on the war they produce. I am satisfied it will ever be preferred to send armed force and make war against the intruders as being more just & less expensive.
— Thomas Jefferson to David Campbell, March 27, 1792

Intrusions upon the lands of the friendly Indian tribes, is not only a violation of the laws, but in direct opposition to the policy of the government towards its savage neighbors. Upon application of any Indian agent, stating that intrusions of this nature have been committed, and are continued, the President requires, that they shall be equally removed, and their houses and improvements destroyed by military force; and that every attempt to return, shall be repressed in the same manner.
— Secretary of War William H. Crawford to Military Commanders, January 27, 1816

The conflict between the whites and Indians that marked American Indian relations was basically a conflict over land. Who was to own and control the land? — this was the elemental question. Land was of supreme importance, outweighing all other considerations in the matter of white-Indian relations.

The anomaly of relations between the white discoverers of the New World and the aboriginal inhabitants has been frequently noted. The Europeans parceled out the land among themselves, thinking of their own rivalries, each trying not to fall behind in the race for power and prestige. Yet the lands that they so freely divided (with but little knowledge of their extent or their condition) were not uninhabited or unencumbered. Over the territory claimed by the Christian kings roamed an undetermined number of pagan redmen in various stages of savage culture. What was to be the relation between the civilized Christians and these savage pagans? What rights to the new land were acquired by discovery?

Although it required many years of actual contact between the groups before settled relations were agreed upon, as European exploration and colonization increased, a theory in regard to the territory in America gained general acceptance. It was a theory developed by the European nations without consultation with the natives, but it did not totally disregard the Indians' rights. According to the theory, the European discoverer acquired the right of pre-emption, the right to acquire title to the soil from the natives in the area, by purchase if the Indians were willing to sell, or by conquest, and to succeed the natives in occupancy of the soil if they should voluntarily leave the country or become extinct. Discovery gave this right against later discoverers; it could hardly make claim against the original possessors of the soil, the native Indians. In practice, nevertheless, and eventually in theory, the absolute dominion or sovereignty over the land rested in the European nations or their successors, leaving to the aborigines the right of occupancy.[1]

Thomas Jefferson relied upon this accepted view when the British minister asked him in 1792 what he understoood to be the American right in the Indian soil. The secretary of state replied: "A right of preëmption of their lands; that is to say, the sole and exclusive right of purchasing from them whenever they should be willing to sell. . . . We consider it as established by the usage of different nations into a kind of *Jus gentium* for America, that a white nation settling down and declaring that such and such are their limits, makes an invasion of those limits by any other white nation an act of war, but gives no right of soil against the native possessors." The following year he was even more emphatic in replying to queries posed by Washington to his cabinet. "I considered our right of pre-emption of the Indian lands," Jefferson remarked, "not as amounting to any dominion, or jurisdiction, or paramountship whatever, but merely in the nature of a remainder after the extinguishment of a present right, which

---

[1] Wilcomb E. Washburn, "The Moral and Legal Justifications for Dispossessing the Indians," in James M. Smith, ed., *Seventeenth-Century America: Essays in Colonial History* (Chapel Hill, 1959), pp. 16–18, points out the "speculative" nature of the claims advanced by the European discoverers.

gave us no present right whatever, but of preventing other nations from taking possession, and so defeating our expectancy; that the Indians had the full, undivided and independent sovereignty as long as they choose to keep it, and that this might be forever." [2]

Henry Knox entertained the same views, although he based them less on theoretical reasoning about the law of nations than did Jefferson. For the secretary of war, the common principles of human decency and the honor and dignity of the nation were reason enough to protect the rights of the Indians. "It is presumable," he wrote to Washington on June 15, 1789, "that a nation solicitous of establishing its character on the broad basis of justice, would not only hesitate at, but reject every proposition to benefit itself, by the injury of any neighboring community, however contemptible and weak it might be, either with respect to its manners or power. . . . The Indians being the prior occupants, possess the right of the soil. It cannot be taken from them unless by their free consent, or by the right of conquest in case of a just war." Knox adverted to the opinion that the Indians had indeed lost their rights by reason of defeat with the British in the Revolution, but he pointed out that Congress in 1788 and 1789 had waived the right of conquest and had conceded to the Indians rights to the lands they possessed. "That the Indians possess the natural rights of man, and that they ought not wantonly be divested thereof, cannot be well denied," Knox declared, and he recommended that these rights be ascertained and declared by law. "Were it enacted that the Indians possess the right to all their territory which they have not fairly conveyed," he wrote, "and that they should not be divested thereof, but in consequence of open treaties, made under the authority of the United States, the foundation of peace and justice would be laid." [3]

---

[2] *Writings of Thomas Jefferson* (memorial edition), I, 340–341, XVII, 328–329; Jefferson to Knox, Aug. 10, 1791, *ibid.*, VIII, 226–227; Jefferson to Knox, Aug. 26, 1790, in *Territorial Papers*, IV, 35. Jefferson's proposed amendment to the Constitution to ratify the Louisiana Purchase contained a statement of respect for Indian rights: "The right of occupancy in the soil, and of self-government, are confirmed to the Indian inhabitants, as they now exist. Pre-emption only of the portions rightfully occupied by them, & a succession to the occupancy of such as they may abandon, with the full rights of possession as well as of property & sovereignty in whatever is not or shall cease to be so rightfully occupied by them shall belong to the U.S." Quoted in Annie H. Abel, "The History of Events Resulting in Indian Consolidation West of the Mississippi," *Annual Report of the American Historical Association for the Year 1906* (Washington, 1908), 1, 241. Miss Abel argues that in 1803 Jefferson looked upon the Indian possession as only temporary.

[3] Knox to Washington, June 15, 1789, and Jan. 4, 1790, in *American State*

Knox was largely following what had been colonial policy. Though differing from one another in methods of extinguishing the Indian title and worrying little about the theoretical questions of ultimate dominion or sovereignty, all the colonies admitted the Indian title and demanded some purchase or agreement by which the title was to pass to a white owner.[4] When, to counteract abuses, the British imperial government restricted to itself all transfer of Indian titles, it further formalized the practice among the colonies of arranging for the purchase of land in a solemn conference and treaty with the tribe.

Treating with the Indians for the extinguishment of land titles on the basis of colony dealing with tribe, together with the diplomatic negotiations of war and peace, gave foundation and strength to the doctrine that the Indian tribes were independent nations with their own rights and sovereignty, rather than subjects of the colony or nation in whose territory they resided. In spite of the fact that the independent-nation theory caused many complications, it became so firmly established in practice that it could not easily be shaken off.

When the United States won its independence from Great Britain, it became heir to an established procedure in Indian relations and in the acquiring of Indian lands. The theory and practice it strengthened by its own actions. It made treaties with the Indian tribes as independent nations at the close of hostilities; in most formal terms it guaranteed the boundary lines separating the Indian lands from the settlements of the whites; it waived the right of conquest in the gaining of Indian lands and continued to seek Indian approval, with compensation paid for lands given up. Despite the ever-increasing encroachment of settlers and speculators onto the Indian lands — and the evident inability of the government to prevent it — there was no official denial that the Indian rights to their lands were inviolate.

In treaty after treaty, both under the Articles of Confederation and under the Constitution, the traditional principles were followed. A formal meeting between the plenipotentiary commissioners of the United States and the leading chiefs and heads-

Papers: Indian Affairs, I, 13, 61. See also Knox to Washington, July 7, 1789, ibid., 53.

[4] See Cyrus Thomas, "Introduction," in Charles C. Royce, comp., Indian Land Cessions in the United States (Eighteenth Annual Report of the Bureau of American Ethnology, Part 2, Washington, 1899), pp. 527–643, for an account of colonial practice in extinguishing Indian title to land.

men of the tribes, a solemn document detailing the compensations, grants, and guarantee, then the approval or ratification by the Senate — this was the established procedure.

Although the accepted policy of the American government recognized the Indian rights to the land and made repeated provision by law and treaty and special proclamation to ensure justice to the aborigines, the views of the frontiersmen, the settlers who were the ones to come into contact with the Indians, were of a different nature altogether. Theorizing about *jus gentium* and rights or pre-emption played little part in the thinking of the settler on the frontier or of the eastern speculator in western lands. Their doctrine was simpler and earthier, and they had their own ideas about *jus gentium*. They saw the rich lands of the Indians and they wanted them. Their philosophy was summed up by John Sevier, one of the most aggressive of the frontier leaders: "By the law of nations, it is agreed that no people shall be entitled to more land than they can cultivate. Of course no people will sit and starve for want of land to work, when a neighbouring nation has much more than they can make use of." [5]

The intercourse acts embodied the policy of the federal government and were intended to guarantee justice to the Indians and provide for the orderly and peaceful settlement of the frontiers. In the conflict with the frontiersmen, who were avaricious for land, the government did not back down in its principles; it in fact tightened its restrictions and strengthened the machinery of enforcement. As the spearhead of settlement fluctuated back and forth across the West, however, driving ever deeper into territories once solely Indian, the pious principles of the legislators ran into the unprincipled practices of the settlers. The men right on the land generally had the better of it, for they again and again deflected the enforcing arm of government and in the end forced the Indians off the lands they coveted. This is the sad story that has attracted so many writers and led to a widely held opinion that the Indians were ruthlessly dispossessed with nothing done to protect their rights. On the contrary, the Indians were not completely deserted. Explicit treaties were made guaranteeing their rights, and stringent laws were enacted to ensure respect for the treaties. Various measures were undertaken to enforce the laws, which were sincere and were by no means ineffective. It is true that in the end the Indians succumbed before

[5] Sevier to James Ore, May 12, 1798, in Robert H. White, *Messages of the Governors of Tennessee* (5 vols., Nashville, 1952–1959), I, 58.

the onrush of the whites, but what order and peace there was on the frontier came in large part from the enforcement of the intercourse acts against unlawful encroachment on the Indian lands.

৯৯

The prohibition of private purchase of lands from the Indians, which had been part of the colonial and imperial policy, continued as a fixed policy of the United States. The Continental Congress, despite serious disregard of Congress on the part of such states as New York, North Carolina, and Georgia, had vindicated the position that treaty making with the Indians for the purposes of extinguishing Indian titles was an exclusive prerogative of the central government. The first Congress under the Constitution incorporated this principle into the Indian trade and intercourse act of July 22, 1790. The restriction entered as section 4 of that law was absolute:

. . . no sale of lands made by any Indians, or any nation or tribe of Indians within the United States, shall be valid to any person or persons, or to any state, whether having the right of pre-emption to such lands or not, unless the same shall be made and duly executed at some public treaty, held under the authority of the United States.

The same prohibition was included in the act of 1793, plus an added clause that provided a fine not exceeding one thousand dollars or twelve months' imprisonment for any person treating directly or indirectly with the Indians for title to land. The law recognized, however, the right of agents of the states, with the approval of the United States commissioners, to be present at the treaty and to propose and adjust with the Indians the compensation for lands within the states whose Indian title would be extinguished by the treaty. This section was re-enacted in the laws of 1796, 1799, and 1802.[6] Little difficulty arose from this section of the laws. The principle was clearly stated and the practice had been uniform for decades. Federal commissioners were appointed to treat with the Indians for their lands, and Congress appropriated funds for compensating the Indians.

The treaties entered into with the Indians for cessions of land had the universal corollary that the unceded lands would be guaranteed against encroachment by the whites. Thus all the treaties entered into by the Continental Congress guaranteed the lands of the Indians not ceded in the treaties and the later ones

⁶ *U.S. Stat.*, I, 138, 330–331, 472, 746, II, 143.

expressly forbade whites to settle on the Indian lands, under sanction of forfeiting the protection of the United States and becoming subject to punishment by the Indians. The same provisions were written into the first treaties made under the Constitution, those with the Creeks (1790) and the Cherokees (1791). Congress, therefore, in drawing up the intercourse act of 1790, considered it unnecessary to make specific prohibition of encroachment on the Indian Country.[7]

The open violations of the treaties, however, necessitated additional legislative measures against the illegal settlers, and the intercourse act of 1793 provided a maximum fine of one thousand dollars and imprisonment of twelve months for anyone who settled on Indian lands or surveyed or marked boundaries on such lands with a view to settlement. The President, furthermore, was authorized to remove all unlawful settlers by such measures as he might judge necessary. From that time on, the successive intercourse acts included sections aimed specifically at the aggressive frontiersmen. The act of 1796, which was copied in substance by the subsequent acts, forbade the whites to cross over the Indian boundary line to hunt or to drive their horses or cattle there to graze, and fines were set up to one hundred dollars or imprisonment up to six months. Even to enter the Indian Country south of the Ohio required a special passport issued by the governor of one of the states or by a commander at a frontier military post. Unauthorized settlers were to lose any claim they might have to the lands they settled on or surveyed and suffer fine and imprisonment as well, and the President was authorized to use military force to remove these settlers.[8]

The federal government was determined to defend the integrity of the Indian Country, but the War Department itself was sometimes forced to seek concessions from the Indians. This occurred particularly in two cases — the acquisition of territory within the Indian Country for military posts, agencies, and trading factories, and for roads connecting important settlements of the whites or major segments of American territory. Getting land for the military posts and the other government establishments caused little trouble. The troops of the United States were generally looked upon with respect by the Indians; military forces within the Indian lands were more a protection than a threat and did not form a wedge for whites to intrude into the forbidden

[7] Kappler, *Treaties*, pp. 7–21, 27, 30.
[8] *U.S. Stat.*, I, 330, 470.

lands. The agencies and factories both worked for the benefit of the Indians.

Formal agreements were made with the Indians that granted or confirmed the right of the United States to particular sites, but the terms of the agreements were sometimes imprecise. Thus Lieutenant Zebulon Pike in his exploration of the upper Mississippi in 1805 signed an agreement with the Sioux for land at the mouth of the Minnesota River and at the mouth of the St. Croix for future military posts, but the two thousand dollars agreed to by the Senate as compensation for the land was not paid to the Indians until 1819, when the troops went up the Mississippi to establish the post at the mouth of the Minnesota that became Fort Snelling.[9] In numerous treaties and conventions with the Indians some provision was made for these government posts, often with discretion as to location and duration left to the President.[10]

The running of roads through the Indian Country was a more controversial question, for the Indians frequently objected to such invasion of their lands. The War Department found it necessary to instruct its agents to proceed with great caution in persuading the Indians to grant permission for the roads and to offer suitable inducements and compensation to the Indians. With requests for the roads also went requests for sites of land on which "houses of entertainment" might be set up for the refreshment of the travelers, and one inducement used to win the agreement of the Indians was that the Indians themselves might profit from running such establishments. Though permission was sometimes delayed, the United States generally won its point, and treaties with the Indians contained specific articles authorizing the roads. Some of the intercourse acts made mention of roads when outlining the lands reserved to the Indians.[11]

---

[9] William W. Folwell, A History of Minnesota (4 vols., St. Paul, 1921–1930), I, 92–94, 136; American State Papers: Indian Affairs, I, 753–755.

[10] For examples see the treaties with the Creeks, June 29, 1796, June 16, 1802, and Nov. 14, 1805, and the treaty with the Sacs and Foxes, Nov. 3, 1804, in Kappler, Treaties, pp. 47–48, 59, 76, 85.

[11] Secretary of War to William C. C. Claiborne, July 9, 1803, in Territorial Papers, V, 221–222; Secretary of War to Benjamin Hawkins, Feb. 11, 1804, ibid., V, 306–307; Albert Gallatin to John Badollet, Aug. 14, 1806, ibid., VII, 378–380. There is considerable correspondence about the difficulties in gaining permission to open a road from the Tennessee settlements to Mobile Bay in 1811 in SW IA LS, vol. C. For examples of treaties, see the treaty with the Cherokees, July 2, 1791, and the treaties with the Chickasaws, Oct. 24, 1801, and the Choctaws, Dec. 17, 1801, in Kappler, Treaties, pp. 30, 55, 56.

Such small and authorized encroachments on the Indian Country were insignificant in comparison with the great illegal onrush of settlers onto the Indian lands, whose force was usually so great that the United States was unable to enforce the intercourse acts with any complete success. The Indians, who made valiant attempts to stave off the onslaught when it became apparent that the federal government was powerless to protect their rights as guaranteed by law and treaty, were little by little crushed, liquidated, or driven west. But the laws of Congress, the proclamations of the President, and the orders issued by the War Department did provide a brake on the westward-rolling juggernaut. Bloody as the frontier was in many instances, where the rapacious whites came up against the Indians making one last stand after another, and unjust and ruthless as some of the expropriation of Indian lands was — conditions would still have been disastrously worse had it not been for the federal government and its insistence on maintaining the integrity of the Indian Country.

The encroachment on the lands of the Cherokees in Tennessee was a noteworthy example of white methods and intentions, and it demonstrated from the very beginning the inability of the new government to control the frontiersmen adequately. To be sure, there were special difficulties in the region. The Cherokees, like the other Five Civilized Tribes, had seen in the Revolution an opportunity to put an end to the encroachment on their lands by the colonists. They believed that the king would win, so they joined his side in the conflict, but the Indians were no match for the aggressive frontiersmen, and ill-supported by the British, they had been defeated. The Cherokees had risked the war and they had lost; it was the beginning of the destruction of their nation. Beginning in 1781, after the collapse of British and Indian resistance to the colonists, settlers poured into the upper Tennessee valley. Many of them continued to carry on an outright war against the Indians.[12]

The settlement with the Indians that the Continental Congress attempted after the Revolution was complicated by the question of the western land claims of the individual states. The

[19] See Randolph C. Downes, "Cherokee-American Relations in the Upper Tennessee Valley 1776–1791," *The East Tennessee Historical Society's Publications*, VIII (1936), 35–53.

regions in eastern Tennessee along the Holston and the French Broad rivers, where the settlers congregated, were lands still under the jurisdiction of North Carolina. Against the Treaty of Hopewell, which the commissioners appointed by Congress had negotiated with the Cherokees in November 1785, North Carolina issued a formal protest, because the treaty drew the Indian boundary line independently of North Carolina's interests, and the state never recognized the treaty. The special Indian Ordinance of August 7, 1786, was conceived as an efficient instrument for Indian control, and the original draft placed substantial powers in the hands of the superintendent and the frontier military commanders. But the Ordinance was emasculated by the promoters of states' rights, leaving in its final form a superintendent with power to license traders but with no real authority to control the trade and no money or military forces to implement his authority to control liquor and illegal traders. The Ordinance itself declared that "the legislative right of any state within its own limits" was not to be infringed or violated.[13]

Thus when the militant frontiersmen along the upper reaches of the Tennessee — so impatient of government action that they set up their own "State of Franklin" — moved aggressively against the Indians, the red men, finding no corresponding congressional force to protect their rights, retaliated with massacres of the frontiersmen, and a general Indian war broke out. To meet this crisis Congress issued the proclamation of September 1, 1788, with its order for the intrusion and outrages to cease. The Cherokees were impressed by this federal support of their claims; they looked upon the proclamation as a promise to remove the settlers, and hence dispersed their war parties. While the proclamation had this salutary effect upon the Indians, it failed to check the illegal settlers it was supposed to remove. In January 1789, in the belief that the Indians were about to attack the frontier again, John Sevier led an invasion of whites into the Indian Country that killed some one hundred and forty-five Indians, and other invasions of a similar nature were reported.[14]

The ineffectiveness of congressional action was due in large part to the fact that the jurisdiction of North Carolina still extended over the area in dispute. Knox continued to condemn

---

[13] William Blount to commissioners, Nov. 28, 1785, and protest of the same date, in *American State Papers: Indian Affairs*, I, 44; Downes, "Cherokee-American Relations," p. 44; *Journals of the Continental Congress*, XXXI, 490–493.

[14] Downes, "Cherokee-American Relations," p. 51.

the illegal settlers and to deplore "the humiliating spectacle of a national treaty being trampled on." Nothing could be done, however, because North Carolina had not yet ratified the Constitution or turned over her western lands to the United States. The report of Knox in July and the proclamation in September 1788 both kept an eye on North Carolina's reaction, and eventually the President and Congress admitted that settlement of matters in eastern Tennessee must wait upon North Carolina's ratification of the Constitution. When commissioners were sent south in August 1789 they were instructed to bypass the Cherokees, merely sending them a message to the effect that the United States would see that the Treaty of Hopewell was enforced and the Indians would be treated with justice if North Carolina joined the union.[15]

When North Carolina finally ratified the Constitution (November 21, 1789) and ceded her western lands to the United States (December 12, 1789), it was too late to remove the entrenched settlers. The government was forced to abandon the Treaty of Hopewell, for in January 1790 Knox recognized that the families south of the French Broad could not be removed. In August 1790 the President asked the Senate for permission to negotiate with the Indians for a new boundary in order to include the settlers who had violated the previous treaty. In July 1791 the Treaty of Holston was signed with the Cherokees, and the boundary line was moved. Article VII of the treaty provided, however, that the "United States solemnly guarantee to the Cherokee nation, all their lands not hereby ceded"; and Article VIII declared, "If any citizen of the United States, or other person not being an Indian, shall settle on any of the Cherokees' lands, such person shall forfeit the protection of the United States, and the Cherokees may punish him, or not, as they please." [16]

After the western lands of North Carolina were made over to the United States, they were organized as the Territory South of the River Ohio, and the provisions of the government for the Northwest Territory were extended over the southern region. The governor, William Blount, who assumed the duties of superintendent of Indian affairs, was commended by the government

---

[15] Knox report, July 7, 1789, in *American State Papers: Indian Affairs*, I, 38, 53; Washington to the Senate, Aug. 22, 1789, *ibid.*, 55; Instructions to commissioners, Aug. 29, 1789, *ibid.*, 67.

[16] Knox to Washington, Jan. 4, 1790, *ibid.*, 60; Washington to the Senate, Aug. 11, 1790, *ibid.*, 83; Kappler, *Treaties*, p. 30.

for his efforts to restrain the settlers who coveted the Indian lands, but he was himself a speculator in western lands and had interests pulling him both ways in the conflict between the Indians and the whites. As governor he was charged to prevent encroachment on the Indian Country; as speculator he wanted a rapid advance of settlement.[17]

The press of frontiersmen continued. The Cherokees pleaded with Washington to remove the whites who had settled on their lands and to prevent the projected settlement at Muscle Shoals. Knox held to his firm policy that the Indians must be shown the power and justice of the United States and that this could be done only by the ejection of the settlers beyond the line determined by the Treaty of Holston, and Secretary of State Jefferson spoke of sending an armed force to make war against the intruders as more just and less expensive than an Indian war incurred to gratify a few intruders. These were high-minded pronouncements, indicating the good intentions of the general government, but they were ineffective in restraining the frontiersmen in the new territory, who took it upon themselves to deal with the Indians and organized armed invasions of the Indian Country. This independent action of the frontiersmen horrified the federal officials. Knox notified Governor Blount in August 1793 of the President's "extreme concern at the late violent and lawless inroads of several parties of whites from the South Western Territory into the peaceable part of the Cherokee Nation." He directed the governor to use his "highest exertions" to bring the offenders to justice. "Unless such crimes shall be punished in an exemplary manner," he wrote, "it will be in vain for the government to make further attempts to establish any plan or system for the administration of Indian Affairs founded on the principles of moderation and justice — Treaties will be at an end and violence and injustice will be the Arbiters of all future disputes between the whites and neighbouring tribes of Indians; and of consequence much innocent blood will be shed, and the frontiers depopulated." [18]

Although active hostilities subsided, the Indians continued to complain. Solicitous letters sent to Knoxville showed the concern

[17] *U.S. Stat.*, I, 132; Thomas Jefferson to Daniel Smith, Dec. 24, 1791, in *Territorial Papers*, IV, 106; William H. Masterson, *William Blount* (Baton Rouge, 1954), pp. 186–187.

[18] Knox to Washington, Jan. 17, 1792, in *Territorial Papers*, IV, 111–115; Jefferson to David Campbell, March 27, 1792, *ibid.*, 130–131; Knox to Blount, Aug. 26, 1793, *ibid.*, 299–300.

of the federal government that justice be done to the Cherokees and the encroachment on their land stopped. Blount in turn wrote to the officers of Blount County, urging them to prevent the settlement of whites across the Indian line. Peace for a time seemed assured. In his first message to the legislature of the new state of Tennessee, Governor John Sevier noted the "pacific colour" of Indian affairs and urged the legislature to adopt suitable measures to prevent violation and encroachment. The lawmakers replied that they would take care that the citizens of the state "commit no encroachments upon the Indians; that the conditions of the treaty of Holston be preserved inviolate on the part of this state." [19]

The intrusions and threatened encroachment on the Cherokee lands in Tennessee had a direct influence on the revision of the intercourse act that became law on May 19, 1796. The secretary of war supplied the chairman of the committee reporting the bill with a copy of Governor Blount's letter about the intended intrusions and suggested to the President that he officially send a copy of the same letter to Congress. "It might have a good effect," Pickering thought, "to enforce the provisions contemplated in the bill to prevent such outrages." [20]

The new law not only prohibited settling on lands beyond the boundary line guaranteed to the Indians, but actually described the boundary line of the Indian Country in detail. Furthermore, it specifically withdrew all support of any claims made to those lands by unauthorized settlers, and it authorized the use of military force to remove the offending settlers. The debate on the bill brought into sharp focus the conflicting viewpoints about Indian rights. In denying the claims of squatters on the basis of North Carolina grants, James Hillhouse, of Connecticut, declared in the House

that though the Indians were men in uncivilized life, and differed in their customs and habits from ourselves, yet they were justly entitled to the lands which they possessed. . . . Indeed, this right and title to the lands had been expressly recognized by the United States in the Treaties they had made with them. The God of Nature had given them the land, and he was sorry to hear any gentlemen on that floor call their right to it in question.

[19] Timothy Pickering to Blount, March 23, 1795, *ibid.*, 386–393; Blount to Alexander Kelley and Littlepage Sims, Dec. 1, 1795, *ibid.*, 408–410; Legislative message of April 22, 1796, in White, *Messages of the Governors of Tennessee*, I, 14; Message to the Governor, April 23, 1796, *ibid.*, 15.
[20] Pickering to Washington, Feb. 2, 1796, in *Territorial Papers*, IV, 419.

He would ask, who were the proprietors of this country previous to its being known to civilized nations (as they were called?) Were not these people? And had they not always been in the peaceful enjoyment of it? Who gave us a right to call their title in question, or forcibly to thrust them out? [21]

Hillhouse asserted that the white claimants to the Indian lands had only a pre-emptive right and that the Indians had the fee simple of the lands.

Such a position was violently opposed by those who supported the claimants to the Indian lands. All title to the lands, they argued, had been in the king and now rested in the states. The Indians, they declared, were mere "tenants at will," and North Carolina had been justified when she opened a land office to dispose of the unappropriated lands after setting apart certain hunting grounds for the Indians.

The conflict was fairly joined, but the "Indian friends" prevailed and the clauses withdrawing all hope of property rights from the illegal settlers were retained.[22]

When word of the passage of this act reached Tennessee, Governor Sevier and the legislators were much incensed, revealing to some extent the lack of sincerity in their previous pronouncements about the inviolability of the Treaty of Holston. The new act was taken, correctly enough, as a frontal attack against the Tennesseans, and on the day of its adjournment the first legislature of the state drew up a long remonstrance to be presented to Congress and the President.

The first sections of the document set forth the basis of Tennessee's rights to its lands: her equal footing with the original states and her succession with them to the sovereignty which Great Britain had over the lands before the Revolution. Citation was made of various acts of North Carolina providing for the sale of the lands in Tennessee and of the protest North Carolina had made against the Treaty of Hopewell. The assembly concentrated its attack on the Treaty of Holston and especially on the act of 1796. It protested that the claims to land could not be

---

[21] *Annals of Congress*, 4 Cong., 1 sess., p. 898 (April 9, 1796).

[22] Governor Blount had written: "You as well as myself are sensible that in the days of folly of this Country, that whoever should attempt to preserve Peace with Indians was instantly denounced as an Indian Friend and the Cry accordingly raised against him; but I rejoice as I wish the future Peace and Happiness of my fellow Citizens that those days are in a great degree over. . . . It is however not to be denied that he who preserves Peace with Indians thereby serves the Indians but it is equally true that by that act he in a much greater degree serves his Fellow Citizens." Blount to Kelley and Sims, Dec. 1, 1795, in *Territorial Papers*, IV, 410.

condemned by the law, since they rested on grants "issued under the faith of North Carolina and the United States." The good faith of the United States, however, had also been pledged to the Cherokees by the Treaty of Holston and by the confirmation of that treaty made at Philadelphia in 1794, and the Tennessee legislators were aware of it. They fell back in their argument then on the same shaky foundation to which Georgia was forced three decades later when the Cherokee lands in that state became the object of white rapacity. "It is believed," they asserted, "that the Indians have no fee simple in the lands alluded to, otherwise the very deed made by North Carolina to the United States would be void. — If the Indians have any claim to the lands in question, it is believed to be the lowest kind of tenancy, namely that of tenants at will." [23]

The remonstrance asked Congress to repeal the prohibitions in the intercourse act that prevented possession of the lands in question and to make provision by law for extinguishing the Indian title to the lands, so that the settlers might be confirmed in the rights and privileges of ownership. When this justice was done to the citizens of the state, the legislature declared, "the officers of government will be enabled to execute the constitutional laws of the United States with ease and convenience." The movement of people into Tennessee and the basis of its prosperity seemed threatened by the act. In his second inaugural address, Governor Sevier painted a pleasant picture of the progress of the new state. "But this happy, this bright prospect of affairs," he added, "is considerably darkened by the extension of the Indian Boundary line and gloomy reflection strikes the mind." For Sevier the 1796 law was an "infamous act," which had given "more

---

[23] Remonstrance to Congress, 1796, in White, *Messages of the Governors of Tennessee*, I, 22–24. Thomas Jefferson in a letter to the secretary of war, August 26, 1790, had made clear what sort of right to the land North Carolina had conveyed to the United States by her cession. "The Cherokees were entitled to the sole occupation of the lands within the limits guaranteed to them. The state of N. Carolina, according to the *jus gentium* established for America by universal usage, had only a right of preemption of these lands against all other nations. It could convey then to it's citizens only this right of preemption, and the right of occupation could not be united to it till obtained by the U.S. from the Cherokees. The act of cession of N. Carolina only preserves the rights of it's citizens, in the same state as they would have been, *had that act never been passed*. It does not make imperfect titles, perfect; but only prevents their being made worse. Congress, by their act, accept on these conditions. The claimants of N. C. then and also the Cherokees are exactly where they would have been, had neither the act of cession, nor that of acceptance been ever made; that is, the latter possess the right of occupation, & the former the right of preemption." *Territorial Papers*, IV, 35.

umbrage to the people of this State than any other act ever passed since the independency of America." [24]

The Treaty of Holston had been signed in 1791, but the actual marking out of the boundary line was long delayed. Finally, to carry out the act of 1796, with its designation of the boundary and the provision that it "be clearly ascertained, and distinctly marked, in all such places as the President of the United States shall deem necessary," three federal commissioners were designated to survey and mark the Cherokee line. This they accomplished shortly before the Tennessee General Assembly met in September 1797. The lawmakers, mindful of the settlers caught within the Indian Country by the line, appointed their own commissioners to check up on the line the federal trio had drawn. The Tennesseans asserted in their report to the Assembly that the line as drawn did not agree with the Treaty of Holston, and that the report of Benjamin Hawkins (one of the federal commissioners) gave "official information which is not true." With this local report in hand the Assembly drew up another remonstrance, protesting the extension of the boundary line as drawn by the United States commissioners. They further protested against the proclamation issued by the commander of federal troops in the area, Lieutenant Colonel Thomas Butler, on August 19, 1797, which required all persons to remove beyond the line by October 25. The Assembly claimed that twenty-five hundred to three thousand persons would be forced to move, and during the inclement season of the year, at that — persons who had settled on the lands in good faith. [25]

Butler seems to have enforced his removal order, but passports were issued to the displaced farmers enabling them to return to their holdings for necessary matters. Meanwhile the wheels were in motion to reinstate the settlers. On December 4 the remonstrance of the Tennessee legislature was presented to Congress. On January 17, 1798, President Adams recommended to Congress that a new treaty be entered into with the Cherokees to acquire from them lands taken over by the whites, and Congress on February 27 appropriated $25,880 for that purpose, the amount estimated as necessary by the secretary of war. [26]

[24] Address of Sept. 22, 1797, in White, *Messages of the Governors of Tennessee,* I, 24; Sevier to Tennessee Senators and Congressman, Jan. 22, 1798, *ibid.,* 53.

[25] The documents are printed *ibid.,* 32–33.

[26] *Annals of Congress,* 5 Cong., 2 sess., pp. 672, 837, 842–845, 847, 1058–60 (Dec. 4, 1797, Jan. 16–18, Feb. 21, 1798); Adams to Congress, Jan. 17, 1798, in Richardson, *Messages and Papers,* I, 260–261; *U.S. Stat.,* I, 539.

At first the Cherokees steadfastly refused to part with their land, and the first commissioners assigned the task of treaty making gave up without success. President Adams addressed the Cherokees in August, explaining to them the situation that the government faced. It had been expected, he pointed out, that the line of Holston would leave most of the settlers on ceded lands. Since this did not prove to be the case, and since many of the settlers were deserving people who had make valuable improvements on the land, the government wanted to make a new purchase in order to avoid distress to the settlers who were being removed.[27]

At length, after much private preliminary negotiating on the part of Governor Sevier and Tennessee commissioners, a new cession of land to cover the settlers was made by the Cherokees at Tellico on October 2, 1798. Tennessee greeted the new treaty with enthusiasm. The House of Representatives of the state spoke of the "acquisition of between Five hundred thousand and one million acres of Territory, a circumstance so obviously advantageous to our Country that a multiplication of language upon that subject is by us deemed unnecessary." The Tennesseans had forced the hand of the federal government, but contentment was short-lived. The complete removal of the Indians from the state was the ultimate design of the whites, and when the Louisiana Purchase was added to the nation, they politely suggested to Congress that there was now a fine opportunity to remove the Indians out of the regions east of the Mississippi to the newly-acquired vastness in the West.[28]

∽❦∽

The advance of settlement in Tennessee was matched by a great push into the rich lands north of the Ohio River, from which the colonists had been restricted by the Indian boundary line of 1763. Treaties made with the Indians after the Revolutionary War by the Continental Congress nominally freed large sections of that territory of its Indian title, but the treaties signed at Fort McIntosh (1785) and at the mouth of the Great Miami (1786) were not satisfactory to the Indians, and the boundary lines were never laid out. The Treaty of Fort Harmar (1789), negotiated

[27] Adams to the Cherokee Nation, Aug. 27, 1798, in *American State Papers: Indian Affairs*, I, 640–641.

[28] Kappler, *Treaties*, pp. 51–54; White, *Messages of the Governors of Tennessee*, I, 70, 153–154.

by Governor St. Clair of the Northwest Territory to reaffirm the cessions of 1785, did not have any better effect. The continuing hostilities of the Indians made peaceful advance into the region impossible until the successful campaigns of General Anthony Wayne in 1794. The Treaty of Greenville, signed by the chastised Indians in 1795, replaced the earlier ineffective treaties and freed the larger part of Ohio and a small triangle of land in Indiana from their Indian titles.

Despite the Indian uncertainties, significant settlements were made in the Ohio country. At Marietta in 1788 began the settlements of the Ohio Company, a group of veterans of the Revolution from New England. On the Miami Purchase, between the Great Miami and Little Miami rivers, the New Jersey promoter, John Cleves Symmes, established a series of settlements in 1788 and 1789. Meanwhile from Kentucky and Virginia came settlers with warrants for land in the Virginia Military District, who made Chillicothe, founded in 1796, their chief center. In the northeast section of the state the Western Reserve of Connecticut drew settlers from New England, and along the upper Ohio squatters from Virginia and Pennsylvania established themselves in large numbers. All these groups suffered from Indian incursions, and the situation was so much in flux before the Treaty of Greenville that there could be no normal operation of the intercourse acts. The incursions of the whites into the Indian regions were often hostile expeditions, causing much grief to the pacific-minded secretary of war, Henry Knox. "The desires of too many frontier white people, to seize, by force or fraud, upon the neighboring Indian lands," he wrote at the end of 1794, "has been, and still continues to be, an unceasing cause of jealousy and hatred on the part of the Indians; and it would appear, upon a calm investigation, that, until the Indians can be quieted upon this point, and rely with confidence upon the protection of their lands by the United States, no well grounded hope of tranquillity can be entertained. The encroachment of white people is incessantly watched, and in unguarded moments, they are murdered by the Indians. Revenge is sought, and the innocent frontier people are too frequently involved as victims in the cruel contest. This appears to be a principal cause of Indian wars." [29]

[29] Beverley W. Bond, Jr., *The Civilization of the Old Northwest: A Study of Political, Social, and Economic Development, 1788–1812* (New York, 1934), chap. I; Knox to Washington, Dec. 29, 1794, in *American State Papers: Indian Affairs*, I, 543–544.

The Treaty of Greenville, although it effectively extinguished the Indian title to a large portion of the Northwest Territory, did not resolve all the problems of peaceful frontier advance. There remained a line of contact between Indians and white settlers to be guarded and watched. The delay in running the boundary line of the Treaty of Greenville (arrangements were made in 1799, but Congress appropriated no money) meant that there were only unmarked frontiers, and the settlers, perhaps often in innocence, settled on lands the Indians still claimed, and so the friction continued. When William Henry Harrison arrived in Indiana as the first governor of the territory, the chiefs begged him to iron out the difficulties. Harrison accordingly issued a proclamation that forbade settling, hunting, or surveying on Indian lands and required the civil and military officers to remove such intruders and to prevent future encroachment. He also wrote to the secretary of war for permission to survey the boundary as a means of avoiding further difficulties. The ultimate running of the lines did not end the process of acquiring land from the Indians, for Harrison himself was zealous in arranging treaties for the extinguishment of Indian land titles. He displayed a fervor to dispossess the Indians by these ostensibly legal means that was in marked contrast with his genuine concern for the rights of the Indians in other matters. The constant pressure on the Indian lands caused renewed warfare that eventually merged with the War of 1812.[30]

The federal government's concern to preserve peace on the frontiers by giving the Indians no cause for irritation was continued in full scope after the War of 1812. The hostilities of the Northwest Indians in that war forced the United States to maintain a firm policy on the one hand of drawing the Indians away from their attachment and allegiance to the British and on the other hand of winning them to friendship and respect for the United States by scrupulous regard for treaty stipulations. In November 1815 Brigadier General Thomas A. Smith, commanding at St. Louis, was directed by the War Department to remove by military force all persons found trespassing on Indian lands. Three months later similar instructions — even more detailed and

[30] Proclamation of May 9, 1801, in *Executive Journal of Indiana Territory, 1800–1816* (*Indiana Historical Society Publications*, vol. III, Indianapolis, 1905), pp. 101–102; George D. Harmon, *Sixty Years of Indian Affairs: Political, Economic, and Diplomatic, 1789–1850* (Chapel Hill, 1941), pp. 89–93; Dorothy B. Goebel, *William Henry Harrison: A Political Biography* (Indianapolis, 1926), pp. 89–127.

specific — were issued to the commanding generals of the military departments.[31]

๑

Among the Creeks and Cherokees in Georgia and Alabama there was continual trouble as whites moved into Indian lands, were removed by the Indian agents and the military officers, then slyly moved back again. Return J. Meigs, the Cherokee agent, and Benjamin Hawkins, agent to the Creeks, and the commanding officers on that frontier were repeatedly directed by the War Department to be vigilant in enforcing the laws against the "licentiousness of daring and unprincipled men" who paid little attention to the rights of the Indians or the authority of the government. Part of the irritation of the Indians came from the grazing of the whites' cattle across the boundary lines. For this problem the government had no ready solution, except to persuade the Indians to bear the trouble patiently. The Creek agent was told to attempt to convince the Indians that "a mere mathematical line in the woods between them and the white people can never prevent the cattle of both parties from ranging where they please." Again and again the secretary of war sought to quiet the Indians by reassuring them that the President intended to pay "the most sacred regard to the existing treaties" and to protect the Indian lands from intrusion. This constant attention of the War Department to the obligations undertaken toward the Indians and the alertness of the agents prevented what might have been a mass invasion of settlers upon the Indian Country.[32] There was, nevertheless, unending tension along the line of demarcation. The whites came in a steady stream, putting more and more pressure on the Indian Country; the agents and military officers (though backed strongly by the sincere intentions of the War Department to prevent violations of the Indian Coun-

---

[31] George Graham to Smith, Nov. 6, 1815, in *Territorial Papers*, XVII, 238; William H. Crawford to Alexander Macomb and other officers commanding military departments, Jan. 27, 1816, *ibid.*, X, 619.

[32] Henry Dearborn to Meigs, June 25, 1801, in SW IA LS, vol. A, p. 71; Dearborn to James Taylor, June 25, 1801, *ibid.*, pp. 71–72; John Newman to Meigs, Aug. 3, 1801, *ibid.*, pp. 106–107; Dearborn to James Wilkinson, April 30, 1802, *ibid.*, p. 206–207; Dearborn to Benjamin Hawkins, Jan. 24, 1803, *ibid.*, pp. 306–308; Dearborn to Hawkins, Feb. 19, 1803, *ibid.*, pp. 325–326; Dearborn to Meigs, Jan. 14, 1804, *ibid.*, pp. 424–425; Dearborn to Hawkins, June 28, 1805, *ibid.*, vol. B, p. 88; Dearborn to Cherokees, July 3 and 7, 1801, *ibid.*, vol. A, pp. 78, 86.

try) did not have sufficient power to be on guard everywhere at once.

In 1809 and 1810 the focus of infection was Mississippi Territory, which witnessed a drive of white settlers into Chickasaw lands north of the Tennessee River in what is now the state of Alabama. Beginning in the early months of 1807 settlers came into the area, thinking (according to their later assertion) that the Indian title had been extinguished by the treaty made with the Cherokees on January 7, 1806. To their dismay, they soon learned that, although the Cherokees had relinquished their claim, the Chickasaws still considered the region theirs. The Chickasaws complained of the continuing influx of whites, but warnings and actual removals failed to stem the onrush. Finally, the Chickasaw chiefs took a stand. They would make one more remonstrance to the President. If he failed to remove the intruders, the nation itself would send an armed force to remove the whites and burn their houses.[33]

The War Department acted at once. Acting Secretary of War John Smith on March 13 and 20, 1809, dispatched instructions to the Cherokee agent Meigs to disperse all intruders on Indian lands. The agent, with a military detachment from Hiwassee Garrison, removed eighty-three families from Cherokee lands and two hundred and one from Chickasaw lands. Some of these had already begun cultivation of their lands and sent a delegation to the Indians, begging leave to remain until their crops were harvested, but to no avail. Meigs reported that they then left quietly without dispute and the removal was completed within a few days "except for one sick person & some women lately in childbed." The whites still hoped, however, that they would be permitted to return to take in their crops. "Altho they came under the description of aggressors," Meigs informed the secretary of war, "it is my duty to say that many of them are reputable well informed, & rich in Cattle & horses — no hunting, agriculture their sole pursuit." They did not want the President to class them with the frontier ruffians who were seeking to escape from regular society.[34]

[33] Kappler, *Treaties*, pp. 90–91; Royce, *Indian Land Cessions*, Plate 54, Cession No. 64; George Colbert to Dearborn, Feb. 18, 1809, in SW LR, C-469 (4); Meigs to Colbert, Feb. 27, 1809, in IA FR, Cherokee Agency; Meigs to intruders, Feb. 27, 1809, *ibid.*; Thomas Freeman to Albert Gallatin, March 4, 1809, in *Territorial Papers*, V, 720–721.

[34] Smith to Meigs, March 13 and 20, 1809, in IA FR, Cherokee Agency; Smith

Meigs's expedition, although he considered it a successful operation, had no more than temporary effect. At the end of June the agent issued another warning to settlers on the Indian lands, "if any such remain, or have returned." He called their attention to the lenient, paternal way in which they had been treated at the time of the recent removal and warned them that the next time things would go badly with them. In October, however, he was forced to repeat the warning to intruders who had appeared on Cherokee lands and to call upon the commander at Hiwassee for another detachment of troops. The agent had by now lost all respect for the illegal settlers who were causing him so much concern. The report he sent to the secretary of war was far from optimistic:

The great length of this frontier, & the few troops in this quarter, puts it in the power of the people of the character mentioned to impose on the Indians & to put the U States to considerable expence. Should this disposition to make intrusions on Indian lands increase, they will perhaps at last put the few troops here at defiance. These intruders are always well armed, some of them shrewd & of desperate character, have nothing to lose & hold barbarous sentiments towards Indians. They see extensive tracts of forrest exceedingly disproportioned to the present or expected population of the tribes who hold them. They take hold of these lands, some of them in hopes the land will be purchased, when they will plead a right of preemption, making a merit of their crimes. With these people remonstrance has no effect, nothing but force can prevent their violation of Indian rights.

Meigs went out with the troops and destroyed the cabins of the intruders. He still refused to take legal action against the offenders, but his patience was wearing thin. "We have hitherto omitted arresting the bodies of these intruders entirely from motives of tenderness to their families because fines & imprisonment would bring extreme distress on them. But if they should be so hardy as make another attempt in defiance of law & contempt of lenity experienced, we must take them into custody & deliver them to the Civil magistracy." Meigs had genuine concern for the rights of the Indians who were his charges, but he was also aware that the Indians would not be amenable to further cessions of land (for which negotiations were then pending) so long as the intruders were not effectively removed.[35]

to commanding officer of Highwassee Garrison, March 13, 1809, in SW LS, Military Book No. 4; Meigs to Smith, June 12, 1809, in *Territorial Papers*, V, 739–740.
[35] Circulars of Meigs to intruders, June 28 and Oct. 11, 1809, in IA FR

In the meantime the removal of intruders on the Chickasaw lands had become the responsibility of James Neelly, the newly appointed Chickasaw agent. He forwarded the complaints of the chiefs to the War Department, and when he got no response to his appeals, beseeched the governor of Mississippi Territory to take some action in his capacity as superintendent of Indian affairs. "I am very much teased with the requests of the King & head men of this Nation," Neelly wrote, "to have the intruders removed off their Land & I cannot do it of myself, without some assistance from the Military Department." Governor Holmes, who declared that between four and five thousand whites had settled within the Indian boundary, sought aid from the War Department, since to send troops from his capital in southwestern Mississippi would be too inconvenient and expensive. Meanwhile Neelly was to inform his charges that the government would certainly remove the intruders by spring or summer.[36]

The secretary of war recognized the difficulty, and he discussed with General Wade Hampton plans for redistributing the troops on that frontier so that they could more effectively police the region. In the middle of June 1810, the secretary of war directed the removal of the squatters. Timely notice was to be given so that the settlers could take away their belongings and the harvest of the year. Then, in the fall or later, if the people had not moved out, troops were to be sent to remove them and to burn their cabins and fences. Parties of soldiers were to return from time to time to make sure that the settlers did not return.[37]

This real threat of removal was getting too close for comfort, and the settlers drew up a long petition to Congress and the President.[38] "A great many of your fellow citizens," the petition began, "have unfortunately settled on what is now Called chickasaw land which has led us into difficultys that tongue cannot express if the orders from the ware department are Executed in removing us off of said land." There followed the usual pleas — the good faith of the settlers in thinking the Indian title had

Cherokee Agency; Meigs to Robert Purdy, Oct. 25, 1809, *ibid.*; Meigs to William Eustis, Oct. 26 and Nov. 16, 1809, *ibid.*

[36] Neelly to Eustis, Oct. 20 and Dec. 30, 1809, in SW LR, N-102 (4) and N-122 (4); David Holmes to Eustis, Feb. 7, 1810, and enclosures, in *Territorial Papers*, VI, 44–46; Holmes to Wade Hampton, Feb. 9, 1810, *ibid.*, 48; Holmes to Neelly, May 20, 1810, *ibid.*, 68.

[37] Eustis to Hampton, May 4 and June 15, 1810, *ibid.*, 63–64, 71; Eustis to Neelly, June 7, 1810, in SW IA LS, vol. C, p. 30.

[38] Petition dated Sept. 5, 1810, in *Territorial Papers*, VI, 106–113.

been extinguished, the misery that would result if the hard order of the War Department were carried out, the injustice that would result if they lost their crops and improvements. "If you could have A true representation of our carractor, the industry we have made, and the purity of our intentions in settling here, together With the Justice of our cause, you would say, in the name of God let them stay on and eat their well earned bread." If this appeal to sentiment did not move Congress, there was a more practical matter: "Perhaps our number may be fare more than you are apprised of; from the best calculation that we can make there is . . . 2250 souls on what is called chickasaw land and all of us could live tollarable comfortable if we Could remain on our improvements." The petition was subscribed to by four hundred and fifty persons.

The pleas of justice and hardship were the standard stuff of which such petitions were made. The true nature of the invasion, however, shines through in other sections of the memorial. The settlers refused to acquiesce in a removal that would, they said, "bring many women and children to a state of starvation mearly to gratify a heathan nation Who have no better right to this land than we have ourselves; and they have by estemation nearly 100,000 acres of land to each man Of their nation and of no more use to government or society than to saunter about upon like so many wolves or bares, whilst they who would be a supporte to government and improve the country must be forsed even to rent poore stoney ridges to make a support to rase their famelies on whilst there is fine fertile countrys lying uncultivated, and we must be debared even from inJoying a small Corner of this land." Such was the economics of frontier settlement.

The force of the intruders was too great to be held back. Temporarily it could be halted, but the intruders were a mobile lot. They had moved in easily the first time, and they could just as easily return. When the troops departed from the area, back streamed the settlers. Although the government again directed the Indian agents and the military commanders to carry out the provisions of the law, little was accomplished. Then came the War of 1812, which turned attention to more serious troubles, and the Creek War of 1813–14. The outcome of it all was what had already come to be expected, an expectation that no doubt took much of the edge off the zeal of officers who were responsible for the removal of the intruders. The more frequently the government acquiesced in the illegal settlements, the more difficult it became to take really effective action. The settlers knew that they would be treated more or less considerately. They knew that the government did not have the troops for a continuing and effective patrol of the Indian lands. They had little fear that civil action would succeed against them, for they could rely on sympathetic courts, and there was an increasing number of examples of government action to cover such settlements by formal treaties to extinguish Indian title. As late as March 19, 1816, the secretary of war was answering complaints of the Chickasaws about intruders by sending instructions to the agent to remove them and turn them over to the United States attorney for prosecution, but by a treaty of September 20, 1816, the land in question was ceded to the United States by the Indians. Though settlers were still prohibited by a law of 1807 forbidding settlement on public lands that had not been surveyed, the matter was no longer one of Indian relations, but pertained instead to the Department of State.[39]

At one spot after another on this section of the frontier the harassment continued, to the exasperation of the Indian agents and officers who were responsible for the enforcement of the intercourse acts. The procedure of moving the illegal settlers off became almost a game and was never completely effective. In 1815, when large numbers of white citizens moved into Cherokee lands in Mississippi Territory with their horses and cattle and made actual settlements on the land, Meigs almost gave up in despair of accomplishing anything under the usual procedure. He wrote finally to the United States attorney in Madison County, Mississippi Territory, to see if some sort of civil action could be instituted against the aggressors. "The mode hitherto practiced to remove such intruders," he wrote, "has been to send troops to remove them burn their Cabins, fences, &c. But in no instance to commit any violence on their persons, or hurt the property of any individual. (Cabbins & fences made by Intruders cannot be denominated their property.) In removing Intruders humanity & tenderness has been always exercised towards those people. But it is now practically found intirely ineffectual. & Some other mode of proceeding to remove the evil must if possible be adopted." He wanted the attorney to institute civil process against the settlers under the intercourse acts. Their mere presence on

[39] Eustis to G. W. Sevier, Jan. 13, 1812, *ibid.*, 260; William H. Crawford to William Cocke, March 19, 1816, *ibid.*, 669–670; George Graham to Andrew Jackson, Jan. 13, 1817, *ibid.*, 747.

the Indian lands without authorization should have been enough to convict them. "If a few examples can be made," Meigs asserted, "it will have ten times the good effect as that of burning Cabbins." Meigs continued to insist that judicial action should be taken against offenders, but little seems to have been done. Still, he was encouraged to some extent by the secretary of war. When intruders on the Cherokee lands in 1819 were to be removed, the military commander was instructed to remove them on requisition from Meigs, and Meigs was told to select "some of the most wealthy and influential from among them" for prosecution under the act of 1802.[40]

Major General Andrew Jackson, then commanding at Nashville, was the officer upon whom Meigs depended for military support in removing intruders. Jackson came to the same conclusion as the agent about the ineffectiveness of the removal procedure. "Experience has proven," he wrote the War Department, "that it is useless to remove . . . [squatters] or stock therefrom, without prosecution for the infraction of the law: The experiment made last fall shewed the inutility of the bare destruction of improvements, and removal of stock; the Intruders returned within a few days after the soldiers had retired, drove back their stock and recommenced their plan of robbery." Jackson had a special problem with the stock that he drove off the Indian lands. Was it liable to seizure or not? He thought that it was and that the only way to stop "the villianies practised within the Indian boundaries" was to seize the cattle, turn them over to the civil authority and make them answerable for the damage. He had attempted to do this, turning the stock over to the marshal if he would receive it, on one occasion at least with beneficial results. Unless the civil authorities would cooperate by prosecuting the offenders, Jackson thought that it was useless for the military to run in pursuit of trespassers and their cattle. "All of the troops on the military peace establishment (without horsemen) could not carry into effect the treaties with the Cherokees and prevent intrusion." Unfortunately, Jackson got very little encouragement from the War Department for his method of procedure. The acting secretary of war, George Graham, pointed out the clear authorization in the act of 1802 for removing *persons* from the Indian Country, but he could find nothing in the act which gave jurisdiction to the federal courts over stock or other personal property

---

[40] Meigs to Louis Winston, Jan. 12, 1815, *ibid.*, 492–493; Calhoun to Meigs, March 25, 1819, *ibid.*, XVIII, 591.

belonging to the intruders. Since the same courts in Tennessee had declined to handle cases over which jurisdiction was specifically given to them, Graham doubted that they would assume jurisdiction "by construction, and on Common law principles" over doubtful cases. He instructed Jackson to drive off the offending stock, then to turn them loose at some point outside the Indian boundary, and to take whatever action he could persuade the state courts to sanction.[41]

A serious weakness in the protection of the Indian Country was the shortage of troops to enforce the removal of intruders. The peacetime establishment of the regular army was altogether inadequate to the task. A plausible solution was to employ Indian troops in the work of removal, since it was the Indians, after all, who were to benefit. General Jackson made the proposal in regard to intruders on the Cherokee lands, and the War Department approved the suggestion. The secretary of war saw decided advantages in the system — the Indian troops would always be within reach of the agent and could continuously guard against the return of the intruders, and the use of Indian troops could save the government money. Meigs employed a detachment of Cherokee light horse troops to aid him in the removal of illegal settlers, but when he submitted a muster roll for payment of the troops, the secretary of war roundly objected. Since the Indians were the beneficiaries of the action, he thought that they had no claim for compensation. Calhoun finally agreed to pay the Cherokees — but only half of what Meigs requested — and in future use of Indian troops he was careful to specify beforehand that no compensation was to be allowed them.[42]

The incessant intrusion onto Cherokee lands in Georgia led finally to the enrollment of volunteer troops at regular army pay to drive the violators out. Joseph McMinn, who replaced Meigs as Cherokee agent, with the approval of the War Department ordered the mustering in of the volunteers and dispatched them

[41] Jackson to Graham, July 22, 1817, in *Correspondence of Andrew Jackson*, John Spencer Bassett, ed. (6 vols., Washington, 1926–1933), II, 308–309; Graham to Jackson, Aug. 14, 1817, in *Territorial Papers*, XVIII, 135–136.

[42] Calhoun to Meigs, April 20, 1820, in SW IA LS, vol. D, p. 406; Calhoun to Meigs, Nov. 14, 1820, and Aug. 4, 1821, *ibid.*, vol. E, pp. 30–31, 140; Calhoun to John Crowell, April 25, 1822, *ibid.*, pp. 245–246. The Cherokees, however, were not satisfied by the arrangement and complained about the "gratuity" they received, which fell far short of regular pay. They argued that it was the responsibility of the United States, not theirs, to remove the intruders who violated the law. Cherokee Delegation to Thomas L. McKenney, May 3, 1824, in IA LR, Cherokee Agency (East).

to drive out the settlers. Armed with large butcher knives to cut down the corn of the intruders and with many mounted on horses that they themselves supplied, the volunteers drove into the trouble spots, destroying the crops and burning fences and houses. The intruders showed considerable hostility, and in the engagement one of the intruders was killed by the troops, for which the officers and two of the privates were haled into court. It was serious business, this use of force to drive out intruders, but the government and the agent were determined that the intercourse acts be rigidly enforced.[43]

෨෧

Where Indian claims to the Indian Country were vague and not seriously pressed by the Indians, white encroachment did not significantly endanger the peace of the frontier, and the intercourse acts, designed to preserve that peace, were not brought into operation.

The settlement of whites north of the Missouri River in the so-called Boone's Lick country is a case in point. In 1808 at the Treaty of Fort Clark, the Osage Indians had relinquished their claims to territory north of the Missouri. The same tract of land, however, was claimed also by the Sacs and the Iowas, although neither tribe apparently made any strong stand on the claims. Beginning about 1810 white settlers appeared along the Missouri on these lands, without molestation from either the Indians or the government, and by 1811 there were perhaps seventy-five families in the settlement. In June 1812 Governor Howard of Louisiana Territory reported that there were one hundred families in the area, respectable people and wealthy by the standards of the country, who wanted to come in under the laws and regulations of the Territory. Howard believed, however, that the land on which they settled was still Indian Country and he refused to organize the settlements or appoint officials for them, lest such action be taken to mean official approval of the encroachment, yet he did not think that he had authority to remove the settlers without specific directions from the President. The country was valuable agriculturally and possessed important salt springs, so the governor urged the government in Washington to acquire

---

[43] The details of this removal are found in the correspondence between McMinn and Calhoun, April–October 1824, in IA LR, Cherokee Agency (East). See also McKenney to McMinn, June 11, July 23, July 29, 1824, in IA LS, vol. 1, pp. 107, 148, 155.

the land from the Indians. A year and a half later, Governor Clark reported four hundred families — "tolerably respectable" — settled along the Missouri "on lands Claimed by the Socks & Ioways." Like his predecessor, Clark noted the desire of these settlers to be organized under the laws of the Territory, and he too recommended extinguishing the Indian title. The governor was soon backed up by a resolution of the Territorial Assembly, which urged the governor to make the proper representations to the President for the extinguishment of the Indian title to the Boone's Lick country.[44]

Clark, however, did not wait for the federal government to get its treaty-making machinery under way. After rereading the 1808 treaty with the Osages, he issued a proclamation on March 9, 1815 (under his authority as governor, commander in chief of the militia, and superintendent of Indian affairs), declaring that the treaty had fully extinguished all Indian title to the lands north of the Missouri. "The pretensions of other nations of Indians to lands lying within these limits, being of very recent date, are utterly unsupported by those usages and that possession and prescription on which the original Inhabitants of this country are accustomed to found their territorial claims," he boldly asserted. He announced that "the proprietary as well as sovereign rights" to the area were regularly acquired by the United States from the Osages at Fort Clark, and he joined the area to St. Charles County for purposes of civil government. This audacious move satisfied the territorial legislature, which organized Howard County to cover the settlements. The Indians, unwilling or unable to stop this sort of aggrandizement, nevertheless made mild complaints, and in 1824 the claims both of the Sacs and Foxes and of the Iowas were finally extinguished. Clark did not seem to be disturbed by acting as commissioner of the United States to extinguish Indian titles that a decade before he had officially and definitely declared did not exist.[45]

Clark, however, was not hostile to Indian claims. Where

[44] Kappler, *Treaties*, pp. 95–99; Royce, *Indian Land Cessions*, Plate 37, Cession No. 69; Cardinal L. Goodwin, "Early Explorations and Settlements of Missouri and Arkansas, 1803–1822," *Missouri Historical Review*, XIV (1920), 400–401; Benjamin Howard to Eustis, June 14, 1812, in *Territorial Papers*, XIV, 567–568; Clark to John Armstrong. Jan. 6, 1814, *ibid.*, 728; Resolution of Jan. 17, 1814, *ibid.*, 731; William Russell to William Rector, April 20, 1814, *ibid.*, 752.

[45] Proclamation of March 9, 1815, *ibid.*, XV, 40–41; Rector to Josiah Meigs, April 17, 1815, *ibid.*, 31; Rector to Edward Tiffin, April 29, 1816, *ibid.*, 131; Session Laws of Missouri Territory, 1815, December session, pp. 81–90; Kappler, *Treaties*, pp. 207–209.

Indian titles seemed clear, he endeavored to carry out the directives and policy of the federal government. On December 4, 1815, he issued one of his strongly worded proclamations warning intruders on the Indian lands in the territory that they were subject to removal. He condemned the violations made on Indian lands and asserted that the practices could no longer be permitted. Whether Clark had some particular intruders in mind, or whether he was merely putting on record his adherence to Presidential directives, is difficult to say. Nevertheless, he seriously frightened the white settlers in the Cape Girardeau region, where the Delawares and the Shawnees had claims dating back to permission given by the Spanish government on January 4, 1793. The Delawares had moved from the area in 1815, settling on a tract set aside from them in southwestern Missouri on the White River, and the Shawnees, too, had begun to move out under assurances that other land would be reserved for them. The Indian claims were still real enough, however, to cast some doubt on the titles of the white settlers. These persons petitioned Congress in January 1816 and again in January 1817 to determine just what lands the Indians were entitled to in the region and then to exchange them for some free and unsettled lands farther west. There is no evidence that any of the white settlers were actually removed, and in treaties with the Shawnees (1825) and the Delawares (1829) all Indian claims to the area were finally extinguished.[46]

More troublesome were the encroachments on the remnants of land still held by the Osages in western Missouri. A delegation of Osages in Washington in July 1820 complained about the white intrusion into their country. "This has become a subject of universal complaint among the Indians," the secretary of war wrote to General Henry Atkinson, "and the honor & justice of the Gov^t require, that it should be prevented." He directed the general to give notice to the whites along the frontier that the intercourse acts would be rigidly enforced, and he directed Governor Clark to cooperate fully with the military commander. Finally, in 1825 the Osages also relinquished all claim to lands in Missouri, and the problem of encroachment in that state was at an end.[47]

⁕

[46] Proclamation of Dec. 4, 1815, in *Territorial Papers*, XV, 191–192; Resolutions of Jan. 22, 1816, and Jan. 24, 1817, *ibid.*, 105–107, 234–236; Kappler, *Treaties*, pp. 262–264, 304–305.

[47] Calhoun to Atkinson, July 21, 1820, in *Territorial Papers*, XV, 629; Calhoun to Clark, July 20, 1820, *ibid.*, 628; Kappler, *Treaties*, pp. 217–221.

In the Territory of Arkansas, which had been established in 1819 by breaking off the lower section of Missouri Territory, there were two centers of trouble from settlers edging into Indian lands — one along the Red River, the other on the Arkansas River near the present western boundary of the state. The Indian agent, George Gray, who moved the agency from Natchitoches to the Sulphur Fork on the Red River in 1821, was instructed by the secretary of war to enforce the intercourse act rigidly against all whites trespassing on the Indian lands and to call upon the military commander of the nearest post for aid in removing intruders if necessary. It was not long before the agent had to act, for whites had begun to move into the lands of the Caddoes. When the agent reported the intrusion to the War Department, he was directed to remove the squatters immediately. He accordingly issued an order to the offending citizens, who, although it was still very early in the year, petitioned to be allowed to remain until fall because their fields were prepared for planting and their stock too scattered to be easily rounded up. Gray allowed them to remain until he got further instructions from the War Department.[48]

When it actually came to removing the intruders, whether settlers or the illegal hunters and traders with whom the region was plagued, Gray had trouble in getting the military help that he needed. Major Alexander Cummings at Fort Towson refused because he disclaimed having any orders and suggested that the agent apply at Fort Jesup instead. Only after correspondence with the War Department and the Office of Indian Affairs was Gray's hand strengthened by an order issued to the Fort Towson commander to give him aid when requested. Gray recommended the stationing of a small command of troops at his agency for better enforcement of the intercourse acts (especially against the "lower class of Whites residing on the Frontier," who plied the Indians with whiskey), but the secretary of war declined to act on the recommendation, urging the agent instead to exercise due vigilance and accomplish all he could under the existing arrangements.[49]

Major Cummings was not to be blamed for his hesitation to

[48] Calhoun to Gray, Nov. 27, 1820, and Nov. 13, 1823, in *Territorial Papers,* XIX, 236–237, 565; Gray to Calhoun, Feb. 28, 1824, *ibid.,* 611–612.
[49] Gray to Calhoun, Jan. 13, 1825, *ibid.,* 745–746; McKenney to Calhoun, March 25, 1825, *ibid.,* XX, 16; McKenney to Gray, July 9, 1825, and Nov. 16, 1825, *ibid.,* 90–92, 152–153; Gray to James Barbour, Sept. 30, 1825, *ibid.,* 110–120.

help. He had his own troubles and could give little support to the Indian agent. In November 1824 he had sent a list of persons who had been hunting in Indian lands west of the Kiamichi River in violation of the second and third sections of the act of 1802 to Samuel C. Roane, the United States district attorney at Little Rock, and he sent also the names of witnesses by whom the fact might be proved. Cummings' action immediately got him in trouble with the men whose names he had sent to the district attorney. They assembled, some two hundred strong, for the purpose of making an attack on the military post. The officer then seized two of the ringleaders and sent them off under guard to Little Rock. On neither the illegal hunters nor the threatened attack on the post, however, did the military commander get any help from the district attorney, who claimed that he had insufficient evidence to undertake a prosecution against the attackers of the post and that it was utterly impossible to do anything about the illegal hunters, since they could not be caught by the marshal and not even the costs of the suits could be collected from them if they were caught and tried. To make matters worse, Roane reported that some of the citizens were preparing to bring charges against the officers of the fort for their action. Cummings saw no way for the act of Congress to be enforced. If the district attorney refused to prosecute, the offenders would escape punishment, and the illegal practices would continue in spite of all the army officers' efforts to prevent them.[50]

When Governor George Izard of Arkansas Territory issued a proclamation in 1825 to stop hunting and trapping on Indian lands, Captain Russell B. Hyde, commanding at Fort Towson, took no action to carry it out, for he had before his eyes the failure of Major Cummings the year before. The frontiersmen were indeed emboldened by the failure of any action to be taken against them. Major Cummings in 1826 reported that these people, finding that they had nothing to fear from the civil authorities, were more open in their transgressions than formerly, and he reported that the whites were organizing an expedition against the Pawnees.[51]

Of even greater seriousness were the sustained settlements made in the region between the Arkansas and the Red rivers on

[50] Cummings to Atkinson, April 8, 1825, and enclosures, ibid., 30–34; Cummings to Charles J. Nourse, April 28, 1825, ibid., 46–47.
[51] Hyde to Izard, Oct. 11, 1825, ibid., 123; Cummings to Edmund P. Gaines, June 22, 1826, ibid., 266–267.

lands set aside for the Choctaw Nation. Here confusion engendered by the emigration of Indians from the east to Arkansas and the consequent necessity to provide the incoming Indians with lands aggravated the problems. The shifting of the western boundary of the territory in 1824 and 1828 added another element of complexity.

On August 24, 1818, the Quapaw Indians ceded to the United States a large tract of land, comprising most of present-day Arkansas south of the Arkansas River and the southern half of Oklahoma. It was the intention of the government not to open all these lands to white settlement but to exchange them and the land north of the Arkansas ceded by the Osages for Indian lands east of the Mississippi. Whites, however, began to move into the region, and in June 1819 the commanding officer at Fort Smith, Major William Bradford, was ordered by General Jackson to remove all the settlers west of a line drawn between the sources of the Kiamichi (which ran into the Red River) and the Poteau (which ran into the Arkansas at Fort Smith). This Bradford proceeded to do, finding about two hundred families, some of whom had crops already growing. But the line that was later marked out ran south from the mouth of the Canadian River and was farther west than the line used by Bradford. Immediately the settlers moved back into the area. When word of this reached the government in Washington, new orders were sent to Colonel Arbuckle at Fort Smith to re-establish the Kiamichi-Poteau line and move all settlers to the east of it, so Arbuckle moved the people a second time. They settled in Miller and Crawford counties of Arkansas Territory.[52]

Despite the presence of these settlers the government soon granted the lands to Choctaws emigrating from the east, for on October 18, 1820, at Doak's Stand, the Choctaws ceded a large section in west-central Mississippi and were given in return a grant of territory in what are now Arkansas and Oklahoma. Thus many white settlers, some of whom had already been removed once or twice, now found themselves again on Indian lands. That they had had no legal right to settle in the region in the first place did not lessen their distress. The Governor of Arkansas Territory declared that it would be necessary to depopu-

[52] Kappler, *Treaties*, pp. 160–161; Royce, *Indian Land Cessions*, Plates 5 and 21, Cession No. 94; Calhoun to Jackson, Dec. 15, 1818, in *Territorial Papers*, XIX, 19; Statement of Bradford, March 25, 1824, in *American State Papers: Indian Affairs*, II, 557.

late two entire counties, that one third of the whole white population lived within the Choctaw cession, that these were the best
lands in the territory ("if I had my choice of the best plantation,
the most eligibly situated and in the highest state of cultivation
. . . I would choose ten within the Indian cession before one
out"), that the cession contained the only salt springs in the
territory, and so on and on.[53]

It was obvious that the intercourse acts could not be enforced
in such a region, and the government began to work for a modification of the Doak's Stand treaty. Pending an inevitable new
agreement with the Indians, no action was taken to remove the
settlers on the Indian lands, who were estimated at five thousand
persons. In November 1824 the Choctaw delegation arrived in
Washington, where negotiations were carried on with them by
Secretary of War Calhoun. The Indians eventually agreed to part
with a section of their Arkansas lands, but they demanded and
got compensation far beyond what Calhoun had initially been
willing to offer. The convention signed in Washington on January
20, 1825, set as the new eastern boundary for the Choctaw Nation
a line running due south from a point on the Arkansas one hundred paces east of Fort Smith to the Red River (approximately
the present western boundary of the state). The United States
agreed to remove white settlers who were west of the new line
and to prevent new settlements in the Choctaw Nation.[54]

The people of Arkansas were far from satisfied, for between
one thousand and two thousand persons were still trapped in
Indian Country and subject to removal. They wanted the eastern
boundary of the Choctaws to be set at the line designated by
Congress in 1824 ás the western boundary of Arkansas — a line
beginning at a point forty miles west of the southwest corner of
Missouri and running due south to the Red River — or, as a last
resort, a line running from the mouth of the Kiamichi to the
mouth of the Poteau. For once Washington officials were firm.
They had done their best in the face of Choctaw intransigence.
If the treaty of January 20, 1825, were not ratified, the President
would be obliged to begin enforcing the original treaty of Doak's

[53] Kappler, *Treaties*, pp. 191–194; Royce, *Indian Land Cessions*, Plate 6,
Cession No. 122; James Miller to Calhoun, Dec. 11, 1820, in *Territorial Papers*,
XIX, 244–246.

[54] Kappler, *Treaties*, pp. 211–214; Royce, *Indian Land Cessions*, Plate 6, Cession No. 122; Edward M. Douglas, *Boundaries, Areas, Geographic Centers and
Altitudes of the United States and the Several States* (Washington, 1930), pp.
178–179.

Stand. There was no other alternative and there would no longer be any excuse for not carrying out the terms of the early treaty if the present convention were rejected by the Senate. It was better to remove two thousand persons than to be obliged to remove five thousand. The government, moreover, did not feel bound in justice to protect settlers who had moved into the region without legal sanction. "The settlements have probably been formed thoughtlessly," Calhoun wrote to Arkansas's delegate in Congress, Henry W. Conway, "under the temptations of fine soil and a genial climate, without reflecting that the lands were not theirs, and that they rendered themselves liable, of course, to be removed as intruders, under the laws of the country. The general mode of forming settlements in our country, no doubt, encouraged the settlements, and the settlers may be considered, under those circumstances, as having claims, not upon the justice, but humanity of the country." [55]

The government was determined this time to uphold the treaty. Provisions were quickly made for running the boundary line, and directions were sent to Governor Izard and to military commanders to see to it that settlers west of the line were removed, after allowing them the customary privilege of harvesting their crops. Beyond that there was to be no further indulgence. "The obligation of the Treaty must be carried into full and complete effect," Secretary of War Barbour wrote to Izard; "and this reaches, as you will see, to a prevention of future settlements from being made on the West of the line, as well as to the breaking up of those already made." [56]

Equally troublesome were the relations with the Cherokees, who began to move into the region of the Arkansas River before any definite provision of land had been made for them there by the federal government. They had begun their migration with the permission of the government during the administrations of Jefferson and Madison, and at first went west only to hunt. As the numbers increased an exchange of lands was contemplated, but as late as 1816 the Cherokees could not be induced to make an exchange, since most of the nation still was east of the Mississippi. Meigs estimated in that year that at least two thousand Cherokees

[55] Conway to Calhoun, Dec. 22, 1824, in *American State Papers: Indian Affairs*, II, 555–556; Calhoun to Conway, Jan. 18, 1825, *ibid.*, 557–558; Barbour to Izard, July 8, 1825, in *Territorial Papers*, XX, 86–87.

[56] Barbour to Izard, March 18, 1825, *ibid.*, 59; Barbour to Jacob Brown, March 19, 1825, *ibid.*, 15–16; Izard to Barbour, June 6, 1825, *ibid.*, 66; Barbour to Izard, July 8, 1825, *ibid.*, 86–87.

were in the Arkansas region and recommended that a factory be established in that area, and in 1813 William L. Lovely, who acted for a time as assistant to Meigs in Tennessee, was appointed agent for the Cherokees in Arkansas. Lovely attempted to maintain peace between the incoming Cherokees and the Osages, who were already in the territory, and with the whites who had started to settle in the region. It was a delicate business, and in such a remote place that connections with government officialdom were tenuous at best. In order to establish some kind of order in the area, Lovely, in July 1813, issued a proclamation which set up a temporary designation of lands for the Cherokees along the Arkansas River.[57]

The white settlers who fell within the projected boundary were soon complaining about this action, which gave to the Cherokees "the best and richest part of the Country," but the Indians were there in considerable number and the federal government was forced to make provision for them. Uppermost in the minds of the government officials in Washington was the prospect of getting the Cherokees in the east to relinquish their holdings in Tennessee, Georgia, and Mississippi. In order to procure these lands, it was necessary to exchange them for an equal amount of land in the West. In fact, by treaties of July 8, 1817, and February 27, 1819, the Cherokees did cede large sections of their lands in the east in return for a tract in Arkansas between the Arkansas and White rivers. The treaty of 1817 provided that all citizens were to be removed, but there were the usual difficulties. Although the War Department early in 1821 again directed the removal of all whites from the Cherokee lands and prohibited settlement on the lands west of the cession, the Cherokees still had grounds for complaint. "We beg leave to inform you," they wrote to the secretary of war in July, "that many of the whites have settled on our land in Arkansas, are killing our game and destroying our range; making farms & planting orchards, as if it were their intention never to quit the Country; which makes our young people very uneasy." [58]

---

[57] Meigs to William H. Crawford, Feb. 17, 1816, enclosed in John Mason to Crawford, March 2, 1816, in *Territorial Papers*, XV, 121–123; Secretary of War to William L. Lovely, Jan. 4, 1813, in SW IA LS, vol. C, p. 153; Lovely to Secretary of War, Oct. 1, 1813, in *Territorial Papers*, XIV, 705–706; Lovely to the Cherokees, July 20, 1813, enclosed in Edward Hempstead to John Armstrong, Dec. 13, 1813, *ibid.*, 721–722.

[58] Hempstead to Armstrong, Dec. 13, 1813, and enclosures, *ibid.*, 719–721; Lovely to Secretary of War, May 27, 1815, and enclosures, *ibid.*, XV, 49–57;

The land especially coveted by the whites was the rich section farther up the Arkansas that was known as "Lovely's Purchase." William Lovely in 1816 had negotiated with the Osages a cession of a triangular piece of territory north of the Arkansas River, beginning a little below Fort Smith and running up to the mouth of the Verdigris River. This cession, of course, had no legal basis, since it had not been negotiated by the federal government, but by a treaty of September 25, 1818, the same tract of land was officially acquired by the United States, and it was always referred to as Lovely's Purchase. The western boundary of the Cherokee grant in Arkansas was not marked out for several years and no one knew definitely whether or not it would eventually run through Lovely's Purchase; the Cherokees, furthermore, were guaranteed an outlet to the west to give them free access to hunting grounds; the government strictly prohibited white settlement on the Purchase.[59]

The policy of exclusion of whites from the Cherokee lands in Arkansas and from Lovely's Purchase was faithfully carried out at first. Governor James Miller reported in 1821 that he knew of only one white person on the Cherokee lands, and special attention was repeatedly directed to the prohibition of settlement in the Purchase and to the removal of intruders. But an abortive running of the western boundary of the Cherokee grant by Governor Miller, the complaints of the Cherokees that they were not getting as much land in Arkansas as they had given up in the east, the repeated assurance of the War Department that the United States intended to do the Indians justice, the urgent pleas of the citizens of Arkansas to be allowed to settle Lovely's Purchase (they argued that by thus blocking off the Cherokees at the east, the Indians would be more easily induced to give up

---

Kappler, *Treaties*, pp. 140–144, 177–179; Royce, *Indian Land Cessions*, Plate 5, Cession No. 143; Calhoun to James Miller, Feb. 21, 1821, in *Territorial Papers*, XIX, 268; Arkansas Cherokees to Calhoun, July 24, 1821, *ibid.*, 305–306.

[59] Kappler, *Treaties*, p. 167; Royce, *Indian Land Cessions*, Plate 21, Cession No. 97; Calhoun to Jackson, Dec. 15, 1818, in *Territorial Papers*, XIX, 19. Documents which tell the story of Lovely's Purchase are found in *House Doc.* 263, 20 Cong., 1 sess., ser. 174. See especially McKenney to Barbour, March 26, 1827, *ibid.*, pp. 27–29. Washington officials soon lost track of the man whose name was given to the region. Governor George Izard of Arkansas Territory referred to him as "one *Lovely,* then an agent or factor in the Osage Country" and was surprised not to find his name anywhere in the 1818 treaty. Izard to Barbour, Jan. 28, 1826, *ibid.*, p. 24. Thomas L. McKenney referred to him as "one Lovely, who was a factor or trader in that country." McKenney to Cooke, Dec. 15, 1826, *ibid.*, p. 26.

their claims in Arkansas altogether and go farther west, instead of hoping that eventually Lovely's Purchase would be given to them) — all this made the question one of great agitation in Arkansas.[60]

Gradually the government weakened in its resolve to keep Lovely's Purchase free of whites. In 1824, when the western boundary of Arkansas Territory was set as a line running due south from a point forty miles west of the southwest corner of Missouri, Lovely's Purchase was contained within the jurisdiction of Arkansas. Still more hope was given the citizens by a law of Congress of April 5, 1826, which extended the land districts of the Territory to include the lands lying west of the Cherokees. This seemed to indicate that Lovely's Purchase would be surveyed immediately and brought into the market. Induced by such a prospect, three hundred families settled on the tract, and a memorial of the Arkansas legislature predicted that by the next planting season, Lovely's Purchase would contain one thousand families.[61]

All this activity in regard to Lovely's Purchase seemed at odds with the orders of the War Department absolutely forbidding settlement, and Colonel Arbuckle voiced his disturbance. He had frequently removed settlers from the tract and was again preparing to send out a detachment for the same purpose. "If it is the intention of Government to permit this tract to be settled," he wrote, "it will spare the military much unpleasant duty & illwill if releived from the obligation of removing them therefrom." The reply was that he should suspend the order prohibiting settlement until further notice. This looked like an open invitation to the citizens of Arkansas, who considered the letter to Arbuckle from the adjutant general as "*permission* of the general government" to go into Lovely's Purchase at long last. They were not slow to act. In February 1828 the territorial delegate declared that the area contained more than three thousand souls and was daily increasing in population.[62]

[60] Calhoun to Cherokee Chiefs, Oct. 8, 1821, in *Territorial Papers*, XIX, 324–325; Calhoun to William Bradford, April 30, 1821, *ibid.*, 286; Matthew Arbuckle to Calhoun, Oct. 27, 1823, *ibid.*, 559–560; *House Doc.* 263, 20 Cong., 1 sess., ser. 174.

[61] *U.S. Stat.*, IV, 40, 153; George Graham to William McRee, June 15, 1826, in *Territorial Papers*, XX, 263–264; *House Doc.* 263, 20 Cong., 1 sess., ser. 174, pp. 29–31.

[62] Arbuckle to Roger Jones, July 31, 1826, in *Territorial Papers*, XX, 277–278; Jones to Arbuckle, Oct. 10, 1826, *ibid.*, 295; A. H. Sevier to Barbour, Feb. 18, 1828, *ibid.*, 603–604.

What a blow it was then to the people of Arkansas when the federal government negotiated a treaty with the Cherokees on May 6, 1828, in which most of Lovely's Purchase was ceded to the Cherokees in return for their lands further east in Arkansas, and the western boundary of Arkansas irrevocably set at a line running from Fort Smith to the southwest corner of Missouri. The citizens could hardly believe their ears when word reached them of the treaty. The bulk and best part of Lovely's Purchase was being given to the Cherokees! From the first appearance of the Cherokee delegation in Washington, the Arkansas delegate to Congress, A. H. Sevier, remonstrated vociferously with the secretary of war against any grant of Lovely's Purchase to the Indians. The government was forced to turn a deaf ear to these pleas, for it had other interests as well to consider — foremost among which was justice to the Indians. Edward W. DuVal, the Cherokee agent, sent forceful arguments to the secretary of war to counteract the arguments of the Arkansas delegate, of whose report he declared, "there is not even the shadow of truth in it: No, — *not the shadow*." [63]

An eloquent plea on behalf of the Indians was entered by Thomas L. McKenney, from the Office of Indian Affairs, who stressed the right the Indians had not to be hemmed in on the west by the whites, a right assured them again and again by the government and written into their treaties. McKenney had some telling points to make. Against the rights of the Indians, so solemnly guaranteed, what rights did the whites possess? "Is the land theirs? Do they own it by purchase? Are they not there this moment by Courtesy?" He had a clinching argument, more practical at the moment than doctrines of abstract right. The year 1828 was a critical time for the southern states in the complicated problem of Indian removal. The chances of getting the remnants of the Five Civilized Tribes to move west could not be jeopardized by a new example of failure to live up to the pledges made to the Indians. "The Cherokees on the East of the Mississippi," McKenney noted, "will soon hear of this failure to maintain the Executive faith as pledged to their Western Brothers — so will the Chickasaws, Choctaws, and Creeks, and then I fear the effect will

[63] Kappler, *Treaties*, pp. 288–292; Sevier to Secretary of War, Feb. 18, April 22, and May 7, 1828, in *Territorial Papers*, XX, 602–605, 651–652, 672–673; Edward W. DuVal to McKenney, April 22, 1828, *ibid.*, 652–653; DuVal to Barbour, April 24, 1828, *ibid.*, 654–656; Memorandum of DuVal, April 25, 1828, *ibid.*, 656–657.

be fatal to our plan of Colonizing the whole." The President was visited, too, by the southern governors, who were anxious that the treaty with the Cherokees should go through without a hitch.[64]

In the end the Cherokees won, at least to the extent that the claims of the white settlers to Lovely's Purchase went unheeded, and the Cherokees were granted much of that section along with adjacent lands in Oklahoma and Kansas to the total of seven million acres. Following a memorandum submitted by the Cherokee agent, DuVal, the western boundary of Arkansas was moved some forty miles to the east of the line set by Congress in 1824, and the new boundary designation was written into the treaty, to become the final western boundary of the state.[65]

By article 3 of the treaty the United States agreed to run the new boundary line by October 1 and as soon as the eastern line was run (that is, from the Arkansas River to the southwest corner of Missouri) to remove all white persons who remained beyond the line. The interests of these whites, however, were by no means neglected by Congress, and Sevier's efforts were not in vain. On May 24, 1828, Congress provided that any person who had settled on the lands that now ceased to be part of the Territory of Arkansas would be given as an indemnity up to three hundred and twenty acres from the public lands within the new bounds of the Territory. Governor Izard issued a proclamation allowing the settlers ninety days to remove or lose the right of pre-emption, but the issuance of the proclamation depended on the completion of the survey of the line, which was delayed so much that considerable confusion resulted. Some of the whites were still on their improvements when the Cherokees began to move in.[66]

◦◦

On the upper Mississippi, meanwhile, major trouble developed over lawless encroachment on the lead lands in the southwestern corner of present-day Wisconsin. These lands attracted a large number of men who sought easy wealth in the lead mines and

[64] McKenney to Barbour, April 12, 1828, *ibid.*, 647–650; *Memoirs of John Quincy Adams*, Charles Francis Adams, ed. (12 vols., Philadelphia, 1874–1877), VII, 516 (April 22, 1828).

[65] Memorandum of DuVal, April 25, 1828, in *Territorial Papers*, XX, 656–657; Kappler, *Treaties*, p. 288.

[66] *U.S. Stat.*, IV, 306–307, 329; Sevier to Graham, July 30, 1828, in *Territorial Papers*, XX, 718–719; Proclamation of Izard, Sept. 27, 1828, *ibid.*, 751–752 and n. 40; Arbuckle to Jones, Jan. 9, 1829, *ibid.*, 831.

cared little for the rights of the Indians or the laws of the government. It was a striking illustration of the pressure of white encroachment on Indian lands, so serious as to threaten an Indian war, yet so determined and on such a large scale that the government's agents after some small show of resistance were forced to acquiesce in the maneuver. Extremely rich in mineral wealth and offering as well inviting agricultural land, the region drew large numbers of men, even though the lands still belonged to the Winnebagoes. McKenney, who toured the Mississippi valley in the autumn of 1827, found the Winnebagoes in a state of great excitement because of the intrusions and reported that two thousand persons had gone over the line. The chief party of the encroaching miners was led by Henry Dodge, who moved into the region with eighty to one hundred armed men, determined to hold out at all costs. Joseph M. Street, the Indian agent at Prairie du Chien, dispatched his subagent, John Marsh, in the dead of winter to order Dodge to move and to threaten him with removal by military force if he persisted in his illegal designs. Marsh sought out Dodge and delivered the agent's orders, which made little impression on the intruders, who argued that since no definite line had been run, there was no way to be sure that they were indeed on Winnebago lands. Street reported to the commanding officer at Fort Crawford that the trespassers consisted of one hundred and thirty men well armed with rifles and pistols and that Dodge's residence had been made into a strong stockaded fort. Suggesting that the defenses were so strong that they might prove formidable to a party sent to remove them, Street requested of Major Fowle a military force of one hundred and eighty men, but Fowle took no action, other than to write to his commanding general for further instructions, for his command was too small to furnish the men and the conditions of the country at that time of year made any movement impossible.[67]

Thus things rode for several months. In July General Atkinson directed the new commandant at Fort Crawford to furnish Street with a military escort. Should the intruders refuse to withdraw under a peaceful order, the officer was immediately to use whatever force was necessary to drive the men off and to keep the lands free from future intrusions. A small detachment, cut

[67] McKenney, *Memoirs*, p. 132; Street to John Fowle, Jan. 24, 1828, in Department of the West, Letters Received, National Archives, Record Group 98; Marsh to Street, Feb. 7, 1828, *ibid.*; Street to Fowle, Feb. 7, 1828, *ibid.*; Fowle to Samuel McRee, Feb. 7, 1828, *ibid.*; Fowle to Street, Feb. 7, 1828, *ibid.*

down to six men so that the whole party could proceed on horseback, went with Street to "Dodge's diggings," only to discover that Dodge and his party had obtained permission for their operations from the United States agent in charge of the mining territory and that all the unlicensed miners had fled on hearing that force would be used to remove them. The success at dispersing the intruders could have been no more than temporary, however, for Marsh reported on July 29, 1828, that the lead mining lands of the Indians had ten thousand men upon them. "The mineral riches of the country," he observed, "have caused people to flock into it with a rapidity altogether unparalleled." [68]

The solution was the old expedient — acquiescence by the government because the whites were on the Indian lands in force and refused to depart. It only remained to legalize the seizure by extinguishing the Indian title to the land by a formal treaty. On August 25, 1828, at Green Bay, the United States commissioners reached a temporary agreement with the tribes, "in order to remove the difficulties which have arisen in consequence of the occupation, by white persons, of that part of the mining country which has not been heretofore ceded to the United States." A provisional boundary was set up and the United States was given permission to occupy the country between the line and the Mississippi. Intruders on the lands were not to be interfered with by the Indians, who were only to report them to the United States officials for action. Meanwhile, until a formal treaty could be arranged, the Indians were to be paid twenty thousand dollars in compensation for any damages sustained by them on account of the intrusions up to time when a treaty could be signed. At Prairie du Chien on July 29, 1829, the Chippewas, Ottawas, and Potawatomies relinquished their claims to the lead regions east of the Mississippi, and three days later the Winnebagoes followed suit. It had been a touch-and-go proposition to restrict the intruders enough to satisfy the Indians until the final treaty of cession could be negotiated. [69]

After the treaties at Prairie du Chien had solved the problem cast of the Mississippi, the difficulty jumped to a new region, as miners now began to make concerted encroachment upon the

[68] Henry Atkinson to John McNeil, July 7, 1828, *ibid.*; McNeil to Atkinson, July 24, 1828, *ibid.*; Marsh to his father, July 29, 1828, quoted in George D. Lyman, *John Marsh, Pioneer: The Life Story of a Trail-blazer on Six Frontiers* (New York, 1930), pp. 143–144.

[69] Kappler, *Treaties*, pp. 292–293, 297–302; Royce, *Indian Land Cessions*, Plates 18 and 64, Cessions No. 147 and 149.

lead regions west of the river in the vicinity of Dubuque. In May 1830, as a result of a disturbance between the Foxes and the Menominees, the Foxes left the lead region at Dubuque (from which they had carefully excluded whites since the death of Julien Dubuque in 1810), and fled to the protection of Fort Armstrong. Immediately on the departure of the Indians, the whites in the Galena country across the Mississippi rushed in to take possession of the mines. The Indian superintendent at St. Louis, General Clark, called upon Henry Atkinson, the military commander at Jefferson Barracks, for troops to remove the intruders. It was a matter of great importance in keeping the Indians in a good mood for a scheduled conference with them at Prairie du Chien. Atkinson directed Major Stephen W. Kearny, who was going up the river to Fort Crawford, to stop at the Dubuque mines and remove any whites found upon the Indian lands, and he directed him on his return to stop again and apprehend persons who had failed to leave and turn them over to the civil authority to be dealt with according to the law.[70]

Lieutenant Colonel Zachary Taylor, commanding at Fort Crawford, on July 4 warned the intruders that they would be forceably removed if they did not leave on their own accord. The threat was apparently strong enough, for when Taylor's soldiers arrived, all but three miners had fled. While the detachment of soldiers remained, the Foxes returned to work the mines. In the following year, when the Indians again departed, the same problem of intruders arose, and troops were again dispatched from Fort Crawford to keep out the illegal miners. This they did with success, and in February 1832 the Sac and Fox agent acknowledged the service of the United States troops in removing the intruders, but it was obvious to the Indians that the whites were poised along the river ready to return as soon as the troops departed.

In September 1832, after their defeat in the Black Hawk War, the Sacs and Foxes ceded their lands in eastern Iowa as an in-

---

[70] Atkinson to Kearny, June 27, 1830, in Western Department Letter Book, vol. V, National Archives, Record Group 98; Atkinson to Alexander Macomb, June 28, 1830, *ibid*. For an account of the intrusions west of the Mississippi, see Jacob Van der Zee, "Early History of Lead Mining in the Iowa Country," *Iowa Journal of History and Politics*, XIII (1915), 3–52. See the sources which he lists, especially the documents found in *Sen. Doc.* 512, 23 Cong., 1 sess., sers. 244–248. There is also considerable correspondence dealing with the subject in Department of the West, Letters Received, January–March, 1833, National Archives, Record Group 98.

demnity, the so-called Black Hawk Purchase.[71] Although the lands were not to be open to the whites until June 1, 1833, through ignorance or wilfulness the whites long before that date started their migration into the area. In October Secretary of War Cass ordered the Indian agent at Fort Armstrong to remove such intruders. At the same time the commissioner of Indian affairs wrote to the Indian agent at Prairie du Chien to call upon the commander at Fort Crawford for military aid in removing the intruders. Street accordingly requested aid from Taylor, who agreed to furnish as many as fifty or sixty men to remove the men and to establish a suitable force on the spot to prevent their return.[72] Many of the miners did leave peaceably, and later petitioned the government for confirmation of their claims, but several times miners had to be removed during the early months of 1833. Finally, after June 1833, the miners were issued licenses to operate in the newly ceded area, and the trouble was over.

Just as military officers who searched the stores of traders for illicit whiskey risked suits for illegal trespass, they were also subject to being called into court for removing squatters on the Indian lands. "Every subaltern in the command knows," reported one civilian traveler in the West, "that if he interferes between an Indian and a white man, he will be sued instantly in the courts of the State. When I was at Prairie du Chien, there were several of the officers who had been cited to appear in court for having, pursuant to order, removed 'squatters' from the Indian lands over the Mississippi. The Indians then despise the agent, because he is clothed with no military authority; and the pioneer despises the military, because their hands are tied by the local civil power, whatever it be." No wonder that agents themselves hesitated to call upon the military commanders, even though the laws and special instructions seemed clear enough that this was the direct procedure to be followed. Thus, the Indian agent at Mackinac felt constrained to request a ruling from the attorney general of Michigan Territory as to whether he could order men out of the Indian Country and call upon troops to enforce his order, or

[71] Kappler, *Treaties*, pp. 349–351; Royce, *Indian Land Cessions*, Plate 24, Cession No. 175.
[72] Street to Cass, Dec. 1832, and enclosures, in *Territorial Papers*, XII, 550–554.

whether it was necessary first to institute a civil process and call out the military only if the civil authority were defied.[73]

Certain elemental conditions formed the basis of these difficulties. Given the nature of American western settlement, there was an inherent antagonism between the frontiersmen and any governmental force that tried to inhibit their activities. There was a deep-seated desire for the land, a hunger (if one can so speak of a nation incredibly land rich) which found the restrictions of the government an obstruction. Americans were expansion-minded; it seemed part of their very nature. Too often the government seemed helpless, even had it had the will, to hold in check the men who squatted on land not yet officially open to them, whether it was public land or Indian Country.

On top of this foundation there was often built a superstructure of personal animosity. Martinets of army officers who expected the free-living citizens on the frontier to jump with military precision at the sound of their voice — commandants little loved by soldier and civilian alike — did not supply the diplomacy necessary for the smooth running of the frontier communities. Indian agents, zealous beyond measure, perhaps, for the interest of their charges, overbearing in their self-importance, who could not get along with either the military or the traders and settlers, added their own measure of intolerance. And frontier entrepreneurs or budding lawyers, who dreamed of their communities as the future pride of the West, with whose ascent they too would be propelled upward, developed fanatical hatred of the army officers who attempted to clamp down restrictions on their manifold operations. It could be an explosive mixture.

Two incidents in Wisconsin in the 1820's and 1830's indicate the disadvantages under which the law-enforcement officers labored. In January 1829 a Green Bay trader named Daniel Whitney sent a party up the Wisconsin River to make shingles at a spot one hundred miles from any settlement and deep in the Indian Country. The army commander at Fort Winnebago, Major David E. Twiggs, looked upon the venture as a definite violation of the act of 1802 and feared that this sort of thing would cause uneasiness and unrest among the Indians. The Winnebagoes, in fact, reported the movement to Street at Prairie du Chien, who sent his subagent to Twiggs for military aid in removing the intruders. Whitney was not one to accept the military

[73] Charles F. Hoffman, *A Winter in the West* (2 vols., New York, 1835), II, 86–87; George Boyd to Cass, July 27, 1824, in *Territorial Papers*, XI, 574–575.

action lightly — he had lost a thousand dollars in the affair — and he brought suit against Twiggs for illegal trespass on his property. Twiggs was arrested by the sheriff and required to furnish sixteen hundred dollars bail for his appearance at the next session of the district court at Green Bay. Not until 1831 was the case cleared, and although Twiggs was freed for want of evidence, he put in a claim against the government for more than a thousand dollars of expense incurred in attending court, lawyers' fees, and other costs. Whitney brought charges against Street as well, but the outcome of that case was not clear. Then Twiggs retaliated by initiating a suit against Whitney for violation of the intercourse acts. An information, drawn up by the United States district attorney and submitted to the Supreme Court of Michigan Territory, was almost immediately withdrawn when the judges gave indications that it would get nowhere. Even the depositions which Twiggs got from members of the shingling party gave little support to his argument that the Indians objected to the intrusion.[74]

Shortly after the Whitney episode, Street became involved in another suit arising out of his eagerness to enforce the intercourse acts. Jean Brunet, a trader at Prairie du Chien who had moved up into Indian Country on a logging expedition, was seized by Street and Major Stephen W. Kearny, the commandant at Fort Crawford, to whom the agent turned for aid. Brunet and his party were kept under guard for a couple of days and then turned over to the civil authority. No sooner was he released than Brunet brought suit against Street and Kearny for their action. Street knew that he must fear the worst, for he was convinced that he would not get a fair trial in Judge Doty's court at Prairie du Chien. The population of the village, Street asserted, was composed "principally of *ignorant Canadian French, and mixed breed Indians, not one in 20* of whom can read or write. Many of these, have been hirelings to go with timber parties, and know little about the law, and *care less,* so long as they are not made to feel its penalties. Of this motley group the Jury will be . . . made up." The case against the defendants was that they had acted without direct orders from the President, which the intercourse law was declared to require, and the jury found them guilty.

[74] Francis Paul Prucha, *Broadax and Bayonet: The Role of the United States Army in the Development of the Northwest, 1815–1860* (Madison, 1953), pp. 64–65 and sources cited there; Alice E. Smith, *James Duane Doty: Frontier Promoter* (Madison, 1954), p. 74.

They were assessed about fourteen hundred dollars for damages and costs and had to petition Congress for a special relief bill to reimburse them.[75]

There seems no doubt that the agent and the officer were unwarrantedly harassed for their enforcement of the law. The outcome was not encouraging, and other agents with frontier experience were less eager than Street to tangle with the local interests. The agent at Green Bay, to whom Twiggs turned for support in his controversy with Whitney, recommended that the major keep his hands out of traders' affairs.

∾

This long recital of intrusions on Indian lands raises the difficult question of the sincerity of the government in its policy of protecting Indian rights to the land. Certainly the legal basis was firm enough, and the doctrines of pre-emption and of Indian sovereignty were endorsed by John Marshall and the Supreme Court in a series of famous decisions. In *Fletcher* vs. *Peck*, in 1810, the Court asserted that the "nature of the Indian title, which is certainly to be respected by all courts, until it be legitimately extinguished, is not such as to be absolutely repugnant to seizin in fee on the part of the State." [76] In 1823, in *Johnson* vs. *McIntosh*, the court expanded this doctrine, when it considered the case of two claimants to the same piece of land, one of whom had received the title directly from the Indians, the other by a patent from the government. Chief Justice Marshall, in giving the decision of the court, furnished a long disquisition about the nature of the Indian title to land and expatiated on the traditional doctrine of pre-emption.

This principle was, that discovery gave title to the government by whose subjects, or by whose authority, it was made, against all other European governments, which title might be consummated by possession. The exclusion of all other Europeans, necessarily gave to the nation making the discovery the sole right of acquiring the soil from the natives, and establishing settlements upon it. . . . In the establishment of these regulations [between discoverer and natives] the rights of the original inhabitants were, in no instance, entirely disregarded; but were necessarily, to a considerable extent, impaired. They were admitted to be the rightful occu-

---

[75] Smith, *James Duane Doty*, pp. 75–76; Prucha, *Broadax and Bayonet*, pp. 65–66. See also Clark to Cass, Feb. 25, 1832, in IA LR, St. Louis Superintendency; Cass to Kearny, Oct. 23, 1832, in IA LS, vol. 9, p. 309.
[76] *Fletcher* vs. *Peck*, 6 Cranch 87 (1810).

pants of the soil, with a legal as well as just claim to retain possession of it, and to use it according to their own discretion; but their rights to complete sovereignty, as independent nations, were necessarily diminished, and their power to dispose of the soil at their own will, to whomsoever they pleased, was denied by the original fundamental principle, that discovery gave exclusive title to those who made it.

With numerous citations of colonial precedents to back up his contention, Marshall maintained that the United States, or the several states, had the exclusive power to extinguish the Indian right of occupancy. Although the "absolute ultimate title" rested with the European discoverers, the Indians kept the right of occupancy. This right, Marshall declared, "is no more incompatible with a seizin in fee, than a lease for years, and might as effectually bar an ejectment." "It has never been contended," he continued, "that the Indian title amounted to nothing. Their right of possession has never been questioned." [77]

The laws and proclamations were explicit, and there were repeated instances of vigorous action to drive off illegal settlers. Yet in the long run, the settlers nearly always won out. Why did the government not take more effective measures to prevent encroachment? The answer lies first in the insufficiency of the forces available to carry out the legislative measures and the executive decisions. Indian agents simply lacked the necessary means. The civil authorities could not be relied upon to prosecute or convict violators; and the army on the frontier was too small to police the whole area successfully. But behind these failures was a larger issue. The federal government was sincerely interested in preventing settlement on Indian lands only up to a point, and it readily acquiesced in illegal settlements when they had gone so far as to be irremediable. The basic policy of the United States intended that white settlement should advance and the Indians withdraw. Its interest was primarily that this process should be as free of disorder and injustice as possible. The government meant to restrain and govern the advance of the whites, not to prevent it forever.[78] It supported Indian claims as far as it could

[77] *Johnson and Graham's Lessee* vs. *McIntosh,* 8 Wheaton 543 (1823).

[78] The desire for orderly settlement on the part of Secretary of War William H. Crawford can be seen in the instructions he sent in 1816 to commissioners to treat with the Indians: "The determination to purchase land only when demanded for settlement, will form the settled policy of the government. Experience has sufficiently proven that our population will spread over any cession, however extensive, before it can be brought into the market, and before there is any regular and steady demand for settlement, thereby increasing the difficulty of protection,

out of justice and humanity to the Indians and above all as far as it was necessary to keep a semblance of peace and to maintain Indian good will so that continuing cessions of land could be evoked from the tribes. In these decades of the century the federal government was convinced that once the Indians had been permanently settled on lands west of the Mississippi, the problems of encroachment and removing intruders would be unhappy memories of the past.

The energy of the government in removing intruders was, in fact, proportionate, either directly or inversely, to a number of other circumstances: to the length of time during which the Indian claims were expected to be maintained; to the seriousness of Indian objections to the intruders, since often removal was the only way to prevent an Indian war; to the necessity of convincing the Indians of the government's good faith, in order to keep them in a proper frame of mind for some impending treaty, at which more concessions of land were to be sought; to the pressures of white settlement, for full-scale drives into an area usually led to new treaties of cession rather than to removal of the whites; to the boldness and aggressiveness of the agents and the military commanders in enforcing the laws; to the military forces available in the area where encroachment was threatened; to the strength of frontier opposition to military action against the intruders; and to the color of title which the settlers on the Indian lands could display and the character of the settlers themselves.

---

embarrassing the government by broils with the natives, and rendering the execution of the laws regulating intercourse with the Indian tribes utterly impracticable." Crawford to William Clark, Ninian Edwards, and Auguste Chouteau, Sept. 17, 1816, in SW IA LS, vol. C, p. 425. See also his letters to these commissioners of May 7 and May 27, 1816, *ibid.*, pp. 340–342, 363.

✧ VIII ✧

CRIMES IN THE INDIAN COUNTRY

It is to be deeply regretted that there are many whites on the
frontiers whose resentments are so keen against all persons
bearing the name of Indians, that they have adopted an opinion
that it is meritorious to kill them on all occasions. The Indians
again conceive themselves bound to retaliate every death by an
indiscriminate murder. With such dispositions on both sides it
it difficult if not utterly impracticable to prevent or even to
punish every irregularity.

> — Secretary of War Henry Knox to the
> Governor of Georgia, July 11, 1792

These laws designate the mode by which trespasses and
offences committed by the white people against the Indians,
as well as those committed by the Indians against the white
people, shall be punished. In making your people well acquainted with these laws, you will render them a great service;
for when they are informed what offences are punishable by the
law, they will take care not to commit such, and when trespasses are committed on them, they will know what reparation
they are to expect, and to whom application should be made to
obtain it. This will have a great effect, in promoting and preserving that friendship and good understanding between his
red and white children, which your father, the President, has
much at heart.

> — Acting Secretary of War George Graham
> to the Creek Delegation, March 17, 1817

When the white and red races met on the American frontier
there occurred innumerable violations of the personal and property rights of one group by members of the other. Murders and
robberies were all too frequent between peoples that were
nominally at peace, and some provision had to be made to preserve law and order or constant warfare would result. If private
retaliation was not to be the rule, then crimes had to be defined
and legal machinery established to mete out justice. These pro-

visions for criminal court procedure formed an essential part of the Indian intercourse acts.

However the sovereignty of the Indian nations might be defined, the establishment of an Indian Country outside the jurisdiction of the states created special problems. Here was another indication of the anomaly of the Indian situation; there were no formal precedents to go by. As in other elements of federal Indian policy, the legislation dealing with crimes in the Indian Country grew bit by bit, until in the act of 1834 the main pieces were finally assembled into one whole.[1]

The first measures taken to regularize criminal procedure in cases arising between Indians and white citizens were special articles included in the early treaties made by the United States with the various tribes. The first treaties, antedating the intercourse acts, which established peace with the Indians after the Revolutionary War, were filled with grand statements about receiving the Indians "into the favor and protection of the United States of America," about burying the hatchet forever, and about the re-establishment of universal friendship. But pains were taken, as well, to include specific provisions for the apprehension and punishment of criminals. Indians or others taking refuge among them who committed murder or other serious crimes against any citizen of the United States were to be delivered up to American authorities by the tribe and punished according to the laws of the United States. If, on the other hand, a white citizen committed the crime against an Indian, he was to be punished just as though the crime had been against another white citizen, and this punishment according to some of the treaties was to be exacted in the presence of the Indians. A special section added the injunction that private retaliation was not to be practiced on either side.[2]

The early intercourse acts, in an attempt to guarantee respect for the treaties on the part of the whites, were concerned particularly with white criminals who committed crimes against the Indians in the Indian Country. The act of 1790 equated a crime against an Indian with the same deed committed against an inhabitant of one of the states or territories. The white of-

---

[1] For a thorough discussion of the legal aspects of criminal jurisdiction over Indians, see Cohen, *Federal Indian Law*.

[2] See, for example, the treaties with the Cherokees (1785), Choctaws (1786), Chickasaws (1786), Shawnees (1786), Wyandots (1789), and Creeks (1790), in Kappler, *Treaties*, pp. 8 ff.

fender was to be subject to the same punishment and the same procedure was to be followed as though the offense had been committed outside the Indian Country against a white. Procedures for apprehending, imprisoning, and bailing in such crimes were to follow the Judiciary Act of 1789.[3]

These basic provisions of 1790 were expanded in succeeding acts because, as Washington pointed out in his annual message of 1792, "more adequate provision for giving energy to the laws throughout our interior frontier, and for restraining the commission of outrages upon the Indians" were necessary. The bill that was introduced in response to the message contained much that the President wished for, but strong opposition developed to the section of the bill which provided for punishment of crimes committed in the Indian Country, the very heart of the measure if it were to bring an end to the outrages caused by the whites. It was argued that the cases were already provided for by treaties or by the laws of the states and that it would be an absurdity to enact them again. The law, furthermore, would operate unfairly by striking the whites without reaching out equally to the Indians. But wiser counsels carried the day; "If the Government cannot make laws to restrain persons from going out of the limits of any of the States, and commit murders and depredations," it was asserted, "it would be in vain to expect any peace with the Indian tribes."[4]

In the act approved on March 1, 1793, "murder, robbery, larceny, trespass or other crimes," were named, and a new section specified the proper courts to be used for offenses of all kinds against the act. Jurisdiction was given to the superior courts of the territories and to the circuit courts of the United States in whose area the offender was apprehended or first brought. Procedure was to be the same as if the crime had been committed within the proper jurisdiction of the court. For noncapital cases the same jurisdiction was given to the county courts of the territories and the district courts of the United States. The President and governors of the territories were authorized to apprehend criminals in the Indian country and to bring them into the states or territories for prosecution. To expedite capital cases, the governors of the territories (for cases in their territories) and the President (for cases in the states) were authorized to issue

---

[3] *U.S. Stat.*, I, 138.

[4] Richardson, *Messages and Papers*, I, 127; *Annals of Congress*, 2 Cong., 2 sess., pp. 750–751 (Dec. 20, 1792).

commissions of oyer and terminer for special hearing of the cases.[5]

The incursions of the whites did not abate. On February 17, 1795, Washington sent another special message to the Senate, and a new bill was introduced to prevent depredations on the Indians. It provided that violators should be punished "in the same manner that enlisted soldiers, committing such an act or acts, without or contrary to orders, may be punished," but the House rejected the bill after the first reading. The House, however, passed resolutions of its own with similar purport. These proposals, considered as supplements to the trade and intercourse act, prescribed punishment by fine and imprisonment for any person found armed with hostile intent on any of the lands guaranteed to the Indians by treaty. An animated debate arose over suggested amendments which would make an exception in the case of citizens pursuing Indians who had recently committed murder or were carrying off captives or plunder. Without such amendment, the argument ran, the proposed measure would stop a man whose family had been murdered from pursuing the savages. Others argued that to allow the exception would destroy the frontier line altogether and that federal troops might as well be withdrawn if the settlers were to settle affairs with the Indians themselves. Debate raged over the resolution, until it was finally agreed to put a limit on the distance that pursuers would be allowed into the Indian Country. A bill was brought in with an amendment worded as follows: "unless it shall be in continuation of a pursuit (not approaching nearer than five miles to any Indian town) of the particular Indians who shall have recently committed murder, or may be carrying off captives." But in the end, after all the talk, the bill failed to pass in the Senate.[6]

The failure of this bill left the problem still to be solved. The President bluntly told Congress in his annual message in December, 1795: ". . . the provisions heretofore made with a view to the protection of the Indians from the violences of the lawless part of our frontier inhabitants, are insufficient. It is demonstrated that these violences can now be perpetrated with impunity, and it can need no argument to prove that unless the murdering of Indians can be restrained by bringing the murderers to

[5] U.S. Stat., I, 329–331.
[6] Sen. Jour., 3 Cong., 2 sess., pp. 160, 164, 170, 171, 184; Annals of Congress, 3 Cong., 2 sess., pp. 1259–61 (Feb. 27, 1795); House Jour., 3 Cong., 2 sess., pp. 344, 346, 349, 350, 351, 352.

condign punishment, all the exertions of the Government to prevent destructive retaliations by the Indians will prove fruitless
and all our present agreeable prospects illusory." [7]

Acting on Washington's recommendation, the Congress wrote
into the intercourse act of 1796 detailed provisions for restraining outrages on both sides. Section 6 of the law decreed the death
penalty for anyone convicted of going into Indian territory and
there murdering an Indian. Under section 4 robbery, larceny,
trespass, and other crimes committed against the person or property of a friendly Indian in the Indian Country — or even being
in the Indian Country with a hostile intention — subjected the
whites to top penalties of a one hundred dollar fine and twelve
months' imprisonment. Furthermore, if the property of an Indian
was taken or destroyed, the offender was to pay the Indian twice
the just value of the property, and if the offender himself could
not pay at least the value of the property, the United States
guaranteed to pay it out of the Treasury. These payments depended on the proviso that the Indian and his tribe did not seek
private revenge or satisfaction. Section 14 dealt with cases in
which Indians crossed over the boundary line and committed
murder or other outrages or stole or destroyed white property.
The injured parties were to report to the superintendent or agent,
who in turn would make application to the tribe for satisfaction.
If satisfaction was not forthcoming within eighteen months, the
President was authorized to take further action. In the case of
property losses, if the Indians did not make good the injury, the
President was authorized to deduct the sum from any annuity
due the Indians. Again, these provisions had no effect if the
whites sought private satisfaction. Court jurisdiction was similar
to that in the act of 1793, but in 1800 a supplementary act provided that, except for murder or other capital offenses, a person
apprehended in the Indian Country for any violation of the
intercourse act could be taken by the military officer who had
him in charge to "some one of the justices of the inferior or
county court of any county nearest to the place of his arrest."
These sections of the 1796 law were re-enacted with little change
in the temporary act of 1799 and in the permanent act of 1802. [8]

It should be noted that section 14 applied only to Indians

---

[7] Richardson, *Messages and Papers*, I, 185.
[8] *U.S. Stat.*, I, 470–473, 744–748, II, 39–40, 141–145. The act of 1802 reduced the time allowed the Indians for making satisfaction from eighteen to
twelve months.

who might pass "across the said boundary line, into any state or territory inhabited by citizens of the United States," and there murder or steal. These early laws made no attempt to legislate against Indians who injured whites *within* the Indian Country itself. Many of the treaties provided for such cases, but without statutory provision there was a loophole that needed to be plugged. When Henry Clay in 1810 introduced a bill in the Senate to provide for such cases, no action was taken on it. Not until the law of March 3, 1817, which provided for crimes in the Indian Country that were not specifically covered by the intercourse acts, did Congress act. Now if "any Indian or other person" committed a crime in the Indian Country which would be punishable in any place "under the sole and exclusive jurisdiction of the United States," he was to suffer the same punishment as if the crime had been committed in such a place. The superior courts of the territories and the United States circuit courts were given jurisdiction over all these cases.[9]

It will be seen at once from this brief résumé that the United States was determined to provide an adequate judicial system for the Indian Country and that the Indians were to be treated with equally scrupulous justice as the whites. In practice, however, there were serious discrepancies. It was the problem again of getting the legal machinery to work with smooth precision. In the early days the universal resort to legal procedures to gain satisfaction and justice which the laws envisioned simply did not obtain. The legislators had in mind the border incursions made by the aggressive whites in eastern Tennessee and the retaliatory raids by the Cherokees and Creeks, and they hoped to prevent on the other frontiers the almost continual state of border warfare that existed for some years along the Tennessee River and its tributaries. Serious chronic disturbances, however, were solved by crushing defeats of the Indians and their removal to lands farther away rather than by a strict enforcement of the laws.

❧

The laws, however, were by no means completely ineffective. Against Indian criminals they were invoked again and again. If an Indian committed a crime against a white — and murder was

---

[9] *Sen. Jour.*, 11 Cong., 2 sess., p. 472; Original bill (S 37), 11 Cong., 2 sess., March 29, 1810; *U.S. Stat.*, III, 383. The provisions of the act of 1817 were incorporated into the act of 1834. The transmission of the 1817 law to the frontier seems to have been unusually faulty. Judge James D. Doty in Michigan Territory did not know of its existence until 1827. Smith, *James Duane Doty*, p. 86.

the offense foremost in mind — the criminal was demanded from the tribe for punishment by the United States. The Indian tribes were recognized as quasi-sovereign nations with jurisdiction over their own members and the usual stipulation of the treaties called for this indirect apprehension of the Indian criminals. If the accused Indian was not delivered up, a military expedition was sent to apprehend him or hostages were seized and held until the criminal appeared. The culprit was guarded by the federal troops and turned over by them to a civil court in a nearby territory or state for trial. If there was no immediate regular session of the court, special commissions of oyer and terminer might be issued for the trials.

In general this procedure worked satisfactorily. However reluctant the Indian tribes might have been to turn over their members to the United States for punishment, they had a remarkably good record in doing so. How much of this was due to their sense of justice and how much to the threat or use of military force cannot be determined. On occasion, too, the agents manifested their appreciation of prompt action in surrendering criminals by presents to the chiefs or warriors who turned over the offenders. At Sault Ste. Marie in 1825, the agent richly rewarded a Chippewa who had persuaded a murderer to surrender and confess. "I have rewarded this noble act," the agent wrote, "by conferring the President's medal upon the deliverer, and investing him with the powers of a chief in his nation. I have also presented to him a small invoice of Indian goods purchased expressly for this purpose, which cannot but prove extremely valuable to him. These little rewards, while they will have a tendency to excite him and his companions to further acts of this kind, will be amply sufficient to prove to him that our government is ever as ready to reward a good, as to punish a bad action." [10]

Personal quirks of the judges or misunderstandings of the import of the laws, however, might cause the procedure to collapse. Such was the case of two Iowa Indians who were tried in St. Louis in 1809. The Indians had been indicted and brought to trial for the murder of a white man in the Indian Country. Governor Meriwether Lewis of Louisiana Territory issued a special commission for a court of oyer and terminer and the Indians were tried and found guilty. Then, to the surprise and

[10] Henry R. Schoolcraft to Lewis Cass, June 27, 1825, in IA LR, Michigan Superintendency; Henry Dearborn to Benjamin Hawkins, June 2, 1802, in SW IA LS, vol. A, pp. 217–218.

dismay of Lewis, the counsel for the Indians moved for arrest of judgment and Judge John B. C. Lucas sustained the motion and threw the case out on the grounds of lack of jurisdiction of the court. He argued that offenses committed on Indian lands by Indians were not punishable in the territorial court because the law of 1802 directed that satisfaction be obtained from the tribe. Lewis violently disagreed with Lucas, but he could not override the court's decision.[11]

The act of 1817 cleared away whatever obscurity there may have been about the jurisdiction of the courts in such cases, but the application of English modes to the Indians caused other trouble. The Indians could not understand the complexity and length of the proceedings, and many men wise in the ways of the frontier were convinced that both justice to the Indians and the status of American authority would fare better under some sort of military trial and execution. The government in Washington, nevertheless, was adamant in maintaining its adherence to civil legal forms.

The procedure can be seen in the case of Winnebago Indians who murdered two soldiers at Rock Island in 1820. Colonel Henry Leavenworth, the regimental commander at Fort Snelling, immediately set out for Fort Armstrong. He had little patience with the slow-turning wheels of justice as required by the laws and wanted to raise a body of Sacs and Foxes to assist him in seizing the Winnebago murderers or at least some hostages. The colonel, however, was persuaded to follow the authorized procedure of making a formal demand for the criminals from the tribe. He made his demand in council with the Indians and retained four chiefs as hostages. Sixteen days later the murderers were turned over to him. Leavenworth's impulse was to shoot them on the spot, convinced as he was that such summary punishment was the only procedure the Indians understood. But his better judgment led him to await directions from the secretary of war, who vetoed the plan and directed that the provisions of the intercourse act for trial and punishment by the civil authorities be followed. So Leavenworth grudgingly followed the legal forms, held a preliminary hearing, and then sent the Indians down the Mississippi for trial in Illinois. Here the Indians were convicted and sentenced to be executed.[12]

[11] Lewis to James Madison, Aug. 27, 1809, and enclosures, in *Territorial Papers*, XIV, 293–312.
[12] I follow here my discussion of the case in *Broadax and Bayonet*, p. 85.

A somewhat similar case occurred in Arkansas Territory in 1824 after a party of whites was murdered by the Osages. The Indian agent, acting on instructions from Robert Crittenden, the acting governor, induced the Indians to attend a conference at Fort Gibson with Colonel Matthew Arbuckle, the commandant. The Indians surrendered five chiefs as perpetrators of the crime, who were confined in jail at Little Rock to stand trial at the next term of the superior court of the territory. Crittenden was convinced of the Indians' guilt and wanted to make examples of them. When the Indians were tried in October, two of them were convicted and sentenced to be executed. The secretary of war, however, received conflicting opinions from the Arkansas frontier. Crittenden repeatedly insisted that if the Indians were not executed their release would be considered a guarantee "for the future impunity for the perpetration of the worst crimes," while Colonel Arbuckle urged pardon of the chiefs. The imprisonment dragged on as some final decision was awaited from the President. The Indians showed great impatience and told Crittenden that they would sooner suffer execution than protracted imprisonment. In the end, the President granted the two chiefs pardon — an "act of Compassion for them as his Red Children" in order to gain their gratitude and future good conduct. This was a fine example of the lack of dispatch that marked the juridical dealings with Indian criminals, but it also indicated the President's desire to be merciful.[13]

It is impossible to tell what percentage of Indian murderers were actually brought to trial. Certainly many murders went unpunished. In 1824 McKenney wrote to both Cass and Clark about the "alarming extent to which murders are committed in the North and the West" and urged them to take special action to prevent recurrence. The Indian agents were to warn the Indians that severe punishment from the United States would be their inevitable lot if they persisted in such conduct.[14]

Even when court action was initiated, the simple frontier communities frequently became tied up in the legal proceedings. To find suitable counsel, to call adequate witnesses, to empanel

[13] This case can be traced in the following documents: Crittenden to Calhoun, Sept. 12, 1824, in *Territorial Papers*, XIX, 692; Samuel C. Roane to Stephen Pleasanton, Oct. 22, 1824, *ibid.*, 712; Matthew Arbuckle to Charles J. Nourse, Nov. 4, 1824, *ibid.*, 719–720; Calhoun to Crittenden, Nov. 17, 1824, *ibid.*, 725; Crittenden to Calhoun, Dec. 25, 1824, *ibid.*, 737; Crittenden to Calhoun, Jan. 29, 1825, *ibid.*, 761–762; Barbour to Crittenden, March 29, 1825, *ibid.*, XX, 17–18.
[14] McKenney to Cass and Clark, Nov. 1, 1824, in IA LS, vol. 1, p. 214.

a proper jury — all this was a complicated and time-consuming process. The local courts had insufficient provisions for confining the prisoners while awaiting trial, it was not always easy to determine which court had proper jurisdiction, and collection of evidence was a difficult and thankless task. The United States district attorney for Michigan Territory met only frustration when he attempted to get a trial under way in 1833 for some Indians confined at Fort Winnebago under the charge of murder. No one assumed any responsibility for gathering evidence or securing witnesses for the special term of the circuit court that had been appointed to be held at Green Bay for the trial. Even the district attorney himself had little luck when he came from Detroit to see what he could do. Although the murders had been committed in plain sight and the chiefs had surrendered the suspects, no one could *prove* who was guilty. At length the Indians were discharged by the Green Bay judge on a writ of habeas corpus on application of the Indians' counsel, former judge James D. Doty.[15]

The whole process was expensive. In 1828, McKenney transmitted a packet of documents to the secretary of war on a case of Winnebago Indians tried before Judge Doty at Prairie du Chien. McKenney noted that the execution of the Indians was awaiting the President's decision as to clemency, but his main concern was not with the outcome of the trial, clemency to the Indians, or satisfaction to the whites, but rather with who was to pay the expenses of the trial. He submitted the expense account of the prosecuting attorney, Judge Doty's account for his special services (the Indians were tried at a special court under a commission of oyer and terminer), and the bill for the counsel for the prisoners. These should be paid, he insisted, by the State Department as arising out of judicial expenditures in Michigan Territory, since the law made no provision for such costs to be charged against the Indian Office or, for that matter, the War Department.[16] Such mundane considerations as the costs of the trial could seriously hamper the execution of justice under the intercourse acts.

It was not the expenses, however, that disturbed the frontier

[15] Doty to Secretary of War, July 22, 1825, in IA LR, Michigan Superintendency; Daniel LeRoy to Cass, Sept. 4, 1833, *ibid.*, Prairie du Chien Agency; John Robb to LeRoy, Oct. 9, 1833, in IA LS, vol. 11, p. 227; D. Goodwin to Cass, July 1, 1834, in IA LR, Prairie du Chien Agency.

[16] McKenney to Peter B. Porter, Oct. 27, 1828, in *Territorial Papers*, XI, 1207–08.

military commanders, upon whose shoulders fell most of the responsibility in the cases — the apprehending of the criminals and their delivery to a civil court. What irked them was the slowness and inconvenience of the procedure and the unpredictability of the outcome. Aware as they were of the importance of impressing the Indians with the rigors of American justice and power, they looked with disfavor upon any course of action which the Indian might interpret as a sign of weakness. That was why Colonel Leavenworth in 1820 urged immediate execution of the Winnebagoes who murdered the soldiers at Rock Island. He did not want the Indians to think that the United States was in any way afraid of the Winnebagoes. Even after he had been dissuaded from shooting the murderers on his own authority, he continued to demand a speedy execution of the sentence. "It would have been better to have *executed* them & *then have tried them* — If they are *tried* they must be *executed* or we shall feel the weight of the Winebago Tomahawk." [17]

Colonel Josiah Snelling, who succeeded Leavenworth on the northwest frontier, was of the same mind. He wanted to throw out the legal procedures of white civilization and punish Indian offenders on the spot. This sort of action the Indians could understand and it would be effective in checking their depredations, but the government refused to modify the policy of treating the Indians on a par with the whites, as far as legal forms were concerned. All along the frontier the army officers were engaged in seeking out criminals in the Indian Country, confining them in the post guard houses, and then sending them under military guard to the civil authorities for trial.[18]

৯⇒

Crimes against the Indians, on the other hand, were so numerous and widespread that their control by judicial means proved impossible. The laws, of course, were on the books and were gradually made more explicit. If the offenses were committed within a territory or a state, the criminal code of that civil jurisdiction sufficed. Within the Indian Country offenses of whites against Indians were punishable in federal courts when the offenses were specified in the federal statutes. The intercourse acts,

---

[17] Leavenworth to Daniel Parker, June 10, 1820, in SW LR, L-12 (14), 1820.
[18] Snelling to Lawrence Taliaferro, Oct. 19, 1824, in Lawrence Taliaferro Papers in the Minnesota Historical Society Library; Prucha, *Broadax and Bayonet*, pp. 86–87.

as we have seen, provided that crimes in any of the states or territories against a white citizen should also be considered crimes if committed in the Indian Country against an Indian.

The frequency of offenses committed against Indians by the frontier whites — among which outright murder was commonplace — was shocking. It was often a question of who was more aggressive, more hostile, more savage — the Indian or the white man. The murders and other aggressions of the whites against the Indians provided one of the great sources of friction between the two races. The problem was clearly seen by the committee of the Continental Congress that reported on Indian relations in July 1787. For the Northwest Territory, which was still without a system of civil laws, the committee recommended that no one be admitted to the new territory for a year without a special permit, that federal troops seize and expel unauthorized intruders and punish with forty stripes those who returned, and that persons committing crimes be tried by court martial. It urged the states bordering on the Indian Country to execute strictly their laws designed to prevent the white citizens from wrongfully invading the rights of the Indians.[19]

The laws and treaties were not effective in themselves, and the lack of enforcement made a mockery of the statutes. The typical frontier community could not be brought to convict a man who injured or murdered an Indian. And confusion as to the status of the federal courts in the territories delayed effective action. One of the federal judges in the Territory South of the Ohio complained in 1791 that there were no United States district attorneys and no courts with federal jurisdiction to prosecute and try violators of Indian treaties. "If the mode of bringing to trial, those who have injured Indians, rests with the people at large," he warned, "the consequence will be the agressors will go unpunished." [20]

North of the Ohio the situation was equally serious, as the white settlers attacked the Indians with violence and offered bounties for Indian scalps. Raiding parties came across the Ohio from Kentucky upsetting the precarious peace which Governor Arthur St. Clair was trying to maintain in the Northwest Territory since the defeat of the Indians by General Wayne. Even Indian prisoners under custody of the civil authorities were not

---

[19] Report of July 26, 1787, in *Territorial Papers*, II, 56–58. The recommendations came to nothing, but they indicate the seriousness of the frontier situation.
[20] David Campbell to Washington, Nov. 9, 1791, *ibid.*, IV, 101–102.

secure from the vengeance of the whites. In one well-reported case from the Illinois country in 1795 two Indian prisoners were taken from their guards and openly murdered. Governor St. Clair did what he could to bring the murderers to justice, but without effect. A court was held in Kaskaskia and compelling evidence was presented to the grand jury, which refused to indict the offenders. When the court moved to Cahokia, St. Clair again had the matter brought up before a grand jury, without success. Another attempt was made, this time to indict them for manslaughter. Again, no action was taken.[21]

The disgrace of the situation was eloquently set forth by St. Clair in his address to the territorial legislature on November 5, 1800:

It has long been a disgrace to the people of all the States bordering upon the Indians, both as men and as Christians, that, while they loudly complained of every injury or wrong received from them, and imperiously demanded satisfaction, they were daily offering to them injustice and wrongs of the most provoking character, for which I have never heard that any person was ever brought to due justice and punishment, and all proceeding from the false principle that, because they had not received the light of the gospel they might be abused, cheated, robbed, plundered, and murdered at pleasure, and the perpetrators, because professed Christians, ought not to suffer for it. What sort of Christianity is this? . . . But it would be criminal to conceal from you that the number of those unhappy people who have been killed since the peace at Greenville, in consequence of this diabolical principle, is great enough to give a very serious alarm for the consequences. A late attempt to bring to punishment a person who, with another, had killed two of the Six Nations, and wounded two of the children, in Trumbull county, proved abortive. Though the homicide was clearly proved, and that it was committed with deliberate malice, the perpetrator was acquitted. Under such circumstances, can it be expected that any people, civilized or savage, will remain at peace? [22]

In Indiana Territory Governor Harrison was again and again directed to see that justice was meted out to violators of Indian rights. In 1801 the secretary of war wrote: "The President requests that in cases of murder committed on any Indians, and the murderer escaping or concealing himself from justice, you will issue proclamations offering a handsome reward for the

[21] William H. Smith, ed., *The Life and Public Services of Arthur St. Clair . . . With His Correspondence and Other Papers* (2 vols., Cincinnati, 1882), II, 327–329; Anthony Wayne to St. Clair, June 5, 1795, *ibid.*, 374; St. Clair to the Secretary to State, 1796, *ibid.*, 396–397.
[22] *Ibid.*, 503.

apprehension of the offender, and use every means in your power for apprehending and bringing him to justice." Two and a half years later the governor was reminded again to be careful of the rights of the Indians.[23]

Letters and directions and official proclamations, even when backed by all the good will in the world, were no match for the singular Indian-hating mentality of the frontiersmen, upon whom depended conviction in the local courts. In Indiana the criminal law broke down, and Governor Harrison lamented the sad state of justice toward the Indians. In his message to the legislature in 1806 he unhesitatingly admitted that, although the laws provided the same punishment for offenses committed against Indians as against white men, "experience . . . shows that there is a wide difference in the execution of those laws. The Indian always suffers, and the white man never." At a later date, when an Indian was murdered by a white at Vincennes, Harrison was unable to get the murderer convicted. He caused the culprit to be apprehended and ordered a special court for the trial, but the man was acquitted by the jury "almost without deliberation." The Indians were much incensed and Harrison sought to quiet them by a present of seventy dollars worth of goods. The success of the whites in escaping punishment for their crimes against the Indians increased the difficulty, of course, of bringing erring Indians to trial, for the chiefs would refuse to turn over the offenders to the whites, preferring to punish them themselves if they were guilty. Not until 1824 was a conviction obtained in Indiana for the murder of an Indian by whites.[24]

The government made repeated efforts to bring white offenders to justice and no doubt the Indians were influenced by the good intentions of the United States, ineffective as they were in keeping white citizens in check. One measure taken to appease

[23] Henry Dearborn to Harrison, Dec. 22, 1801, in *Territorial Papers*, VII, 37–38; Dearborn to Harrison, July 2, 1804, *ibid.*, 204–205. Harrison's difficulties in bringing the murderers of Indians to punishment are related in Moses Dawson, *A Historical Narrative of the Civil and Military Services of Major-General William H. Harrison* (Cincinnati, 1824), pp. 31–33, 45–46.

[24] Philbrick, *Laws of Indiana Territory, 1801–1809*, p. clxxxiv; *Messages and Letters of Harrison*, I, 199–200; Harrison to Secretary of War, June 6, 1811, *ibid.*, 515. The details of the murder in 1824 of nine Indians — which "for cold blooded cruelty baffles all description, and in point of atrocity surpasses any thing that has ever disgraced the settlement of this Country" — and the difficulties involved in the guarding of the murderers, their trial, and execution are described in a series of letters from John Johnston, the Piqua agent, to Calhoun and Mc-Kenney, April 28, 1824, to July 16, 1825, in IA LR, Piqua Agency.

the Indians was to issue a proclamation in the name of the President, offering a handsome reward for the apprehension of the criminal. On the occasion of the murder of a Cherokee woman in 1801, the agent was directed to publish the proclamation in the Tennessee papers, to have copies of it stuck up in public places, and to use his "best endeavours to have its contents explained throughout the Cherokee Nation." When a Cherokee boy was shot by a white man on the frontier of North Carolina in 1804 and the Indians threatened immediate retaliation unless the murderer was taken up and punished, the President issued a similar proclamation, offering a five hundred dollar reward for the apprehension of the murderer.[25]

The ineffectiveness of such proclamations in actually bringing the criminals to justice in the frontier communities may be presumed, and the government more frequently resorted to compensation to the families of the murdered Indians by payment of a fixed sum of money or goods. The War Department directed the Indian agents to offer such pecuniary satisfaction in cases where the murderers could not be apprehended, in order to satisfy the families and show the willingness of the government to do justice. The payment was intended to quiet the Indians' complaints and was not intended to absolve the government from taking active measures to bring the murderers to trial. A sum of one to two hundred dollars for each Indian murdered by the whites was suggested by the secretary of war in 1803, and this amount was regularly given.[26]

How the system operated can be seen in a report sent to the War Department in 1819 by Return J. Meigs, the Cherokee agent.

A considerable number of Indians have been killed (generally speaking murdered) since I have been in this agency, & the Cherokees had a debt of eight lives (their phrase) against us when I came here in 1807.

Having communicated the, some recent, killing (or murdering) of indians to the then Secretary of War, I received instructions on that subject, & have acted on those instructions in sundry instances, by making presents to the relatives of those killed, &c on their solemnly promising to cease all thoughts of taking satisfaction as they call it, on the vile principle of retaliation. Those presents have in every instance had the desired effect by

[25] Dearborn to Meigs, Dec. 2, 1801, in SW IA LS, vol. A, p. 128; Proclamations dated Feb. 27 and March 1, 1804, ibid., pp. 443, 447.

[26] Dearborn to Meigs, May 30, 1803, ibid., pp. 352–353; Dearborn to Silas Dinsmoor, Sept. 7, 1803, ibid., p. 373; Dearborn to Dinsmoor, Jan. 7, 1804, ibid., p. 417; Calhoun to Thomas Forsyth, March 15, 1819, ibid., vol. D, p. 269; Calhoun to John McKee, July 21, 1819, in Territorial Papers, XVIII, 657.

[removing] all after complaint. I never gave presents to the full amount authorized — the sums given I called Peace Offerings, & graduated them according to my opinion of their attrociousness after due consideration of all the attending circumstances.[27]

Calhoun, although he approved the payment of such compensation in particular cases, objected to it as repugnant to the principles of the government, and he instructed the agents to inform the chiefs that the practice could not be continued in the future.[28]

৯৹

As the intercourse acts sought to maintain peace on the frontiers by guaranteeing satisfaction for murders committed by either party in order to prevent lawless private retaliation, so they attempted to eliminate conflict arising out of thefts. Here the chief concern was horses. Aside from outright murders and massacres by the Indians, there was nothing so likely to embroil the two races on the frontier as horse stealing.

Historians have described the ease and speed with which the Indians took to the horse, once it reached this continent with the European discoverers. The red man, it should be noted, was as adept at stealing horses as he was in converting them to his use. On the other hand, horses were of elemental necessity for the frontiersman. Without them he could not farm, he could not move about, he could not survive. The white's necessity and the Indian's cupidity and stealth made for an explosive combination that threatened to blow up one frontier after another. The petitions that reached the War Department regularly coupled horse stealing with murder as the scourge of living near the Indians. A memorial from Tennessee in 1791 reported that "the Indians kill[d] nine of Our Citizens and Stole fifty or Sixty head of Horses"; Governor Blount in 1792 hoped to induce the Indians "to desist from murdering and horse-stealing"; the militia officers of St. Clair Country in Illinois Territory complained of the depredations of the Indians "by stealing horses to a very considerable amount, plundering of other property, and by the massacre of many of the inhabitants." [29]

A flood of complaints welled up from all sections of the

[27] Meigs to Calhoun, Nov. 14, 1819, in SW IA LR.
[28] Calhoun to Meigs, Jan. 6, 1820, in SW IA LS, vol. D, p. 354; Calhoun to William Ward, July 8, 1823, ibid., vol. E, p. 462.
[29] Territorial Papers, IV, 72, 129, XVI, 188-189.

frontier. Governor Harrison, in urging the establishment of troops at Kaskaskia in December 1801, noted: "In the article of stolen horses, these depredations have become very frequent and vexatious — and my remonstrances to the chiefs have hitherto been attended with no good effect." The Osages in Missouri were notorious for their horse stealing, although General Clark appears to have had some success in getting back the horses through his demands upon the chiefs, and the Cherokees in Arkansas slipped into the ways that had caused trouble back in Tennessee.[30]

The settlers in the Territory South of the Ohio were especially plagued by the horse thieves. Their relations with the Cherokees were already at the breaking point and some action was needed to correct the evil. "Horse Stealing is a Subject of complaint (almost continual) to me without my being able to give any redress," Governor Blount wrote to the secretary of war in May 1792. "The only thing I can do is to give passports to the Sufferers to go into the nation in Search of their horses and letters to the chiefs, which as yet has never been attended with recovery. . . . Horse Stealing is the grand Source of Hostility between the white and red people in this district and I fear will actually produce it if not desisted from — It is a Subject on which the whites are very sore and with difficulty restrain themselves from taking what they call Satisfaction, that is from killing Some of the Indians." The situation was especially bad because of the ease with which the stolen horses could be disposed of. The Indians were not in the business by themselves but were urged on by unscrupulous whites who stood to profit by the sale of the illegal booty. The stolen horses would be conveyed through the Indian Country to the Carolinas or Georgia and sold there on the seaboard. It was a sizable operation — Blount asserted that at least five hundred had been stolen in 1792 in the Southwest Territory and later spoke of thefts as "without number" — and there was little hope of recovery. To demand the stolen horses from the chiefs did no good. Even if the chiefs discountenanced the thefts, which some thought likely, they did not exert enough authority over the young men of the tribes to prevent the horse stealing that was so profitable to the braves and to their white instigators.[31]

[30] Harrison to Jefferson, Dec. 30, 1801, *ibid.*, VII 42; George Peter to James Wilkinson, Sept. 8, 1805, *ibid.*, XIII, 232; Clark to Dearborn, Sept. 23, 1808, *ibid.*, XIV, 224–228; Clark to Dearborn, Dec. 2, 1808, *ibid.*, XIV, 242; Clark to William L. Lovely, Aug. 21, 1814, *ibid.*, XV, 54.

[31] Blount to Knox, May 5, May 16, and Nov. 8, 1792, *ibid.*, IV, 149, 151–152, 210; Blount to James Seagrove, Jan. 9, 1794, *ibid.*, 320.

It was necessary to get at the evil indirectly, first of all by stopping up the market for the stolen stock. If the Indians could not dispose of the horses by ready sale, there would be no further incentive for large-scale thefts. Such seems to have been the logic behind the provisions that were written into the intercourse acts, beginning with the act of 1793 and repeated in the subsequent acts of 1796, 1799, and 1802.

According to these laws, to purchase a horse from any Indian or from any white person within the Indian Country required a special license, and a special report of all horses purchased was to be made to the agent who issued the license. For every horse purchased or brought out of the Indian Country without a license, a fine of thirty to one hundred dollars was to be imposed. Furthermore, to plug another loophole, any person who purchased a horse which he knew had been brought out of the Indian Country without a license was to forfeit the value of the horse — one half to the informer and one half to the government. Although the law was aimed directly at the situation obtaining in the Cherokee country, it was not successful. Governor Blount continued to warn of dangers of hostility rising from the thefts, and recommended that special government agents be sent to the places in the Carolinas and Georgia where the horses were regularly sent for sale. He was taken to task, however, by the secretary of war, who was as much concerned about the encroachments of the whites onto Cherokee lands as about the theft of horses by the Indians. "The stealing of Horses by the Indians you have represented as a great Source of hostility," he answered Blount, "but of this we shall with an ill grace complain while we suffer our own Citizens to rob them of their Lands, especially, if, as you inform, our own Citizens encourage the practice of the Indians by purchasing the stolen Horses on the frontiers of South Carolina, North Carolina and Georgia and one Species of robbing affords as just ground of hostility as the other." It was a stern rebuke to the frontiersmen for their disregard of justice to the red men.[32]

There were no convictions under these licensing and forfeiture provisions of the intercourse acts, and the laws soon became a dead letter. The provisions died hard, however, and were continued almost by inertia. When Governor Cass and General Clark submitted their proposals in 1829 for new legislation to govern

[32] *U.S. Stat.*, I, 330; Blount to Knox, Nov. 10, 1794, in *Territorial Papers*, IV, 365; Timothy Pickering to Blount, March 23, 1795, *ibid.*, 392.

the Indian department and regulate relations with the Indians, they included in their draft the licensing provisions for buying horses that were found in the early laws. They commented in the margin, however: "These prohibitions and regulations concerning the purchase of horses from the Indians, in the Indian Country, are not perhaps very important, but they are continued here because they are found in the act of March 30, 1802." The House committee which drew up draft bills in 1834, out of which came the acts of that year, copied Cass and Clark except for some minor details. But somewhere between the committee's report and the final acts these outdated and useless provisions were scrapped.[33]

∽●∾

The intercourse act of 1796, while continuing the restrictions on the purchase of horses in the Indian Country, tried a new approach to the problem — one aimed less at justice than at preventing injustice from causing frontier disturbances. These were the guarantees in sections 4 and 14 of government compensation for theft of horses or other injuries if satisfaction could not be obtained from the guilty parties themselves, either by application to the tribe in the case of thefts by Indians or by recourse to the courts in the case of injuries perpetrated by whites.

Such provisions with regard to stolen horses had already been written into treaties with the Indians. The pattern was set in the treaty with the Cherokees at Philadelphia, June 26, 1794, in which the Cherokees, "in order to evince the sincerity of their intentions in future, to prevent the practice of stealing horses, attended with the most pernicious consequences to the lives and peace of both parties," agreed that for every horse stolen from the whites and not returned within three months, the sum of fifty dollars would be deducted from their annuity. In the new treaty with the Cherokees at Tellico in 1798, the provision was made mutual and the value of the horses was increased to sixty dollars. If a white man stole a horse from an Indian, the United States would pay the Indian proprietor sixty dollars in cash; if the white man were the victim, the amount would be paid to him out of the Indian annuity. Similar provisions were written into later treaties with other tribes.[34]

<hr/>

[33] *Sen. Doc.* 72, 20 Cong., 2 sess., ser. 181, p. 36; *House Rep.* 474, 23 Cong., 1 sess., ser. 263, pp. 28–29.

[34] Kappler, *Treaties*, pp. 34, 54, 75, 96–97, 161, 231.

The frontiersmen were quick to call for satisfaction under section 14 of the intercourse law, and they were restless until it was assured. The tinderbox situation in the Northwest Territory caused the acting governor there to submit claims without positive proofs as to which Indians were the thieves. "I trust legal ones may not be required," he wrote, "for they are almost impossible to be obtained in actual Thefts of horses by the Indians and the people will in Consequence assume the 'Lex Talionis' — indeed it is with extreme Difficulty I have hitherto prevented it, though I have been quite as lavish of my promises and assurances to Sufferers as the most liberal Construction of *the Law* authorises, or Mischief inevitably would have ensued, tending to produce another War, for which I am truly sorry to say there seems many white as well as red, Savages most ardently longing —" [35]

The War Department was eventually flooded with claims for stolen horses and occasionally for other property. The Department did not know just what to do about the claims, since it soon became apparent that they were being submitted on the least provocation without clear evidence that the Indians were the real culprits and without going through the procedure prescribed by the laws. Claims that came in from Indiana Territory languished in the files of the War Department until at length they were sent back to Governor Harrison with the instruction that since he was on the spot, he should sort out the evidence and make the awards. If his reports on the awards were not full or complete enough, however, the payments were held up in Washington, pending more information. The delay in settlement was sometimes excessive. Annuity payments to the Shawnees made in 1810, for example, were cut down by three hundred and ten dollars (out of a total annuity of a thousand dollars) because of awards rendered by Governor Harrison for horses stolen in the years 1796–1797. Conflict of jurisdictions, too, was a cause for confusion. Claims of inhabitants of Missouri who sought redress from the secretary of Missouri Territory for horses stolen by the Kickapoos were directed to Governor Edwards of Illinois Territory, on the grounds that the Kickapoos resided under his jurisdiction. Edwards himself hesitated to act because he thought the law required him to have previous instructions from the President.[36]

[35] Winthrop Sargent to the Secretary of State, May 23, 1797, in *Territorial Papers*, III, 468–469.
[36] Dearborn to Harrison, Nov. 24, 1803, and July 18, 1806, *ibid.*, VII, 157, 370; William Eustis to John Johnson, May 12, 1810, *ibid.*, VIII, 21; Dearborn

The War Department eyed the claims that reached it most critically. In 1804, when a claim came in against the Kickapoos for a stolen mare that amounted to practically the full annuity for the year, the secretary of war refused to approve the claim because he doubted that the horse was that valuable; at least, he thought, the exceptional value would have to be proved. "We ought to be as careful of the rights & property of the Indians as we are of our own Citizens," he wrote to Governor Harrison; "they have in many instances too much reason to complain of injustice on the part of our Citizens, and even of our public tribunals in cases of Indians being murdered by white persons; we ought therefore to be cautious how we give them new cause of Complaint." [37]

The great difficulty that faced the Department in an equitable adjustment of the claims was the vague manner in which they were supported. Again and again the claims were returned to the Indian agents for their judgments on the value of the evidence and for a stricter compliance with the provisions of the law. In some areas a practical investigation of the claims was made by the agents without any attempt to adhere strictly to legal forms, and the judgments of the agents were honored by the War Department. Return J. Meigs, the Cherokee agent, found it necessary to adopt a workable system of his own, which he explained to Secretary of War Eustis in 1811, after Eustis had returned a batch of claims to Meigs for his decision. "I have done the best in my power," Meigs wrote, "to decide them equitably: without being sure that in every case I have done so. . . . I believe it is impossible to distribute justice perfectly between the citizens and Indians; all that can be done, is to do the best that can be done. If in determining these claims, law & evidence is strictly adhered to, the greatest part of those brought forward by citizens would be thrown out, and it would be still worse with those brought by Indians, as their testimony is worth nothing in the eye of the law." Meigs told how in 1808 he had submitted a number of claims to the attorney general, Caesar A. Rodney, for his opinion. Rodney refused to decide on them because he felt that he would have

---

to William Hull, May 12, 1806, and May 28, 1808, *ibid.*, X, 56, 224; Petition to Frederick Bates, Aug. 3, 1810, *ibid.*, XVI, 115; Ninian Edwards to Dearborn, Sept. 1, 1810, *ibid.*, XVI, 114; Bates to Edwards, Aug. 2, 1810, in Thomas M. Marshall, ed., *The Life and Papers of Frederick Bates* (2 vols., St. Louis, 1926), II, 149–150.

[37] Dearborn to Harrison, July 2, 1804, in *Territorial Papers*, VII, 204–205.

to decide against them on legal grounds. Meigs then sat down with Henry Dearborn, the secretary of war, and the two men decided the cases — "in the same extra-judicial way that has now been in use for ten years past." The agent admitted there might be errors in the judgments, but he thought they were few. If the claims had all been thrown out for want of formal legal evidence, he saw inevitable reprisals on the frontier and the shedding of blood.[38]

The War Department, however, was not satisfied with such informal arrangement, and in 1818 it issued a special circular to the Indian superintendents and agents which outlined the precise action to be taken:

In case of injury to our citizens, after making the demand for a redress of the injury, as pointed out by the act, you will, if it is not redressed in the time specified, forward the claim properly testified, stating the time, place, and circumstance of the Injury complained of, to the 5th Auditor [of the Treasury] for his examination. Your opinion on the truth of the claim, and the amount of damage, will accompany your report.

In case of injury done to the Indians you will make a similar report, accompanied with your opinion, to this Department and to the District Attorney where the person who has done the injury resides; so that proper legal steps may be taken against the wrong doer, in order to make the reparation at his expense and not at the expense of the public, which should if possible, be avoided. No payment, except thro' the order of this Department, will be allowed.

I observe that, in most of the applications made for reparation of injury, no care is taken to comply with the requisitions of the act; but it is hoped, that, in future they will be made more regular, as none will be admitted but such as the law or treaties provide for, and in which the provisions of the act have been complied with.[39]

The fifth auditor performed the duty of checking the claims for a brief period only and then the duty again fell upon the War Department directly.[40] The secretary of war himself wrote to the

[38] Eustis to Meigs, Sept. 16, 1811, in SW IA LS, vol. C, pp. 97–98; Meigs to Eustis, Dec. 12, 1811, in IA FR, Cherokee Agency. These field office records contain considerable correspondence on claims, but the records of the formal claims themselves could not be found.

[39] Circular to superintendents and agents, Sept. 5, 1818, in SW IA LS, vol. D, p. 210.

[40] For action taken by the fifth auditor in approving and rejecting claims, see Stephen Pleasanton to Comptroller of the Treasury, Jan. 19, 1819, in Fifth Auditor's Office, Auditors' Reports, vol. I, National Archives, Record Group 217; Pleasanton to Calhoun, Feb. 9, 1819, in Fifth Auditor's Office, Letter Books, vol. I, p. 107, National Archives, Record Group 217.

agents, sometimes authorizing the payment of the claims but more often rejecting them for lack of proper procedure or insufficient evidence. "Great caution ought to be exercised in admitting claims of this sort," Calhoun wrote to the Choctaw agent in 1821, "either on the part of individuals of the whites or the Indians, unless upon the most positive evidence, otherwise, it is not unreasonable to suppose, that frauds will be frequently practised upon the government." [41]

When the Indian Office was established in 1824, the duty of checking the claims fell to McKenney, who faced the same troubles. "Claims of Indians against Citizens, under the 4th Sec. of the law of intercourse, and of citizens against Indians under the 14. Section, have accumulated so in Department as to become quite a burden to the files," he wrote soon after taking office, "and none or very few of them appear to have gone thro' any of the formalities requisite to constitute a legal claim against the Government." In 1828 the secretary of war issued another circular, directing adherence to the procedures outlined in the act of 1802, but four years later the commissioner of Indian affairs was still returning claims to William Clark because the stipulations of the law had not been followed. [42]

Faulty as the operation of the law was, it regularized this point of contact between the two races. By providing machinery for recovery of losses by peaceful means, it eliminated any justification for private retaliation and was largely successful in removing this friction, except on the rawest frontiers before they were amenable to juridical procedures. [43] In numerous cases the injured

[41] Calhoun to John McKee, Feb. 17, 1821, in SW IA LS, vol. E, p. 54. See also, as examples, Calhoun to Clark, Feb. 10, 1820, ibid., vol. D, p. 367; Calhoun to McKee, Feb. 16, 1821, ibid., vol. E, pp. 53–54; Calhoun to Richard Graham, July 12, 1821, ibid., vol. E, pp. 128–129; Calhoun to Clark, Dec. 9, 1823, ibid., vol. F, p. 15; Calhoun to Joseph McMinn, Dec. 18, 1823, ibid., vol. F, p. 20.

[42] McKenney to Benjamin F. Smith, Aug. 5, 1824, in IA LS, vol. 1, pp. 164–165; McKenney to Cass, Oct. 26, 1826, ibid., vol. 3, p. 202; Circular of James Barbour, March 25, 1828, ibid., vol. 4, p. 365; Elbert Herring to Clark, April 16, 1832, ibid., vol. 8, p. 296. Two other technicalities came into play. Claims, even if well attested, made against Indians to whom no annuities were due could not be paid under the intercourse acts. McKenney to Barbour, May 12, 1828, ibid., vol. 4, pp. 442–443. Nor did the law apply if the Indians stole white property within the Indian Country. McKenney to Hugh Montgomery, Feb. 5, 1830, ibid., vol. 6, p. 254.

[43] Some of the difficulties that occurred when the whites burst into Tennessee and Ohio were repeated when the whites came in contact with the Indians in Arkansas. The chief clerk of the War Department wrote to the governor of Arkansas in 1820: "The restless and predatory conduct of the Indians generally, within your superintendence is viewed with regret; to check which, the pro-

whites received compensation for their losses out of the annuities due the Indians, and in some cases — although apparently far fewer — the Indians were paid for injuries sustained from the whites.[44] It should be noted, however, that frequently large numbers of claims on both sides were summarily provided for in treaties made with specific tribes.[45]

Since it was generally admitted that offenses among the Indians within the tribe or nation were tribal matters that were to be handled by the tribe and were of no concern to the United States government, crimes committed by Indians against other Indians did not fall within the scope of the intercourse acts. The sovereignty of the Indian tribes, no matter how it might be circumscribed in other respects, was certainly considered to extend to the punishment of its own members. Up to the middle of the nineteenth century, indeed, there were no laws or treaty provisions which limited the powers of self-government of the tribes with respect to internal affairs. This hands-off policy rested upon the doctrine of tribal self-government. Indian tribal sovereignty existed long before the coming of the whites and did not depend upon federal legislation. Yet the United States formally indicated its respect for this tribal authority by embodying in the act of March 3, 1817, which established federal jurisdiction over Indian offenses, the declaration that the law did not extend "to any offense committed by one Indian against another, within any

---

visions of the law of intercourse will have to be rigidly enforced against all offenders. Lest you should not have a copy of it at hand, I herewith enclose one. You will see by it, that injured citizens by seeking or attempting to obtain private satisfaction or revenge, forfeit all claim upon the U.S. for indemnification. You will inform them of this, and caution them against proceeding to violence for the recovery of property stolen from them by the Indians." C. Vandeventer to James Miller, Sept. 12, 1820, in SW IA LS, vol. E, p. 11.

[44] It is impossible to determine the total amounts paid to Indians under section four of the intercourse act or to the whites under section fourteen. Indian Office and Treasury Department records do not provide complete information. It seems true to say that only a small percentage of the claims submitted were actually approved and paid. The fullest extant data on compensation claims is found in the record books kept by William Clark for the St. Louis Superintendency, in which he recorded the names of the injured parties, the objects stolen or damaged, the amounts claimed and recommended to be paid, etc. Copies of depositions made before justices of the peace in regard to losses are also preserved. See volumes 3 and 11, Records of the Superintendency of Indian Affairs, St. Louis, in the possession of the Kansas State Historical Society, Topeka.

[45] See, for example, article 6 of the treaty with the Quapaws, August 24, 1818, and article 5 of the treaty with the Cherokees, May 6, 1828, in Kappler, Treaties, pp. 161, 289–290.

Indian boundary." [46] Intertribal wars, however, were of continuing interest to the United States, for they could endanger the lives and property of white citizens on the frontier. Indian agents were directed to use whatever advice, persuasion, or presents might be necessary to prevent hostilities between tribes, but they were not to involve the United States on either side.[47]

[46] *U.S. Stat.*, III, 383. After the Mexican War several treaties abandoned the long-established distinction between internal and external affairs, and certain internal affairs were declared subject to federal control. In an act of March 3, 1885, certain specified crimes (notably murder, manslaughter, rape, assault with intent to kill, arson, burglary, and larceny) were brought under federal jurisdiction. Cohen, *Federal Indian Law*, pp. 46, 362–363.

[47] John Smith to William Clark, Sept. 8, 1810, in SW IA LS, vol. C, pp. 49–50; Calhoun to James Miller, June 29, 1820, *ibid.*, vol. D, pp. 458–459.

ᐫ IX ᐬ

CIVILIZATION AND REMOVAL

As it has ever been a favorite object with the government, to wean the Indians from their attachment to their barbarous customs and pursuits and turn their attention to the cultivation of the arts of civilized life, and gradually prepare them for a full participation and enjoyment with its citizens of all their most valuable moral and political rights, every thing, therefore, that has a tendency to promote these ends, will have the most decided approbation of this Department.

— Secretary of War Calhoun to the Creek
Agent, September 29, 1818

It is decidedly my opinion . . . that the plan of collocating the Indians on suitable lands West of the Mississippi, contains the elements of their preservation; and will tend, if faithfully carried into effect, to produce the happiest benefits upon the Indian race. I have not been able to perceive in any other policy, principles which combine our own obligations to the Indians, in all that is humane and just, with effects so favorable to them, as is contained in this plan.

— Secretary of War Barbour to Congressman
William McLean, April 29, 1828

The United States was interested in more than the mere avoidance of conflict. It attempted a positive program of aid to the Indians in order to persuade them to adopt the white man's civilization and way of life. As time passed and experience deepened, it became ever clearer that it was not possible for the two races — the one civilized, the other savage — to exist together in some sort of amalgam; the Indians must become civilized if they were to form an integral part of American society. This was a basic assumption which governed the thinking of the men who molded American Indian policy, remote from the brutal outlook of many frontiersmen, who would happily have accepted the total destruction of the aborigines.

The process of civilization was to be marked by — indeed it was to be brought about by — transition from the nomadic life of the hunter, who depended on the chase, to the settled life of the farmer, who depended on the surer sustenance provided by agriculture. It was assumed that as soon as the Indians learned the ways of agriculture and domestic manufacture they would see the advantages of this way of life over their old habits and readily, if not eagerly, adopt them. The Indians would then become absorbed into American society.

It was understood that the whites, already blessed with a high civilization, had a responsibility to bring these blessings to their less fortunate red brethren. In the early days of the Continental Congress the doctrine received formal approval in a resolution of 1776, which declared that "a friendly commerce between the people of the United Colonies and the Indians, and the propagation of the gospel, and the cultivation of the civil arts among the latter, may produce many and inestimable advantages to both," and it directed the commissioners for Indian affairs to investigate places among the Indians for the residence of ministers and teachers. Henry Knox, in his first long report on Indian affairs to President Washington admitted that the civilization of the Indians would be "an operation of complicated difficulty" which would require deep knowledge of human nature and patient perseverance in wise policies, but he did not doubt its possibility. It could begin, he thought, with an attempt to instill in the Indian a "love for exclusive property"; and to this end he recommended gifts of sheep and other domestic animals for chiefs and their wives and the appointment of persons to show the Indians how to manage them. Missionaries should be appointed to reside among the Indians, supplied with the necessary implements and stock for farming. In his instructions to General Rufus Putnam, who was sent in 1792 to treat with the Indians near Lake Erie, Knox directed him to make clear to the Indians the desire of the United States to impart to them "the blessings of civilization, as the only mean[s] of perpetuating them on the earth," and that the government was willing to go to the expense of teaching them to read and write and to practice the agricultural arts of the whites.[1]

President Washington was moved by similar considerations

[1] *Journals of the Continental Congress*, IV, 111; Knox to Washington, July 7, 1789, in *American State Papers: Indian Affairs*, I, 53–54; Knox to Putnam, May 22, 1792, *ibid.*, 235.

when he outlined an Indian policy for the new nation. He had asked Congress in 1791 to undertake experiments for bringing civilization to the Indians and in the following year repeated his plea. Congress, in the intercourse act of 1793, provided that "in order to promote civilization among the friendly Indian tribes, and to secure the continuance of their friendship," the President might furnish them with "useful domestic animals, and the implements of husbandry," as well as other goods and money. Temporary agents, too, could be sent to reside among them for the same purposes, and the sum of $20,000 a year was allowed for the gifts and payment of the agents. Washington, in his annual message of 1795, noted with pleasure that the results of the law seemed promising, and in the act of 1796 the provision was retained, although the appropriation was cut down to $15,000. This measure was continued in the intercourse acts of 1799 and 1802.[2]

Among the Cherokees, especially, the work got well under way, and the agents to that nation were told that it was a principal object of their work to introduce among the women the art of spinning and weaving and among the men "a taste for raising of stock and Agriculture." They were enjoined to operate a school to teach the women and were promised the spinning wheels and other apparatus necessary for producing linen and cotton cloth and the agricultural implements and live-stock essential for the farms. A specified sum of money was authorized to be spent on these projects.[3]

The civilization of the Indians by instructing them in agricultural and household arts received the vigorous support of Thomas Jefferson. In his first annual message to Congress he enthusiastically reported success in the program under the intercourse acts — that the Indians had already come to realize the superiority of these means of obtaining clothing and subsistence over the precarious resources of hunting and fishing, and that instead of decreasing in numbers they were beginning to show an increase. In 1803 Jefferson noted the growing reluctance of the Indians to make further cessions of land to the whites. To counteract this reluctance, the President advocated the establishment of trading houses that would get the Indians used to the white

[2] Messages of Oct. 25, 1791, Nov. 6, 1792, and Dec. 8, 1795, in Richardson, *Messages and Papers,* I 104–105, 127, 185; *U.S. Stat.,* I, 331, 472, 746–747, II, 143.
[3] James McHenry to Thomas Lewis, March 30, 1799, and Henry Dearborn to Return J. Meigs, May 15, 1801, in SW IA LS, vol. A, pp. 29–35, 43–49. The importance of these civilizing measures can be seen from the prominent position given to them in the long instructions to the agents.

man's goods and lead them away from their primitive life, but he proposed first of all that the United States encourage the Indians to abandon hunting and to apply themselves to raising stock, to agriculture, and to domestic manufacture — and thereby prove that less land and labor would support them better than their former mode of living. "In leading them thus to agriculture, to manufacture, and civilization; in bringing together their and our sentiments, and in preparing them ultimately to participate in the benefits of our Government," Jefferson concluded, "I trust and believe we are acting for their greatest good." [4]

The President reiterated these views freely in his "talks" to the Indians, for example, in his message to the Miamis, Potawatomies, and Weas on January 7, 1802: ". . . we shall with great pleasure see your people become disposed to cultivate the earth, to raise herds of useful animals and to spin and weave, for their food and clothing. These resources are certain, they will never disappoint you, while those of hunting may fail, and expose your women and children to the miseries of hunger and cold. We will with pleasure furnish you with implements for the most necessary arts, and with persons who may instruct how to make and use them." [5]

Jefferson's views were ardently promoted by his secretary of war, Henry Dearborn, who kept up a constant battery of instructions to the agents on the use of implements made available under the intercourse act. He wrote in the name of the President to the territorial governors of the Northwest Territory, Mississippi Territory, and Indiana Territory to encourage them to promote energetically the government's plan for civilizing the Indians, and he authorized the employment of blacksmiths and carpenters, who were necessary to keep the plows and other implements in working order.[6]

Dearborn expressed his optimism to the Creek agent in 1803:

The progress made in the introduction of the arts of civilization among the Creeks must be highly pleasing to every benevolent mind, and in my opinion is conclusive evidence of the practicability of such improvements

[4] Messages of Dec. 8, 1801, and Jan. 18, 1803, in Richardson, *Messages and Papers*, I, 326, 354–355.
[5] SW IA LS, vol. A, p. 143.
[6] Dearborn to William Lyman, July 14, 1801, and to Charles Jouett, Sept. 6, 1802, *ibid.*, pp. 92–93; Dearborn to William C. C. Claiborne, William H. Harrison, and Arthur St. Clair, Feb. 23, 1802, *ibid.*, p. 166. See also Dearborn to Silas Dinsmoor, May 8, 1802, in which the intentions of the government in its Indian policy are again clearly stated. *Ibid.*, pp. 207–208.

upon the state of society among the several Indian Nations as may ultimately destroy all distinctions between what are called Savages and civilized people. The contemplation of such a period however distant it may be is highly pleasing, and richly compensates for all our trouble and expense; and to those Gentlemen who have and shall be the individual agents in effecting such an honorable and benevolent system it must not only afford the most pleasant self approbation, but command the warmest plaudits of every good man.[7]

When word reached the War Department that one of the Indian agents was obstructing the work of civilization being carried on within his agency by a missionary establishment, he was warned that if he did not cease his opposition to the views of the government in this matter, he would be removed from his position.[8]

Jefferson, as he neared the end of his administration, saw in the state of Indian affairs a vindication of the policy of civilization. Those tribes who were "most advanced in the pursuits of industry" were the ones who were most friendly to the United States. The southern tribes, especially, were far ahead of the others in agriculture and the household arts and in proportion to this advancement identified their views with those of the United States.[9]

It is impossible to detail the full operation of the annual $15,000 authorized by the intercourse acts, for the Treasury Department kept no special account under that heading, and when the Senate in 1822 asked for information on the annual disposition of the fund, little was forthcoming from either the War Department or the Treasury. Secretary of War Calhoun, however, reported that he thought the principal expenditure had been made through the Cherokee, Creek, Chickasaw, and Choctaw agents for spinning wheels, looms, agricultural implements, and domestic animals.[10]

The annual fund provided by the intercourse acts for promotion of civilization among the Indians was not the only source from which the government could draw in providing plows and looms, blacksmiths and carpenters, for many of the treaties signed

[7] Dearborn to Benjamin Hawkins, May 24, 1803, *ibid.*, pp. 349–350.

[8] John Smith to William Wells, July 9, 1807, *ibid.*, vol. B, p. 324. For a full account of the case see Joseph R. Parsons, Jr., "Civilizing the Indians of the Old Northwest, 1800–1810," *Indiana Magazine of History*, LVI (1960), 208–213.

[9] Message of Oct. 27, 1807, in Richardson, *Messages and Papers*, I, 427–428.

[10] Calhoun to James Monroe, Feb. 21, 1822, and Report of William Lee, Feb. 19, 1822, in *American State Papers: Indian Affairs*, II, 326.

with the tribes also made provision for such aid. In the Treaty of New York with the Creeks in 1790, article XII provided that in order that "the Creek Nation may be led to a greater degree of civilization, and to become herdsmen and cultivators, instead of remaining in a state of hunters, the United States will from time to time furnish gratuitously the said nation with useful domestic animals and implements of husbandry," and the Treaty of Holston with the Cherokees in the following year contained the same provision. In a treaty with the Six Nations in 1794 the United States agreed to a perpetual annual expenditure of $4500 to purchase clothing, livestock, and agricultural implements for the tribes and to hire "useful artificers" for the benefit of the Indians. The Delawares in 1804 were promised a yearly sum "to be exclusively appropriated to the purpose of ameliorating their condition and promoting their civilization" plus the employment of a person to teach them how to build fences, cultivate the earth, and practice the domestic arts. In addition, the United States agreed to deliver draft horses, cattle, hogs, and agricultural implements. Similar arrangements were made with other tribes, and sometimes the tribes were allowed to choose between annuities in the form of goods or money or special aids for developing agriculture. Furthermore, provisions were often made for blacksmiths or other artificers and for teachers in agricultural or domestic arts.[11]

Abortive attempts were made in 1821 and 1822 to make the licensed traders responsible for promoting the agricultural advance of the tribes they served. A bill introduced in January 1821, while aiming primarily at the abolition of the factories and the tighter control of independent Indian traders, included special features to promote the civilization of the Indians. According to the bill, traders were to have fixed abodes on land leased from the Indians and were to set up blacksmith shops there for the Indians. They were to cultivate grain and fruit and raise domestic animals, sell seed and stock to the Indians, and induce the Indians to become cultivators and livestock breeders. Each trader was to pay an annual fee for his license, which was to be used to buy seed and stock for the Indians and to build mills for them. The bill, however, was not acted upon, and when it was reintroduced in January 1822, it again made no progress through the House.[12]

[11] Kappler, *Treaties*, pp. 28, 31, 36, 42, 70–71, 75, 93, 95, 186, 200.
[12] The 1821 bill is printed in *Annals of Congress*, 16 Cong., 2 sess., pp. 958–959 (January 25, 1821). *House Jour.*, 17 Cong., 1 sess., ser. 62, pp. 157, 543; Original bill (HR 41), 17 Cong., 1 sess., Jan. 17, 1822.

Encouragement in agriculture and household arts came also from the Indian factory system, especially under Thomas L. McKenney, who became superintendent of Indian trade in 1816. The factors were expected to be more than tradesmen; they were to be key men in spreading the gospel of agriculture and domestic arts as well, to be the source of supplies and information, and to furnish models of what could be done in taming the wilderness.[13]

As the years progressed and humanitarian concern for the Indians deepened, still other aid came from missionary groups, who established missions among the tribes and who by and large subscribed to the principle that there was little hope of Christianizing the savages without first building a foundation of stable civilized existence. The missionaries were agricultural agents as well as messengers of Christ's Gospel and their centers were model establishments and practical schools which augmented the work of the government.

A second phase of the civilization program — though not always distinct from the promotion of agriculture and spinning and weaving — was the establishment of schools for the Indian children. Here the missionary groups were indispensable. They were pioneers in the field of educating the Indians in the basic skills of reading and writing, and it was through them that the government acted when it came to encourage the work by special appropriations. Missionary work among the Indians began of course with the coming of the European discoverers in the sixteenth century, and throughout the colonial period there were noble attempts made to Christianize and educate the aborigines. Government aid and encouragement of such enterprises came slowly, however, although individuals in influential posts were able to do something to promote the work of education. Thus when the Presbyterian missionary Gideon Blackburn approached President Jefferson and Secretary of War Dearborn in 1803 about aid for a school among the Cherokees, he was warmly received and permitted to open his school. Although Blackburn was told that he could expect no compensation from the government for his services, the secretary of war nevertheless instructed the Cherokee agent to erect a school house and to give necessary aid to start the project, "which should not require more than two

[13] See, for example, McKenney to George C. Sibley, Oct. 21, 1816, in IT LS, vol. D, pp. 152–153.

or three hundred dollars for the first six months of its application." [14]

The establishment of schools among the Indians began with Protestant missionary groups, but there was little growth until government aid was provided. McKenney in August 1819 reported that he knew of only four schools for Indian children in the Indian Country — two among the Cherokees (a flourishing school of perhaps one hundred pupils at Brainerd, in Tennessee, supported by the American Board of Commissioners for Foreign Missions and a small school of five students conducted by the Moravians) and two among the Senecas, run by the Quakers. To this enumeration he added three schools for Indians outside the Indian Country (run by the Baptists, the Methodists, and the American Board of Commissioners for Foreign Missions) and several "minor and fugitive" schools among the southern tribes of which he knew neither the location nor the sponsoring groups.[15]

McKenney in his position as superintendent of Indian trade was an ardent advocate of schools for the Indian children. He carried on an extensive correspondence with individual missionaries and with missionary groups, and again and again recommended government aid in establishing schools for the Indians. In writing to Isaac Thomas, chairman of the House Committee on Indian Affairs in 1817, McKenney coupled a strong proposal for schools with his urgent recommendation that the factory system be extended.[16] McKenney's views were enthusiastically adopted by the committee, which reported a bill on January 22, 1818, to extend the factory system by the authorization of eight new factories and to provide schools for the Indians.

Your committee are aware that many plausible objections may be raised against the proposed measure; but we believe that all difficulties on this subject may be surmounted, and that the great object may be carried into practical effect. In the present state of our country, one of two things seems to be necessary: either that those sons of the forest should be moralized or exterminated. Humanity would rejoice at the former, but shrink with horror from the latter. Put into the hands of their children the primer and the hoe, and they will naturally, in time, take hold of the plough; and, as their minds become enlightened and expand, the Bible

[14] Dearborn to Meigs, July 1, 1803, in SW IA LS, vol. A, pp. 354–355; Dearborn to Gideon Blackburn, July 1, 1803, *ibid.*, pp. 355–356; Dearborn to Blackburn, Jan. 12, 1804, *ibid.*, pp. 422–423. Blackburn continued his school until 1810, when ill health and financial difficulties forced him to withdraw.
[15] McKenney to Calhoun, Aug. 14, 1819, in IT LS, vol. E, pp. 298–302.
[16] McKenney to Thomas, Dec. 14, 1817, *ibid.*, vol. D, pp. 201–209.

will be their book, and they will grow up in habits of morality and industry, leave the chase to those whose minds are less cultivated, and become useful members of society.

Great exertions have, of late years, been made by individuals and missionary societies in Europe and America; schools have been established by those humane and benevolent societies in the Indies, amongst the Hindoos, and the Hottentots; and, notwithstanding that superstition, bigotry, and ignorance have shrouded those people in darkness for ages, thousands of them have already yielded to instruction.

The Government has no such difficulties to encounter, no Bibles nor books to translate into foreign or other languages — only to establish some English schools. The experiment may be tried at a very small expense.

The committee believe that increasing the number of trading posts, and establishing schools on or near our frontier for the education of Indian children, would be attended with beneficial effects both to the United States and the Indian tribes, and the best possible means of securing the friendship of those nations in amity with us, and, in time, to bring the hostile tribes to see that their true interest lies in peace, and not in war. . . .[17]

The bill submitted by the committee proposed to use profits from the factory system to support the schools for the Indians both by directly endowing schools and by helping missionary societies to support their schools. The second provision was removed by amendment and a limit was set on the first of $10,000 annually, but the bill was still not passed. Perhaps it departed too much from the basic principle of the factory system, which specified that no profits were to be made out of the government trade with the Indians in order to undersell and gradually force out the petty traders.[18]

This was but a temporary delay, for the movement for some government aid to Indian schools continued to advance. President Monroe reasserted the need to civilize the Indians, and Congress gave his words serious attention. The special House committee reporting on the President's message in January 1819 praised the successful work being done by missionary societies among the Indians, but it asserted that "a more energetic and extensive system is necessary, to improve the various Indian tribes, in agriculture, education, and civilization." On the same date the House Committee on Indian Affairs reported a bill which would have authorized the President to select such tribes as he

[17] Report of Jan. 22, 1818, in *American State Papers: Indian Affairs*, II, 150–151.
[18] *House Jour.*, 15 Cong., 1 sess., ser. 4, p. 169; Original bill (HR 50), 15 Cong., 1 sess., Jan. 22, 1818.

thought best prepared for the change and to use whatever means seemed proper to civilize them. On February 19 the Senate introduced its own version of a civilization bill, which replaced the House bill and which passed with little opposition.[19]

The "Act making provision for the civilization of the Indian tribes adjoining the frontier settlements" became law on March 3, 1819. It appropriated $10,000 annually to be used at the President's discretion to further the civilization of the tribes wherever practicable by employing "capable persons of good moral character, to instruct them in the mode of agriculture suited to their situation; and for teaching their children in reading, writing, and arithmetic." The President and the secretary of war decided not to use the fund directly, but rather to spend it through the "benevolent societies" that had already or would in future (under the encouragement of the fund) establish schools for the education of Indian children. Secretary of War Calhoun issued a special circular which invited interested individuals or groups to apply for a share in the fund, submitting information about their resources, the kind of education they proposed to impart, and the number of students to be instructed.[20]

The civilization fund was not without its critics. Congress repeatedly asked for reports on the functioning of the program and passed resolutions inquiring into the expediency of repealing the act. On May 4, 1822, Congressman Thomas Metcalfe of Kentucky sought to eliminate the measure altogether by amendments that he proposed to the supplementary intercourse act of 1822. He inveighed against the civilization fund on the grounds of inutility and cited numerous historical examples to show that all such attempts to civilize the Indians had ended in failure. Despite such attacks the annual appropriations continued, and the House Committee on Indian Affairs in 1824 reported enthusiastically on the program. The committee noted the twenty-one schools then in existence, all but three of which had been established after the act of 1819, and the more than eight hundred pupils, "whose progress in the acquisition of an English education exceeds the most sanguine expectations that had been formed." It was the opinion of the committee that the large contributions

[19] *House Doc.* 91, 15 Cong., 2 sess., ser. 22; *Sen. Jour.*, 15 Cong., 2 sess., ser. 13, pp. 288, 289, 323; *House Jour.*, 15 Cong., 2 sess., ser. 16, pp. 188, 331, 333, 339.

[20] *U.S. Stat.*, III, 516–517; Report of Calhoun, Jan. 15, 1820, in *American State Papers: Indian Affairs*, II, 200–201; Circular of Sept. 3, 1819, *ibid.*, 201.

made towards the schools by the missionary societies had been stimulated by the annual appropriation of the government.[21]

When McKenney was appointed to head the Office of Indian Affairs in 1824, he continued to fight aggressively for the program. One of his early acts was to send a blistering circular to the Indian superintendents and agents reminding them of the solicitude of the government for the improvement of the Indians by means of the school system and the $10,000 annual appropriation for its support. It was their duty, McKenney declared, to *"sanction, and second,* this plan of renovating the morals and enlightening and improving these unfortunate people." Those who opposed the program were opposing the government itself, paralyzing the government's program, and bringing it into contempt in the eyes of the Indians, whom it was designed to benefit. McKenney continued to be enthusiastic about the program and its salutary effects. In November 1824 he reported thirty-two schools in operation, with nine hundred and sixteen children, and he accepted the optimistic reports of the school directors as proof that there was no insuperable difficulty standing in the way of a complete reformation of the life of the Indians. A year later he had still lost none of his enthusiasm, and in 1826 he recommended that the annual allotment be increased, so great were the benefits being derived from the schools. The annual reports of the commissioners show a steady increase in the number of schools, the enrollment of Indian pupils, and the religious groups taking part. These groups, encouraged by the government aid, devoted more and more from their private funds to the enterprise.[22]

The direct appropriations of Congress for schools were aug-

---

[21] *House Jour.,* 16 Cong., 1 sess., ser. 30, pp. 413, 452; *House Jour.,* 17 Cong., 1 sess., ser. 62, pp. 94, 102, 115, 126, 175, 258; *House Jour.,* 18 Cong., 1 sess., ser. 92, pp. 119–120; *Annals of Congress,* 17 Cong., 1 sess., pp. 1792–1801 (May 4, 1822); Report of March 23, 1824, in *American State Papers: Indian Affairs,* II, 457–459.

[22] Circular of Aug. 7, 1824, in IA LS, vol. 2, p. 170; McKenney to Calhoun, Nov. 24, 1824, in *American State Papers: Indian Affairs,* II, 522–524; McKenney to Barbour, Dec. 13, 1825, in IA LS, vol. 2, pp. 298–306; McKenney to Barbour, Nov. 20, 1826, in *American State Papers: Indian Affairs,* II, 671–672. The annual reports of the head of the Office of Indian Affairs, included in the annual reports of the secretary of war, contain data on the Indian schools. A summary of the data can be found in Alice C. Fletcher, *Indian Education and Civilization* (*Sen. Exec. Doc.* 95, 48 Cong., 2 sess., ser. 2264, Washington, 1888), p. 197. In 1824 the missionary schools received $12,708.48 from the government, $8,750.00 from Indian annuities and under treaty provisions, and $170,147.52 from private contributions. In 1825 the figures were $13,620.41, $11,750.00, and $170,700.44, respectively. *American State Papers: Indian Affairs,* II, 669.

mented by provisions in the treaties with various tribes, for after the act of 1819 had stimulated the movement for Indian schools, numerous treaties contained provisions to aid in the education of the young. The Treaty of Doak's Stand with the Choctaws in 1820 provided that some of the land ceded by the Indians was to be sold by the President in order to provide funds for the support of the Choctaw schools on both sides of the Mississippi. Treaties with the Chippewas and with the Potawatomies in 1826 authorized an annual grant for schools, to be continued as long as Congress thought proper. And the policy continued, with sizable sums due each year under treaty arrangements for the Indian schools.[23]

Although the agricultural and educational program did not slacken, there gradually developed another program for the "preservation and civilization" of the aborigines. This was the policy of removal.

Despite the optimism of supporters of the civilization fund, an uncomfortable fact was becoming increasingly obvious: the contact of the Indians with white civilization had deleterious effects upon the Indians that far outweighed the benefits. The efforts at improvement were vitiated or overbalanced by the steady pressure of white vices, to which the Indians succumbed. Instead of prospering under white tutelage, the Indians were degenerating and disappearing.

It cannot be denied that the land greed of the whites forced the Indians westward and that behind the removal policy was the desire of eastern whites for Indian lands and the wish of eastern states to be disencumbered of the embarrassment of independent groups of aborigines within their boundaries. This selfish drive can explain the radical position and demands of a George M. Troup or a Wilson Lumpkin, and the legislatures of Georgia or Alabama. We know, too, that American frontiersmen developed a peculiar Indian-hating mentality, which, combined with avarice for the Indian lands, made many hope and work for

[23] Kappler, *Treaties*, pp. 193, 270, 274, 282, 287, 304, 307. Harmon, *Sixty Years of Indian Affairs*, pp. 380–381, reprints tables showing the amounts available in 1834 and 1845 for civilization promotion under various treaty arrangements. For the later history of government aid to schools for the Indians, see Fletcher, *Indian Education and Civilization*, and Evelyn C. Adams, *American Indian Education: Government Schools and Economics Progress* (New York, 1946).

the day when the Indians would disappear. But these selfish economic motives were not the only force behind the removal policy. That men as knowledgeable in Indian ways and as high-minded as Thomas L. McKenney, Lewis Cass, and William Clark were long-time and ardent promoters of Indian removal should give us pause in seeing only Jacksonian villainy behind the policy. The promoters of the program argued with great sincerity that only if the Indians were removed beyond contact with whites could the slow process of education, civilization, and Christianization take place. Insofar as removal was necessary to safeguard the Indian, to that extent the intercourse acts had failed.

A dramatic shift in attitude can be seen in Thomas L. McKenney. His enthusiastic reports on the progress of the Indian schools and Indian civilization in general were replaced by more dismal reporting. The tour of the Indian Country that he made in 1827 opened his eyes to the degradation of the eastern tribes, and when asked to report in 1830 on the previous eight years of operation of the program of civilizing the Indians, he no longer considered salvation possible in the present location of the tribes. The condition of the Florida Indians he described as "in all respects truly deplorable. It is not known that they have advanced a single step in any sort of improvement; and as to the means of education, when offered to them, they were refused." The Indians in the Northwest, he reported, "pretend to nothing more than to maintain all the characteristic traits of their race. They catch fish, and plant patches of corn; dance, paint, hunt, get drunk, when they can get liquor, fight, and often starve." Their condition, however, was far better than that of the Creeks and better than most of the Choctaws. McKenney agreed that those Choctaws who had benefited by instruction were better off than they had been before. "But these were, to my eye," he said, "like green spots in the desert. The rest was cheerless and hopeless enough. Before this personal observation, I was sanguine in the hope of seeing these people relieved, and saved, where they are. But a sight of their condition, and the prospect of the collisions which have since taken place, and which have grown out of the anomalous relations which they bear to the States, produced a sudden change in my opinion and my hopes." [24]

The proposal to move the Indians to a permanent reservation west of the Mississippi, which McKenney now so warmly es-

[24] Report of McKenney, March 22, 1830, in *Sen. Doc.* 110, 21 Cong., 1 sess., ser. 193, pp. 2–3.

poused, was not new and had been gradually gaining momentum in governmental circles.[25] It had originated with Thomas Jefferson in 1803, when the addition of the vast Louisiana Territory created conditions that would make removal feasible. Before the end of Jefferson's administration there was gentle pressure put upon the Cherokees — to introduce to them at least the notion of exchanging their present country for lands west of the Mississippi. The Indian agent was directed by the secretary of war to sound out the chiefs on the idea and to let the subject be talked about the nation, so that the prevailing opinion could be ascertained. Those who chose to live by hunting were to be especially encouraged to emigrate, but care was to be taken that the removal was the result of their own inclinations, and not the result of pressure.[26]

Although some of the Cherokees did go west, at first to hunt and then to settle, there was no exchange of lands until the treaty of 1817, in which provision was made for the Cherokees who had gone to the Arkansas River. The problems of the War of 1812 had crowded out any serious thought of orderly emigration of the tribes, but with Monroe's administration, the proposal began to be agitated again in earnest. In January 1817 the Senate Committee on the Public Lands reported on the expediency of making an exchange of lands with the Indians and proposed that an appropriation be made to enable the President to enter into treaties with the Indians for the purpose of exchanging lands. The aim of the measure would be to obviate the "irregular form of the frontier, deeply indented by tracts of Indian territory," to consolidate the settlement of the whites, and to remove the Indians from intimate intercourse with the whites, an intercourse "by which the civilized man cannot be improved, and by which there is ground to believe the savage is depraved." [27]

James Monroe and his secretary of war, John C. Calhoun, worked earnestly for a change in the enduring situation of the Indians. The anomaly of large groups of savage or semicivilized tribes surrounded by civilized whites struck them with special force. The solution was either removal to the open West or a change from the hunter state. In a letter to Jackson in October

---

[25] For a detailed history of the removal policy, see Annie H. Abel, "The History of Events Resulting in Indian Consolidation West of the Mississippi River," *Annual Report of the American Historical Association for the Year 1906*, I, 233–540.

[26] Secretary of War to Meigs, March 25, 1808, in SW IA LS, vol. B, p. 364; Secretary of War to Meigs, May 5, 1808, *ibid.*, p. 377.

[27] *Sen. Jour.*, 14 Cong., 2 sess., p. 95; Report of Senate Committee on Public Lands, Jan. 9, 1817, in *American State Papers: Indian Affairs*, II, 123–124.

1817, Monroe asserted that "the hunter or savage state requires a greater extent of territory to sustain it, than is compatible with the progress and just claims of civilized life, and must yield to it." He returned to the same views in his annual message to Congress in December, adding that it was right that the hunter should yield to the farmer, "for the earth was given to mankind to support the greatest number of which it is capable, and no tribe or people have a right to withhold from the wants of others more than is necessary for their own support and comfort." The prickly question of land tenure would disappear if only the Indians could be removed beyond the Mississippi, and the War Department authorized its commissioners to make liberal offers to the eastern tribes in an attempt to induce them to accept willingly an exchange of lands. Monroe and Calhoun, as well as Jackson, were convinced that the good of the Indians demanded an end to their independent status within the white settlements and urged some action on Congress, but no general measure was immediately forthcoming.[28]

The removal question was then given a new and dangerous twist by special circumstances surrounding the Cherokees in Georgia (and to a lesser extent, the Creeks, Chickasaws, and Choctaws in Alabama and Mississippi). The Cherokees were settled within the boundaries of Georgia on lands which they had always held. These Indians were not nomads. They had a developed agricultural economy, able political leaders, and laws modeled on those of the whites. And — of great importance in the controversy — they had an abiding attachment to their lands and were determined to hold them at all costs, no matter what the federal government might offer them as an inducement to move.

Georgia and the United States had signed a compact on April 24, 1802, by which Georgia ceded to the United States her western land claims. In return the United States agreed to extinguish the Indian title to lands within the state, as soon as it could be done peaceably and on reasonable terms, and turn them over to

[28] Monroe to Jackson, Oct. 5, 1817, in *Correspondence of Andrew Jackson*, II, 331–332; Message of Dec. 2, 1817, in Richardson, *Messages and Papers*, II, 16; C. Vandeventer to Cass, June 29, 1818, in SW IA LS, vol. D, pp. 176–179; Calhoun to Joseph McMinn, July 29, 1818, *ibid.*, pp. 191–194; Monroe's message to Congress, Nov. 10, 1818, in Richardson, *Messages and Papers*, II, 46; Calhoun's report of Jan. 15, 1820, in *American State Papers: Indian Affairs*, II, 200–201.

Georgia.[29] As the land greed of the Georgians increased through the years, the federal government was accused of failing in its part of the bargain, for the Cherokees were in the East, and the government had not extinguished their title to the Georgia lands. Complaints reached Washington both from the Cherokees — who looked with apprehension on the threats of Georgia and on the federal government's renewed appropriations for a treaty to extinguish the Indian claims — and from the Georgians. The governor of Georgia censured the federal government for its tardiness and weakness, asserted that the Indians were mere tenants at will who had only a temporary right to use the lands for hunting, and insisted that Georgia was determined to gain the Cherokee lands.[30]

To these criticisms Monroe replied in a special message to Congress on March 30, 1824, defending the course of the government, asserting that the Indian title was in no way affected by the compact with Georgia, and denying any obligation on the part of the United States to force the Indians to move against their will. He reiterated his own strong opinion that removal would be in the best interests of the Indians, but he refused to be pushed by Georgia beyond the strict import of the compact. The President's message did nothing to soothe the irritation of the Georgians, whose governor in another communication to the President commented with much severity upon the bad faith that for twenty years had characterized the conduct of the executive officers of the United States.[31]

As Monroe neared the end of his term in office, he increased his insistence that steps be taken to preserve the fast-degenerating tribes, now increasingly threatened by Georgia. He told Congress in December 1824 of the Indians' deplorable conditions and the danger of their extinction. To civilize them was essential to their survival, but this was a slow process and could not be attained in the territory where the Indians then resided. Monroe had no thought of forceful ejection; even if it aimed at the security and happiness of the Indians it would be "revolting to humanity, and utterly unjustifiable." There was only one solution:

[29] The compact of 1802 is printed in *Territorial Papers*, V, 142–146.
[30] Charles C. Royce, "The Cherokee Nation of Indians: A Narrative of Their Official Relations with the Colonial and Federal Governments," *Annual Report of the Bureau of Ethnology, 1883–1884* (Washington, 1887), pp. 233–238.
[31] Monroe's message and numerous documents relating to the compact of 1802 are printed in *Sen. Doc.* 63, 18 Cong., 1 sess., ser. 91. See also Royce, "The Cherokee Nation of Indians," pp. 238–240.

the Indians must be invited and induced to take up their home in the West. The plan would be expensive, Monroe admitted, but he saw no other solution.[32]

Before Congress had time to act, Monroe addressed a new, special message to Congress on the subject of removal, based upon a report of Calhoun dated January 24, 1825. The President insisted upon a liberal policy that would satisfy both the Cherokees and the Georgians. He asked for "a well-digested plan" for governing and civilizing the Indians, which would not only "shield them from impending ruin, but promote their welfare and happiness." The President was convinced that such a plan was practicable and that it could be made so attractive to the Indians that all, even those most opposed to emigration, would be induced to accede to it in the near future. The essence of his proposal was the institution of a government in the West for the Indians, one that would preserve order, prevent the intrusion of the whites, and stimulate civilization. To his mind the promise of such a state was the most powerful consideration the government had to offer as an inducement to the Indians to relinquish their old lands and move to new ones designated in the West. "It is not doubted," Monroe told Congress, "that this arrangement will present considerations of sufficient force to surmount all their prejudices in favor of the soil of their nativity, however strong they may be." To convince the Indians of the sincere interest of the government in their welfare, he asked Congress to pledge the solemn faith of the United States to fulfill such arrangements as he had suggested, and he recommended sending commissioners to the various tribes to explain to them the objects of the government.[33]

Congress acted at once to implement the President's message. On the day following the message, Thomas Hart Benton wrote to Secretary of War Calhoun that the Committee on Indian Affairs in the Senate had unanimously adopted the system recommended by Monroe, and Calhoun sent Benton a draft of a bill.[34] The bill, introduced by Benton on February 1, followed precisely the recommendations Monroe had made, authorizing the President to acquire land from the western Indians and to treat with the

[32] Message of Dec. 7, 1824, in Richardson, *Messages and Papers*, II, 261.

[33] Report of Calhoun, Jan. 24, 1825, in *American State Papers: Indian Affairs*, II, 542–544; Message of Monroe, Jan. 27, 1825, in Richardson, *Messages and Papers*, II, 280–283.

[34] Benton to Calhoun, Jan. 28, 1825, in IA LR, Miscellaneous; Calhoun to Benton, Jan. 31, 1825, in IA LS, vol. 1, pp. 334–335.

eastern tribes for removal to the West. The bill directed the President, furthermore, "to pledge the faith of the nation" that the emigrating tribes would be guaranteed permanent peace, protection from intrusion, and aid in improving their condition and in forming a suitable government, and to appoint commissioners to visit the tribes to induce them to move. One hundred and twenty-five thousand dollars was to be appropriated to carry out the provisions of the act. It was a promising beginning, but although the bill passed the Senate, it failed in the House.[35]

The matter, however, was by no means dead. In December 1825 a House resolution charged the Committee on Indian Affairs to inquire into the expediency and practicability of establishing a territorial government for the Indians west of the Mississippi. In February 1826 a new bill was introduced.[36] This bill represented the current view of the administration, for John Cocke, the chairman of the House Committee on Indian Affairs, had sent a copy of the earlier bill to Secretary of War Barbour, asking for his opinion. "The Committee are desirous," Cocke said, "to cooperate with the views of the President in relation to the Indians within the limits of the U. States." Barbour in reply sent a long letter to Cocke, in which he argued for removal of the Indians as the only means to preserve the Indians. He suggested the following outline for a bill:

(1) The country west of the Mississippi to be set aside for the exclusive use of the Indians.

(2) Removal of the Indians as individuals, instead of as tribes.

(3) Establishment of a territorial government for the Indians, to be maintained by the United States.

(4) When circumstances permitted, extinction of tribes and distribution of property among individuals.

(5) To leave unchanged the condition of those Indians who remained in the East.[37]

Barbour's letter was read and discussed in a cabinet meeting on February 7. The report of the meeting which President John

[35] *Sen. Jour.*, 18 Cong., 2 sess., ser. 107, pp. 124, 130, 164, 185, 187; *House Jour.*, 18 Cong., 2 sess., ser. 112, pp. 264, 265, 269; Original bill (S 45), 18 Cong., 2 sess., Feb. 1, 1825. A similar bill was introduced in the House on February 7 (HR 320), but it was dropped in favor of the Senate bill. *House Jour.*, 18 Cong., 2 sess., ser. 112, p. 211.

[36] *House Jour.*, 19 Cong., 1 sess., ser. 130, pp. 97, 276; Original bill (HR 113), 19 Cong., 1 sess., Feb. 21, 1826.

[37] John Cocke to James Barbour, Jan. 11, 1826, in IA LR, Miscellaneous; Barbour to Cocke, Feb. 3, 1826, in *American State Papers: Indian Affairs*, II, 646–649.

Quincy Adams entered in his diary indicated the perplexity with which the administration faced the Indian problem.

Messrs. Rush, Barbour, Southard, and Wirt were here in Cabinet meeting upon Mr. Barbour's letter to the Chairman of the Committee on Indian Affairs of the House of Representatives. The letter was read, and variously commented upon by the other members of the Administration. Mr. Clay was absent, confined to his house by a relapse of influenza. Mr. Barbour's plan is differently modified from that which he had at first prepared. He has given up the idea of incorporating the Indians into the several States where they reside. He has now substituted that of forming them all into a great territorial Government west of the Mississippi. There are many very excellent observations in the paper, which is full of benevolence and humanity. I fear there is no practicable plan by which they can be organized into one civilized, or half civilized, Government. Mr. Rush, Mr. Southard, and Mr. Wirt all expressed their doubts of the practicability of Governor Barbour's plan; but they had nothing more effective to propose, and I approved it from the same motive.[38]

The bill failed to pass, however, and at the beginning of the following session of Congress, the House called upon the secretary of war for detailed information on the condition of the Indians and their willingness to migrate and the probable expense of removal. McKenney answered the request for the secretary of war in a serious and reasonable document, in which he honestly admitted lack of information on much of what the House wanted to know and recognized the difficulties involved in carrying out removal. But he insisted strongly that the program was possible and that the Indians could be brought to accept it if they were approached in the right way.[39]

On July 26, 1827, the Cherokee Nation adopted a written constitution patterned after that of the United States, which asserted that the Cherokees were one of the sovereign and independent nations of the earth with complete jurisdiction over their own territory. This move on the part of the Indians caused great alarm. The secretary of war wrote to the Cherokee agent, warning that the constitution could not be understood as changing the relations that then existed between the Indians and the government of the United States. In the House of Representatives the

---

[38] *Memoirs of John Quincy Adams*, VII, 113. William Clark in his long comments on Barbour's letter showed general agreement. Clark to Barbour, March 1, 1826, in *American State Papers: Indian Affairs*, II, 653–654.

[39] *House Jour.* 19 Cong., 2 sess., ser. 147, pp. 61, 66, 80; McKenney to Barbour, Dec. 27, 1826, in IA LS, vol. 3, pp. 273–285.

Committee on the Judiciary and then the Committee on Indian Affairs were directed to inquire into the matter, and a special report was requested from the President. Georgia, of course, was indignant and angered by the "presumptuous document." [40]

Since Congress failed to pass any measure to relieve the situation, Georgia itself finally began to move against the Cherokees, contending that it could not abide an *imperium in imperio* in the state, as it considered the Cherokees with their constitution and laws. Georgia's line of action was to extend the authority of the state and its laws over the Cherokee lands. This would in effect withdraw the Cherokee lands from the status of "Indian Country," bring control of the lands into Georgia's hands, and by overt as well as subtle pressure, force the Indians off most of the land.

The resolutions of a committee of the Georgia legislature approved on December 27, 1827, gave an indication in which direction the wind was blowing. After condemning the bad faith of the federal government for not having extinguished the Cherokee title, the committee put forth Georgia's position, that the lands within the limits of the state belonged to it absolutely, and that since the Indians were merely tenants at will, the state could end that tenancy at any time. The committee insisted that Georgia had the right to extend its authority and laws over the whole territory and to exact obedience to them from all. Another of the resolutions was a thinly veiled threat of the use of force, if necessary, to accomplish Georgia's aims. [41]

The situation was growing steadily more serious. How could the claims of the state of Georgia be reconciled with justice to the Indians? John Quincy Adams in his final message to Congress reviewed the problem:

As independent powers, we negotiated with them [the Indians] by treaties; as proprietors, we purchased of them all the lands which we could prevail upon them to sell; as brethren of the human race, rude and ignorant, we endeavored to bring them to the knowledge of religion and of letters. The ultimate design was to incorporate in our own institutions that portion of them which could be converted to the state of civilization. In the practice of European States, before our Revolution, they had been considered *as*

---

[40] The Cherokee Constitution is printed in *House Doc.* 91, 23 Cong., 2 sess., ser. 273, pp. 10–19. For congressional action, see *House Jour.*, 20 Cong., 1 sess., ser. 168, pp. 114, 130, 136, 168, 325, 332, 359, 370, 436, 452. The President's report with accompanying documents is in *House Exec. Doc.* 211, 20 Cong., 1 sess., ser. 173.

[41] *Acts of the General Assembly of the State of Georgia, 1827* (Milledgeville, 1827), pp. 249–250.

children to be governed; as tenants at discretion, to be dispossessed as occasion might require; as hunters to be indemnified by trifling concessions for removal from the grounds from which their game was extirpated. In changing the system it would seem as if a full contemplation of the consequences of the change had not been taken. We have been far more successful in the acquisition of their lands than in imparting to them the principles or inspiring them with the spirit of civilization. But in appropriating to ourselves their hunting grounds we have brought upon ourselves the obligation of providing them with subsistence; and when we have had the rare good fortune of teaching them the arts of civilization and the doctrines of Christianity we have unexpectedly found them forming in the midst of ourselves communities claiming to be independent of ours and rivals of sovereignty within the territories of the members of our Union. This state of things requires that a remedy should be provided — a remedy which, while it shall do justice to those unfortunate children of nature, may secure to the members of our confederation their rights of sovereignty and of soil.[42]

The House Committee on Indian Affairs, which considered the proposals of President Adams and Secretary of War Porter, concurred in the opinion that removal was necessary in view of the crisis growing out of the controversy with the states. The elementary question to be answered was, How are the Indians to be preserved? The committee found only one way: to remove the Indians from the states and establish them on lands beyond the limits of any state or territory. "The policy of urging them to leave their country for another would be deplored," the committee asserted, "if it were not believed to be the only effectual measure to secure the prosperity and happiness of themselves and their posterity." A bill was reported by the committee to appropriate fifty thousand dollars to enable the President to aid the Indians in their migration to the west, but it was not enacted into law.[43]

꙳

Then Andrew Jackson became President of the United States. He was a man of forthright views who did not hesitate to speak his mind and a man who had ample Indian experience to give weight to his utterances. He had early decided that it was farcical to treat with the Indian tribes as though they were sovereign and independent nations, and he could point to considerable evidence to show that treaties had never been a success.

[42] Message of Dec. 2, 1828, in Richardson, *Messages and Papers*, II, 415–416.
[43] *House Rep.* 87, 20 Cong., 2 sess., ser. 190, pp. 1–3; Original bill (HR 449), 20 Cong., 2 sess., Feb. 18, 1829.

Jackson himself had been a United States commissioner in drawing up treaties with the southern Indians. As his experience with the Indians grew, he began to question openly the wisdom of the traditional procedure. In March 1817, while military commander in the South, he had complained to President Monroe about the absurdity of making treaties with the Indians, whom he considered subjects of the United States with no sovereignty of their own. Congress, Jackson maintained, had as much right to legislate for the Indians as for the people in the territories, and he strongly urged — for the good of the Indians, he insisted, as well as for the good of the nation — that Congress make use of this right to prescribe the Indian bounds, to occupy and possess parts of their lands when the safety, interest, or defense of the country should render it necessary. Due compensation was to be given, of course, just as in any exercise of the right of eminent domain, but to treat with the Indians as though they were independent nations rather than subjects was nonsense. The Indians had been thrown on the bounty of the government after the Revolution and after their defeat in subsequent Indian wars. They had no right of soil or domain except for the mere possessory right that had been granted to them by the liberality and humanity of the United States. Treaties would be all very well if the Indians were in fact independent nations, possessing the rights of sovereignty and domain, but Jackson flatly denied that this was the case. The Indians, he said, "have only a possessory right to the soil, for the purpose of hunting and not the right of domain, hence I conclude that Congress has full power, by law, to regulate all the concerns of the Indians."

Jackson saw no validity in the argument that the United States, following in the path of Great Britain, had always treated with the Indians as independent nations. To his mind, this was a policy that had grown out of weakness and special circumstances and was not based on any rights acknowledged to be possessed by the Indians. The policy of making treaties with the Indians grew up out of necessity at a time when the government was not strong enough to enforce its regulations among the Indians or to keep peace in any other way. Now, under changed circumstances, a more just procedure would be the forceful reduction of the Indian lands, so that the natives, confined to close limits, would adopt the civilized existence of the white man.[44]

---

[44] *Correspondence of Andrew Jackson*, II, 279–281.

Monroe had found Jackson's view "new but very deserving of attention," and encouraged, no doubt, by the favorable reception of his views in high circles, Jackson had stuck to his position. In 1820 he wrote to Secretary of War Calhoun on the subject of Indian affairs. The message was the same. It was absurd to treat with Indians rather than legislate for them. It was "high time to do away with the farce of treating with the Indian tribes." Again his views were approved, but Calhoun was unable to get Congress to modify the treaty system.[45] During the seven and one-half years that Calhoun held the position of secretary of war, with the conduct of Indian affairs under his department, forty treaties were signed with the Indian nations. The picture had not changed. The solemnities were still observed; the documents spoke formally of grants and guarantees, as though the great powers of the world were negotiating.

When he entered the White House, Jackson was convinced that the Indians could no longer exist as independent enclaves within the states. Either they must move west or become subject to the laws of the states. Assured of presidential sympathy, Georgia then made a new move against the Cherokees. At the end of 1828 the Georgia legislature passed a law which added Cherokee lands to certain northwestern counties of Georgia. A second law, a year later, extended the laws of the state over these lands, effective June 1, 1830. Thereafter the Cherokee laws and customs were to be null and void.[46]

The Cherokees immediately protested and made representations to the President and to Congress.[47] Jackson, whatever his shortcomings in dealing with the Indians, was not one to hide his realistic intentions behind pleasant phrases, for, as he had written to an Indian commissioner a few years earlier, "with all Indians, the best plan will be to come out with candor."[48] Through the instrumentality of his secretary of war, Jackson answered the Cherokees. Bluntly he told them that they had no

[45] Monroe to Jackson, Oct. 5, 1817, *ibid.*, 331–332; Jackson to Calhoun, Sept. 2, 1820, and Jan. 18, 1821, *ibid.*, III, 32, 36–38; Calhoun to Jackson, Nov. 16, 1821, *ibid.*, 132.

[46] William C. Dawson, comp., *A Compilation of the Laws of the State of Georgia* (Milledgeville, 1831), pp. 198–199.

[47] The letter of the Cherokee Delegation to the President, Feb. 17, 1829, could not be located. See Cherokee memorial to Congress, Feb. 27, 1829, in *House Doc.* 145, 20 Cong., 2 sess., ser. 187; Cherokee memorials presented in the House, Feb. 15, 1830, in *House Rep.* 311, 21 Cong., 1 sess., ser. 201.

[48] Jackson to John D. Terrill, July 29, 1826, in *Correspondence of Andrew Jackson*, III, 308–309.

hope of succor from the federal government. The address made by Secretary of War John H. Eaton to the delegation of the Cherokees on April 18, 1829, was an unequivocal statement of the Jackson policy. It informed the Indians that by the Declaration of Independence and the treaty of 1783 all the sovereignty which pertained to Great Britain had been conferred upon the states of the Union. "If, as is the case," Eaton told the Indians, "you have been permitted to abide on your lands from that period to the present, enjoying the right of the soil, and privilege to hunt, it is not thence to be inferred, that this was any thing more than a permission, growing out of compacts with your nation; nor is it a circumstance whence, now to deny to those states, the exercise of their original sovereignty."

The treaties with the Indians, which for the supporters of Indian rights were a great arsenal of arguments, were turned to his own uses by the secretary of war. The "emphatic language" of the Treaty of Hopewell, he told the Cherokees, could not be mistaken. The United States *gave peace* to the Indians and took them again into favor and under her protection. The treaty *allotted* and *defined* the hunting grounds. It secured to the Indians the privilege of pursuing game and protection from encroachment. "No right, however, save a mere possessory one, is by the provisions of the treaty of Hopewell conceded to your nation. The soil, and the use of it, were suffered to remain with you, while the Sovereignty abided precisely where it did before, in those states within whose limits you were situated." Later treaties, after renewed hostilities, were similar to the Treaty of Hopewell, guaranteeing occupancy and possession of the Indian Country. "But the United States, always mindful of the authority of the States, even when treating for what was so much desired, peace with her red brothers, forbore to offer a guarantee adverse to the Sovereignty of Georgia. They could not do so; they had not the power." The compact of 1802, Eaton added, had nothing to say about sovereignty. Both parties to the compact knew well where it lay — with the state. There was nothing to be offered to the Cherokees but the urgent recommendation that they move west of the Mississippi.[49]

The same doctrine was bluntly set forth by Jackson's attorney general, John M. Berrien, who insisted that the United States had granted peace to the Cherokees in 1785 as a "mere grace of the

---

[49] Eaton to Cherokee Delegation, April 18, 1829, in IA LS, vol. 5, pp. 408–412.

conqueror." [50] The argument might have sounded plausible in 1830, but it should be considered in the light of the actions of the Continental Congress in 1783 and the years following, when a most nervous anxiety to get peace signed with the Indians was indicated. Congress did not look much like a conqueror imposing terms on the conquered Indians. She was seeking to keep the Indians at peace at all costs, rather than risk any more hostilities, which the new weak nation could ill afford.

Opposition quickly arose to the treatment of the southern Indians as missionary groups with establishments among the Five Civilized Tribes began to protest the removal of their charges, whom they had been directing along the road toward civilization. Although the secretary of war in 1828 had reprimanded the missionaries for having plans diametrically opposed to those of the government, the opposition did not slacken. Prominent church groups in the North and East began to speak out against the government's policy, working toward that full-throated cry that was to resound in the halls of Congress as the debate on removal got under way in April, 1830. The charge of being unchristian was not one to be lightly shrugged off, and the administration undertook to counteract the opposition. Thomas L. McKenney, using his position as head of the Office of Indian Affairs, enlisted in support of Jackson's policy and program a group of New York clergymen, who organized on July 22, 1829, the Board for the Emigration, Preservation, and Improvement of the Aborigines. When McKenney addressed the Board on August 12, his argument for removal was couched in humanitarian and religious terms; his concern was only to preserve the Indians from complete degradation and to enable them to improve and civilize themselves outside of contact with the whites. [51]

Jackson moved ahead boldly. In his first message to Congress, on December 8, 1829, he addressed himself to the problem of the "condition and ulterior destiny of the Indian tribes within the limits of some of our States." He called attention to the fact that

[50] "Opinion of the Attorney General as to the right acquired to the soil under existing treaties with the Cherokees," March 10, 1830, in House Exec. Doc. 89, 21 Cong., 1 sess., ser. 197, pp. 45–46.

[51] Report of Secretary of War Peter B. Porter, Nov. 24, 1828, in Sen. Doc. 1, 20 Cong., 2 sess., ser. 181, p. 22. Documents relative to the New York Board are printed in Documents and Proceedings Relating to the Formation and Progress of a Board in the City of New York for the Emigration, Preservation and Improvement of the Aborigines of America (New York, 1829). Some of the essential material is also printed in McKenney, Memoirs. See also the correspondence in the Office of Indian Affairs records.

some of the southern Indians had "lately attempted to erect an independent government within the limits of Georgia and Alabama," that the states had countered this infringement on their sovereignty by extending their laws over the Indians, and that the Indians in turn had appealed to the federal government. Did the federal government have a right to sustain the Indians in their pretensions, he asked. His answer was unequivocal. The Constitution forbade the erection of a new state within the territory of an existing state without that state's permission. Still less, then, could it allow a "foreign and independent government" to establish itself there. On these grounds, he told Congress, he had informed the Indians that their attempt to establish an independent government would not be countenanced by the Executive of the United States, and he advised them either to emigrate beyond the Mississippi or to submit to the laws of the states. He came back to the old argument: if the Indians remained in contact with the whites they would be degraded and destroyed. "Humanity and national honor demand that every effort should be made to avert so great a calamity." The solution was to set apart an ample district west of the Mississippi, to be guaranteed to the Indian tribes as long as they occupied it. There they could be taught the arts of civilization.

Jackson denied any intention to use force. "This emigration should be voluntary, for it would be as cruel as unjust to compel the aborigines to abandon the graves of their fathers and seek a home in a distant land." The protestation had a hollow ring, for the Indians were to be informed that if they remained they would be subject to the state laws and would lose much of their beloved land. With more than a touch of sarcasm, the President pronounced it visionary for the Indians to hope to retain hunting lands on which they had neither dwelt nor made improvements, "merely because they have seen them from the mountain or passed them in the chase." [52]

Following the suggestion of the President, both the House and the Senate introduced an Indian removal bill. The bills were similar in nature and the House version was dropped in favor of the Senate bill. This bill, like the President's message, made no mention of coercion to remove the Indians, and on the surface it seemed harmless and humane enough, with its provisions for a permanent guarantee of possession of the new lands, compensa-

[52] Richardson, *Messages and Papers*, II, 456–459.

tion for improvements left behind, and aid and assistance for the emigrants.[53] But those who knew the policy and practice of Jackson and the Georgians understood that force would be inevitable.

The bill occasioned a long and bitter debate in Congress. In the Senate the attack was led by Senator Theodore Frelinghuysen of New Jersey who spoke for six hours against the administration bill, bringing in all possible arguments to support the Indians and fighting to establish their claim to independent authority over the lands and to protection of these rights from the federal government against the pretensions of Georgia. Frelinghuysen was ably supported by Senator Peleg Sprague of Maine, and in the House of Representatives Henry R. Storrs of New York, William W. Ellsworth of Connecticut, and Edward Everett of Massachusetts, among others, gave long speeches of the same tenor.[54]

The administration, of course, did not lack supporters in Congress. These men repeated and amplified the Jacksonian doctrine that removal was in the best interests of the Indians, and that the Indian title to the lands was at best only a possessory title, dependent upon the good will of the ultimate sovereign.[55] The right to dispossess the Indians to which the Jackson party appealed was almost a part of the American atmosphere, so universally had it been accepted and promoted — now openly and with apostolic vigor, now subconsciously under the guise of protecting and preserving the Indians. It was a question of civilization versus the savage state, and no one was ready to preach that savagism should be perpetuated.[56] Friends of Indian rights,

---

[53] *U.S. Stat.*, IV, 411–412.

[54] The speeches of both sides are reported in condensed form in *Register of Debates in Congress*, 21 Cong., 1 sess., pp. 305 ff and 580 ff (February 24, 1830, and following, in the House, and April 6, 1830, and following, in the Senate). The speeches of Frelinghuysen, Sprague, Everett, and others were circulated in pamphlet form, and a collection of speeches against the Removal Bill was edited by Jeremiah Evarts in *Speeches on the Passage of the Bill, for the Removal of the Indians, Delivered in the Congress of the United States, April and May, 1830* (New York, 1830).

[55] The reports of the Senate and House Committees on Indian Affairs, which accompanied the bills, were long and able expositions of the administration views. *Sen. Doc.* 61, 21 Cong., 1 sess., ser. 193; *House Rep.* 227, 21 Cong., 1 sess., ser. 200. The extreme Georgia position is fully developed in Wilson Lumpkin, *The Removal of the Cherokee Indians from Georgia* (2 vols., New York, 1907).

[56] An extremely interesting and provocative study of white attitudes toward the Indian is that of Roy Harvey Pearce, *The Savages of America: A Study of the*

such as Knox and Jefferson, had agreed that the very course of civilization would ultimately reduce the Indian holdings as game grew scarcer and the hunting grounds receded to the west. This was an outcome to be hoped for, for the Indians would come to realize the advantages of the settled agricultural state over the insecurity of the hunter's life. The repeated talk of bringing "the blessings of civilization" to the Indians was an expression of concern and pity for less fortunate sons of the one Creator. But the frontiersmen, who had experienced at first hand the atrocities of Indian warfare and looked with impatience on the rich lands claimed by these savages as their hunting grounds, cared little about being purveyors of civilization. Their motivation was often vindictiveness and avarice, and they speeded by direct and hostile action what the others would accept as the inevitable and peaceful outcome of the meeting of a superior with an inferior race. Nor did they operate in a philosophical vacuum, for dispossessing the Indians of their lands had a fully developed rationalization, stretching from the establishment of first colonies through the prolonged debate over the removal bill.[57]

The first and ultimate argument for dispossessing the Indians was religious. The Puritan John Winthrop, first governor of Massachusetts Bay Colony, declared: "The whole earth is the lords Garden & he hath given it to the sonnes of men, wth a general Condicion, Gen: 1.28. Increase & multiply, replenish the earth & subdue it. . . . And for the Natives of New England they inclose noe land neither have any settled habitation nor any tame cattle to improve the land by, & soe have noe other but a naturall right to those countries Soe as if we leave them sufficient for their use wee may lawfully take the rest, there being more than enough for them & us."[58] The argument passed down through the decades. "There can be no doubt," Lewis Cass asserted in 1830, ". . . that the Creator intended the earth should be reclaimed from a state of nature and cultivated," and Thomas Hart Benton proclaimed

Indian and the Idea of Civilization (Baltimore, 1953). See also his "The Metaphysics of Indian-Hating," *Ethnohistory*, IV (1957), 27–40.

[57] I am indebted to Albert K. Weinberg, *Manifest Destiny: A Study of Nationalist Expansionism in American History* (Baltimore, 1935), for ideas and references in regard to arguments for dispossessing the Indians of their land. See also Washburn, "The Moral and Legal Justifications for Dispossessing the Indians," for a stimulating treatment of the problem in the colonial period.

[58] From *Conclusions for the Plantation in New England*, quoted in Weinberg, *Manifest Destiny*, pp. 74–75.

that the white race had the superior right to the land because it "used it according to the intentions of the CREATOR." [59]

Figuring even more prominently in the debate over Indian rights to the land was a second argument, based not on God's revealed word, but upon natural reason, the natural law which God had ordained within his creation. The doctrine was expressed in a myriad of forms. Semi-literate frontiersmen justified their encroachment on Chickasaw lands by challenging the government to remove them from "fine fertile countrys lying uncultivated." [60] Learned orators and writers cited the great Swiss jurist, Vattel, whose doctrine on the supremacy of the cultivator over the hunter became a classic weapon in the arsenal of the dispossessors:

There is another celebrated question, to which the discovery of the new world has principally given rise. It is asked if a nation may lawfully take possession of a part of a vast country, in which there are found none but erratic nations, incapable by the smallness of their numbers, to people the whole? We have already observed in establishing the obligation to cultivate the earth, that these nations cannot exclusively appropriate to themselves more land than they have occasion for, and which they are unable to settle and cultivate. Their removing their habitations through these immense regions, cannot be taken for a true and legal possession; and the people of Europe, too closely pent up, finding land of which these nations are in no particular want, and of which they make no actual and constant use, may lawfully possess it, and establish colonies there. We have already said, that the earth belongs to the human race in general, and was designed to furnish it with subsistence: if each nation had resolved from the beginning, to appropriate to itself a vast country, that the people might live only by hunting, fishing, and wild fruits, our globe would not be sufficient to maintain a tenth part of its present inhabitants. People have not then deviated from the views of nature in confining the Indians within narrow limits.[61]

[59] "Removal of the Indians," *North American Review*, XXX (1830), 77, and *Congressional Globe*, 27 Cong., 3 sess., Appendix, p. 74, quoted in Weinberg, *Manifest Destiny*, pp. 85, 73. An excellent example of the argument that the savages did not have a right to hold back the progress of cultivation and civilization was the flowery oration delivered by John Quincy Adams at Plymouth, Massachusetts, December 22, 1802, quoted in Jedidiah Morse, *A Report to the Secretary of War of the United States, on Indian Affairs* (New Haven, 1822), Appendix, pp. 281–288.

[60] Petition of intruders on Chickasaw lands, Sept. 5, 1810, in *Territorial Papers*, VI, 107.

[61] Emmerich de Vattel, *The Law of Nations; or Principles of the Law of Nature, Applied to the Conduct and Affairs of Nations and Sovereigns*, book I, chapter XVIII, paragraph 209 (edition published by Simeon Butler, Northampton, Mass., 1820, pp. 158–159).

It mattered little to the American proponents of this view that much of their argument was applied to situations — the Cherokees in Georgia were not hunters, but farmers — where Vattel's doctrine did not hold.

The appeal to the natural law was augmented by more down-to-earth considerations. The history of past dealings with the Indians — the treaty guarantees and legal stipulations — from which Marshall abstracted his doctrine of unassailable Indian rights to their land until they chose to part with them, yielded a far different doctrine for those whose one concern was to justify driving the Indians out if they refused to depart voluntarily. Jackson's reading of the treaties found that they were not based on any set principle of recognition of Indian sovereignty or of Indian rights, but on the peculiar necessities of the moment. Secretary of War Eaton's address to the Cherokees asserted that whatever the Indians possessed had been given to them by the United States at the end of the Revolution. "Treaties," proclaimed Governor George G. Gilmer of Georgia, "were expedients by which ignorant, intractable, and savage people were induced without bloodshed to yield up what civilized peoples had a right to possess by virtue of that command of the Creator delivered to man upon his formation — be fruitful, multiply, and replenish the earth, and subdue it." [62] To the House Committee on Indian Affairs, which reported the removal bill in 1830, the practice of extinguishing Indian titles by money payments was "but the substitute which humanity and expediency have imposed, in place of the sword, in arriving at the actual enjoyment of property claimed by the right of discovery, and sanctioned by the natural superiority allowed to the claims of civilized communities over those of savage tribes." [63]

The administration supporters insisted that the opposition to the Indian removal bill was a matter of party politics and that the sudden feeling for the Indians was a ruse to defeat the President on an important measure. Wilson Lumpkin of Georgia declared that there was not one of the supporters of the Cherokees but was an opponent of Jackson on political grounds. Jackson himself claimed that the opposition to the bill was part of the "secrete workings of Duff Green, Calhoun and Co." [64]

[62] Governor Gilmer is quoted by Weinberg, *Manifest Destiny*, p. 83, from *Journal of the House of Representatives of the State of Georgia*, 1830.
[63] *House Rep.* 227, 21 Cong., 1 sess., ser. 200, pp. 6–7.
[64] Lumpkin, *Removal of the Cherokees*, I, 74; Jackson to John Coffee, April 24, 1831, in *Correspondence of Andrew Jackson*, IV, 269.

While debate was proceeding in Congress on the bill, both houses were deluged with memorials, praying that the government of the United States protect the Indians from injustice and oppression in the possession of their lands and the full enjoyment of their rights, and in the exercise of their own laws and customs. The memorials, which increased in number as the debate on the bill progressed, were all of a pattern and came mainly from New England and the East. New Jersey was heavily represented, and Maine and Massachusetts, with a sprinkling from Pennsylvania. There was a memorial from the faculty and students of Amherst and numerous petitions from the Quakers. Many groups did not identify themselves, but they were obviously part of the general opposition to Jackson's measure that came from the Methodists and Congregationalists. The motives of these memorialists are hard to determine. They no doubt, as Secretary of War Porter suggested, had a material interest in the maintenance of their missionary establishments among the Cherokees in Georgia. More likely, their concern for the Indians was part of the genuine moral upsurge of the period, akin to the temperance movement, opposition to the Sunday mails, and African colonization of the Negroes. That these men so fully explored and so loudly proclaimed the Indian rights to the soil and the status of the Indians as quasi-independent nations may well have been an important force in keeping that view and practice dominant in the United States for many decades more.[65]

The arguments in Congress and in the memorials were duplicated in the periodical press. Lewis Cass, in a long article in the *North American Review*, presented a moderate statement of the case for removal. He was answered point by point, with a good deal more invective than he himself had used, by an article in the *American Monthly Magazine*. Jeremiah Evarts, in a series of short articles in the *National Intelligencer* under the name of William Penn, presented a more or less dispassionate statement of the Indians' position. Many of the congressional speeches and the magazine articles were circulated in pamphlet form, in order to spread and keep the agitation going.[66]

---

[65] The Removal Bill had its own memorialists — church groups, too, like the Baptists and the New York Board for Emigration, Preservation, and Improvement of the Aborigines — but they were but a drop compared with the flood unloosed by the opposition. See the indexes to the *House Jour.* and *Sen. Jour.*, 21 Cong., 1 sess., for the presentation of these memorials. A good number of the memorials were ordered printed and appear in the serial set of congressional documents.

[66] [Lewis Cass], "Removal of the Indians," *North American Review*, XXX

When the votes were counted, the removal bill passed by a small majority, but the controversy was not resolved. If anything, the agitation against the administration measure grew stronger as Jackson began to get the movement under way. Memorials continued to pour down upon Congress, and the President was further goaded by the Senate, which demanded an accounting of his enforcement of the intercourse act in Georgia. Jackson replied with a strong vindication of his course of action in withdrawing federal troops from the Cherokee lands as soon as Georgia extended her laws over the area.[67]

Jackson's victory was a practical one. He got what he and Georgia wanted: the removal of the Indians on the basis of his interpretation of Indian rights. Theoretically, however, the Georgia position that the Indians were mere tenants at will and that state laws could be extended over their territory — a position with which Jackson agreed and which he backed with his executive authority — did not stand the test of court action. When the Cherokee Nation in 1831 brought suit against the State of Georgia to defeat the operation of Georgia laws, it is true, the Supreme Court decided (without determining the validity of Georgia's action) that an Indian tribe or nation in the United States was not a foreign state in the sense of the Constitution and could not maintain an action in the courts of the United States. The Indians were, Marshall decided, "dependent domestic nations." The Cherokees soon had the matter again before the Supreme Court. One of Georgia's laws required that all white residents in the Cherokee territory take an oath of allegiance to the state and obtain a license from state authorities. When two missionaries refused to abide by the law, they were arrested and imprisoned. They challenged the action of Georgia, and their case was taken before the Supreme Court. In the famous case of *Worcester* vs. *Georgia*, John Marshall declared the law of Georgia extending her authority over the Cherokee lands null and void, as contrary to treaties and to the Constitution. In the course of the long argument, he

(1830), 62–121; Anonymous, *The Removal of the Indians: An Article from the American Monthly Magazine, An Examination of an Article in the North American Review; and an Exhibition of the Advancement of the Southern Tribes, in Civilization and Christianity* (Boston, 1830); [Jeremiah Evarts], *Essays on the Present Crisis in the Condition of the American Indians; First Published in the National Intelligencer, Under the Signature of William Penn* (Boston, 1829).

[67] Jackson's message to the Senate, Feb. 22, 1831, and accompanying documents, in *Sen. Doc.* 65, 21 Cong., 2 sess., ser. 204.

reasserted the existence of Indian tribes as independent nations: "From the commencement of our government, Congress has passed acts to regulate trade and intercourse with the Indians; which treat them as nations, respect their rights, and manifest a firm purpose to afford that protection which treaties stipulate. All these acts, and especially that of 1802, which is still in force, manifestly consider the several Indian nations as distinct political communities, having territorial boundaries, within which their authority is exclusive, and having a right to all lands within those boundaries, which is not only acknowledged, but guaranteed by the United States." [68]

Jackson, it is well known, refused to enforce John Marshall's decision. He and his administration proceeded firmly to follow the policy he had so long promoted. It is unfair, however, to charge them with cynical expediency and complete disregard for Indian rights and feelings, despite the later miseries of the "Trail of Tears." It was their confident hope, as Secretary of War Eaton expressed it to Governor George R. Gilmer of Georgia shortly after the passage of the removal bill,

that these people, now, when their expectations of an interference on the part of Congress has failed, will awaken to a sense of their condition and true interest, and to a knowledge that their utter and entire extinction as a people, must be the consequence of remaining at their present homes. Pending the examination of these questions before Congress the suggestion has been frequently made that the Indians if placed in the West, may again be subject to intrusions and interruptions. This is assuming too much, and more I should fain hope, than the good faith of this Government will even authorize to be conjectured. This unfortunate race of people have strong claims to our justice and to our sympathies, and should be protected from all interruption after they shall reach their new Homes. If Congress shall do no more, in legislating for them, they will doubtless place at the disposal of the Executive, authority sufficient, to prevent the white people from every interfering with or intruding upon their soil and their rights. This can be done, and this I have no hesitation in believing will be done. If so, a state of things more propitious to our red friends will be produced, than has been witnessed at any former period of their history.[69]

[68] Cherokees vs. Georgia, 5 Pet. 1 (1831); Worcester vs. Georgia, 6 Pet. 515 (1832).
[69] Eaton to Gilmer, June 1, 1830, in IA LS, vol. 6, pp. 436–439. Cohen, Federal Indian Law, p. 123, remarks: "John Marshall's analysis of the basis of Indian self-government in the law of nations has been consistently followed by the courts for more than a hundred years. The doctrine set forth in this opinion has been applied to an unfolding series of new problems in scores of cases that have come before the Supreme Court and the inferior federal courts. The doctrine

Having admitted the inability of the federal government to interfere in Georgia's actions, the administration did whatever it considered helpful to persuade the Indians to move willingly out of the scope of state jurisdictions. Secretary of War Eaton cut off the $2500 annual allotment made to the American Board of Commissioners for Foreign Missions for its Indian schools among the southern Indians on the grounds "that the Government by its funds should not extend encouragement and assistance to those, who thinking differently upon this subject, employ their efforts to prevent removals." [70] The War Department offered what it considered liberal inducements in the way of annuities, schools and other civilization aids, financial help in the emigration, and the like, to the emigrating Indians.

Jackson's administration was embarrassed by the failure of the Indians to accept the inducements to emigrate. Many Indians, it is true, did cede their lands in the East and withdraw, and Secretary of War Lewis Cass, who replaced Eaton in 1831, and Elbert Herring, who got McKenney's job in the same year, reported that the program of removal was "progressively developing its good effects." [71] The Cherokees, nevertheless, refused to depart. Although Cass repeatedly met with the Cherokee delegations and explained to them the President's sincere desire to aid them, he continued to insist that if they chose to remain, they must then accept both the privileges and disabilities of other citizens. He worked earnestly to implement the pledges made to the Indians in regard to their new home and outlined a policy to protect the Indians in the West. He instructed the commissioners sent to examine the country set apart for the Indians in

---

has not always been so highly respected in state courts and by administrative agencies. . . .

"The whole course of judicial decision on the nature of Indian tribal powers is marked by adherence to three fundamental principles: (1) An Indian tribe possesses, in the first instance, all the powers of any sovereign state. (2) Conquest renders the tribe subject to the legislative power of the United States and, in substance, terminates the external powers of sovereignty of the tribes, e.g., its power to enter into treaties with foreign nations, but does not by itself affect the internal sovereignty of the tribe, i.e., its powers of local self-government. (3) These powers are subject to qualification by treaties and by express legislation of Congress, but, save as thus expressly qualified, full powers of internal sovereignty are vested in the Indian tribes and in their duly constituted organs of government."

[70] Eaton to McKenney, June 7, 1830, in IA LS, vol. 6, p. 459.

[71] See reports of Herring, Nov. 19, 1831, in House Exec. Doc. 2, 22 Cong., 1 sess., ser. 216, p. 172; Nov. 22, 1832, in House Exec. Doc. 2, 22 Cong., 2 sess., ser. 233, p. 160; Nov. 25, 1834, in Sen. Doc. 1, 23 Cong., 2 sess., ser. 266, p. 239.

the West "to locate them all in as favorable positions as possible, in districts sufficiently fertile, salubrious, and extensive, and with boundaries, either natural or artificial, so clearly defined as to preclude the possibility of dispute. There is country enough for all, and more than all; and the President is anxious that full justice should be done to each, and every measure adopted be as much to their satisfaction as is compatible with the nature of such an arrangement." [72]

The unwillingness of the Cherokees to emigrate exasperated the secretary of war. "It was hoped that the favorable terms offered by the Government would have been accepted," he wrote to Wilson Lumpkin, who was by then governor of Georgia. "But some strange infatuation seems to prevail among these Indians. That they cannot remain where they are and prosper is attested as well by their actual condition as by the whole history of our aboriginal tribes. Still they refuse to adopt the only course which promises a cure or even an alleviation for the evils of their present condition." In seeking to remove all possible obstacles to Indian acceptance of removal, Cass privately requested Lumpkin to pardon the imprisoned missionaries so that one more pretext for not accepting the government's proposals might be removed. Little by little Cass grew less patient in his dealing with the Cherokees, telling them curtly in 1834 that there was little use in reviving discussion with them, since the government's position had not changed. [73]

Jackson himself in a long address to the Cherokees in March 1835 restated his position: "I have no motive, my friends, to deceive you. I am sincerely desirous to promote your welfare. Listen to me therefore while I tell you you cannot remain where you now are. Circumstances that cannot be controlled and which are beyond the reach of human laws render it impossible that you can flourish in the midst of a civilized community. You have but one remedy within your reach. And that is to remove to the west and join your countrymen who are already established there. And the sooner you do this the sooner will commence your career of improvement and prosperity." [74]

[72] Cass to Cherokee chiefs, Jan. 10, 1832, in IA LS, vol. 8, pp. 4–7; Cass to Jackson, Feb. 16, 1832, ibid., pp. 264–291; Cass to commissioners, July 14, 1832, in House Exec. Doc. 2, 22 Cong., 2 sess., ser. 233, p. 34.

[73] Cass to Lumpkin, Dec. 24, 1832, in IA LS, vol. 9, pp. 486–489; Cass to Cherokee delegation, Feb. 2, 1832, and March 18, 1834, ibid., vol. 10, pp. 18–21, vol. 12, pp. 187–188.

[74] Jackson to the Cherokees, March 16, 1835, ibid., vol. 15, p. 168.

The Indians could not hold out forever. Those who wished to stay were given small reservations where they were. The rest were moved to the West, amidst inevitable hardships, which have been repeatedly retold.[75]

In 1828 Secretary of War Porter had complained that there was no clear definition of the nature of the relations between the United States and the Indians. On one side were the advocates of "primitive and imprescriptible rights in their broadest extent," contending that the tribes were independent nations with sole and exclusive right to the property and government of the territories they occupied. On the other side were the extremists who considered the Indian "mere tenants at will, subject, like the buffalo of the prairies, to be hunted from their country whenever it may suit our interests or convenience to take possession of it." [76]

The debate of 1830 should have widened the split between the opposing forces, for each side presented an extreme position, but when the dust stirred up by the debate began to settle, the definition that Porter had asked for began to appear. It is true that the supporters of the removal bill won their point in Congress and that the Indians were ejected from the southern states. In practice on the frontier, too, the attitude that looked without sympathy on Indian rights was often victorious, but it did not for that reason reflect the official Indian policy of the United States as it developed through almost fifty years. For that policy we must turn to the treaties made with the Indians, which uniformly guaranteed Indian rights; to the intercourse acts, which implemented the treaties in protection of Indian rights and restricted the contacts between whites and Indians; and to the Supreme Court decisions of 1831 and 1832, which vindicated Jackson's opponents.[77] The tremendous weight of the argument put forth

---

[75] See Grant Foreman, *Indian Removal: The Emigration of the Five Civilized Tribes of Indians* (Norman, Okla., 1932), and *The Last Trek of the Indians* (Chicago, 1946).

[76] Report of the Secretary of War, Nov. 24, 1828, in *American State Papers: Military Affairs*, IV, 3.

[77] For a discussion of judicial decisions in regard to Indian rights to the soil, rights of sovereignty, etc., see Cohen, *Federal Indian Law*. In the matter of rights to the soil, Cohen remarks: "Cases and opinions subsequent to the McIntosh case oscillate between a stress on the content of the Indian possessory right and stress on the limitations of that right. These opinions and cases might perhaps be classified according to whether they refer to the Indian right of occupancy as a 'mere' right of occupancy or as a 'sacred' right of occupancy. All the cases, however,

in the 1830's by the supporters of the Cherokees stirred the conscience of the nation. What new authority it gave to the traditional principles behind American Indian policy cannot have been insignificant.

---

agree in saying that the aboriginal Indian title involves an exclusive right of occupancy and does not involve an ultimate fee." *Ibid.*, p. 293.

THE LAWS OF 1834

The policy of the Government on the subject of its Indian relations, as indicated by our various treaties with that people, and by the laws regulating our intercourse with them, has never been very distinctly marked; nor, indeed has it at different times been very uniform or consistent in its character. The regulations, too, of the Department, so far as it may be said to have any, have been equally undefined and vacillating; and there appears to have been scarcely any other rule to guide the officers and the agents in the discharge of their functions — particularly in regard to the disbursement and application of the contingent fund — than their own several notions of justice and policy.

> — Secretary of War Porter to Lewis Cass, 1828

The acts of the last session of Congress on the subject of Indian affairs, have introduced important changes into those relations. Many of the provisions of former laws had become inappropriate or inadequate, and not suited to the channel which time and circumstances had made. In the act regulating the intercourse with the various tribes, the principles of intercommunication with them are laid down, and the necessary details provided. In that for the reorganization of the department, the number of officers employed has been much reduced, and the current expenses diminished.

> — Annual Report of Secretary of War Cass, 1834

The emptying of the eastern states of the Indians and the establishment of the tribes west of the Mississippi re-emphasized the need, which had gradually become increasingly evident, for a reorganization of Indian affairs and a restatement of Indian policy. In 1834 a wholesale revamping was undertaken, a triple attack made upon current problems: (1) a reorganization of the

Indian department; (2) a new trade and intercourse act; and (3) a proposed organization of a western territory to provide a government for the Indians who had emigrated to the west. The first of these put a firm legislative foundation under the Indian service, made explicit provision for Indian agents whose status had been somewhat irregular before, and established systematic accounting procedures in order to eliminate the confusion and embarrassment that had frequently arisen in financial matters. The second was a restatement and codification of Indian policy as it had developed during the preceding four and one-half decades of United States history, the fruit of earlier legislation, ripened now in the bright light of frontier experience and the warm winds of congressional debate. The third was intended to fulfill the pledges made to the Indians upon removal, that adequate provision would be made for their protection and for their government.

These proposals for the most part were not revolutionary. Their ultimate source was earlier legislation based on past experience and the numerous recommendations made through the years to perfect United States policy toward the aborigines. There were, morever, important proximate sources through which the past was brought to focus on the present. Such were the detailed recommendations submitted to the secretary of war by Governor Lewis Cass and General William Clark in February 1829, Cass's report as secretary of war in 1831, the report of the commissioners sent out by Cass in 1832 to investigate the new home allotted to the emigrating Indians, and finally, the report of the House Committee on Indian Affairs, which presented the draft of the new Indian bills to Congress in 1834.

The intercourse act of 1802, which was little more than a permanent re-enactment of the temporary acts of 1796 and 1799, had long been subject to criticism, as events showed how little effective it was in meeting recurring problems in the contacts between the Indians and the whites. The regulation of traders needed to be tightened, the restrictions on liquor in the Indian country needed more adequate enforcement, and encroachment on Indian land had not been prevented. Piecemeal corrective legislation and executive directives needed to be augmented and pulled together in a single piece of legislation. This need, plus the frustrating difficulties arising from the lack of well-founded administrative procedures in the War Department for handling Indian affairs, struck Peter B. Porter with special force when he became secretary of war in the spring of 1828. "In the few weeks that have elapsed since I had the honor to be called to this Department," Porter wrote to Governor Cass in July 1828, "I have found no portion of its extensive and complicated duties so perplexing, and the performance of which has been less welcome, than those which appertain to the Bureau of Indian Affairs." It was not due to any deficiencies in the character of the men charged with the duties, he asserted, but came rather from "the want of a well digested system of principles and rules for the administration of our Indian concerns." His purpose in writing Cass and in sending a similar letter to William Clark at St. Louis was to invite the two men to Washington to draw up a code of regulations for Indian affairs which could be presented to Congress for its action. "The long and intimate acquaintance which you have both had with the Indian character," he told them, "— your knowledge of their interests, their habits, wants, wishes and capabilities would render your aid and advice in the formation of such a system, peculiarly useful and desirable." [1]

Both Cass and Clark responded enthusiastically to Porter's proposal. Clark thought that the existing laws were "not sufficiently explicit & consistent" to punish offences against the laws and regulations, and Cass wanted "some established principles to regulate the discretion which now exists." Working together in Washington, they produced a long report, which Porter sent to the Senate on February 9, 1829. [2]

The first of three items which Cass and Clark presented answered Porter's demand for a bill which would "embrace the whole policy of the government, and comprise all its legislation on Indian intercourse, and every other subject connected therewith, in one statute." The bill they submitted was composed of fifty-six sections and was entitled "An Act to provide for regulating trade and intercourse with the Indian Tribes and for the general management of Indian affairs." It was made up in large part of transcriptions — more or less literal — from previous laws, incorporating most of the intercourse act of 1802, a law of 1800 providing for visits of Indians to the seat of Government, the

[1] Porter to Cass, July 28, 1828, in IA LS, vol. 5, pp. 56–57. See also Report of the Secretary of War, Nov. 24, 1828, in Sen. Doc. 1, 20 Cong., 2 sess., ser. 181, pp. 20–21.
[2] Clark to Porter, Aug. 27, 1828, in IA LR, St. Louis Superintendency; Cass to Porter, Sept. 8, 1828, ibid., Michigan Superintendency. The report of Cass and Clark is in Sen. Doc. 72, 20 Cong., 2 sess., ser. 181.

provisions of the law of 1816 excluding foreigners from the Indian trade, the act of 1817 providing for crimes committed in the Indian Country, the law of 1818 concerning the manner of appointing Indian agents, the 1819 law which appropriated the annual $10,000 civilization fund, the supplementary intercourse act of 1822, the provisions of 1824 designating sites for the trade, as well as sections of other laws which touched upon Indian trade, Indian agents, or the accounting for public funds.

There was also much that was new; the additions and the modifications of previous provisions embodied the views of the two men in regard to ameliorating the then-existing state of affairs The first sections of the bill concerned the appointment and duties of Indian department personnel, a serious omission in previous legislation. There was to be a commissioner of Indian affairs in the War Department who was to have responsibility for Indian matters, handle Indian department accounts, and in general direct Indian relations. In this proposal Cass and Clark merely incorporated provisions of the bills which had been introduced in previous sessions of Congress by the Committee on Indian Affairs.[3] The superintendent of Indian affairs at St. Louis who had been authorized in 1822 was continued, and the governors of the territories were still to be charged with Indian affairs, but the proposed law specified their responsibilities more precisely. Indian agents and subagents, whose legal status was most hazy, were directly provided for in the bill, and the President was authorized to discontinue agencies when no longer needed. Commissioners to hold Indian treaties with extensive police powers were provided for. A set method for handling financial accounts in the Indian department was outlined, to bring this activity in line with that in other departments.

The new proposals kept the traditional idea of the boundary line between the Indian lands and those of the whites, but it recognized the impossibility (in the new and changing circumstances of the Indians) of drawing the line in detail as had been done in the laws of 1796, 1799, and 1802. It substituted instead a general provision that the limits of the various cessions should be the boundary line, which would change as new cessions were made.

In the matter of granting licenses to trade with the Indians

---

[3] *House Jour.*, 20 Cong., 1 sess., ser. 168, p. 105; Original bill (IIR 29), 20 Cong., 1 sess., Jan. 2, 1828.

and indeed of entering the Indian Country for any reason, the proposed bill went considerably beyond the earlier legislation and was an explicit expression of the view that had been gradually gaining ground. A chief element of the new policy was the discretionary authority to be granted to agents in issuing licenses, so that they would have power to refuse licenses to men of bad character, with recourse to higher authority if necessary. This, together with the continued prohibition against foreign traders and the limiting of the trade to specific designated sites, was considered essential for keeping close watch on the traders so as to prevent abuses in the trade. Once the dependence of the Indians on licensed traders was established, the President was then to be given authority to prohibit all trade with certain tribes, if public interest required, as a means of bringing pressure upon hostile or recalcitrant tribes in extraordinary cases.

Beyond requiring a license of traders who desired to enter the Indian Country (a traditional provision of Indian laws), Cass and Clark proposed that a passport be required of *anyone* who desired to enter Indian lands. Such a provision for the region south of the Ohio had been included in the acts of 1796, 1799, and 1802, and foreigners needed a passport under the act of 1816; Cass and Clark now made it an essential part of their policy for the whole Indian Country. "It will be difficult, if not impracticable," they commented, "to enforce many of the regulations contemplated by this act, unless the entrance itself into the Indian country is prohibited."

Cass and Clark wrote their report at a time when exclusion of whiskey from the Indian Country still rested on the discretionary power given the President in the act of 1802. "No distinct substantive provision forbidding the introduction of spirituous liquors into the Indian country, exists in our statute book," they noted, "and the propriety of introducing it here, will scarcely be questioned." They proposed a flat prohibition on the use of liquor in the trade and they repeated with clarification the search and forfeiture procedures of the act of 1822, but they would still allow whiskey to be taken in under license for the use of the traders' boatmen.

The proposed bill was accompanied by a set of "Regulations for the Government of the Indian Department," of which the general objects were declared to be the following:

1st. To carry into effect the provisions of the laws, and the instructions of the government, relating to Indians and Indian intercourse.

2nd. To ensure a faithful disbursement of the public money applicable to these objects, and a zealous and upright performance of their duties, by the officers of the Department.

3d. To enforce a strict accountability and a prompt settlement of accounts.

The regulations in many places repeated the provisions in the bill but also added details of procedure for carrying the law into effect. It had sections governing the civil and the fiscal administration of the Indian department, prescribed the limits of the agencies, listed the designated trading posts, provided rules for treating with the Indians, paying annuities, issuing licenses, processing claims for indemnification for losses suffered by either race, use of the civilization fund, the prohibition of liquor, and the accounting for funds.[1]

A third item was a bill to consolidate into one statute all the provisions for payment of annuities due from the United States to the Indians. This was a sensible proposal, intended to eliminate the unnecessary complications attendant upon accounting for funds under diverse headings.[5]

The work of Governor Cass and General Clark bore witness to their competence in Indian affairs. They included, it is true, a few items which no longer were of current importance, but they suggested adequate provisions for a workable department and proposed new legislation and regulations to correct evils not taken care of by the earlier laws, and they skillfully worked into one bill and one set of regulations diverse matters which had been scattered through the statutes and War Department directives. They attempted in their regulations to codify existing practice where it was satisfactory and introduce new procedures where greater clarity or strength was needed. The proposed bill was accompanied by an extensive section by section commentary which makes clear the thinking behind the proposals and gives a fine insight into Indian affairs at the time.

The work of Cass and Clark was submitted to the Senate by Secretary of War Porter with the earnest recommendation that it

---

[1] The Regulations are printed in *Sen. Doc.* 72, 20 Cong., 2 sess., ser. 181, pp. 75–82. The article in the Regulations dealing with fiscal administration of the Indian department bears the following footnote: "The regulations here proposed, respecting the settlement of accounts, &c. have been introduced at the suggestion of the officers of the Treasury Department, who are charged with this branch of business. It is a subject which is not understood by the persons who have prepared this report." *Ibid.*, p. 59.

[5] *Ibid.*, pp. 52–57.

receive early consideration. McKenney, too, praised the proposals; the report was, he declared, "able and judicious," and the accompanying bill, "ample and apposite," although he objected to the mode of accounting that Cass and Clark had proposed and offered alternative suggestions. McKenney picked out for special emphasis the provisions in the bill and regulations that would grant discretion to the agents in granting licenses to traders. That this discretionary power was a crucial point in the regulation of Indian intercourse can be seen from the violent opposition it stirred up in the American Fur Company.[6]

Congress took no action on the Cass-Clark report as it stood, but it was not ineffectual, for it served as a ready reference for those who advocated some updating of the laws governing relations with the Indians, and much of it was incorporated into the acts which became law in 1834.[7]

A second document of importance was the first annual report of Lewis Cass as secretary of war, dated November 21, 1831. Between the submission of the report that he and Clark had prepared in the winter of 1828–29 and this report as secretary of war, there had occurred the momentous debate in Congress on removal. With the adoption of Jackson's policy by Congress in May 1830 and the beginning of removal in 1830 and 1831, the Indian situation in the United States was rapidly changing from that which had obtained in 1802. Cass realized this change and proposed to provide a positive policy to cope with it.

"A crisis in our Indian affairs has evidently arrived," Cass declared, "which calls for the establishment of a system of policy adapted to the existing state of things, and calculated to fix upon a permanent basis the future destiny of the Indians." He hoped by careful planning for the future to repair the errors and unpleasantness of the past. The basis of his deliberation was the

[6] *Ibid.*, p. 1; Report of McKenney, Nov. 17, 1829, in *Sen. Doc.* 1, 21 Cong., 1 sess., ser. 192, pp. 167–168; McKenney to John H. Eaton, Jan. 21, 1830, in IA LS, vol. 6, pp. 237–238. The *Senate Journal* makes no mention of presentation of the Cass-Clark proposals in the Senate. They were attached to and printed with the secretary of war's reply to two requests for information sent to the War Department by the Senate — one on Indian agents and one on lands ceded by the Indians. See *Sen. Jour.*, 20 Cong., 2 sess., ser. 180, p. 114.

[7] See recommendations for changes in Report of S. S. Hamilton, Nov. 26, 1830, in *Sen. Doc.* 1, 21 Cong., 2 sess., ser. 203, p. 163; Report of Eaton, Dec. 1, 1830, *ibid.*, pp. 32–33; Report of Herring, Nov. 19, 1831, in *House Exec. Doc.* 2, 22 Cong., 1 sess., ser. 216, pp. 174–175.

policy of removal, accepted by Congress and promoted by the President. Cass was convinced that this was the only means — given the circumstances in the East and the character of the Indians — by which the Indians could be preserved and improved. Granted the migration to the West, what steps should be taken to protect and encourage the Indians there? Cass suggested a seven-point program — a list of principles to govern relations with the Indians in their new circumstances.

1. A solemn declaration that the country assigned to the Indians would be theirs forever and a determination that white settlement should never encroach upon it.

2. A determination, accompanied by proper surveillance and proper police, to exclude all liquor from the Indians' new territory.

3. The employment of adequate military force in the vicinity of the Indians in order to prevent hostility between the tribes.

4. Encouragement to the Indians to adopt severalty of property.

5. Assistance to all who needed it for opening farms and procuring domestic animals and agricultural implements.

6. Leaving untouched as much as possible the peculiar institutions and customs of the Indians.

7. Employment of persons to instruct the Indians, as far and as fast as they were capable.

This, it was apparent, was not a detailed blueprint for Indian laws or regulations, but it offered a general policy background which the law makers would find useful.[8]

෴

Then in 1832 special commissioners were appointed to examine the country set apart for the emigrating Indians, to treat with the Indians for adjustment of difficulties between tribes, to ascertain and report on the condition of the country and the proper locations for the different tribes, and to propose plans for the improvement, government, and security of the Indians. The commissioners were given detailed instructions by Secretary of War Cass and were charged to gather the information which would be essential in developing a sound policy for governing future relations with the Indians. "In the great change we are now urging them [the Indians] to make," Cass warned the commis-

[8] Report of Secretary of War, Nov. 21, 1831, *ibid.*, pp. 27–34.

sioners, "it is desirable that all their political relations, as well among themselves as with us, should be established upon a permanent basis, beyond the necessity of any future alteration. Your report upon this branch of the subject will be laid before Congress, and will probably become the foundation of a system of legislation for these Indians." [9]

The commissioners submitted a long and useful report, full of details on the condition of the western tribes and the character of the territory to be allotted to the emigrating Indians. They emphasized the necessity for governmental action to suppress hostilities between the Indian groups and recommended in detail the military posts in the West which they considered essential. They noted the high prices charged the Indians for goods by white traders and urged that the government care for Indian wants by supplying annuities in goods at reasonable cost. They stressed the importance of freeing the Indian Country of white citizens and preventing whites from grazing their livestock or trapping on Indian lands. They strongly suggested the organization of the Indian territory with a governor, a marshal, a prosecuting attorney, and a judiciary, who could enforce the laws of the United States within the Indian Country, and an annual convention of the Indians in a grand council. So anxious were the commissioners to avoid contacts between the whites and the Indians that they recommended a neutral strip of land five miles wide between the lands of the two races, on which all settlement was to be prohibited. [10]

Meanwhile piecemeal attempts to shore up the sagging Indian system continued to be made in Congress. John Bell of Tennessee, of the House Committee on Indian Affairs, in March 1832 introduced "a bill in addition to the several acts regulating the Intercourse with the Indian tribes." It struck at the whiskey traffic by prescribing punishments for any one introducing or attempting to introduce ardent spirits into Indian Country and authorized all persons in the United States service to destroy any found there. Licenses were to be required of any persons entering the Indian Country, whether to trade or not, and extensive powers were put into the hands of the President to stop or prevent hostilities between tribes. A final section in the bill directed the

<hr/>

[9] *U.S. Stat.*, IV, 595–596; Instructions of Cass, July 14, 1832, in *House Exec. Doc.* 2, 22 Cong., 2 sess., ser. 233, pp. 32–37.

[10] Report of commissioners, Feb. 10, 1834, in *House Rep.* 474, 23 Cong., 1 sess., ser. 263, pp. 78–103.

secretary of war to report a plan for governing the emigrated Indians and a plan for improving the Indians and for regulating intercourse with them. The bill, however, died in the Committee of the Whole.[11]

Jackson in his annual message to Congress in December 1833 returned again to Indian removal, restating his old position and asserting that the Indians who had already emigrated were prosperous and contented. He was mindful, however, that the demands for some reorganization of Indian affairs in the light of new conditions had not yet been met. He directed the attention of Congress to the forthcoming report of the commissioners who were then "engaged in investigating the condition and prospects of these Indians and in devising a plan for their intercourse and government." The report, Jackson hoped, would furnish ample information on which to base legislative action.[12]

From the report of the commissioners, when it arrived, and from the Cass-Clark proposals of five years earlier, the House Committee on Indian Affairs prepared their full-scale report, which was presented on May 20, 1834. The report was accompanied by the trio of bills for organizing the Indian department, for a new trade and intercourse act, and for organizing a government for the Indians in the West.

Since the authorization in 1832 of the commissioner of Indian affairs met the demand that had been made for a centralized office to handle Indian affairs, the Committee turned immediately to the problem of Indian superintendencies and agencies. What they discovered was a situation of legislative and administrative confusion. They found four superintendents, eighteen agents, twenty-seven subagents and thirty-four interpreters on duty with the Indian department, drawing a total annual compensation of $57,222. They were dismayed by the lack of legal foundation for the offices that these men filled, and insisted that the creation of the offices and the fixing of the salaries "should not be left to Executive discretion or to legislative implication." For help in drawing up a suitable bill, the Committee turned to Secretary of War Cass, asking him "to furnish them with a general bill, re-organising the Indian Department & in fact defining as far as

[11] *House Jour.*, 22 Cong., 1 sess., ser. 215, p. 505; Original bill (HR 483), 22 Cong., 1 sess., March 17, 1832.
[12] Message of Dec. 3, 1833, in Richardson, *Messages and Papers*, III, 32–33.

possible the Indian service." Cass replied with alacrity and made arrangements to meet personally with the Committee.[13]

The bill reported by the Committee on May 20 withdrew the superintendence of Indian affairs from the governors of Florida and Arkansas territories and from the governor of Michigan Territory as soon as a new territory was organized west of Lake Michigan. It continued, however, the superintendency at St. Louis for all Indians west of the Mississippi who were not within the bounds of any state or territory. The superintendents were authorized to have general direction over agents and subagents and were given the power to suspend them for misconduct. Authorized agencies were listed in the bill, a terminal date for some was set, and all others were declared abolished. The establishment of subagencies, however, and the appointment of subagents was left in the hands of the President. The powers and the responsibilities of the agents and subagents, especially in regard to issuing licenses, was extended. To care for miscellaneous needs, the President was authorized to require military officers to perform the duties of Indian agent. The limits of the agencies were to be determined by the secretary of war according to tribes or by geographical boundaries. Provision was made, too, for the hiring and for the compensation of interpreters, blacksmiths, and other mechanics.

A second concern of the Committee in the Indian department bill was the payment of annuities. Henceforth no payments were to be made on an individual basis, but the whole annuity was to be paid to the tribe, that is, to its chiefs or to other persons delegated by the tribes. If the Indians requested, the annuity might be paid in goods, and all goods for the Indians were to be purchased by an agent of the government and under sealed bids if time permitted, in an attempt to prevent the exorbitant mark-up on the goods which the western commissioners had reported.

The bill contained additional items collected from previous legislation: the prohibition that no person employed in the Indian department might engage in trade with the Indians; the authorization for the President to furnish domestic animals and implements of husbandry to the Indians in the West; and the granting of rations to Indians who visited military posts or agencies on the

[13] Lewis to Lewis Cass, Feb. 25, 1834, in IA LR, Miscellaneous; Cass to Lewis, Feb. 26, 1834, in Office of the Secretary of War, Reports to Congress, vol. 3, National Archives, Record Group 107. No copy of a written report to the committee including a detailed bill could be found.

frontier. The President was also authorized to prescribe the necessary rules and regulations for carrying out the act.

The committee pushed this bill as an economy measure, as well as a clarification of former uncertainties, and it submitted data to show that the bill would "effect an annual saving of the expenditure of over $80,000."

The bill became law on June 30 exactly as it had been submitted by the committee.[14]

The new legislation established a well-organized Indian department with a considerable reduction in personnel, effecting its economy in part by placing additional burdens upon the military officers on the frontier. The post commanders were often called upon to assume the duties of Indian agent, and the quartermaster officers were frequently responsible for the funds disbursed to the Indians in annuity payments. To govern the officers in these tasks the adjutant general sent them copies of the 1834 laws and special sets of regulations; he directed them to follow instructions given them by the commissioner of Indian affairs, by order of the secretary of war.[15]

꩜

The second bill of the committee, which on June 30 became the intercourse act of 1834, is a good example of the continuity of American Indian policy. It offered no sharp break with the past but embodied, occasionally in modified form, the principles that had developed through the previous decades. One who has seen the provisions of the earlier laws feels much at home here. Where changes did occur they were by and large the culmination of long-term agitation for correction of abuses. The committee in drawing up this bill relied heavily on the proposals made by Governor Cass and General Clark.

The act began with a definition of the Indian Country. The principle of the earlier intercourse acts, in which "the boundary of the Indian Country was a line of metes and bounds, variable from time to time by treaties," was rejected by the committee because the multiplication of treaties made it difficult to ascertain

[14] For action in Congress, see *House Jour.*, 23 Cong., 1 sess., ser. 253, pp. 645, 833, 852, 869; *Sen. Jour.*, 23 Cong., 1 sess., ser. 237, p. 376.
[15] Circular to post commanders, July 12, 1834, in Adjutant General's Office, Letters Sent, vol. 11, pp. 42–43, National Archives, Record Group 94. A list of officers appointed to pay annuities is included in Herring to Thomas S. Jesup, July 21, 1834, in IA LS, vol. 13, p. 230. A circular letter from Herring to the post commanders was sent on August 4, 1834, *ibid.*, pp. 301–302.

just what was Indian Country at any given moment. Instead, the new law declared: "That all that part of the United States west of the Mississippi, and not within the states of Missouri and Louisiana, or the Territory of Arkansas, and also, that part of the United States east of the Mississippi river, and not within a state to which the Indian title has not been extinguished, for the purposes of this act, [shall] be taken and deemed to be the Indian country." The law accepted the removal of the Indians as an accomplished fact. The Indians in the southern states were no longer considered to be in Indian Country, and in territories east of the Mississippi, as Indian titles were extinguished, the lands would cease automatically to be Indian Country. West of the Mississippi the designation of Indian Country could be changed only by legislative enactment.

The licensing system for trading with the Indians was continued, of course. The superintendent of Indian affairs at St. Louis and the agents and subagents could issue the licenses, which were to run for two years east of the Mississippi and for three years in the West. A bond not exceeding five thousand dollars was required for faithful observance of the laws and regulations. Power to revoke and cancel the licenses was given to the superintendent when he judged the person had violated the laws or "that it would be improper to permit him to remain in the Indian country." As a further means of eliminating troublesome traders the law incorporated the proposal of Cass and Clark that discretion be given to the issuing agent, who might now refuse an application "if he is satisfied that the applicant is a person of bad character, or that it would be improper to permit him to reside in the Indian country, or if a license, previously granted to such applicant, has been revoked, or a forfeiture of his bond decreed." To prevent arbitrary action on the part of the agent, however, appeal could be made to the commissioner of Indian affairs. The traders were obliged to carry on their operations at "certain suitable and convenient places," to be designated by the superintendent, agent, or subagents and inserted in the license. The use of presidential authority to withhold goods from certain tribes and to revoke licenses to trade with them, which Cass and Clark had proposed as a means of bringing pressure to bear on the Indians when the public interest demanded it, became part of the new law.[16]

[16] The Cass and Clark version of the licensing provision read: "No person shall be permitted to trade with any of the Indians, [in the Indian country] without a license. . . ." They explained in their comments that the brackets indicated an

Any person who without a license lived in the Indian Country as a trader or introduced goods to trade there was subject to forfeiture of all his goods and a fine of five hundred dollars. The prohibition against foreign traders was continued; no licenses were to be granted to any but United States citizens, but permission to employ foreign boatmen and interpreters at the discretion of the President that had been part of American policy since the regulations issued by Calhoun in 1818 was now specifically provided for in the law. The requirement that foreigners obtain a passport before entering Indian Country, which had been part of the act of 1816, was repeated in the new act, with the fine set at one thousand dollars. The extension of the passport requirement to United States citizens for which Cass and Clark had called, however, was not accepted by the committee, who argued that such suspicion ought not to be shown toward mere travellers in the Indian Country and that the inconvenience of obtaining passports had made the provision in the act of 1802 requiring them south of the Ohio a dead letter for years.

The improvidence of the Indians was guarded against by the restriction which forbade anyone, under a fifty dollar penalty, to purchase or receive from an Indian guns, traps, other articles used in hunting, implements of husbandry, cooking utensils, or clothing. This section was a repetition of a clause first included in the intercourse act of 1796.

The integrity of the Indian Country was guaranteed in several ways, each a repetition or amplification of provisions already included in earlier laws. In the 1834 act, however, restrictions were made more explicit and fines were often increased. No white persons were permitted to hunt, trap, or take and destroy any peltries or game in the Indian Country except for subsistence. Violators were to forfeit $500 and all the traps and guns and ammunition used or procured for the purpose as well as any peltries taken. This was an attempt to halt or arrest an increasing evil, pointed out in clear terms by the commissioners, who had reported that licenses to trade were construed into licenses to trap and that the mountains were filled with men employed to catch beaver and kill other game. The grazing of livestock on

---

alternative reading upon which they thought Congress should decide — that is, whether the trade regulations should apply to Indians everywhere or only in the Indian Country. The committee submitted its bill with parentheses in place of brackets, thus limiting the operation of the section to the Indian Country. The same thing occurred in the section prohibiting the sale of liquor to Indians.

Indian lands without the consent of the Indians, an evil that had existed from early times but which in the opinion of the commissioners was destined to become an increasing evil because the Indian range would long remain the best, was to be punished by a fine of one dollar for each animal thus violating the Indian Country.[17] All intruders into the Indian Country in violation of the law were to be removed by the agents, and the President could authorize the use of military force to effect the removal.

Although it was the intention of the administration and of Congress to make a final guarantee to the Indians against encroachment on their lands by white settlers, no provision beyond those already in force were included in the new intercourse act, which restated the established formula: "If any person shall make a settlement on any lands belonging, secured, or granted by treaty with the United States to any Indian tribe, or shall survey or shall attempt to survey such lands, or designate any of the boundaries by marking trees, or otherwise, such offender shall forfeit and pay the sum of one thousand dollars." The President, as before, was authorized to have the illegal settlers removed by the military troops. The traditional policy of acquiring Indian lands by formal treaty was restated with no modification, except for changes in the penalties assigned.

The dangers of intrigue among the Indians on the part of foreign powers and the machinations of malintentioned individuals to stir up the Indians to violate treaties with the United States or to give other evidences of hostility had been legislated against in 1800 in "An Act for the preservation of peace with the Indian tribes." This act, which had expired after two years, had been aimed at British and Spanish intrigue, and had established fines and imprisonment for three offenses: sending talks or messages to any Indians "with an intent to produce a contravention or infraction of any treaty or other law of the United States, or to disturb the peace and tranquillity of the United States"; carrying messages of such a nature between the Indians and any United States citizen or subject or agent of a foreign power; or inducing a foreign nation to incite the Indians against the United States or in any way alienating or attempting to alienate the confidence of the Indians from the government of the United States. Now, as a further means of insuring tranquillity of the Indians in their new home west of the Mississippi, these three prohibitions were res-

---

[17] The committee report recommended a fine of five dollars for each animal, but the sum was reduced to one dollar before the bill became law.

urrected and included as three separate sections of the act of 1834.[18]

The provisions of the fourth and fourteenth sections of the act of 1802, which dealt with indemnification for thefts or damages done to property of either race by members of the other race, were incorporated into the new act, after strong endorsement by Cass and Clark. The object of the promise to the Indians, of course, was to quiet them and prevent them from seeking private satisfaction; the promise of eventual indemnification to the whites, they remarked, "is a wise and prudent one, and is in daily practical operation upon the frontiers. When persons are injured by the aggression of Indians, and can look confidently to the government for compensation, they feel disposed to submit patiently, and to await the operation of the laws. Were it otherwise, every injury would be followed by a corresponding revenge, and our whole border country would be agitated by a series of partial hostilities, leading eventually to Indian wars." The committee added a proviso to the effect that claims had to be presented within three years and it provided further that the indemnification would be paid to the whites out of the Treasury of the United States in cases where there were no annuities due the Indians which could be drawn upon. To facilitate the taking of proof in cases of claims, the Indian superintendent, agents, and subagents were authorized to administer oaths to witnesses in the taking of depositions.

Indian department officials were charged specifically in the new law with responsibility in bringing Indian criminals to justice, in a section taken from the Cass-Clark report: "It shall be the duty of superintendents, agents, and sub-agents, to endeavour to procure the arrest and trial of all Indians accused of committing any crime, offence, of misdemeanor, and all other persons who have committed crimes or offenses within any state or territory, and have fled into the Indian country, either by demanding the same of the chiefs of the proper tribe, or by such other means as the President may authorize, and the President may direct the military force of the United States to be employed in the apprehension of such Indians, and also, in preventing or terminating hostilities between any of the Indian tribes."

Cass and Clark saw the danger involved in wholesale use of military force in the Indian Country, but they foresaw that the

[18] *U.S. Stat.*, II, 6–7. These sections had been included in the Cass-Clark proposals without any comment to explain the reason for reviving them.

employment of troops might be required in cases of "more than ordinary atrocity or importance." They felt, however, that by leaving the discretion of use of the military in the hands of the President no danger would come from the authority granted. In the act of 1834 the military forces were relied upon in numerous instances: to remove illegal settlers or surveyors, to apprehend Indian criminals, to search for and to seize liquor, to break up distilleries, to apprehend persons violating the intercourse act and convey them to the civil authorities for trial, and to prevent or terminate hostilities among the Indian tribes.

The final clause in the section of the act quoted above marked a new direction in United States relations with the tribes. The War Department had been careful not to interfere in purely Indian squabbles. Although it deprecated the hostilities which frequently broke out between tribes, it had adopted a hands-off policy. In the act of 1834, as it had already done to some extent in particular treaties with the Indians, the government committed itself to the opposite policy. Hostilities were stimulated by the closer contacts between tribes that resulted from the emigration of Eastern Indians to the West, and these hostilities were an increasing cause of concern to the frontiersmen and to the fur traders.

Cass and Clark argued in 1829 that "no well founded objection can be foreseen" to the President's use of military force to prevent or terminate hostilities between tribes. They based their proposal on the principle that "the relation of the government of the United States to the Indian tribes, is, in many respects, a paternal one, founded upon the strength and intelligence of the one party, and the weakness and ignorance of the other." They charged the Indians with wars "as ceaseless as they are causeless, originating they know not why, and terminating they care not when," arising often out of the desire of the young men of the tribe to prove their valor. The government had a direct interest in suppressing such wars, both to protect American citizens who fell in the way of the war parties and to preserve the Indians themselves. The commissioners, too, insisted that humanity as well as justice demanded that hostilities between tribes stop and they declared that "it remains for the Government of the United States *alone* to determine when they shall end."

Just as the bill was being considered in Congress, in fact, the War Department was disturbed by reports of hostilities between the Sacs and Foxes and the Sioux. William B. Astor, president of the American Fur Company, sent to Secretary of War Cass a report of the difficulties and urged the government to take steps to prevent an outbreak of war between the tribes. "To our trade in their country it must be disastrous, beyond all doubt," Astor lamented; "but that is of little moment when compared with the safety of the frontier families who will be exposed to great danger in such a state of things." The Indians wanted to be allowed to settle their quarrel by themselves; if that were to be allowed the fur company would be forced to withdraw all its traders. "The strong arm of the Government can alone preserve peace among these Indians, and secure the repose of the frontiers," Astor asserted.[19]

Cass replied that under no circumstances would the Indians be given a free hand to settle their dispute with the tomahawk. What action the government could take, however, remained a problem. "The best practical method of preventing these hostilities becomes sometimes a matter of difficulty," Cass admitted. "And perhaps it will take some time before the object is fully accomplished. But every proper effort will be used to effect it as speedily as possible. And it will hereafter be a cardinal principle in our Indian relations." The "proper effort" made by the War Department was to demand through the Indian agents the surrender of the offenders from each side and their confinement at military posts — the Sacs and Foxes at Fort Armstrong, the Sioux at Fort Snelling. If the criminals were not turned over to the military commanders, hostages were to be taken, and as a last resort dragoons were to be sent into the Indian Country to maintain peace. It was Cass's hope that the confinement of the malefactors or hostages would lead both sides to request their release and to adjust their difficulties amicably. He had no intention of turning over the criminals to the opposing side, since that would lead to their summary execution without any sort of trial.[20] Cass based his action upon treaties made with the Indians, but in the act of 1834, the Department had general statutory authorization, under the direction of the President, to use military force to end or prevent Indian wars.

The importance that Cass and Clark attached to further restrictions on the whiskey traffic we have already noticed. They insisted upon a positive prohibition of its use in the trade and a strengthening of the searching and forfeiture procedures found

[19] Astor to Cass, May 22, 1834, in IA LR, Sac and Fox Agency.
[20] Cass to Astor, May 30, 1834, in IA LS, vol. 12, pp. 389–390; Herring to Clark, May 29, 1834, *ibid.*, pp. 387–388.

in the act of 1822, although they would still permit the use of liquor among the *engagees*. The bill presented by the committee, while basically adopting the Cass-Clark article, tightened the law still more. It established a fine of five hundred dollars for distributing liquor to Indians and a fine of three hundred dollars for bringing whiskey into the Indian Country or attempting to do so. The committee rejected the exception in the case of the boatmen, and it further authorized "any person, in the service of the United States, or . . . any Indian, to take and destroy any ardent spirits or wine found in the Indian country," except for military supplies, which were specifically permitted by the act. The commissioners in their report had adverted to the attempt of McKenzie of the American Fur Company to distill liquor within the Indian Country, and they discovered that the Indians themselves were operating distilleries in the Cherokee country. The committee resolved to put an end to such contravention of government policy and added a separate section to the law which set a one-thousand dollar fine for anyone, Indian or white, who set up or operated a distillery in the Indian Country and which authorized the agents of the Indian department to destroy any distillery found within their agencies and to call upon the military forces, if necessary, for help.

The complicated sections in the earlier intercourse acts that prescribed the courts and procedure to be used in prosecuting violators of the intercourse acts and that had been taken over as they stood by Cass and Clark were much simplified by the committee. For the purposes of the act, the Indian Country was annexed to the judicial districts of the adjoining territories or states. Offenders might be apprehended in other states or territories and transported to the territory or judicial district having jurisdiction. The provision of the act of 1817 that declared that laws providing punishment of crimes committed within any place within the sole and exclusive jurisdiction of the United States should be in force also in the Indian Country was continued, along with the proviso that these laws did not extend to crimes committed by one Indian against another.

In the act of 1834 for all violations where the punishment by previous laws had been fine or imprisonment, the imprisonment was omitted, leaving the penalty to be recovered in an action of debt, to be prosecuted in any district where the offender might be found. Goods or other property to be seized for violation of the act were to be proceeded against in the manner directed by the revenue laws. In all trials about right of property between Indians and whites, the burden of proof, as in the act of 1822, was to rest upon the white persons whenever the Indian made out a presumption of title in himself from the fact of previous possession or ownership.

To enforce the act reliance was still placed upon the military garrisons on the frontier under regulations from the President — in apprehending persons found in the Indian Country in violation of the act and in examining and seizing the stores and boats in which liquor was found. This section was taken directly from the act of 1802 and contained the same prescriptions for limited confinement and gentle treatment.

The law as approved on June 30, 1834, differed little from the bill introduced by the committee, although there had been amendments in both the House and the Senate. The House took out of the bill the obsolete provisions, which Cass and Clark without reason had retained, concerning the purchase of horses from the Indians under license and also a section providing for commissioners to treat with the Indians. It added to the section on indemnification for Indian destruction of white property outside the Indian Country offenses committed against whites who were lawfully within the Indian territory. The Senate, on motion of Mr. Frelinghuysen, added the provision that the new act would not "impair or affect the Intercourse Act of 1802 so far as the same relates or concerns Indian tribes residing east of the Mississippi," and the Senate added as well the final section of the act, which provided for the duties of Indian agents among the western Indians until such time as a western territory might be established.[21]

❧

The third object of the committee, "the obligations of the United States to the emigrant tribes," was to be attained by a "bill to provide for the establishment of the Western Territory and for the security and protection of the emigrant and other Indian tribes therein." This bill and the two already discussed were considered to be "parts of a system" and the committee in its report urged that all three be passed together.

[21] *House Jour.*, 23 Cong., 1 sess., ser. 253, pp. 645, 833, 852, 869; *Sen. Jour.*, 23 Cong., 1 sess., ser. 237, pp. 376, 389, 394; *Register of Debates in Congress*, 23 Cong., 1 sess., pp. 2125, 4763–64 (June 30, 1834, June 25, 1834); Engrossed bill, showing Senate amendments, Records of the United States Senate, National Archives, Record Group 46.

The first two bills passed with little commotion. The third floundered in the House. This is not surprising, for it was the most radical of the three and had no real precedents to rest on. The Indian department bill was a regularization and simplification of an already operating system; the new intercourse act consisted largely in a re-enactment of previous legislation, with some foreseen modifications. But the bill for the western territory for the Indians took the House by surprise. The legislators were not ready for the unprecedented departure.

The bill provided for a new political arrangement in the West, yet it was not without a history, for there had been intimations from time to time that some provision would have to be made for the Indians within the framework of the United States government.[22] Early treaties had suggested the admission into Congress of delegates from the Indian nations, but it was not until the removal of the Indians became a viable concept that the matter of their government in the West became important. In response to President Monroe's annual message of 1824, in which he spoke of laying out districts in the West for the tribes and establishing civil governments in each, the House passed a resolution on December 17, instructing the Committee on Indian Affairs "to inquire into the expediency of organizing all the territory of the United States lying west of the state of Missouri and territories of Arkansas and Michigan, into a separate territory, to be occupied exclusively by the Indians." And Monroe's special message on removal of January 27, 1825, spoke of the necessity of providing in the West "a system of internal government which shall protect their property from invasion, and, by the regular progress of improvement and civilization, prevent that degeneracy which has generally marked the transition from the one to the other state." The promise of a government that would serve as a bond of amity between the tribes and preserve internal order in the tribes, would prevent intrusions on their property, and would promote civilization Monroe thought was the most powerful inducement the United States could offer to the tribes to emigrate. Advantages to the United States would not be lacking in such a plan of permanent peace. The bill that Senator Benton introduced on February 1 in accordance with the President's recommendations for removal included a provision that the United States would

[22] See Annie H. Abel, "Proposals for an Indian State, 1778–1878," *Annual Report of the American Historical Association for 1907* (Washington, 1908), I, 87–104, for a careful, well-documented survey of the subject.

aid in forming a suitable government in the western region, and a similar bill was introduced in the House. Benton's bill was passed by the Senate, but neither bill was approved by the House.[23]

At the beginning of the next Congress, a resolution in the House introduced by James C. Mitchell of Tennessee proposing removal of the eastern Indians, included the proposition to establish for the Indians in the West "a territorial Government . . . of the same kind, and regulated by the same rules, that the Territories of the United States are now governed." In the same session John Cocke of Tennessee, of the Committee on Indian Affairs, reintroduced the removal bill of the previous year, with the changes suggested by Secretary of War Barbour and with the provision for the organization of a government for the emigrated Indians whenever the President should think proper. Congress did not act, however, despite the reintroduction of Mitchell's resolution on December 17, 1827.[24]

Meanwhile removal treaties entered into with the Indians looked toward a governmental setup for the Indians in the West, which would free them permanently from the jurisdiction of any state or territory and place them under some sort of government of their own.[25] Certainly the removal bill of 1830 required some sort of government in the West if the pledges therein were to be fulfilled.

When the commissioners were sent west in 1832 they were charged by the law which authorized their appointment and by the special instructions of Secretary of War Cass to report information regarding a plan "for the Government and security of the Indians." The commissioners fulfilled this obligation in considerable detail, and the committee in drawing up its bill relied heavily on their report.[26]

[23] Treaty with the Delawares, 1778, in Kappler, *Treaties*, p. 5; Treaty of Hopewell with the Cherokees, 1785, *ibid.*, p. 10; *House Jour.*, 18 Cong., 2 sess., ser. 112, p. 56; Richardson, *Messages and Papers*, II, 281–282.
[24] *House Jour.*, 19 Cong., 1 sess., ser. 130, pp. 97, 276; Original bill (HR 113), 19 Cong., 1 sess., Feb. 21, 1826, printed in *House Rep.* 474, 23 Cong., 1 sess., ser. 263, pp. 76–78; Barbour to Cocke, Feb. 3, 1826, in *American State Papers: Indian Affairs*, II, 648; *House Jour.*, 20 Cong., 1 sess., ser. 168, pp. 63, 68.
[25] See treaties with the Cherokees, May 6, 1828, the Choctaws, Sept. 27, 1830, and the Creeks, March 24, 1832, in Kappler, *Treaties*, pp. 288–292, 310–315, 341–343. These are discussed in *House Rep.* 474, 23 Cong., 1 sess., ser. 263, pp. 15–17.
[26] *U.S. Stat.*, IV, 596; *House Exec. Doc.* 2, 22 Cong., 2 sess., ser. 233, p. 85; *House Rep.* 474, 23 Cong., 1 sess., ser. 263, pp. 100–102.

The bill established boundaries for an Indian territory west of Arkansas and Missouri which was to be reserved forever for the Indian tribes. It pledged the faith of the United States to guarantee the land to the Indians and their descendants. Each of the tribes was to organize a government for its own internal affairs, and a general council was to be established as a governing body for the voluntary confederation of the tribes which the bill envisioned. There was to be a governor appointed by the President who had a veto over acts of the council, power to reprieve offenders sentenced to capital punishment (with pardoning power reserved to the President), and considerable authority in settling difficulties between tribes, in executing the laws, and in employing the military forces of the United States. The confederation was to send a delegate to Congress and the committee expressed a hope of eventual admission of the territory as a state into the union.[27]

The three bills of the committee, although introduced in the House on May 20, 1834, were not debated until June 24, close to the adjournment of Congress on the 30th. The lateness in the session may well have enabled the first two bills to be pushed through without much change, but strong opposition arose to the bill on the western territory, and after considerable and violent debate, it was postponed to the next session and to ultimate failure. [28]

The bill was severely criticized. John Quincy Adams immediately assailed it on the basis of unconstitutionality. "What constitutional right had the United States to form a constitution and form of government for the Indians?" he demanded. "To erect a Territory to be inhabited exclusively by the Indians?" Samuel F. Vinton, of Ohio, spoke with much severity against almost every part of the bill, charging that it would establish an absolute military despotism in the West, in the hands of the President, ruling through the appointed governor. Critics like Adams and Vinton were not to be hurried into acceptance of the bill and demanded that it be postponed to a later time when full consideration could be given to it. Adams admitted that he had read neither the committee's report nor the bills before that very day and had not suspected that any such bill as this was included among them. The admission of an exclusively Indian state to the Union was a

[27] The bill (HR 490) is printed *ibid.*, pp. 34–37; discussion of the bill in the committee report is on pp. 14–22.

[28] *House Jour.*, 23 Cong., 1 sess., ser. 253, pp. 645, 833, 834.

seminal idea, he said, and might set a dangerous precedent. Was the House prepared, he asked, upon a half hour's notice "totally to change the relations of the Indian tribes to this country?" He objected, too, to the power given to the President by the bill — power that rightly belonged to Congress. William S. Archer of Virginia argued that the bill did not provide an Indian government, but would "establish and enforce the Government of the United States within the sacred territory set apart as the exclusive abode" of the Indians. Millard Fillmore of New York doubted the propriety of the bill as a piece of legislation. To him it seemed to be more nearly an act of treaty-making.

Horace Everett of Vermont calmly and ably defended the report of the committee and the western territory bill, answering point by point the arguments of the critics, denying in large part that the criticisms had any validity when applied to the circumstances of the Indians and their present state of civilization. Everett was seconded by other members of the committee, but the demand to postpone consideration of the bill was too strong to withstand.[29]

The bill was taken up again at the beginning of the second session of the 23d Congress in December 1834, but once more Congress adjourned before action was taken. Later attempts to organize a territory for the Indians met no greater success.[30]

Without the organization of the western territory for the Indians there was little hope that the pledge given to the Indians upon removal that they would be protected in the permanent enjoyment of the western lands could be fulfilled or that the new intercourse act would enjoy much better enforcement than its predecessors.

[29] *Register of Debates in Congress*, 23 Cong., 1 sess., pp. 4763–79 (June 25, 1834).

[30] *House Jour.*, 23 Cong., 2 sess., ser. 270, pp. 65, 425, 430–433. The post-1834 attempts and recommendations are discussed in Abel, "Proposals for an Indian State."

EPILOGUE

A milestone in American Indian policy had been reached in 1834. The formative years were over, and the United States looked to the future with an Indian policy that was considered reasonable and adequate. The two laws passed in 1834 summed up the experience of the past; they offered the well-grounded legal basis for the Indian service which had been so long in coming and embodied the principles for regulating the contacts between the whites and the Indians that had proved necessary through the preceding decades. The continually changing boundaries of the Indian Country that had kept Indian relations in a state of flux were now stabilized, it was hopefully assumed, by the removal of the Indians to the West. With a tempered enthusiasm the President and the secretary of war could commend the nation for what had been accomplished and look forward to less troubled times, although in 1834 the worst of the tribulations for the emigrating Indians were yet to come.

The failure of Congress to provide a new governmental setup in the West for the emigrated tribes, it is true, still disturbed the policy makers. Benjamin F. Butler, acting secretary of war, called attention to this need in the annual report of 1836:

Connected with the general subject of our Indian relations are two measures, proposed by the commissioner, which I deem of great moment. They are, the organization of an efficient system for the protection and government of the Indian country west of the Mississippi, and the establishment of military posts for the protection of that country and of our own frontiers. . . .

These measures are due to the numerous tribes whom we have planted in this extensive territory, and to the pledges and encouragements by which they were induced to consent to a change of residence. We may now be said to have consummated the policy of emigration, and to have entered on an era full of interest to both parties. It involves the last hopes of humanity in respect to the Indian tribes; and though, to the United States, its issues cannot be equally momentous, they yet deeply concern our prosperity and honor. It therefore behooves us, at this juncture, seriously to examine the relations which exist between the United States and the inhabitants of the Indian country, to look into the duties which devolve on us, and to mature a system of measures for their just and constant execution.[1]

Although nothing had been accomplished to date, the need was apparent and no doubt would soon be met.

Optimism about the future might well have been moderated by a look backward from 1834 to 1790. If one sought to evaluate the success of the Indian intercourse acts there were embarrassing questions to face. Laws and proclamations had multiplied, drawn up in ever stricter fashion as they became more inclusive in the actions they prohibited. But had there been commensurate improvement in the situations which the laws had been designed to remedy? Whiskey flowed as freely in the 1830's as it had in 1800. The pressure of encroaching whites had driven the Indians farther and farther west.

Protection of the rights and persons of the Indians remained more an ideal than a reality because the means applied had been out of all proportion to the magnitude of the problem. The expanse of the frontier and the multitudes of oncoming settlers were the basis of the problem. Neither the one nor the other had been adequately faced. A frontier bordering the Indian Country thousands of miles in length and an Indian Country itself of great depth presented an enforcement area that required a numerous and mobile police force. The United States had neither. A few scattered frontier posts, manned by foot soldiers of questionable distinction, could not cope with sly traders who were able to break across the line anywhere and be deep in Indian Country before their presence was even suspected nor with squatters on the Indian lands who returned as quickly as they were driven off. To patrol the frontier adequately was close to impossible with the small number of troops allowed by Congress. And in 1821, just as the frontier was moving west and the need increasing, the total force of the army was reduced from ten to six thousand men.

Although the agents of the Indian department were often persuasively effective with the Indians themselves, they lacked any substantial power to enforce their decisions. They had to call upon the military commanders to apprehend offenders, and then both agent and commandant were forced to apply to the civil courts for the accomplishment of justice. To say that the territorial court system was rudimentary is to comment on only the

[1] Report of the Secretary of War, Dec. 3, 1836, in *Sen. Doc.* 1, 24 Cong., 2 sess., ser. 297, pp. 123–125.

beginning of the difficulty. The courts reflected the milieu in which they existed. The courts and juries were frontier-minded, opposed both to the Indians and to the federal army officers who were on hand to protect the red men. The Indians were a physical hindrance to the advance of white settlement, whose mere presence on the land was bad enough, but whose savage ways (breaking out again and again into atrocities under the repeated sting of injustice and hatred from the whites) seemed to justify extermination. The army with its authoritarian ways was said to be inimical to American democracy, which flourished in a somewhat undomesticated variety on the frontier.

One reason for lack of complete success in carrying out the Indian program was the continuing necessity for economizing under which the Indian department operated. It was true, no doubt, that expenses could easily have run to great extremes without the bridle of War Department caution, but when the need for economy actually meant cutting down the number of agents or prevented the establishment of new military posts, then the enforcement of the intercourse acts was bound to suffer. Throughout the whole formative period there was seldom if ever an opportunity for an all-out campaign of enforcement because of the lack of money.

The secretary of war wrote to William Clark in August 1809, for example, ordering him to cross off the names of some of the interpreters and agents whom Clark had submitted in his estimate of expenditures. "It does not appear to be necessary," he was told, "that the expense of attending our Relations with the Indians in the Territory of Louisiana, should be four times as much as the whole expense of supporting its civil government." Five months later Governor William Hull at Detroit was told that a general reduction in the expenditures of the Indian department was "absolutely indispensable." The governor had to decide what services and personnel to dispense with and where to cut down. After the War of 1812 the conditions were no better, and the agents were warned that expenditures had to be kept within limits, "however desirous the executive may be to pursue a liberal policy towards the Indians." In 1829 Secretary of War Eaton had to write to the Indian superintendents to tell them that "the most rigid economy" was necessary and to direct them to enjoin the same course upon all the agents under them. Indeed, one of the strong arguments put forth in support of the bill in 1834 for reorganizing the Indian department was the monetary saving it would effect.[2]

Weaknesses and inadequacies are easy to catalog. Harder to judge is the over-all effect of the intercourse acts in these early years. That they prevented much open conflict between the races and allowed the inevitable westward advance of white settlement to proceed with a certain orderliness is perhaps judgment enough.

[2] William Eustis to Clark, Aug. 7, 1809, in SW IA LS, vol. C, p. 4; Eustis to William Hull, Jan. 1, 1810, *ibid.*, pp. 9–10; George Graham to Thomas Posey, June 26, 1817, *ibid.*, vol. D, p. 50; Eaton to Clark, March 10, 1829, in IA LS, vol. 5, p. 327.

BIBLIOGRAPHICAL NOTE

This is not an exhaustive bibliography on Indian policy or Indian affairs and does not include every item cited in the footnotes. I have tried only to indicate the principal sources upon which my study is based, grouping them by type of material in the first seven sections below, and by particular subject matter in the remaining sections. It did not seem worthwhile to list numerous books and articles on American Indian affairs that contributed only slightly or indirectly to my own work. So many of them, in fact, are written from some particular point of view, often an uncritical and sentimental support of the Indian cause, that they are of questionable value in arriving at a balanced account of the Indian policy in the early years of the United States. I hope, however, that this bibliographical note, together with the footnote citations, will guide an interested reader to the most important primary sources as well as to the basic secondary works.

An extensive study of United States Indian affairs in the first decades after the adoption of the Constitution is George D. Harmon, *Sixty Years of Indian Affairs: Political, Economic, and Diplomatic, 1789–1850* (Chapel Hill, 1941). This work covers much of the same ground as the present study, but it is quite different in its organization and focus of interest. Harmon's bibliography, on pp. 383–414, lists manuscript sources as well as numerous secondary works.

An important listing of dissertations dealing with Indian matters is published in Frederick J. Dockstader, comp., *The American Indian in Graduate Studies: A Bibliography of Theses and Dissertations* (New York, 1957).

1. MANUSCRIPT MATERIALS IN THE NATIONAL ARCHIVES.

The chief sources for the history of American federal Indian policy are first of all the official records of the federal government — the correspondence and reports of the President, the secretary of war, and of other persons within the War Department who were charged specially with the management of Indian affairs. The following groups of records are fundamental.

Record Group 75, Records of the Office of Indian Affairs (also called Records of the Bureau of Indian Affairs). This collection contains letters sent and received by the War Department or its subordinate branches that pertain to Indian matters. The following items were of special value for the present study.

(1) Office of the Secretary of War, Letters Sent, Indian Affiairs — comprising letter books that contain copies of correspondence from 1800 to 1824.

(2) Office of the Secretary of War, Letters Received, Indian Affairs — comprising correspondence from Indian superintendents, agents, and others, from 1800 to 1824. These files of letters are less complete than the letters

sent and can be supplemented by the regular files of secretary of war's letters in Record Group 107.

(3) Office of Indian Affairs, Letters Sent — comprising books of letters sent after the establishment of the Bureau of Indian Affairs in 1824. The volumes contain letters on Indian matters from the secretary of war as well as from the men who headed the Office (or Bureau) of Indian Affairs.

(4) Office of Indian Affairs, Letters Received — comprising files of correspondence received by the secretary of war or the head of the Office of Indian Affairs from superintendents, agents, army officers, members of Congress, and others concerned with Indian matters. These letters are indexed in bound volumes of Registers of Letters Received and are filed by superintendency or agency or by some specific subject matter, such as Schools.

(5) Office of Indian Trade, Letters Sent — comprising bound volumes of letters sent from 1807 to 1822. The contents pertain largely to the operation of the factories, but there is much also on general Indian trade policy and other Indian matters.

(6) Office of Indian Affairs, Field Office Records — comprising correspondence files, fiscal records, and other reports maintained at the superintendency or agency level. Those of the Michigan Superintendency and Cherokee Agency were especially helpful.

Record Group 107, Records of the Office of the Secretary of War. Most of the strictly Indian material has been segregated into Record Group 75, but some items are still found here. The following items offer information, especially on the role of the army in enforcing the Indian policy of the government.

(1) Office of the Secretary of War, Letters Sent — comprising letter books of outgoing correspondence from 1800 on. There is one volume of letters for the period 1791–1794, but all other eighteenth century records were destroyed by fire in 1800.

(2) Office of the Secretary of War, Letters Received — comprising files of incoming correspondence indexed in Registers of Letters Received.

(3) Office of the Secretary of War, Reports to Congress — comprising letter books of reports prepared in answer to resolutions of Congress and letters and reports sent to members of Congress. The volumes contain information on Indian policy in the letters sent to the chairmen of the committees on Indian affairs.

Record Group 98, Records of United States Army Commands — comprising a variety of correspondence, orders, and reports originating in territorial commands. Some material showing the concern of frontier army commanders with Indian affairs is found here.

The following record groups contain material that throws light on some special aspects of Indian affairs.

Record Group 46, Records of the United States Senate, and *Record Group 233*, Records of the United States House of Representatives, contain original bills and committee reports dealing with Indian matters. These items are necessary for a complete account of legislative action.

Record Group 59, General Records of the Department of State, contains the Papers of the Continental Congress, which are useful in supplementing the published *Journals of the Continental Congress*.

Record Group 60, General Records of the Department of Justice, contains manuscript volumes of opinions of the attorney general, which include some statements on Indian laws and policy.

Record Group 206, Records of the Solicitor of the Treasury, contains volumes of Attorneys' Returns and Letters Received from United States Attorneys, Clerks of Courts, and Marshals, which offer some slight data on court action arising under the intercourse acts.

Record Group 217, Records of the General Accounting Office, contains Reports and Letter Books of the Fifth Auditor's Office, which give a little information on claims for compensation arising under the intercourse acts.

Note: Indian materials can be located by consulting the *Guide to Materials in the National Archives* (Washington, 1948) and the check lists prepared for the various collections. A brief introduction to Indian materials in the National Archives is given by Gaston Litton, "The Resources of the National Archives for the Study of the American Indian," *Ethnohistory*, II (1955), 191–208. See also the discussion of sources in William N. Fenton, *American Indian and White Relations to 1830: Needs & Opportunities for Study* (Chapel Hill, 1957).

2. OTHER MANUSCRIPT MATERIALS.

The Records of the United States Superintendency of Indian Affairs, St. Louis, 1813–1855, are in the library of the Kansas Historical Society in Topeka. They are incomplete but contain letter books and account books kept by William Clark and his successors in office. They also include accounts and reports of agents dependent upon the St. Louis superintendent. I used microfilm copies of these records in the library of the National Archives.

Three volumes of American Fur Company Letter Books, 1816–1830, originating at the Company's post at Mackinac, contain valuable information on the trading activities of the Company and its reactions to the various laws and regulations established by the federal government. Photostatic copies of the volumes are in the library of the State Historical Society of Wisconsin, in Madison.

3. FEDERAL AND TERRITORIAL PAPERS.

Among published government documents two general series are of outstanding value. *American State Papers: Indian Affairs* (2 vols., Washington, 1832–1834) contain numerous legislative and executive documents relating to Indian affairs from 1789 to 1827. Clarence E. Carter, ed., *The Territorial Papers of the United States* (24 vols. to date, Washington, 1934 —) is a superbly edited selection of documents from the National

Archives and other sources, illustrating the administrative history of the territories. Although the editor has professedly limited the amount of Indian matter, enough pertinent and typical matter is included to give a fairly complete picture of Indian affairs. Footnote references to other material not printed in this series are very helpful.

4. CONGRESSIONAL DOCUMENTS.

The development of Indian policy can be followed in the journals and debates of Congress. The *Journals* for the first thirteen Congresses exist in reprint: *Journal of the Senate* (5 vols., Washington, 1820–1821) and *Journal of the House of Representatives* (9 vols., Washington, 1826). The *Journals* of the 14th Congress were printed by William A. Davis, Washington, 1815–1816. The *Journals* for the 15th and subsequent Congresses appear in the serial set of congressional documents. Useful indexes to the early *Journals* are Albert Ordway, *General Index of the Journals of Congress, from the First to Tenth Congress Inclusive* (*House Report* 1776, 46 Cong., 2 sess., ser. 1939, Washington, 1880), and *General Index of the Journals of Congress, from the Eleventh to Sixteenth Congress Inclusive* (*House Report* 1559, 47 Cong., 1 sess., ser. 2071, Washington, 1883). Debates on the various reports and bills are found in *Annals of the Congress of the United States* (42 vols., Washington, 1834–1856) and *Register of Debates in Congress* (29 vols., Washington, 1825–1837).

Bound volumes of printed bills for the Senate and the House, beginning with the 6th Congress, are in the Library of Congress. They are incomplete, however, and must be supplemented by the original bills, preserved in Record Groups 46 and 233 in the National Archives. Many congressional reports dealing with Indian affairs are in the serial set of congressional documents. They are a rich source of evidence because of the numerous documents that are frequently appended. Individual reports are listed in the sections below dealing with particular aspects of American Indian policy and others are cited in the footnotes.

Note: Two useful articles on congressional action are by Kenneth W. Colgrove, "The Attitude of Congress toward the Pioneers of the West from 1789 to 1820," *Iowa Journal of History and Politics*, VIII (1910), 3–129, and "The Attitude of Congress toward the Pioneers of the West, 1820–1850, I, Relations between the Pioneers and the Indians," *ibid.*, IX (1911), 196–302.

5. PAPERS OF PRESIDENTS AND OTHER OFFICERS.

The annual messages of the Presidents to Congress (which frequently included extensive sections on Indian affairs) and other special messages are in James D. Richardson, comp., *A Compilation of the Messages and Papers of the Presidents* (10 vols., Washington, 1896–1899). Annual reports of the secretary of war are in *American State Papers: Military Affairs* (7 vols.,

Washington, 1832–1861) and after 1823 are attached to the annual message of the President in the serial set of congressional documents. After 1824 the annual report of the head of the Office of Indian Affairs appears with the report of the secretary of war. A listing of the Indian office reports is in J. A. Jones, "Key to the Annual Reports of the United States Commissioner of Indian Affairs," *Ethnohistory*, II (1955), 58–64.

See also the following collections: *The Writings of George Washington from the Original Manuscript Sources, 1745–1799*, John C. Fitzpatrick, ed. (39 vols., Washington, 1931–1944); *The Writings of Thomas Jefferson*, Memorial Edition (20 vols., Washington, 1903–1904); *The Works of John C. Calhoun*, Richard K. Crallé, ed. (6 vols., New York, 1853–1855); *Memoirs of John Quincy Adams, Comprising Portions of His Diary from 1795 to 1848*, Charles Francis Adams, ed. (12 vols., Philadelphia, 1874–1877); *Correspondence of Andrew Jackson*, John Spencer Bassett, ed. (6 vols., Washington, 1926–1933).

6. FEDERAL LAWS AND CASES.

The laws dealing with Indian affairs are in *United States Statutes at Large*. For Indian treaties, see Charles J. Kappler, ed., *Indian Affairs: Laws and Treaties*, II, *Treaties* (Washington, 1904), or Volume VII of the *Statutes*. The cessions of land made by the Indians in the treaties are carefully described in text and maps in Charles C. Royce, comp., *Indian Land Cessions in the United States* (Eighteenth Annual Report of the Bureau of American Ethnology, Part 2, Washington, 1899). Supreme Court decisions on Indian cases can be found in standard editions of United States reports. Cases in inferior courts are reported in *The Federal Cases, Comprising Cases Argued and Determined in the Circuit and District Courts of the United States, from the Earliest Times to the Beginning of the Federal Reporter* (30 vols., St. Paul, 1894–1897). For a topically arranged digest of cases concerning the Indians, see Kenneth S. Murchison, comp., *Digest of Decisions Relating to Indian Affairs*, vol. I, *Judicial* (*House Document* 538, 56 Cong., 2 sess., ser. 4190, Washington, 1901).

Note: An indispensable reference work for Indian legal history is Felix S. Cohen, *Handbook of Federal Indian Law, with Reference Tables and Index* (Washington, 1942). This work was revised and brought up to date through 1956 in United States Department of the Interior, Office of the Solicitor, *Federal Indian Law* (Washington, 1958). All references in the present study have been made to Cohen's original work. Valuable discussions of the legal position of the Indian are found in the following articles: W. G. Rice, "The Position of the American Indian in the Law of the United States," *Journal of Comparative Legislation and International Law*, 3d ser., XVI (1934), 78–95; Austin Abbott, "Indians and the Law," *Harvard Law Review*, II (1888), 167–179; William B. Hornblower, "The Legal Status of the Indians," *Report of the Fourteenth Annual Meeting of the American Bar Association*, 1891; Gerald Gunther, "Governmental Power and New York Indian Lands — A Reassessment of a Persistent Problem of Federal-State Relations," *Buffalo Law Review*, VIII (1958), 1–26.

7. TERRITORIAL AND STATE RECORDS.

Legislative action of the territorial and state governments, which supplemented federal action, can be found in compilations of territorial laws such as the following: Louis B. Ewbank and Dorothy L. Riker, eds., *The Laws of Indiana Territory, 1809–1816 (Indiana Historical Collections,* vol. XX, Indianapolis, 1934); Francis S. Philbrick, ed., *The Laws of Indiana Territory, 1801–1809 (Collections of the Illinois State Historical Library,* vol. XXI, Springfield, 1930); Francis S. Philbrick, ed., *The Laws of Illinois Territory, 1809–1818 (Collections of the Illinois State Historical Library,* vol. XXV, Springfield, 1950); Theodore C. Pease, *The Laws of the Northwest Territory, 1788–1800 (Collections of the Illinois State Historical Library,* vol. XVII, Springfield, 1925). For the rest, one must rely on individual session laws or early volumes of statutes. I have used the extensive collection preserved in the Treasure Room of the Harvard Law Library. Guides to these laws are Grace E. MacDonald, *Check-List of Session Laws* (New York, 1936), and *Check-list of Statutes of States of the United States of America* (Providence, 1937). An exhaustive microfilm collection of early state and territorial records has been prepared by the Library of Congress under the direction of William S. Jenkins. See the mimeographed *Guide to the Microfilm Collection of Early State Records* (Photoduplication Service, The Library of Congress, 1950).

Also of use for a knowledge of territorial and early state action in Indian matters are Logan Esarey, ed., *Messages and Letters of William Henry Harrison (Indiana Historical Collections,* vol. VII, Indianapolis, 1922); *Executive Journal of Indiana Territory, 1800–1816 (Indiana Historical Society Publications,* vol. III, Indianapolis, 1905); Thomas M. Marshall, ed., *The Life and Papers of Frederick Bates* (2 vols., St. Louis, 1926); Dunbar Rowland, ed., *The Mississippi Territorial Archives, 1798–1803* (Nashville, 1905); William H. Smith, ed., *The Life and Public Services of Arthur St. Clair, Soldier of the Revolutionary War; President of the Continental Congress; and Governor of the North-Western Territory, with His Correspondence and Other Papers* (2 vols., Cincinnati, 1882); Gayle Thornbrough and Dorothy Riker, eds., *Journals of the General Assembly of Indiana Territory, 1805–1815 (Indiana Historical Collections,* vol. XXXII, Indianapolis, 1950); Robert H. White, *Messages of the Governors of Tennessee* (5 vols., Nashville, 1952–1959).

The system of courts in the territories — both federal and territorial — on which enforcement of the intercourse acts depended was not well defined and its operation often haphazard. There is an excellent discussion of the courts of Michigan Territory in the editor's introductions in William W. Blume, ed., *Transactions of the Supreme Court of the Territory of Michigan* (6 vols., Ann Arbor, 1935–1940). The volumes include valuable documents showing the operation of the territorial courts. Francis S. Philbrick, ed., *The Laws of Illinois Territory, 1809–1818,* (Springfield, 1950), has a long introduction which describes the working of the territorial court system. William B. Hamilton, *Anglo-American Law on the Frontier: Thomas Rodney and His Territorial Cases* (Durham, 1953), describes the uncertain operation of the courts in Mississippi Territory. Alice E. Smith, *James Duane Doty: Frontier Promoter* (Madison, 1954), includes a good deal on Doty's activities as frontier lawyer and territorial judge.

8. COLONIAL AND IMPERIAL INDIAN POLICY.

No comprehensive history of colonial Indian policy has yet been written. Laws and documents dealing with Indian affairs must be extracted from the compilations of documents that have been published for the separate colonies, since *Laws of the Colonial and State Governments Relating to Indians and Indian Affairs from 1633 to 1831* (Washington, 1832) is not complete enough to be of value. E. B. O'Callaghan, ed., *Documents Relative to the Colonial History of the State of New-York* (15 vols., Albany, 1853–1887), is especially rich in materials on the Six Nations and for imperial documents. Leonard W. Labaree, ed., *Royal Instructions to British Colonial Governors, 1670–1776* (2 vols., New York, 1935), has a section devoted to Indian affairs. Peter Wraxall, *An Abridgment of the Indian Affairs Contained in Four Folio Volumes, Transacted in the Colony of New York, from the Year 1678 to the Year 1751,* Charles H. McIlwain, ed. (Cambridge, Mass., 1915), is an important source for Indian affairs in New York. Colonial treaties with the Indians have been summarized in Henry F. DuPuy, ed., *Bibliography of the English Colonial Treaties with the American Indians, Including a Synopsis of Each Treaty* (New York, 1917). See also Carl Van Doren, ed., *Indian Treaties Printed by Benjamin Franklin, 1736–1762* (Philadelphia, 1938).

McIlwain's long introduction to Wraxall's *Abridgment* is an excellent description of the Indian trade and Indian policy for the vital New York area. Verner W. Crane, *The Southern Frontier, 1670–1732* (Durham, 1928), is a definitive study of Indian relations and western policy in the South, at least as far as South Carolina is concerned. George A. Cribbs, "The Frontier Policy of Pennsylvania," *Western Pennsylvania Historical Magazine,* II (1919), 5–35, 72–106, 174–198, includes a discussion of Indian affairs. A tentative study of Pennsylvania Indian policy is Julian P. Boyd, "Indian Affairs in Pennsylvania, 1736–1762," in Van Doren's *Indian Treaties Printed by Benjamin Franklin,* pp. xix–lxxxviii. Francis X. Moloney, *The Fur Trade in New England, 1620–1676* (Cambridge, Mass., 1931), although very brief, gives essential information on New England Indian policy. The "Introduction," by Cyrus Thomas, in Charles C. Royce, comp., *Indian Land Cessions in the United States* (Washington, 1899), pp. 527–643, is a detailed study, with long passages from documents, of colonial practice in extinguishing Indian land titles. James A. James, "English Institutions and the American Indian," *Johns Hopkins University Studies in Historical and Political Science*, XII (1894), 460–519, is a competent survey of colonial Indian policy, with emphasis on precedents for later American policy. He draws his examples from Massachusetts, New York, and Virginia.

The imperialization of British Indian policy has been more fully treated. Clarence W. Alvord, *The Mississippi Valley in British Politics: A Study of the Trade, Land Speculation, and Experiments in Imperialism Culminating in the American Revolution* (2 vols., Cleveland, 1917), although criticized in some sections by later scholars, is a basic work. Oliver M. Dickerson, *American Colonial Government, 1696–1765: A Study of the British Board of Trade in Its Relation to the American Colonies, Political, Industrial, Administrative* (Cleveland, 1912), has an excellent section in the final chapter, which deals with "Indian Relations," pp. 336–356. See also Lawrence H. Gipson, *The British Empire Before the American Revolution*, vol. IX, *The Triumphant Empire: New Responsibilities within the Enlarged Empire, 1763–1766* (New York, 1956). John R. Alden, *John Stuart and the Southern Colonial Frontier: A Study of Indian Relations, War, Trade, and Land Problems in the Southern Wilderness, 1754–1775* (Ann Arbor, 1944), has an immense amount of information on the southern frontier after the establishment of the superintendencies. Helen L. Shaw, *British Administration of the Southern Indians* (Lancaster, Pa., 1931), is based on study in the Public Records Office, but it has been largely superseded by Alden's work.

Studies in specific aspects of British imperial policy toward the Indians are numerous. John R. Alden, "The Albany Congress and the Creation of the Indian Superintendencies," *Mississippi Valley Historical Review*, XXVII (1940), 193–210, argues that the creation of the superintendency system and the appointment of William Johnson as northern superintendent were due to the report of conferences at the Albany Congress and not to Peter Wraxall, Thomas Pownall, or anyone else. Clarence E. Carter, "The Significance of the Military Office in America, 1763–1775," *American Historical Review*, XXVIII (1923), 475–488, and "The Office of Commander in Chief: A Phase of Imperial Unity on the Eve of the Revolution," in Richard B. Morris, ed., *The Era of the American Revolution* (New York, 1939), pp. 170–213, sees a connection between the superintendents and the military commander that is challenged by Alden, *John Stuart*, chap. IX. For data on Edmond Atkin, first superintendent for the southern colonies, see Wilbur R. Jacobs, ed., *Indians of the Southern Colonial Frontier: The Edmond Atkin Report and Plan of 1755* (Columbia, S. C., 1954), and John C. Parish, "Edmond Atkin, British Superintendent of Indian Affairs," in *The Persistence of the Westward Movement and Other Essays* (Berkeley, 1943), pp. 147–160. For William Johnson, see Arthur Pound, *Johnson of the Mohawks: A Biography of Sir William Johnson, Irish Immigrant, Mohawk War Chief, American Soldier, Empire Builder* (New York, 1930). A more recent life, to be accepted with reservations, is James T. Flexner, *Mohawk*

Baronet: Sir William Johnson of New York (New York, 1959). Johnson's papers are printed in *The Papers of Sir William Johnson* (12 vols., Albany, 1921–1957).

The Proclamation of 1763 is treated by Clarence W. Alvord in "The Genesis of the Proclamation of 1763," *Michigan Pioneer and Historical Collections*, XXXVI (1908), 20–52. Alvord revised his views somewhat in his *Mississippi Valley in British Politics* (2 vols., Cleveland, 1917), but both of his works are corrected by R. A. Humphreys, "Lord Shelburne and the Proclamation of 1763," *English Historical Review*, XLIX (1934), 241–264. The Proclamation is printed in Adam Shortt and Arthur G. Doughty, eds.; *Documents Relating to the Constitutional History of Canada, 1759–1791* (Ottawa, 1907), pp. 119–123. Details on the boundary line of 1763 can be found in Max Farrand, "The Indian Boundary Line," *American Historical Review*, X (1905), 782–791, and John C. Parish, "John Stuart and the Cartography of the Indian Boundary Line," in *The Persistence of the Westward Movement*, pp. 131–146.

9. THE CONTINENTAL CONGRESS.

The Indian policy of the new nation during the Revolution and under the Articles of Confederation can be discovered in the *Journals of the Continental Congress, 1774–1789* (34 vols., Washington, 1904–1937). These printed *Journals*, however, should be supplemented by the Papers of the Continental Congress in the National Archives.

Walter H. Mohr, *Federal Indian Relations, 1774–1788* (Philadelphia, 1933), is a scholarly study of Indian affairs in the period, based on exhaustive research. See his bibliography, pp. 203–224. Merrill Jensen, *The Articles of Confederation: An Interpretation of the Social-Constitutional History of the American Revolution, 1774–1781* (Madison, 1940), has some material on Indian matters and is good on the interrelation of the Indian and western land problems. Edmund C. Burnett, *The Continental Congress* (New York, 1941), has scattered references to Indian matters. Helen L. Shaw, *British Administration of the Southern Indians, 1756–1783* (Lancaster, Pa., 1931), treats of the southern Indians during the Revolution, but from the British, not the American side. Merritt B. Pound, *Benjamin Hawkins — Indian Agent* (Athens, Ga., 1951), in its early chapters discusses Hawkins' work in Indian affairs as a member of the Continental Congress and commissioner to the Indians. Randolph C. Downes, "Cherokee-American Relations in the Upper Tennessee Valley, 1776–1791," *East Tennessee Historical Society's Publications*, VIII (1936), 35–53, is an excellent article on frontier conditions. See also his article, "Creek-American Relations, 1782–1790," *Georgia Historical Quarterly*, XXI (1937), 142–184, and Reginald Horsman, "American Indian Policy in the Old Northwest, 1783–1812," *William and Mary Quarterly*, XVIII (1961), 35–53.

10. THE CONSTITUTION.

The limited concern for Indian affairs in the Constitutional Convention can be traced in Max Farrand, ed., *The Records of the Federal Convention of 1787* (4 vols., New Haven, 1911–1937). The constitutional basis for Indian relations is discussed in W. G. Rice, "The Position of the American Indian in the Law of the United States," *Journal of Comparative Legislation and International Law*, 3d ser., XVI (1934), 78–95. See also Felix S. Cohen, *Handbook of Federal Indian Law* (Washington, 1942), pp. 89–100, and the decisions referred to there.

11. THE INDIAN DEPARTMENT.

General accounts of the development of the Indian department can be found in Laurence F. Schmeckebier, *The Office of Indian Affairs: Its History, Activities and Organization* (Institute for Government Research, *Service Monographs of the United States Government*, no. 48, Baltimore, 1927), pp. 1–42; Felix S. Cohen, *Handbook of Federal Indian Law* (Washington, 1942), pp. 9–12; Ruth A. Gallaher, "The Indian Agent in the United States Before 1850," *Iowa Journal of History and Politics*, XIV (1916), 3–55; *Annual Report of the Commissioner of Indian Affairs*, 1892, pp. 12–25. An extensive historical account of legislation dealing with Indian agencies is in *House Report 474*, 23 Cong., 1 sess., May 20, 1834, ser. 263. *House Document 60*, 23 Cong., 1 sess., Jan. 22, 1834, ser. 255, gives data on persons employed in the Indian department. The work of the agents is discussed in Edgar B. Wesley, *Guarding the Frontier: A Study of Frontier Defense from 1815 to 1825* (Minneapolis, 1935), pp. 16–30; Gallaher, "The Indian Agent in the United States Before 1850"; R. S. Cotterill, "Federal Indian Management in the South, 1789–1825," *Mississippi Valley Historical Review*, XX (1933), 333–352. The work of one agent is discussed in detail in Merritt B. Pound, *Benjamin Hawkins — Indian Agent* (Athens, Ga., 1951). See also *Letters of Benjamin Hawkins, 1796–1806* (*Collections of the Georgia Historical Society*, IX, Savannah, 1916). For information on Return J. Meigs, Cherokee agent, see Henry T. Malone, *Cherokees of the Old South: A People in Transition* (Athens, Ga., 1956), pp. 57–73. Some of the work of the Office of Indian Affairs can be traced in Thomas L. McKenney, *Memoirs, Official and Personal; with Sketches of Travels among the Northern and Southern Indians* (New York, 1846).

The frontier military posts, whose commanders and troops enforced Indian laws and regulations, are all accounted for in Henry P. Beers, *The Western Military Frontier, 1815–1846* (Philadelphia, 1935). This is the best source for data on the establishment and abandonment of the forts. See also Wesley, *Guarding the Frontier;* Francis Paul Prucha, *Broadax and Bayonet: The Role of the United States Army in the Development of the Northwest, 1815–1860* (Madison, 1953); Grant Foreman, *Advancing the Frontier, 1830–1860* (Norman, Okla., 1933).

12. INDIAN TRADE.

Wayne E. Stevens, *The Northwest Fur Trade, 1763–1800* (Urbana, 1928), is a careful study of the early period. The two series of documents edited by Reuben Gold Thwaites, "The Fur Trade in Wisconsin, 1815–1817," *Wisconsin Historical Collections*, XIX (Madison, 1910), 375–488, and "The Fur Trade in Wisconsin, 1812–1825," *ibid.*, XX (Madison, 1911), 1–395, contain much information on trade policy, the exclusion of foreigners, the liquor traffic, and the like. Kenneth W. Porter, *John Jacob Astor: Business Man* (2 vols., Cambridge, Mass., 1931), is valuable for its discussion of the part played by the American Fur Company in the Indian trade. For the Missouri River trade the basic work is Hiram M. Chittenden, *The American Fur Trade of the Far West: A History of the Pioneer Trading Posts and Early Fur Companies of the Missouri Valley and the Rocky Mountains and of the Overland Commerce with Santa Fe* (3 vols., New York, 1902). Ida A. Johnson, *The Michigan Fur Trade* (Lansing, 1919), is a detailed study based on sound sources, but it is somewhat romantic in its treatment. Secretary of War Calhoun's Report on a System of Indian Trade of December 5, 1818, is in *House Document* 25, 15 Cong., 1 sess., ser. 17. Abuses in the Indian trade are detailed in *Senate Document* 47, 16 Cong., 1 sess., Feb. 16, 1820, ser. 26. Documents relative to the condition of the fur trade are in *Senate Document* 67, 20 Cong., 2 sess., Feb. 9, 1829, ser. 181, and *Senate Document* 90, 22 Cong., 1 sess., Feb. 9, 1832, ser. 213. Otto F. Frederickson, *The Liquor Question Among the Indian Tribes in Kansas, 1804–1881* (*Bulletin of the University of Kansas, Humanistic Studies*, vol. IV, no. 4, Lawrence, 1932), is an excellent study of the liquor problem.

For material on the origin, development, and failure of the United States factory system of trading houses for the Indians, see Katherine Coman, "Government Factories: An Attempt to Control Competition in the Fur Trade," *Bulletin of the American Economic Association*, 4th ser., no. 2 (April 1911), pp. 368–388; and Royal B. Way, "The United States Factory System for Trading with the Indians, 1796–1822," *Mississippi Valley Historical Review*, VI (1919), 220–235. The most satisfactory brief account is chapter IV, "The Factory System," in Edgar B. Wesley, *Guarding the Frontier*. Ora Brooks Peake, *A History of the United States Indian Factory System, 1795–1822* (Denver, 1954), is the most complete published study of the factory system, but it is disappointing in its handling of the sources and in its style and organization.

13. INTRUDERS ON INDIAN LANDS.

Correspondence about encroachment upon the Indian lands fills the official files and is a frequent subject in the papers of Presidents, governors, and other officials. The problem is discussed in all the general works on Indian relations. For particular areas the following references are helpful: Randolph C. Downes, "Cherokee-American Relations in the Upper Tennessee Valley 1776–1791," *East Tennessee Historical Society's Publications*, VIII (1936), 35–53; William H. Masterson, *William Blount* (Baton Rouge, 1954); Beverley W. Bond, Jr., *The Civilization of the Old Northwest: A*

Study of Political, Social, and Economic Development, 1788–1812 (New York, 1934); Dorothy B. Goebel, *William Henry Harrison: A Political Biography* (Indianapolis, 1926); R. S. Cotterill, *The Southern Indians: The Story of the Civilized Tribes before Removal* (Norman, Okla., 1954); Cardinal L. Goodwin, "Early Explorations and Settlements of Missouri and Arkansas, 1803–1822," *Missouri Historical Review*, XIV (1920), 385–424; Grant Foreman, *Indians and Pioneers: The Story of the American Southwest before 1830* (New Haven, 1930). Documents dealing with Lovely's Purchase are in *House Document* 263, 20 Cong., 1 sess., April 30, 1828, ser. 174. Information on the intrusions on the lead regions can be found in George D. Lyman, *John Marsh, Pioneer: The Life Story of a Trail-blazer on Six Frontiers* (New York, 1930), and Jacob Van der Zee, "Early History of Lead Mining in the Iowa Country," *Iowa Journal of History and Politics*, XIII (1915), 3–52.

See Number 15, below, for references to the debate in 1830 over the Removal Bill, which gave full expression to both sides of the question of the property rights of the Indians. The policy of the colonies in regard to Indian land tenure is discussed in Cyrus Thomas, "Introduction," in Charles C. Royce, comp., *Indian Land Cessions in the United States* (Washington, 1899), pp. 527–643. A general history of land tenure is J. P Kinney, *A Continent Lost — A Civilization Won: Indian Land Tenure in America* (Baltimore, 1937). His general purpose is to counteract the criticism heaped upon the federal government for unfair and unjust treatment of the Indians. A provocative study of American attitudes toward the Indian is Roy Harvey Pearce, *The Savages of America: A Study of the Indian and the Idea of Civilization* (Baltimore, 1953). See also his article, "The Metaphysics of Indian-Hating," *Ethnohistory*, IV (1957), 27–40. The arguments for dispossessing the Indians are discussed in Albert K. Weinberg, *Manifest Destiny: A Study of Nationalist Expansionism in American History* (Baltimore, 1935), and Wilcomb E. Washburn, "The Moral and Legal Justifications for Dispossessing the Indians," in James Morton Smith, ed., *Seventeenth-Century America: Essays in Colonial History* (Chapel Hill, 1959), pp. 16–32. A valuable comparative study by an anthropologist is A. Grenfell Price, *White Settlers and Native Peoples: An Historical Study of Racial Contacts between English-speaking Whites and Aboriginal Peoples in the United States, Canada, Australia and New Zealand* (Melbourne, 1949).

14. INDIAN EDUCATION AND CIVILIZATION.

The early attempts of the government to aid in the establishment of schools for the Indians are discussed in George D. Harmon, *Sixty Years of Indian Affairs* (Chapel Hill, 1941), pp. 157–166, 351–360; Alice C. Fletcher, *Indian Education and Civilization* (*Senate Executive Document* 95, 48 Cong., 2 sess., ser. 2264, Washington, 1888); Evelyn C. Adams, *American Indian Education: Government Schools and Economic Progress* (New York, 1946). Reports on Indian civilization are in *House Document* 91, 15 Cong.,

2 sess., Jan. 15, 1819, ser. 22; *House Document* 46, 16 Cong., 1 sess., Jan. 17, 1820, ser. 33. See also Joseph A. Parsons, Jr., "Civilizing the Indians of the Old Northwest, 1800–1810," *Indiana Magazine of History*, LVI (1960), 195–216.

15. INDIAN REMOVAL.

The removal policy of the federal government is carefully treated in Annie H. Abel, "The History of Events Resulting in Indian Consolidation West of the Mississippi," *Annual Report of the American Historical Association for the Year 1906* (Washington, 1908), I, 233–450. Charles C. Royce, "The Cherokee Nation of Indians: A Narrative of Their Official Relations with the Colonial and Federal Governments," *Annual Report of the Bureau of Ethnology, 1883–1884* (Washington, 1887), pp. 121–378, gives a chronological account with full paraphrasing of pertinent documents. Ulrich B. Phillips, "Georgia and State Rights: A Study of the Political History of Georgia from the Revolution to the Civil War, with Particular Regard to Federal Relations," *Annual Report of the American Historical Association for the Year 1901*, II, 3–224, contains an excellent section on the Cherokee removal question. Thomas V. Parker, *The Cherokee Indians, with Special Reference to Their Relations with the United States Government* (New York, 1907), is a small book, pro-Cherokee, but based on official sources. Richard Peters, *The Case of the Cherokee Nation against the State of Georgia, Argued and Determined at the Supreme Court of the United States, January Term 1831* (Philadelphia, 1831), gives a full account of the case, with the arguments of counsel and supplementary documents.

The arguments over removal, focused on the Removal Bill of 1830, were extensive and widely disseminated. The full scope of the argumentation can be seen in the long speeches made by both sides in the House and the Senate, in *Register of Debates in Congress*, 21 Cong., 1 sess., pp. 305 ff and 580 ff (February 24, 1830, and after, in the House, and April 6, 1830, and after, in the Senate). Speeches against the bill were edited by Jeremiah Evarts under the title, *Speeches on the Passage of the Bill, for the Removal of the Indians, Delivered in the Congress of the United States, April and May, 1830* (Boston and New York, 1830). The most important writings against the bill were [Jeremiah Evarts], *Essays on the Present Crisis in the Condition of the American Indians; First Published in the National Intelligencer, under the Signature of William Penn* (Boston, 1829). See also *The Removal of the Indians; An Article from the American Monthly Magazine: An Examination of an Article in the North American Review; and an Exhibition of the Advancement of the Southern Tribes, in Civilization and Christianity* (Boston, 1830). This article has been attributed to various authors.

The Georgian position on removal is set forth in Wilson Lumpkin, *The Removal of the Cherokee Indians from Georgia* (2 vols., Wormsloe, Ga., and New York, 1907), which is made up largely of his speeches and correspondence. A calm, moderate article supporting removal is [Lewis Cass], "Removal of the Indians," *North American Review*, XXX (1830), 62–121. The records of the group of New York clergymen who organized to support removal are printed in *Documents and Proceedings Relating to the Formation and Progress of a Board in the City of New York for the Emigration, Preservation, and Improvement of the Aborigines of America* (New York, 1829). Thomas L. McKenney's part in this board is described in his *Memoirs, Official and Personal* (New York, 1846).

General histories of the Cherokees all touch on the removal controversy. See Marion L. Starkey, *The Cherokee Nation* (New York, 1946), and Rachel C. Eaton, *John Ross and the Cherokee Indians* (Menasha, Wis., 1914). The actual process of removal is described by Grant Foreman in *Indian Removal: The Emigration of the Five Civilized Tribes of Indians* (Norman, Okla., 1932), and *The Last Trek of the Indians* (Chicago, 1946).

16. THE LAWS OF 1834.

Two basic reports lay behind the laws of 1834. One, the proposals for reorganizing the conduct of Indian affairs submitted by William Clark and Lewis Cass, is in *Senate Document* 72, 20 Cong., 2 sess., Feb. 10, 1829, ser. 181. The report of the House Committee on Indian Affairs, which introduced the bills, is in *House Report* 474, 23 Cong., 1 sess., May 20, 1834, ser. 263. See also Annie H. Abel, "Proposals for an Indian State, 1778–1878," *Annual Report of the American Historical Association for 1907* (Washington, 1908), I, 87–104.

INDEX

INDEX

Accounting for funds, 57, 59, 93–94, 253

Act of 1800 concerning criminals, 192

Act of 1800 concerning Indian visits, 252

Act of 1800 for preserving peace, 264

Act of 1807 concerning public lands, 163

Act of 1816 concerning foreigners, 77–78

Act of 1817 concerning crimes, 193, 195, 211

Act of 1822 supplementing intercourse acts, 63, 93–94, 110

Act of 1824 designating sites, 98–101

Act of 1832 prohibiting liquor, 115, 127

Acts, see Intercourse acts

Adams, John, 154, 155

Adams, John Quincy: and removal policy, 230–231, 232–233; and western territory, 272–273

Additional Court of Michigan Territory, 131

Agents, Indian: of the British, 9, 22, 26, 52; in Franklin draft, 29; recommended by Washington, 47; appointment and duties, 52–57; and enforcement, 60; proposed by Knox, 61; conflicts with military officers, 64–65; and licensing of foreigners, 78–79, 80; discretionary power, 95–97; to civilize Indians, 215; in Cass-Clark Plan, 253; in law of 1834, 259–260; lack of power, 275

Agriculture promoted among Indians, see Civilization program

Albany Congress, 10, 12, 15, 29

Alcohol, see Liquor traffic

American Board of Commissioners for Foreign Missions, 220, 246

American Fur Company, 71, 79, 81; suits against officers, 83–84; and factory system, 88–89, 92; and licensing system, 95–96; and designated sites, 99–100; and liquor traffic, 110–117, 119–120, 130–134, 135–137. See also Astor, John Jacob; Astor, William B.; Stuart, Robert

Annuities, 57, 86; deductions from, 192, 206, 207; in Cass-Clark Plan, 255; in act of 1834, 260

Appalachian Mountains as boundary line, 18

Arbuckle, Matthew, 121–125, 171, 176, 196

Archer, William S., 273

Ardent spirits, see Liquor traffic

Arkansas Territory: liquor traffic in, 121–126; encroachment in, 167–178; boundary changes, 171, 172, 176, 177, 178; murders in, 196

Army of the United States, see Military force

Arrests of criminals, 62

Articles of Confederation, 29–31. See also Continental Congress

Astor, John Jacob, 66, 79, 99; and liquor traffic, 110–111, 113–114, 119–120. See also American Fur Company

Astor, William B., 99, 266–267

Atkin, Edmond, 11

Atkinson, Henry, 168, 179, 181

Attorney General of Michigan Territory, 182

Attorney General of the United States, 81. See also Berrien, John M.; Rodney, Caesar A.; Taney, Roger B.

Ballard, James H., 74

Barbour, James, 63, 120, 173, 271; and removal policy, 230–231

Baptist schools, 220

Bell, John, 258

Bent, Silas, 74

Benton, Thomas Hart: and factory system, 92; and removal policy, 229; on Indian rights, 240–241; and western territory, 270–271

Berrien, John M., 236–237

Blackburn, Gideon, 219–220

Black Hawk Purchase, 182

Black Hawk War, 130, 181

Blount, William, 69, 149–150, 151; and horse stealing, 203, 204, 205